Social Change in Contemporary China

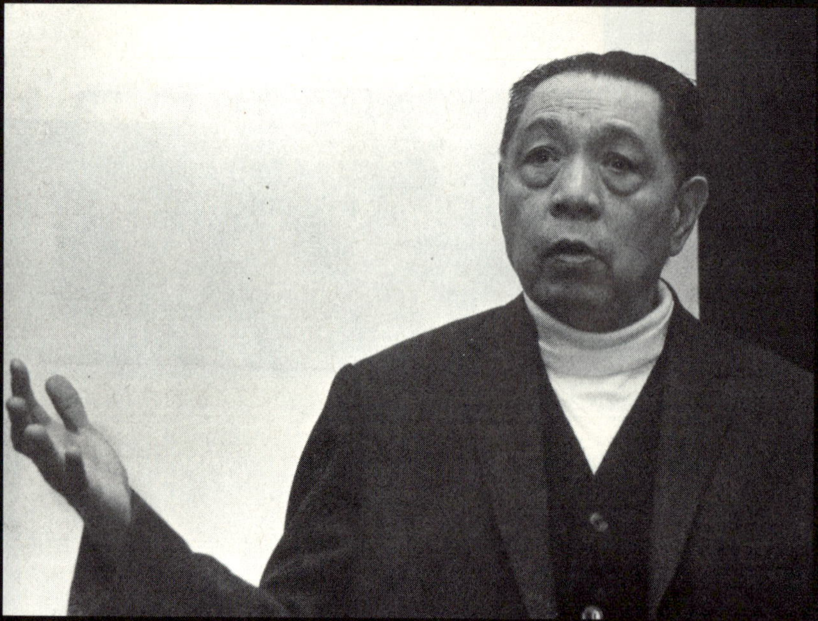

Social Change in Contemporary China

C. K. Yang and the Concept of Institutional Diffusion

EDITED BY WENFANG TANG
AND BURKART HOLZNER

UNIVERSITY OF PITTSBURGH PRESS

This book is the result of a collaboration between the University of Pittsburgh and The Chinese University of Hong Kong and the support and efforts of the administrators, faculty, and staff of those institutions, especially: Professor S. K. Lau, Professor T. S. Cheung, Vice Chancellor Professor Arthur Li, Professor Ambrose Y. C. King, Professor Fei Xiao-tung, and Chancellor Mark Nordenberg.

Published by the University of Pittsburgh Press, Pittsburgh PA 15260

Manufactured in the United States of America
Printed on acid-free paper
10 9 8 7 6 5 4 3 2 1

Library of Congress Cataloging-in-Publication Data

Social change in contemporary China : C.K. Yang and the concept of institutional diffusion / edited by Wenfang Tang and Burkart Holzner.
p. cm.
Includes bibliographical references and index.
ISBN 0-8229-4297-6 (cloth : alk. paper) — ISBN 0-8229-5933-X (pbk. : alk. paper)
1. Social change—China. 2. Organizational change—China. 3. Culture diffusion—China. 4. China—Social conditions. 5. China—Economic conditions. 6. Yang, C. K., 1910- I. Tang, Wenfang, 1955- II. Holzner, Burkart.
HN733.5.S623 2006
306.0951'09045—dc22

2006019184

CONTENTS

TABLES AND FIGURES

TABLES

FIGURES

Social Change in Contemporary China

1

WENFANG TANG

Introduction

The Diffusion of Institutions in Contemporary China

C. K. Yang and the Theory of Institutional Diffusion

C. K. YANG PIONEERED the application of the functionalist approach to the study of China. One of his primary contributions is his assertion that formal institutions are only one way to serve social functions. As long as other, informal practices serve the same functions, they should be treated as diffused institutions and not be neglected (Yang 1961). By identifying the common functions any society has to serve, Yang used China as a case study under a comparative structure-functionalist framework.

Yang's important contribution to the study of China and institutional change was not a random finding but flowed directly from his solid intellectual training both in Chinese history and culture and in Western social science theory and research. As Burkart Holzner describes in his biographical chapter, Yang was born in 1911 during the nationalist revolution that overthrew the Qing dynasty. He received his BA and MA from Yenching University (later Peking University), one of China's elite schools, and his PhD in sociology from the University of Michigan. During this time, modern Western ideas were being introduced to China in an unprecedented flood, and Chinese intellectuals were desperately searching for a solution to China's modernization. They launched the "new culture" movement to replace traditional practices that were seen as barriers to modernization. Yang's writings clearly reflected this intellectual trend (see, for example, his 1959 analysis of the Chinese family and village). More importantly, because of Yang's cross-cultural educational experiences, he was frustrated with the way China was characterized in Western social science literature —for example, as being a civilization without religion. Yet Yang, on the basis of his knowledge of Chinese history and culture, could clearly see the influence of religion in people's lives and in Chinese social institutions. He felt a great need to integrate modern social science and the Chinese experience.

Yang was a productive researcher and writer, and from 1933 to 1989 he published a dozen books and numerous articles. Chong Chor Lau's chapter articulates the nature of Yang's writings, describing it as an "institutional theory of social system change." The Chinese "system" consists of interrelated elements: economic, familial, communal, spiritual, and state-society relationships. Each element is governed by an institution or a set of rules—for example, the economic institution was once governed by a set of periodic rural markets. Yang was interested in the effects external factors have in changing these institutions, such as the effect commercialization and modernization have on rural markets; the effect traditional values, Westernization, and communism have on family, community, and religion; and the impact perceived effectiveness in governance has on mass action.

While writing mostly in the early years of the Communist transition, Yang had limited data to test the success of the new institutions. The Communist Party's more than half a century's rule and market reforms since the late 1970s and early 1980s allow us to examine not only the direction but also the speed of change. For example, did family relationships "modernize" faster in China than in market economies at similar levels of economic development? If modernization was slower, perhaps socialism is less effective at promoting family equality than market democracies are. Yang would be happy to see that many chapters in this volume are aimed in one way or another at testing the institutional effectiveness of socialism. He would perhaps also envy the much larger amount of data available to today's researchers on China.

Perhaps no other work is more important in Yang's institutional theory than his 1961 study of religion in China, summarized by Ambrose Y. C. King and Lizhu Fan. They tell us that Yang's motivation was to solve the discrepancy between the common view that China was a country without religion and yet temples and shrines could be seen in every corner of the Chinese landscape.

Yang found that the two institutional religions, Buddhism and Taoism, were weak and did not provide the source of ethical values for secular social relations that Christianity did (Yang 1961, 303). However, the "classical religion," Confucianism, functioned as a form of diffused religion (304). Confucian beliefs carried religious meanings "in a society in which gods and spirits were thought to lurk in every corner" (255). This diffused religion had no independent institutional base, and its religious functions were performed by the state and the kinship network. While diffused in the state and the kinship system, the classical religion was also diffused in institutional religions. It drew on Buddhism and Taoism for theological concepts and symbols and at the same time legitimized these institutional religions (295). What we see in Yang's analysis is the diffusion of classical religion in religious institutions, such as Buddhism and Taoism, and in secular social institutions. In this study, Yang showed us how culture could influence and interconnect social institutions.

An institution provides a set of rules that define the social, political, economic, and spiritual aspects of an individual's life. It is more than a set of values based on cultural traditions, is often incorporated by the state, and has both moral and legal significance. Yet an institution is not complete without interacting with its members. An individual holds memberships in various institutions: a voter in the electorate, an employee in the labor force, a wife or mother in the family, a member of a church. The survival of an institution depends on its members' participation. As Isabelle Thireau and Hua Linshan discuss in their chapter, an institution is not a passive entity; it is a dynamic, interactive, and constantly evolving process.

Contemporary institutionalists focus on how institutions constrain individual behavior (Peters 1998, 122), a basic function of institutions. Yet if we accept that an institution is an interactive process, institutionalism only explains why individual behavior changes, not why institutions themselves change. The cultural school tends to emphasize the importance of cultural values and interpersonal ties in understanding outcomes. For example, political factions based on personal ties are seen as a more effective means to understanding policy changes in China than are formal institutional arrangements (Nathan 1990). But even though this perspective points out the role of culture in institutions, it is unsatisfactory because it does not explain the obvious constraints the formal structure places on individual behavior.

A theory of institutional diffusion based on studies by C. K. Yang and the contributors of this volume can interpret institutional constraints on individual behavior and institutional change itself. Institutional diffusion includes two interrelated processes. First, institutions, while constraining behavior through external punishment and reward, are diffused in people's minds and become part of a society's value system. Thus, past experiences in traditional lifestyle, market economy, and socialism all left their imprints in today's Chinese mind, formulating a distinctive set of ideas and values. Second, this set of ideas and values, or culture, is diffused in existing institutions. This diffusion occurs most noticeably when institutional rules are being implemented. Those participating in the institution make demands, interpret the articles in a law, or boycott an unreasonable item. These behaviors further define and legitimize the institution with cultural characteristics. An institutional blueprint can be copied from another society, but the process of implementing institutional rules provides opportunities to revise the original design through local understanding and interpretation. For example, establishing an electoral system based on such principles as free nomination, secret balloting, universal suffrage, and term limits could result in a single-party democracy (as was the case in certain periods in post–World War II Japan), a two-party democracy (as is the case in the United States), and a multiparty democracy (as is the case in Russia).

The key assumption of institutional diffusion is that the public can participate in institution building. This is easy to see in a democracy where voters express their desire through elections. Yet for institutional diffusion to hold, it must also be applicable to nondemocratic societies. In other words, it has to show that the public in a nondemocratic society can also express their preferences in institution building. Governments, democratic or nondemocratic, all deliver services, including economic growth, jobs, income, social security and safety, health care, and education. Failure to deliver these services would result in public dissatisfaction and demands for change. The hundreds or even thousands of public protests reported each year in China show that the lack of open elections and institutional checks and balances does not stop the public from demanding change. Indeed, protest is no surprise even in a nondemocratic society if one has nothing to lose, as is the case for an unemployed worker without insurance. No government can last very long without some legitimacy, even nondemocratic governments. Lacking open elections, the Chinese state sees the effective delivery of services as a way to increase its legitimacy. Thus, effectively delivering services becomes a necessity. Allowing public participation is the only way to get policy feedback. It is not the state's altruistic desire but the need to survive that makes the state listen to public opinion. Therefore, as long as public demand does not lead to the destruction of the state, it is a necessary element of institution building. In this sense, public opinion and cultural characteristics are useful means to predict institutional outcomes in a nondemocratic society.

Public Institutions

Thireau and Hua's elegant study of the interaction between migrant workers and labor law vividly describes institutional diffusion. Quoting Yang's work, they show that there is no necessary relationship between policy innovations and institutions. Only through interacting with members of a society can institutions come alive. Thus, they advance the definition of institution from rule-setting to practice.

After a detailed discussion of the restructuring process of China's labor institution and the eventual passage of the 1995 Labor Law, Thireau and Hua show how the making of the new labor institution was an interactive process. Through their analysis of 123 complaint letters sent by migrant workers to Shenzhen's municipal labor bureau in 1996 and 1997, the authors find that knowledge of the institutional framework (the Labor Law) increased workers' tendency to demand that employers follow the rules. Knowledge is a result of improved education under modernization. A more general conclusion based on this finding is that modernization increases one's likelihood to seek institutional solutions. Another finding in this chapter is that expectation matters. The concerns of migrant workers in Shenzhen were different from those of the permanent urban residents; for example, migrant workers' main concern was whether they were paid rather than whether their pay met the minimum wage standard. In this case, institutional constraint only goes as far as the participants' expectations.

Thireau and Hua provide concrete examples of how the Labor Law was defined, expanded, and legitimized through the complaint letters. For example, some workers defined the right to negotiate equally with an employer as the right to participate in managerial decision making. Others extended their legitimate right as workers to include acceptable living conditions. Still others cited social norms—such as egalitarianism, filial piety, human dignity, and keeping one's word—to justify their complaints and, thus, gave new interpretations to the Labor Law. To put the new law in the context of socialist norms, workers referred to such values as "support the building of socialism," "implement a socialist legal system," "no one should be able to breach the laws decided by the Chinese Communist Party," and demanded that local authorities follow the law. Finally, Thireau and Hua present evidence that union leaders discussed adjusting the law in response to workers' complaints, an important point because it shows that the public does participate in institution building even in a single-party authoritarian system.

The Thireau and Hua study shows us that China's new labor institution, though seemingly not that different from such institutions in other societies, is injected with doses of modernization, traditional values, and the socialist legacy. Laws that look identical from one society to another can have different meanings because members in each society carry a different set of historical, cultural, and institutional experiences. And these different meanings affect the way societies implement their laws. The importance of this study lies in its concrete description of how popular norms affect institutional development. Traditional values and socialist norms both play a role in the new labor institution. The common perception of the polarization between institution and culture is melted under the authors' pen.

Thomas G. Rawski's chapter is another example of how culture can pervade in China's economic institution. He shows that China was successful in reducing poverty from 50 percent of its population in 1978 to less than 5 percent in 1998. Economists, on the one hand, attribute this rapid improvement in living standards to incentives under the household responsibility system; political scientists, on the other hand, praise rural leadership for China's economic growth. Rawski argues instead that cultural factors underlie its economic growth. A market-oriented rural culture originating in the Imperial and Republican eras contains important traits that facilitated the post-1978 economic growth. Among these are a historic experience of markets for land, labor, and funds and a long history of trade. Also developed during the Imperial era were such market institutions as monetization, brokerage, shareholding, agency functions, business associations, and customary law. The recent rural economic boom was further facilitated by the early development of such complex organizations as kinship groups, village associations, government, and the educational system. Interaction with these organizations and structures enabled ordinary citizens to develop such business skills as management and accounting and to understand and redefine the economic institution. Rawski's study shows how historical market experience formulated an economic culture that, once the new economic structure was set up, facilitated China's post-1978 economic boom. One other research topic for the future is how the socialist experience affected the post-Mao boom.

Zhanxin Zhang's chapter explores the effect of market forces and the socialist legacy on income distribution since 1978. Zhang disagrees with Victor Nee's (1989) prediction that markets can automatically replace the state, proposing instead a "rights-power interaction" perspective. The state has transformed itself from being a redistributor to being a regulator during marketization, granting private property of labor but maintaining the power to intervene. Zhang uses the urban sample of the 1988 and 1995 China Income Surveys (a joint effort by Western and Chinese researchers) to assess the effects of marketization. For example, labor-contract firms offered higher wages than "semibureaucratic" firms (state-owned and urban collective firms). The return to education increased over time and was higher in contractual labor organizations than in semibureaucratic ones. Yet market is not the only force determining income distribution; Zhang's data show that bureaucratic intervention still played an important role. For example, the state sector offered better pay to workers than did collectively owned firms. Employees in higher level bureaucratic organizations were paid more than those in lower level ones. Monopolistic state firms could afford to pay their employees more than competitive state firms could over time.

Wang Feng and Tianfu Wang's study on income inequality in urban China offers another perspective on income distribution during marketization. Drawing on data from the 1986–1995 Urban Income Survey collected by the State Statistical Bureau in China and from the authors' field interviews, Wang and Wang find that the rising income gap in China more likely reflects group distinctions than individual characteristics. For example, the gap between rural and urban incomes still accounts for as much as 50 percent of the total inequality; there is more equality within rural or urban populations, and urban income is still more equal than rural income. According to Wang and Wang, the interprovincial gap increased from less than 2 percent of total inequality in 1986 to over 40 percent in 1995. The Intercity gap increased from 10 percent in 1986 to 50 percent in the mid-1990s. The interownership gap stayed at the 6–7 percent level from 1986 to 1995. The interindustry gap stayed at 6 percent from the mid-1980s to the mid-1990s. The share of category variables in income distribution (ownership, industry, province, city) is very noticeable. The share of these variables in income distribution increased from 1988 to 1995. The authors attribute the importance of group distinctions to local governments' strong ties with firms during reform because of the need for political legitimacy and personal economic gain; continued and strengthened welfare subsidies within the *danwei* (work organization); the limitation of managerial power by institutional checks and balances such as the party, the union, employee congress, stock owners' congress, and the board of directors; and, finally, to the moral sentiment for equality, harmony, and stability.

Both Zhang and Wang and Wang remind us that group variables are as important as individual variables in explaining income gaps during reform. Their chapters show that marketization does not automatically eliminate traditional categories created during socialism. Many of these categories survived and will continue to affect income distribution. The common theme running through both chapters is that new institutions are defined by old and new players, cultural values, socialist legacies, and migrant workers' market competition. The value of these studies lies in the authors' efforts to identify sources of income distribution. They find a clear confluence of market stratification and bureaucratic hierarchy. They differ in that Wang and Wang find more socialist-bureaucratic influence than market influence, whereas Zhang finds bureaucratic and market influences developing simultaneously. One possible explanation may lie in the different data sources these authors used.

Ka-ho Mok's chapter tackles China's educational institution. Like Zhang, he follows the transformationist perspective: the role of government during globalization and marketization has changed from a "provider of welfare benefits" to "the builder of markets." He discusses how globalization and marketization challenged the traditional state-controlled education system. Accordingly, education policy shifted in the 1980s and 1990s from direct state control to macro guidance—that is, control through legislation, funding, planning, and advice. Drawing from field research in Beijing, Shanghai, Wenzhou, and Guangzhou, Mok presents examples of decentralization and marketization in higher education, including user fees, private higher education, increased competition among higher education institutions, emphasis on consumer choice in education, and pressure to generate revenue. While the state remains in control in education, marketization is a powerful force in changing China's education institutions and even in changing the state itself.

Empirical evidence indicates that the state still plays a role in maintaining equal access to education while allowing limited market influence. For example, a 1992 urban survey shows that throughout the 1950s, 1960s, and 1970s, the effect of parents' education on their children's education consistently declined. In the 1980s and the 1990s, as result of marketization, parental influence returned as a factor. But the return was slow, and by the mid-1990s, parental influence had returned only to its pre-Cultural Revolution level and was still far less than in 1949 (Tang and Parish 2000, fig. 3.3). In any case, Mok's study and the empirical evidence both suggest that globalization can only have its root in China through local adaptation and thus carries distinctive local characteristics.

Rance P. L. Lee examines China's health care institution. He creatively applies the distinction C. K. Yang makes in religion between diffused and institutional religions to health care in Hong Kong, with traditional Chinese medicine (TCM) representing diffused health care and biomedicine representing institutional health care. Under British rule TCM was diffused in nonmedical institutions, such as religion (spiritual healing, praying for an end to SARS), family life (self-medication, diet), media (health information, healing methods), and community life (tea houses, herbal restaurants, fitness programs).

The post-1997 Hong Kong government legalized TCM. This institutionalization modernized TCM and brought more research, training, state funding, economic opportunities, professionalism, and regulation. These features, borrowed from the existing institutional health care system, promoted a greater public acceptance of TCM, a willingness from the government to incorporate it into the official health care system, and opportunities for TCM to compete in a global market. According to household surveys in Hong Kong in 1992, only about 6 percent of those visiting doctors consulted TCM doctors; by 1999, however, this number had risen to about 20 percent. In other words, a dual model of health care in Hong Kong was emerging. Lee's study is a good example of institutional diffusion. The influence of biomedicine during the institutionalization of TCM shows how traditional culture can be significantly influenced by Western ideas, particularly when those in the traditional culture seek acceptance by the public and the state and desire viable economic means to survive in a global market. Yet the continued diffusion of TCM in other institutions suggests that the health care institution, though dominated by biomedicine, carries its cultural characteristics when being implemented in Chinese society.

Family and Community

Deborah S. Davis, in her study of housing consumption, reports the results of her two-wave survey among one hundred households in post-socialist Shanghai in 1987 and 1998. She explains how the liberalization of property rights changed the gender of urban housing consumption. The pre-1978 socialist policy placed housing at a low priority. Although China was more successful in providing basic and equal access to housing than market societies at similar levels of economic development, this policy resulted in small apartment boxes and dilapidation (also see Whyte and Parish 1984). Yet the gender tilt, as Davis explains, favored women because, under socialism, both husband and wife had equal claim to ownership of their apartment. Furthermore, household settings were "feminized" because women were at home as housekeepers and mothers, whereas men were often away on business, so items of a masculine character, such as chess sets and souvenirs from business trips, were generally less visible. The author's detailed descriptions of household arrangements vividly portray daily life under socialism. The privatization of the housing market and the rapid growth of the construction industry since 1978 have dramatically improved housing conditions in urban China. But marketization has reversed the socialist gender balance. Today, the husband is generally the legal owner of the apartment. He also plays a central role in home renovation projects; Davis observed in bookstores that there were as many men as women reading home decorating magazines. Davis's study serves as an example of the chain reactions that occur during institutional change. Marketization is a double-edged sword; in this case, it improved housing consumption but also widened gender inequality in domestic space.

Yanjie Bian, Deborah S. Davis, and Shaoguang Wang's study of family social capital in urban China shows how culture, markets, and bureaucracy shape a social network. Citing the inadequacy of earlier studies that found kinship less significant than coworkers in a network, the authors propose an "event-based position-generator" approach and use a cultural event and its participants' status to measure a network. This approach is more accurate in measuring network capacity. The authors, thus, measure a family's network capacity, or family social capital, by the number of greeters and their occupational and organizational status during a family's lunar New Year celebration. In their 1998 sample of four hundred households in Shanghai, Wuhan, Tianjin, and Shenzhen, they find kinship by far played the most important role in an individual's social network. For example, 44 percent of New Year's greeters were kin members, and only 20 percent were coworkers. In addition, bureaucratic control continued to affect a family's accumulation of social capital. Government officials and managers possessed more administrative resources and had better networks than other occupations. The effect of marketization on social capital is mixed. Families who were private entrepreneurs, had higher incomes, and were more educated had more social capital. Professional families were less competitive than those whose members were officials and managers, indicating "a lower return on expertise."

The conceptual importance of this chapter is the authors' innovative approach to measuring social capital. Bian, Davis, and Wang suggest that cultural events like the lunar New Year can be used for such pragmatic purposes as networking and show how this process is shaped by the social and political environment, namely, family and kinship ties, marketization, and continued bureaucratic control of resource distribution. One question that deserves further attention is how this pattern of accumulating social capital has changed over time. In fact, one reason for the inconsistency between earlier studies that found a less significant role for kinship and Bian, Davis, and Wang's study showing a strong kinship influence may be the reduced role of the work unit in people's life, the crumbling of the centrally planned economy and the social safety net, and increased economic uncertainty during market reform. More than before, people must rely on family and kinship for support during difficult times.

Jieming Chen examines another important aspect of the family institution: the care of the elderly. Using the 1994 survey data on 731 parent-child pairs in Baoding, Chen finds that most people supported the idea of old age support and frequently visited their parents. Support in service was more common among older parents with functional limitations. Financial support increased with the child's income and the parent's financial need. In-kind support was not need-based and mostly carried symbolic meaning. Chen also finds a short-term exchange relationship. Grandparents provided childcare for grandchildren and, in some cases, housing in exchange for their children's financial support. Chen shows that, overall, the traditional value of intergenerational support (family altruism) and family solidarity persisted regardless of the dramatic social changes taking place but that by 1994 most old age support was need-based, indicating a declining social safety net during reform.

Chen addresses the relationship between modernization and old age support. He finds, for example, that economic growth and affluence created more nuclear families and less coresidency between adult children and their parents. This finding suggests that coresidence-based old age support stems from the need to pool family resources, as well as from traditional values. According to a 1989 nationwide survey of women and family, Parish and Farrer (2000, 247–48) find that while most parents expected to live with their children in their old age, fewer than 5 percent anticipated financial support. This is an indication of the extensive pension system established in the socialist period. Five years later, Chen's 1994 survey shows a significantly higher percentage of urban parents' tendency to depend on their children financially in the future, perhaps indicating a decline of the urban social safety net. In short, old age care in China is influenced by cultural values, economic development and modernization, and government policy on old age care.

Cho-yun Hsu's chapter on community life describes local communities as the building blocks of Chinese society. He carefully reviews works by C. K. Yang, William Skinner, Mei-rong Lin, and Jinqing Cao and shows how traditional communities perform economic, political, religious, and ritual functions and how they served as a buffer between the state and society. Hsu believes that the return of the traditional community and communal solidarity in rural China since 1978 has facilitated China's economic growth.

Similar to Chen's study of old age support, Hsu's analysis reminds us of the resilience of the Chinese traditional community, even under the radical social reforms during socialism. Future research may further explore other sources of threat to the traditional community, such as industrialization and globalization.

Most contributors to this volume agree that institutional change in today's China is a complex interaction among culture, market, bureaucracy, and modernization. Some contributors endeavor to explain the combined effects of these factors, such as Thireau and Hua in their chapter on labor institution, Zhang in his study on urban income distribution, Mok in his analysis of education, and Bian, Davis, and Wang in their study of social networks. Some pay more attention to culture, such as Chen in his study of old age care and Hsu in his discussion of the community. Yet culture is not immune to external influence. It is itself shaped by past and present institutional experience. This is shown by Rawski's explanation of the post-1978 economic boom and by Lee's study of traditional Chinese medicine. Other authors shift our attention more explicitly to socialism's legacy, such as Wang and Wang's study on group and individual income inequality. Several authors suggest that the market cannot automatically replace the state. Yet others, such as Davis in her discussion of the housing market (and also Rawski and Mok), more explicitly suggest the impact of marketization on institutional change. To be fair, while focusing on the importance of a single factor, each of these authors agrees that other factors also play a role.

Although the chapters in this volume cover a wide range of institutions, most contributors suggest, whether directly or indirectly, that China's institutions require public participation and are modified by local conditions. Studying these local conditions and the individual values and behavior derived from them will produce valuable insights in understanding institutional change.

Part I

C. K. YANG AND HIS THEORY OF INSTITUTIONS

2

BURKART HOLZNER

C. K. Yang

Sociology in China and the Encounter of Civilizations

The Life of C. K. Yang and its Historical Context

YANG CH'ING-K'UN, known in the West as C. K. Yang and among his friends simply as C. K., lived and worked during one of history's greatest intercivilizational encounters: that between China and the West. I am using the term *intercivilizational encounter* in the strict sense the sociologist Benjamin Nelson uses it:

> Sociology is at a turning point in respect to the horizons it is obliged to confront and the perspectives and methods it is obliged to adopt in order to make sense of the perplexing and tumultuous sociocultural processes of our time. We dare no longer suppose that these processes can effectively be gotten at by confining ourselves to settings which are local, parochial, or instantial. . . . We are obliged to see that many of the most important phenomena of processes and productions of our time are occurring across the world, and they are occurring most intensely in those levels and those settings which have been least systematically studied by sociologists or anthropologists. I refer to the *societal level*, the *civilizational level*, and the *intercivilizational settings and encounters.* (Huff 1981)

Indeed, Yang's life was shaped by the encounter between China and the emerging modern world in the twentieth century, and his sociology and his institution building contributed in important ways to advancing this encounter from confrontation to understanding. This fact places Yang's sociological work at the center of change in the discipline of sociology.

Sociology was born in the West in the mid-nineteenth century, and by the turn of the twentieth century its basic concepts had been formulated. In the last century it focused heavily on the study of Western national societies. Today, it is obliged, as Benjamin Nelson said, to become a social science of global scope. Sociologists must work from a global frame of reference, and their studies must create knowledge linking the world's civilizations. Yang was a pioneer in this effort.

He was born in Canton, the city now known as Guangzhou in 1911, a year of revolution. The Manchu dynasty fell, the Chinese Republic was proclaimed, and Sun Yat-sen was elected president. China began to leave its feudal past behind. Yang was born into a traditional and patrician household of considerable wealth. His father owned the wholesale fish market of Canton, as well as extensive real estate and farm land. As the son of a wealthy and traditional family he was tutored at home in Confucian learning, but he reached out for more education. He decided to enter Yenching University, a move his father, who had hoped his son would follow him in the family business, strongly opposed (Schluchter 1983).

Young Yang, we are told, was a rebellious youth. He had seen the arrogance of British colonialists and the deprivations of poverty in China. He saw indentured laborers marching in chains and once witnessed a British gunboat fire on a crowd. The experiences of his youth made lasting impressions on him, and though later he transcended them, he remained firmly committed throughout his life to the idea of China and its place in the world.

While at Yenching University he was much impressed by the visit of the sociologist Robert Ezra Park. Park represented a sociological generation that had learned from the classical masters. He was a student of Georg Simmel, the great German sociologist and contemporary of Max Weber. There are reasons to believe that Park was a powerful influence in Yang's career choice and his decision to come to America. It is important to note that Yang lived only one generation of scholars away from the founding generation that created the framework of sociological theory.

Yang completed his bachelor of arts degree in sociology at Yenching University in 1932 and his master's two years later, in 1934. While at Yenching, he and China's other great sociologist, Fei Xiao Tong, studied and lived together, forming a life-long friendship. Yang came to the United States the year he graduated. Soon thereafter Japan attacked China, marking the beginning of many years of war in China, Asia, and, later, the rest of the world. In 1939, the year World War II began in Europe, Yang completed his doctorate in sociology at the University of Michigan. And on December 10 of the same year he married Louise Chin, who became his companion for life. They had two sons, Wallace and Wesley Yang. He and his family stayed in the United States until 1948.

He moved his family to New York to become the editor of the *Chinese Journal* in New York City. His choice of this assignment reflected not only his dedication to serving his people but also, perhaps, the influence of Robert E. Park, who began his own graduate studies after working as a reporter for eleven years. Yang was an adventurous journalist, promoting the interests of the Chinese community in New York and, especially, campaigning against crime that was victimizing this community. Several times he was threatened by criminals he exposed. He began his academic career as an assistant professor of sociology at the University of Washington in Seattle, where he taught from 1944 until 1948.

He was asked to join the faculty of Lingnan University in Canton in 1948, and he served as an associate professor and head of the sociology department. It was from that vantage point that he witnessed the early phase of China's transition to communism. True to his commitments to sociology, he chronicled the changes occurring in the early phase of the revolution, and it was during this time that he collected the material for several important books. Doing fieldwork during the revolution was no doubt courageous. It may well have been motivated by his sociological conviction that no significant change could come to China without revolution, a conclusion Weber himself had reached long before. His work may also have been inspired by another influential figure in his early academic life: the anthropologist Robert Redfield (son-in-law of Robert E. Park).

Sociology was under some suspicion by the early 1950s in China, and in 1951 he and his family returned to the United States, where he became a research associate at the Center for International Studies at the Massachusetts Institute of Technology and in 1952 at Harvard.

Yang moved to Pittsburgh in 1953 to serve as associate professor of sociology at the University of Pittsburgh and became a full professor in 1958. He wrote prolifically during the 1950s and 1960s, and his books *A Chinese Village in Early Communist Transition, The Chinese Family in the Communist Revolution,* and *Religion in Chinese Society* appeared during that period.

Yearly during the 1960s Yang visited what he termed "the outer fringe of the Asia mainland, namely Hong Kong, Taiwan, and Japan." "I noted the woefully backward state of the field of sociology in Hong Kong," he wrote at the time, "and I started to help a local college in setting up field investigation centers as a first step to direct their attention to examining indigenous social facts in the light of sociological knowledge that they were studying from books, mainly Western sociology books with their theoretical base in the Western civilization, particularly North American civilization, which holds wide discrepancies from facts of other societies such as Hong Kong." (The "local college" mentioned here was Chung Chi College, now part of the Chinese University of Hong Kong.)[1]

Yang was also a student of American society even though most of his writing centered on China. He was aware of the "enormity of America's industrial might," as he called it, and that Pittsburgh was right in the center of its industrial capitalism. In the 1960s Pittsburgh's riverbanks were lined with steel mills, and the night sky glowed red from the fires of their furnaces; it was the classic symbol as well as reality of heavy industry.

Yang took a leave of absence from the University of Pittsburgh in 1964 to join the faculty of the Social Research Center at the University of Hawaii. It was here he began plans for an ambitious program of intellectual cooperation between China, Japan, and the United States, linking social science colleagues at the University of Hawaii and the University of Pittsburgh with leading scholars in Japan, Taiwan, and Hong Kong.

In late 1965 the founding vice chancellor of the Chinese University of Hong Kong, C. M. Li, called Yang to enlist his help in developing the sociology program at the then fledgling university. Yang asked me to be his partner in this venture, and in January 1966 we traveled to Hong Kong to meet our colleagues in the sociology department.

Charles H. Peake, then vice chancellor for academic disciplines at the University of Pittsburgh, readily understood the benefits of partnering with the Chinese University of Hong Kong and specifically with C. M. Li. He supported the establishment of a formal program of cooperation between the two universities. Yang spent much effort in designing the cooperation program and managed much of it himself. These years were Yang's most creative period in building the academic bridges linking scholars across the Pacific.

A critical event in the emerging partnership was a travel seminar to Japan, Taiwan, and Hong Kong that Yang organized in February 1967 and that Peake and I participated in. It deepened Peake's and my understanding of Asia and his committment to the international studies program.

In 1968 the University of Pittsburgh's University Center for International Studies (UCIS) was founded; it was designed to be the central, integrative framework for all the international programs and centers of the university. Yang was the leading advisor in matters Chinese to the leadership of UCIS and of the university. UCIS and the department of sociology were the institutional anchors of the interuniversity linkage between the Chinese University of Hong Kong and the University of Pittsburgh, but the university's chancellor, Wesley W. Posvar, took a direct and personal interest in this program as well. The Lingnan board of trustees and the Rockefeller Brothers Fund decided to help the Pittsburgh–Hong Kong partnership. In subsequent years, many young scholars from the Chinese University of Hong Kong came to the University of Pittsburgh for their graduate education, and many Pittsburgh faculty served in Hong Kong. In fact, today several of Hong Kong's universities have University of Pittsburgh alumni among their top leadership, in part due to this program.

Yang returned to Pittsburgh from Hawaii in 1968 and served as professor of sociology at both Pittsburgh and Hong Kong. He actively participated in planning the future of the Chinese University of Hong Kong and in planning the international profile of the University of Pittsburgh. In 1971 Yang was among the first social scientists from America to be invited to visit the People's Republic of China, a turning point both for Yang and for Chinese-American relations. Reflecting in 1972 on his ambitious plans for research on China, he wrote:

> All the foregoing efforts seemed to come to a halt when I unexpectedly received the invitation from Peking to visit China in October 1971. It seems to be a project that has priority and urgency over all the rest of the things I have been doing. I made my China trip in October–November 1971. The consequences were anything but expected: innumerable requests for speaking, for communication in the mass media, for consultations, and for publications by publishers. For the period between the end of November and the present, I hardly could keep my feet on my home base in Pittsburgh, with developments in the future still to be conjectured. But there is little doubt of the significance of whatever effort I can make to present the realistic China as it exists under the Communist rule to the American public, and to the students in 1,000 classes (John Lindbeck's figure) carrying on Chinese studies in the country. To formulate and to convey an accurate image of China with its massive population, extensive territory, and highly strategic political significance in the present era has overriding significance beyond many of the projects that have occupied my attention up to now.[2]

Yang was appointed Distinguished Service Professor of Sociology by the University of Pittsburgh in 1972, and in that year he made a second visit to the People's Republic of China. In 1974 the Chinese University of Hong Kong awarded him an honorary doctorate. In 1979 Professor Fei Xiao Tong invited Yang, Wesley Posvar, Jiri Nehnevajsa, and me to Beijing to deliver the first lectures on American sociology; these were the first such lectures since the Chinese government had closed down professional sociology in 1952.[3] The lectures focused on applications of sociology and the field's usefulness in modernization. The time was a turning point in China. The Cultural Revolution had come to its end with the arrest of the "Gang of Four." Deng Xiaoping, who had become China's leader, decided to open China to at least part of the world. Our lectures were an element in this opening. In this context, Vice Premier Yao Yi-lin officially invited our group, led by Fei Xiaotong and C. K. Yang. He endorsed the project of reestablishing sociology in China's universities, stating on Chinese national television that China's modernization effort needed professionals educated in the discipline of objective recording and analyzing facts and that for this reason sociological training was important. A period of engaged institution building followed for Yang. He retired from the University of Pittsburgh in 1981 and became Distinguished Service Professor Emeritus. He died on January 10, 1999.

C. K. Yang's Sociology

A Global and Comparative Perspective

Yang traveled the world, and his travels were part of his sociological self-education. He traveled through all of China and Mongolia and made two field trips to the People's Republic of China in the early 1970s. He visited many other countries in Asia as well: Japan, the Philippines, Singapore, Malaysia, Thailand, Burma, India, Iran, and Lebanon. In Europe he traveled in Greece, Italy, Switzerland, Germany, Finland, Denmark, Sweden, Holland, England, France, Spain, Portugal, and the former Soviet Union. For him, sociology was a world enterprise, albeit a woefully incomplete work in progress. He read widely and engaged other sociologists on a range of issues. But the study of China and the building of an authentic Chinese sociology were the center of his intellectual commitments.

Building on the Sociological Traditions

Yang joined the main traditions of sociological theory: he built on the foundations laid by Max Weber and his conception of sociology as the science of social action. He carefully read Weber's works in pursuit of the answer to why economic rationality, modern capitalism, had originated in the West. Yang's study of Weber's work on China was a fundamental component in the development of his sociological thinking. In Yang's introduction to Hans Gerth's translation of Weber's *The Religion of China* (Weber 1964) he stressed the significance of Weber's insistence on understanding the "dynamic disposition of a religion toward the socioeconomic order" (p. xliii). He agreed with Weber's conclusion that significant change could not come to China without a revolution.

Yang respected the work of Talcott Parsons and drew on his systematic study of the theory of action, which built on Weber, of course. He also used Parsons's general idea of the "social system" as a guiding principle to understanding the dynamic interconnectedness of institutions, groups, and their cultures. It served as a broad framework for Yang's monumental study of religion in Chinese society, as did the carefully selected "pattern variables" of *diffuseness* and *specificity* that helped him in structuring the work. Although Parsons wrote an insightful foreword to Yang's book *The Chinese Family in the Communist Revolution* (Yang 1959), Yang was not a "Parsonian." He developed his main vision of sociology from the work of what came to be known as the Chicago school of human ecology, community studies, and studies of relations among groups. Again, the perspectives of Robert E. Park and Robert Redfield came into play, as well as the heritage of Weber. His own background as a well-grounded scholar in the Chinese tradition was influential as well. In fact, he mastered two high traditions of scholarship: the ancient traditions of China and the young tradition of sociology.

Yang was challenged by Weber's interpretation of religion in China. Weber focused on Confucianism and Taoism, treating them as major cultural religions. Yang, however, revised this image in his celebrated book *Religion in Chinese Society* (Yang 1961). His analysis was the first to go beyond the study of specific religious doctrines, describing instead religious activity throughout Chinese society. He used Parsons's *pattern variables of specificity versus diffuseness* as the conceptual framework, which allowed him to study *specific* religious institutions separate from the *diffuse* religion that pervaded society. The focus of Western scholars, seeking analogies to the well-delimited Christian-specific institutions of the church and clergy, had overlooked the significance of diffuse religion in China. He was able to show that religion in its diffuse form permeated Chinese society. This work enabled him to contribute to the ongoing debate about Weber's explanation for China's long history of stagnation.

A scholarly consensus has emerged on at least a few points in this debate. Confucianism and Taoism as such did not exhaust the spectrum of Chinese religion, as Yang showed. Weber's belief that China did not advance in the process of rationalization because of the persistence of magical thinking—viewing the world as a *Zaubergarten* (magic garden)—was somewhat of an exaggeration. In fact, the development potential of Chinese intellectual accomplishments had been seriously underestimated.[4] However, although China was, for a long period in history, technologically ahead of Europe, the fact remains that China did not develop modern science in the strict sense of that modern institution.

Yang was much concerned with Weber's understanding of the role of cities in the process he calls rationalization. Weber's thesis is that the European "free cities" were unique in the world and were enclaves of freedom within the fabric of feudal domination; they were economic hubs as well as military and political powers in their own right. Yang sought to examine the actual history of Chinese cities. Subsequent work showed that there were, indeed, significant economic centers in China but not like the politically and militarily autonomous "free cities" of Europe.

Yang's Practice of Sociology

Observing Social Reality Directly

Yang insisted on observing social reality through direct, personal contact with it. He respected the skills of journalists and instilled this respect in his students. In his early work in Hong Kong and later in Pittsburgh he insisted that those doing fieldwork and community studies learn how to observe and record social facts. He was passionate about grasping social reality "live," much in the spirit of Robert E. Park and Robert Redfield, whom he admired. He was a careful investigator, always looking for quantifiable data in addition to his qualitative understanding, and his vivid and accurate village studies reflect his exceptional ability to observe and analyze.

Making Sociology Useful

Another principle of his sociology was that it be made useful. He discovered that community studies, studies of demographic facts, could be of great practical use locally. For instance, in Pittsburgh he advised city planners and made recommendations about planned roads and tunnels that would be obsolete before they were even begun. He wanted sociology to be useful in Hong Kong and China as well. His Kwun Tong study was a project dear to his heart and useful for Hong Kong. The study investigated how the many immigrants with peasant background would adapt to the very different, emerging urban social reality. The development of this industrial satellite of Hong Kong fascinated him. Similarly, he immersed himself in the planning of the study of "hawkers," as the street vendors in Hong Kong were called. Hong Kong's government tried to persuade the "hawkers" to move into neat marketing buildings. But to the annoyance of the government, they did not leave their street marketing. Different policies would have to be created. It was this spirit of applied sociology that informed his efforts to rebuild sociology and social anthropology in China beginning in 1979. He did see sociology as essential to China's path of modernization.

Correcting the West's View of China

Early on, Yang saw that Western sociologists' view of China was inaccurate and needed to be corrected. His first publication in English, *A North China Local Market Economy* (Yang 1944), was a brief but path-breaking work. In his foreword Herbert Blumer wrote, "The study fills a significant gap in our knowledge of native Chinese economy and adds to our knowledge of Chinese rural life. . . . Little has been known of local trade and its institutionalization in the form of the 'periodic' market. . . . From the meticulous accounts given by Dr. Yang of the kinds and quantities of goods sold in the market one can see the limited economic world of the people and can perceive the confines placed on their structure of living." This excerpt from *A North China Local Market Economy* clearly illustrates Yang's style as a sociologist:

> A periodic market is composed of a group of sellers and buyers meeting in a fixed place and at regular time intervals. The place may be a village or a town. The length of the time interval differs with local conditions. . . . Outside of the market date, a market village or town is usually quiet and peaceful. . . . There may be several stores

on the street corners, or even scores of stores lining its main street, but business is exceedingly slow. The doors of some of them are half closed or even entirely closed. Streets are deserted save for a few sauntering loiterers. The barking of the dogs and the crowing of the chickens, together with the occasional rumbling of a passing cart and the shouting of the driver to the animals, break the silence now and then. The scene is cool and calm, and life is slow paced. Such is the general appearance of the town or village and the narrow sphere of its social and economic services to the surrounding territory. . . . But on the day when the market meets it is like the dead come to life. Shortly after dawn breaks over the horizon, farmers, craftsmen, and professional traders, each taking their vendible articles in hand, on back, on packing animals, in wheelbarrows, on carts, begin to stream in from roads, from paths, from all highways and by-ways that lead to the market site. . . . Meanwhile, buyers also start to pour in from all directions. Approaching noon, both sellers and buyers are collected in great multitudes. The quiet and lonely village or town is drowned in the din of high market voices, turning it into a roaring scene. The usually empty streets are packed with whirling and milling crowds. The sleepy and stoic faces of the peasants wake up and are animated with excitement in haggling and bargaining. . . . Toward late afternoon, the heat of the day is over, and the busy market is drawing to its close, until one sees only a few lonely souls wearily packing their remnants in the dusky shadows of an empty street. (Yang 1944)

Insisting on Historical Context

A fourth principle guiding Yang's work was his rule to apply a thoroughly historical perspective to his sociological investigations and reflections. This may have been rooted in his classical Chinese education and his deep familiarity with Chinese history and literature. He sensed early on, for example, the importance of markets and cities. About his study of the town of Foshan, he wrote,

> In addition to the contribution [this study makes toward] understanding Chinese society, such a study holds significance for the general theoretical framework of urban sociology on a comparative basis. A well-known theme in this direction came from Max Weber, claiming that the *economic* city is peculiar to Europe alone, leading to the development of industrial civilization. Elsewhere in the world, Weber claimed, cities were only administrative centers with very limited significance in economic production. My study seeks to prove the contrary: that economic production centers have long existed as one of the many types of cities in Chinese civilization, and the explanation of the absence of industrialization in the Chinese social history may not be explained by the Weberian theme.[5]

Although he did not complete this study, another imaginative foray into Chinese history did yield results. It was the study of "mass actions" in nineteenth-century China. This research program was a quantitative study of mass unrest and social movements during the late Ch'ing period (1796–1911). The data were extracted from the "Veritable Records" of the Ch'ing emperors and yielded information about more than six thousand incidents, primarily riots and battles of rebellion; it yielded a picture of social movements and unrest that brought about increasingly drastic changes in Chinese society. Yang appears to have written only one paper on this work (Yang 1975). Here is how he summarized the study's main (preliminary) findings:

> In all major phases of analysis the data clearly converge on the political institution as the primary sector which failed to maintain the traditional social order and thus bred social unrest. The predominance of suppressive measures and the prominence of government military success had only questionable effectiveness in restabilizing the traditional socio-political order. Suppression and victories in one decade did not forestall the further rise of mass action incidents in the next decade. . . . The ineffectiveness of suppression as a means to quell unrest is also emphasized by the internal deterioration of the ruling class of late Ch'ing China. It is important to note from the . . . statistical information that the ruling class and its supporting elements supplied the bulk of leadership for incidents of social unrest. In this sense, government suppressive actions may well be viewed as an internal strife or civil war among the rulers and their henchmen. (Yang 1975, 208)

Sociology for Modernization

When in 1979 Yang accepted the invitation of Professor Fei Xiao Tong of the Chinese Academy of Social Science to help reintroduce the disciplines of sociology and social anthropology to China, a decisive moment had occurred in Chinese modernization. Yang enlisted me and our colleague Jiri Nehnevajsa to devise a program to assist in Fei's assignment. We decided to offer a series of overview lectures at the Chinese Academy of Social Science on the role of sociology and social research in the United States. I had done much work on social systems for knowledge creation and use, and Jiri Nehnevajsa was a well-established sociological survey researcher with expertise in technology assessments and planning for change. We called the program "The Sociology for

Modernization" rather than "sociology *of* modernization," which we saw as a descriptive enterprise.

The many strands of Yang's sociological vision came together in this, his last major project, which we and many others helped him carry out. And it was an undertaking of genuine service. Sociology for the modernization of China, while built on the experience of sociology in the West, would become an endogenous enterprise in China and would help it master the difficulties of the social transformation that needed to be addressed.

Much has changed in China, in the world, and in sociology since that time twenty-five years ago. There is a new phase of modernization in progress now, a phase of modernity called by some "reflexive modernization" or "phase II modernization." It is characterized by global interconnections, rapid technological and economic changes, and the emergence of entirely new modes of communication and, indeed, of institutions. This phase of modernity has altered the web of social relations, the role of the nation-state, and the modalities of social identities. Sociology is not only affected by but also a part of these changes. There is now a strong sociological profession in China. It plays a role in the challenges China is facing today. And it plays a role in the world. For China, as for other parts of the world, the rapid changes brought on by globalization pose challenges that sociology for modernization can help to deal with. I believe that the vision C. K. Yang had for sociology in China can also serve as a guide for its future.

Building Bridges Between East and West

China was Yang's birthplace and his cultural home, yet the United States had accepted him, respected him, and granted him citizenship. He was a Chinese patriot, but he was also an American patriot. Being a person of dual but sincere loyalty is a difficult feat, but he accomplished it. He saw both cultures with clear eyes and understood intimately how each viewed itself and the world. His sense of history was keen, and his commitment to building bridges between China and the United States never wavered.

Yang's effort to rebuild sociology in Hong Kong and later in China required not only telling China's story of change to America but also creating opportunities for Chinese scholars and students to study sociology. It also required finding ways to adapt sociology to the Chinese reality, and he created programs both at the University of Pittsburgh and at the Chinese University of Hong Kong for this purpose. Many of Yang's Chinese graduate students are now significant figures in Chinese sociology. And many of his American graduate students are significant figures in Chinese studies and international education in the United States.

Yang's Legacy as an Institution Builder

Yang knew institutions and understood their dynamics, and he used this knowledge to enhance the institutions he served. The high profile the University of Pittsburgh enjoys today in international scholarship owes much to his pioneering work in the 1960s and 1970s. He recognized early in the development of the Chinese University of Hong Kong that bringing the initial three colleges together to create one university would be a crucial step in the university's success, and as a senior advisor in all matters of sociology, he pressed for the realization of the central university approach.

Yang's institutional thinking was much concerned with time and demographics. He knew that rebuilding an academic discipline would take time and that even highly gifted graduate students would need years to become recognized scholars and professors in their own right. He understood the importance of budgets and the commitment of university leaders, without which nothing would flourish. So he stayed with the overall project of the Chinese University of Hong Kong for as long as he could, enjoying the immense satisfaction of seeing it evolve into one of the world's leading research universities.

3

CHONG CHOR LAU

Institutional Restructuring, Organizational Integration, and the Chinese Revolution

C. K. Yang's Theory of Social System Change

THE CHINESE REVOLUTION and the social changes that followed constitute the central theme in the lifetime work of C. K. Yang. From the early 1930s to the late 1980s Yang conducted extensive empirical research on the radical changes occurring in Chinese society. Although his intellectual interests shifted over the years, he remained focused on the transformation of the social system. The system perspective guided his studies on the various aspects of social life.

Institutional and organizational change are the key concepts in Yang's social system theory. Social institutions are reconstituted in different phases of revolutionary movements. This process in China gave rise to an organizational pattern that facilitated China's national integration. Institutional restructuring and organizational integration are thus integral components of the modernization of the Chinese social system.

Yang carefully examined evidence of these changes during the six decades of his work. He began his academic career with a large project to study an entire marketing community in 1932. He then moved on to studying the family and the village, conducting extensive fieldwork in rural China for twenty years. After the Communist revolution of 1949, fieldwork became difficult, so Yang turned his attention to historical studies of Chinese religion and social movements. But as soon as China reopened its doors to outside researchers in the 1970s, Yang returned to China to gather empirical data for his study of national integration. Yang's uninterrupted academic career provides an empirical foundation for his system theory of social change.

Central to Yang's research agenda was a desire to identify the salient aspects of social transformation brought about by the Chinese revolution. He believed that the century-long revolution was not a random, uniquely Chinese response to the challenge of modernity but rather was similar to the pattern of social change in the West identified by Max Weber.[1] Institutions and organizations in every domain of social life in China were to undergo processes of rationalization that were similar to those experienced in the modern history of the West. This comparative view allowed Yang to document in detail the discontinuity of the hold of the traditional order and to closely examine the rise of new patterns, some of which he would witness with his own eyes. The opening up of China in the early 1980s gave rise to a significant amount of empirical data that allow for theoretical verification of Yang's ideas.

Sources of Yang's Theory

Market Studies

Yang began his academic career in 1932 when he undertook a large field study of a rural market area in North China (Yang 1944). The site, in Zouping County, Shantung Province, was chosen because of its traditional, preindustrial features, as well as its proximity to Jinan and Qingdao, two large cities in Shantung Province, from where forces of industrialization made inroads into the district. The site provided a good opportunity to study the traditional structure of a Chinese agricultural community and the influence of industrialization on the transformation of local society.

The focus of Yang's study was the marketing community. At the center of the community was the periodic market: a group of sellers and buyers meeting at a fixed place and at regular time intervals. Depending on the local conditions, these markets were held every five or six days.

The market system of Zouping consisted of twenty-six markets, ten small markets, thirteen medium markets, and three large markets. None of the markets on its own could meet all the demands of the local population. The small and medium markets were close to the buyers, but they sold only the bare necessities for daily consumption. The large markets possessed all the goods and services required by the local economy, but they were too far away from most villages. The three types of markets together, however, functioned in an interdependent fashion to serve the local economy quite adequately.

In addition to the transaction of consumer products, the markets were closely related to local production by providing the means of production. More production goods were transacted in the larger markets. The market system was equally important as an outlet for local production. While the periodic market served as the main venue through which outside goods reached the local population, it was also the chief focal point where local products were gathered up to be shipped outside and ultimately used in exchange for community needs from distant regions.

The market system served to satisfy the social needs of the local community. It provided local people with entertainment through the performance of professional storytellers, various theatrical troupes, singers, magicians, and boxers, as well as patent medicine peddlers. People used the services of fortune tellers in the market, not only for fortune telling but also for the reading and writing of letters. The market system also served as a center of information—that is to say, a place for disseminating ideas and social movements among the rural population.

The market in Zouping evolved from the formation of service areas for buyers and sellers. Different principles governed each area. The size of each area was small, since walking distance was a governing principle. In Zouping and the surrounding counties, there was an unwritten law that no new market could be established within 1.8 miles of an already existing market.

Another organizing principle was the complementality of the small, medium, and large markets in the system. In Zouping, the mean radius of the service area of the small markets, providing only daily necessities, was 1.3 miles, serving an average population of 3,847 people. For luxuries, the populace turned to larger markets. The mean radius of the medium-sized market was 2.5 miles, serving an average population of 8,000. The largest market in Zouping had a radius of 8.2 miles and served 50,000 people. The large markets complemented the smaller ones by providing expensive consumption items, such as draft animals and fancy wedding clothing.

The size of the sellers' area was usually two to three times that of the average service area. A seller was willing to spend more time and energy than a buyer to travel to an area in order to sell his goods. This is especially so in the case of highly perishable goods like fruits and vegetables.

The markets in Zouping were also governed by a set of social institutions. The core arrangements involved the public regulation of weights and measures. Yang provides evidence from a case study detailing the organizational process for the maintenance of public weights and measures. The focus of his attention, however, was on institutional change—namely, the replacement of the "communal market," where the rules were maintained by the local community, with government tax regulations.

Changes were also taking place in the relationship between towns and markets. While Yang's study shows that the markets were still more important to the population of Zouping than were towns, towns were gaining in two ways. The number of stores in towns was increasing, while attendance at markets was decreasing. The motivation behind this shift was the growing commercialization of agriculture that forced people to purchase commodities that formerly had been produced or made at home.

At the core of the commercialization of agriculture was the replacement of grain production with cotton planting, a trend common to all of North China. Along with this trend, modern forces from outside of Zouping gradually approached the local community. This was most observable in the market system.

Yang's research strategy for his market studies involved selecting a periodic market system in which to observe the traditional order, the invasion of extrasystemic forces, and the balance between them. Yang's findings from his empirical research on market systems can be summarized as follows:

> The pattern of life self-sufficiency in the local community is found only in the social system consisting of villages and their populations, the periodic markets of different sizes, and the market towns. The periodic market plays an important role in the traditional order.
>
> The forces of modern change began to be felt by the local social system as the nation underwent its revolutionary transformation. Among other factors, the commercialization of agriculture broke down local self-sufficiency and the traditional balance. Towns, especially those close to modern transportation, increased in significance, undermining the role of the periodic market and gradually integrating the local social system into the national society.
>
> This new order brought about a new set of social arrangements and, as a result, new attitudes among the local population. The following three arrangements are the most salient: (1) Commercialization of cotton planting gave rise to a calculating attitude among a significant segment of the Zouping population. Cotton was one-third to two-thirds more profitable than traditional grain crops. In a matter of two decades after the 1932 study, cotton acreage multiplied. (2) Commercialization of local production gave rise to a new set of organizational

patterns in the local economy. Cotton was shipped to large cities in exchange for machine-made goods, undermining the production of homemade products and eventually local self-sufficiency. Mechanized modes of transportation became more important for the local population. Towns gradually replaced the periodic markets as the centers of business. Although a rational bureaucratic form of organization did not take hold, examples of calculation could be found in the development of the new organizational pattern in the Zouping economy. (3) The commercialization of local life gave rise to a merchant class. As the boundaries of the market system expanded, merchants gradually came to dominated local life. With the ongoing decline in local self-sufficiency, there emerged a new social system in which the peasants were increasingly subjected to the whims of the merchants and landlords as well as to the vicissitudes of the business cycle.

The Changing Family

Yang's market studies provided glimpses into both the emerging pattern of the social system and the forces combining to undermine China's traditional social order. At the core of that order was the Chinese family, and this became the focus of Yang's next research project (Yang 1959).

As an institution the family performed a multiplicity of functions and played a vital role in the organization of social life in traditional China. To carry out its functions, the small nuclear family relied on a large kinship network. The organizational principles of the household and kinship network were dictated by Confucianism, which assigned roles and responsibilities based on gender, age, and generation. These are the structural principles of the dominance of parents over children, the old over the young, and men over women, principles of traditional familism that were written into law and enforced by the dynastic regimes. Furthermore, this familism early on acquired a sacred character, ensuring compliance from the people very similar to the obedience to the commandments in Judaism and Christianity.

Yang's research found that the fading of familism derived from three areas of social system change: structural changes that diminished the traditional organizational principles and consequently altered familial relations, the transformation of patterns of marriage and divorce and family decision making, and changes in the status and role of family members and in people's values and ideology about the family.

The crumbling of the age hierarchy began before the Communist revolution. During the Republican period, it was fashionable to acquire Western knowledge and technology as part of the attempt to save China. In this respect, the young had a distinct advantage over the old in the acquisition of new ideas and skills. The rise of the young was aided also by increased educational opportunities in the early twentieth century. The authority of the elders was further attacked during the May Fourth Movement of 1919 as Confucianism was targeted as the root of China's political and social crises.

After the victory of the Communist revolution, the status of youth was even further elevated by the emergence of youth organizations. In September 1951, less than two years after the founding of the People's Republic, national membership in the New Democratic Youth League exceeded five million people. The Chinese Communist Party, the governing party, was also dominated by young people. With their newly gained political power, the youth rose in status, whereas the older generations generally lost power and status. Dramatic changes in political institutions and organizations caused the rapid decline in the veneration of age in the Chinese family.

The transformation of gender inequalities was no less dramatic. The most fundamental source of change came from a new marriage law, promulgated in May 1950. The principle of gender equality, espoused in the law, was enforced by the government. After the law was enacted, the Communists attempted mass education to teach women how to exert their rights. Thus, with both legal and political help, the status of women in the family reached unprecedented heights.

The kinship networks supported the dominance of traditional principles, especially the authority of clan elders, in local communities. But the rise of the Communist regime meant an end to the power of the clans. The Communist regime was the first Chinese government not to rely on clans for the maintenance of local peace and order. Instead, the regime organized poor peasants' associations to compete with clan authority. During the land reform movement, the Communists targeted "familism and clanism" as obstacles to modern development, and there were concerted efforts to dissolve the clan organizations. With the crippling of clans' organization and functioning, clan elders lost their authority and power in the local communities.

Parents and clan leaders also lost decision-making authority related to marriage, divorce, and births. Control by the family and the clan in these matters was weakened, and young couples gained more freedom and autonomy. Yang provides ample data to show this central trend in the fading away of traditional parental control in the dynamics of the family institution.

The result of these changes was a new pattern of familial relations. The family and clan heads lost their dominant position as the autonomy of individual members grew. This means that the dominance of the old over the young, the control of parents over children, and the superior status of men over women had come to an end. The ascendancy of women in the family was the most important outcome of the transformation of the Chinese family. It altered all key relationships in the family, giving rise to a new family institution that was similar to the modern family of the West.

In his research on the changing family, Yang pays considerable attention to the place of ideas, social movements, and organizations in the process of social system change. His findings regarding the changing family can be summarized as follows:

New ideas, mostly from the West, constitute a force in the institutional transformation of marriage, divorce, and equality between men and women as well as between the old and the young. Ideas are incorporated into instruments of change, such as the new marriage law and the government's propaganda to promote it.

Widespread mass movements—whether spontaneous, such as the women's movement in the pre-Communist period, or planned, such as the political campaigns of the Communists—played pivotal roles in the extensive transformation of the social system.

Organized power was used as a weapon in the Communist revolution; it was also used to improve individual status, the most obvious example of this being the young's increased power over the older generation.

Social Change in the Village

The village studies, which Yang and his colleagues began in 1948, continued until 1951, two years into the Communist regime's rule (Yang 1959). They provided an opportunity to examine the changes in the institutional system at the village level as the local community was integrated into the national community. Yang's observations of these changes provide vivid pictures about the initial stage of the modernization of social life at the grassroots level of the social system.

All significant components of the village institutional system were transformed by the whirlwind campaigns initiated by the Communist regime. There was a succession of movements during the first decade of Communist rule: land reform and efforts to organize peasants' associations throughout the country and various stages of agricultural collectivization, culminating in the Great

Leap Forward and the rise of the people's communes. As a result of these changes, the traditional village institutions were radically changed, and life on the farm was never the same again.

The kinship system was attacked on both sides: from the land reform movement and the collectivization movement. The destruction of the clans and the rise of the peasants' associations meant that the local political order was transformed from a decentralized pattern of balance among clan elders, rich families, and old gentry groups into a centralized pattern of direct and systematic control by the central government. Unlike the old clans and gentry groups, the peasants' associations and other organizations were mere instruments of the local government.

Collective farming also weakened the control of the kinship system by stripping away most of its economic functions. During the process of collectivization, land and major farm equipment were removed from family ownership, eroding the foundation of the family as a production center. Together with changes in the family institution, the kinship system was no longer at the core of the village structure.

The new core derived its status and authority from the national system. At the center was the rapidly expanding Communist Party. Very quickly, village committees were established in almost every one of China's one million villages, and through the village committees, the party was able to set up new organizations, such as the Communist Youth League, the peasants' association, and the women's association, to support its rule. As a result, the village community was closely integrated into the state. For the first time in Chinese history, the entire national system could be transformed in a uniform manner. Here in summary is Yang's empirical finding on social change in the village:

> Through the organization of the Communist Party, the Communist Youth League, the peasants' association, and the women's association, the formerly decentralized power structure of the village was centralized under the control of the national government. This integration of the local community and the state allowed for the transformation of the national social system in a concerted and uniform manner.

Religion in Chinese Society

The central theoretical construct of Yang's studies of religion is the continuum between institutional and diffused religion (Yang 1961). The pair is taken from

Talcott Parsons's sociological concepts of diffuseness and specificity and applied to an interpretation of the structure of China's religious institution.

Institutional religion has a system of theology, rituals, and organization of its own, independent of other secular social institutions. It is a social institution by itself, having its own basic concepts and structure. The world's great religions, except Confucianism, are institutional religions. In traditional China, Buddhism and Taoism represented institutional religion.

Diffused religion has its own theology, rituals, and symbols, as well as an organization intimately merged with the concepts and structure of secular institutions and other aspects of the social order. In traditional China, diffused religion was found in all major social groups and institutions. It was represented in the family and clan system by ancestor worship: Belief in the souls of one's departed ancestors was part of perpetuating the family; mortuary and sacrificial rites formed an inseparable part of family rituals; and the head of the family acted as an officiating priest, with family members as the congregation. In terms of theological concept, ritualistic practice, and personnel structure, ancestor worship was an integral part of the family and the wider kinship system. As a component of all major social institutions, the diffused religion affected every significant aspect of social life in China.

The use of the concept of diffuseness in his analysis of traditional Chinese religion enabled Yang to examine the moral character of the social institutions in traditional China. In other societies dominated by institutional religions, religious influence is limited to believers. The case of traditional China is unique as its indigenous religion merged into its secular institutions and consequently affected almost all members of the society. This inclusion transformed the secular organization. Thus the clan and the family were not ordinary social groups but religious corporations. Because the secular institutions and social and political groups have similar religious elements, a moral character can be found in them. This character was a significant source of the stability of the social order in traditional China.

The fading of this moral character in many aspects of life in modern China is a key to understanding social system change over the last two centuries. Research on the changing family shows that the disappearance of the religious element was the cumulative result of conceptual and structural institutional changes as well as changes in the larger system. In the larger system a shift occurred in the center of loyalty from the kinship organization to the nation-state, weakening the influence of such core values as filial piety. The disintegration of the clan and the weakening of family functions resulted in a loosened grip over individual members. In the contemporary period, most religious practices have been suppressed by the state, thus bringing an end to the long relationship between religion and the Chinese institutional system.

The effect of the loss of this integrative force on the social system is an important research question for students of contemporary China. When communism rode to victory in China, it was natural to consider it as a new integrative force in society. Although communism is not theistic, its role as the ideological guidepost of the Chinese revolution was even more fundamental than Confucianism's in the traditional period. Traditional Confucianism accepted Chinese indigenous religions, while Sung Neo-Confucianism absorbed many Buddhist ideas. But with communism as the guiding ideology, all forms of religious activities were suppressed. Theistic religions are regarded by Marxism-Leninism as the "opiate of the people." Together with exploitation by the clan, they were not to be tolerated. Unlike the Confucianists, who learned how to live with theistic religions, the Communists were resolute in the eventual elimination of these faiths.

This is the reason for anticipating a clash between the Communist ideology and other religious faiths. The materialistic premise of the Communist ideology precludes the development of its own mythological content, similar to the mythological content of Buddhism and Taoism, or Confucianism, which developed many myths and cults based on such supernatural notions as heaven and fate. Because the Communist regime believed that theistic religion would eventually become extinct, it organized systematic efforts to accelerate the process. Was it possible for the Communist faith to replace the theistic religions as an integrative force in the social system?

Yang anticipated great difficulties with regard to this. One difficulty rests in communism itself. It is difficult for the humanitarian values of the first generation of Communists to be transmitted to later generations because there are no mythical and cultic vehicles for doing so. The new generation, nurtured in a completely demythologized doctrine, may enjoy a sense of fulfillment in terms of economic security and national power. But should the Communist program succeed, the Communists would be anemic in terms of moral integrative values. Once the Communist regime is faced with crises, and the people subjected to extreme distress, the new generations will reach beyond the finitude of empirical experience and rational thought for relief. This difficulty renders communism no substitute for theistic faiths.

This limitation of communism as a faith may force the new regime to develop a permanent tolerance of theistic religion so that theism can perform the moral integrative function of stabilizing the new social order. Will there be a peaceful coexistence between communism and theistic faiths? Only time will tell. But the emphasis on moral integration in the social system provides the following finding:

> The particular nature of the diffused religion of China's indigenous faith gave rise to the moral character of the traditional institutions and social groups. The religious elements in the secular system played an integrative role in the social order in the absence of institutional religion. During the last two centuries, modern forces eroded this integrative force of the social system. The Communist faith cannot substitute for it because of its nontheistic beliefs. A theory of social system change must pay special attention to the lack of a moral character and the absence of an integrative force, as well as the consequences thereof.

Nineteenth-century Social Movements

Yang made it clear that his purpose in studying social movements in nineteenth-century China was to understand social system change in China (Yang 1975). A central theoretical concern in his social movement studies was the gradual decomposition of China's political and religious institutions. It was postulated that only during major social movements do actors consciously evaluate social values. Widespread, conscious reorientations of values indicate strains in institutional arrangements. Therefore, social movements are observable facts that reveal a deep-seated institutional dissatisfaction that becomes a source of social system change.

Yang's research project on social movements was extensive, covering the last six reigns of the Ch'ing dynasty, from 1796 to 1911. Data on social movements and social change were extracted from 2,247 chuan (volumes) of the *Ta Ch'ing Shih Lu* (The Factual Records of the Ch'ing). Four kinds of information were culled from the volumes: (1) mass action incidents; a total of 6,643 incidents were collected, each involving five or more participants and creating public issues, ranging from famine riots to battles of rebellion; (2) imperial honors awarded to exemplary persons in support of such critical traditional values as loyalty, filial piety, and chastity; a total of 2,112,846 people were honored; (3) government relief for famines and disasters; during the 116 years, a total of 18,743 calamities were recorded; and (4) cases of punishment of officials, which were used as indicators of political ineffectiveness; during the century a total of 31,899 officials were punished for various offenses. Together, the data showed the prevalence of social movement incidents that forced increasingly drastic changes on Chinese society in modern times, the system's responses, and the ineffectiveness of the political and economic institutions.

The selection of historical social movements for an empirical study of social system change has a strategic significance: through analysis of the cumulative effects of mass incidents over a long period of time, the interlinking of institutions as sources of systemic dissatisfaction becomes observable, and, at the same time, the organizational responses to such crises can be evaluated. Yang's findings on social movements are summarized here:

Faced with widespread rebellion, the political and economic administration of the old regime became a source of change in the social system through its inability to restore social order and reverse the accelerating imperial decline.

Traditional organizational responses do not adequately explain the uninterrupted revolutions of the twentieth century. The government was ineffective in maintaining traditional values and suppressing uprisings. It lost control of the situation, precipitating increased systemic dissatisfaction among the populace. The ineffectiveness of the institutional and organizational responses of the old regime reinforced changes in the social system that ushered in a period of modern transformation.

Emerging National Integration

Yang's final research project focused on the Chinese community and national integration. In the early 1970s, as Sino-American relations were normalized, he returned to China and by the mid-1970s launched research to "identify the saliently significant changes in community structure and in the institutional system of Chinese society within the context of a systematic, sociological framework."

There are two theoretical foci in this research: on the one hand, it emphasizes the interlinking of institutions and their changes in studying the development of national integration; on the other, it uses an organization-intensive model as a tool for understanding the modern transformation of Chinese society. The major findings on these institutional and organizational changes can be summarized as follows: Fieldwork and documentary research show that the family is no longer the core of the Chinese social structure due to the diminished importance of the economic, educational, and other social functions of the family as an institution. In traditional China, the triangular struggle between the central government, its appointed officials in the local governments, and local interest groups gave rise to the strategic role of kinship solidarity and the social influence of the family organization. After the Communist revolution, the government suppressed local interests and the family lost its political function. A similar growth of organizational power can be observed in economic and educational institutions, resulting in the reduced role of the family in these activities. In the span of one generation, China's family-centric institutional pattern came to an end.

The interlinking of institutions can be observed in China's economic transformation. In both agriculture and industry, politics has taken command. For example, the communists frequently used mass mobilization campaigns in such planned social changes as the collectivization movement, the commune movement, and the movement to nationalize commerce and industry.

The same pattern can be found in the process of restratification. Each family and individual members are assigned a politically defined "class status." This was accomplished by a political campaign that accompanied the land reform movement. One's status would affect opportunities at work and in school as well as in one's political career.

This interlinking institutional pattern of change is intertwined with an organization-intensive feature. In both the rural and urban transformations, organization-building was the tool of choice. This is most obvious in the process of the collectivization of agriculture. Indeed, organization was a weapon for all endeavors. The "organization fad" climaxed in the commune movement of the late 1950s when the entire rural society was organized into 26,000 communes, with an average population of 25,000 people per commune. Here, in summary, are Yang's findings on national integration:

> The interlinking institutions and their changes characterized the period of the radical transformation of the Chinese social system. The Communist regime utilized this multi-institutional approach to carry out many planned social changes. The process climaxed in a systemwide transformation: the Cultural Revolution.
>
> The organization-intensive model was the weapon of choice in various modernization efforts. "Organization-building" climaxed in the commune movement of the rural areas. In the cities, industrialization was carried out under "bureaucratic industrialization," similar to the pattern found in the West.

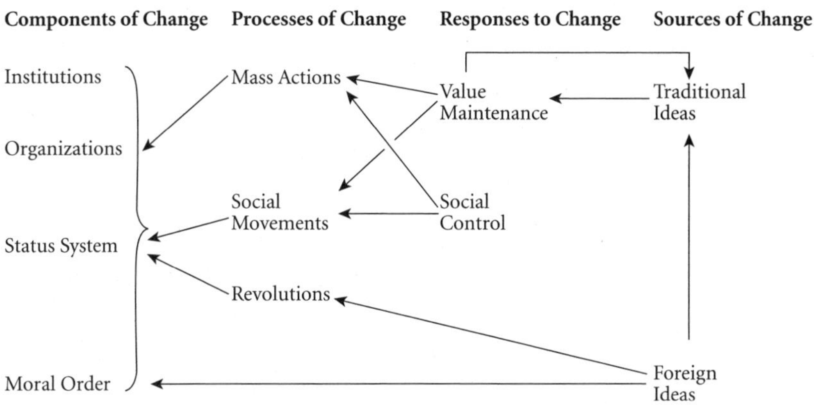

Figure 3.1. C. K. Yang's theory of social system change: A systematization

The Systematization of Yang's Theory

The major concepts of Yang's research-inspired theory are presented in figure 3.1. The central component of the social system under transformation is the interlinking institutions. The role of the institutional system is significant in three respects. First, the other major components—namely, organization, status, and culture—are intimately related to the institutions. Second, the various processes of social change, such as mass actions, social movements, and revolutions, primarily act on the institutions and force their changes. Finally, institutional changes are targets of both traditional ideas, which are brought about by value maintenance, and foreign ideas, which are brought about by intercultural contacts. Because of this key role of the institutional system in his theory, it can be called an institutional theory of social system change.

From the systematized theory as represented in figure 3.1, we can see that the changing processes originated from the weakening influences of indigenous ideas and the introduction of foreign ideas into the system. Social movement studies provide indications that traditional values lost their power to guide social behavior by showing the concomitant increases in the distribution of imperial honors and mass action incidents. The power of Western ideas can be found in the processes of family and religious changes. The following propositions summarize the role ideas play in social system change:

Social system change begins when the orientations of a segment of the population have been significantly altered.

Social orientations may change because traditional values lose their influence, new ideas are introduced, or both. An example of such a shift in orientation is a change in the identity structure of a population segment, as social movement studies hypothesize. This proposition links an unstable identity structure with the rise of social movements, especially institution-oriented movements.

These propositions explain social system change as people wanting things to be done differently from how they were done before. One reason people make this decision is that the traditional norms once preventing such a choice have been weakened. Yet change also occurs from the opposite direction: people are threatened by inconsistencies as a result of an ideological reorientation. When vastly different social systems encounter each other, such reorientations became inevitable. Delineating the role of ideas in initiating social system change is one of the great sociological contributions of Max Weber. Yang points this out in his introduction to Weber's *The Religion of China*: "Ideas, and ideals, instead of always being reflections of materialistic conditions, can be independent, voluntaristic forces in initiating socioeconomic change" (Weber 1964).

Most of the time, a social system and its organizations operate according to routines. They solve new problems based on conventional patterns. Studies of nineteenth-century China show that the social system responded to challenges by utilizing value promotion (such as the old regime increasing the number of honors given to people who upheld the value of loyalty) and military suppression of the previous administrations. Even when such efforts failed, the old regime found it difficult to change tack. This difficulty can be explained in part by a lack of know-how but more often by a reluctance or resistance to change because of vested interests. This sort of resistance in the social system is a major reason why "business as usual" persists. The following propositions summarize this finding:

Social systems respond to challenges according to customary patterns.

Even if traditional solutions fail, institutional changes are difficult to initiate unless widespread massive social movements threaten the survival of the system.

The role of social movements in the theory of social system change can be seen in their substitution function for the factor analysis of the variables of social change. In a social movement, empirical interdependence of the initiating factors can be found. By examining waves of social movements, it is possible to trace the repercussions of a change once it has been initiated throughout the social system. Such repercussions are functional alternatives to the empirical investigations of the processes of institutional change. The following proposition summarizes this finding:

> Social movements can serve as a locale for studying the processes of social system change because they represent long-range processes through which a society collectively controls the aspirations and values of its members and their identity structure, the distribution of authority and rewards, the institutionalization of collective goals, and its response to situations confronting the society as whole.

Central to the components of change is the institutional system. Yang found that weak traditional institutional responses to new challenges caused widespread rebellions that provided the background for social system transformation. New institutional arrangements are also essential to the rise of modern behavioral patterns. It is around the social institutions that the specific content of social behavior is organized. This organization changes human action from random tendencies into a coherent pattern. It is because of this function that the change of institutions becomes the central facet of social system change. The following proposition summarizes this finding:

> For the social system to be fundamentally transformed, social institutions must be significantly altered.
>
> If the institutional arrangements favorable to the economic development of a society are in place, the material construction phase of modernization can be completed quickly.

Yang places equal emphasis on the organizational transformation in a society under modernization. He uses the "organizational-intensive" concept to summarize the early efforts of the Chinese Communists to change the Chinese economy. Widespread organization-building activities were observable in such areas as the rise of the bureaucratic state, bureaucratic industrialization, and even in the failed efforts at collective farming. The trend was toward big, formal, rational organizations. Empirical research, however, also shows the complexity of organizational changes. Organizations have been used to restrict changes even though these changes may represent facets of the general movement of rationalization in society. These observations are generalized in the following propositions:

In social system change related to modernization, the rise of a rational form of organization in important areas of social life is an inevitable trend and therefore part of the change process.

All organizations, particularly rational organizations, are tools that masters, either formal and informal groups or individuals, use to generate valued outputs that they can then appropriate.[2]

Yang uses the concept of "restratification" to describe the outcome of the Chinese revolution. He pays sufficient attention to the structural and substantial aspects of changes in the status system. This includes the changing rules of the game, the social standing of groups and individual actors, and the mechanisms of stratification. This aspect of social system change is the most relevant to the individuals who comprise the system. The following proposition summarizes this finding:

One important outcome of social system change is the rise of a new status system that has a radical and inescapable impact on the individuals within the social system.

Yang pays special attention to the moral sentiments of the social system. In this respect he shares Parsons's belief that moral sentiments underlie any institutional pattern (Parsons 1954, 60). In his studies of religion, Yang carefully compares the moral sources of institutional enforcement of various religions. In his analysis of modern change, he points out the basic shift in the secularization of the moral order and the resultant loss of faith in institutional patterns. Without a moral character, social institutions are stripped of their awe-inspiring quality and thereby weakened in their enforcement capacity. The following proposition summarizes this finding:

The moralization of institutions, organizations, and status systems are essential processes in the functioning of a social system. Therefore, transforming a social system requires altering its moral order.

Contemporary Evidence

Yang predicted that, in order for China to modernize, a broader field would have to be cleared for the free play of economic rationality, and a normative code would have to be constructed to regulate this rationality. Of strategic importance in modernization were three structural components: the extension of the market system and the attendant differentiation in the economic sectors of the social structure, the institution building and organizational change in the community and family system, and the fundamental transformation of the moral order. These components are crucial to rebuilding a social system based on rational premises. The three decades of radical change prior to reform are relevant to understanding China's modernization because the Chinese Communists removed those characteristics of the Chinese social structure and the dominant values that Weber saw as inhibiting China's socioeconomic development (Weber 1964). With traditional forces minimized, the work of rebuilding could begin with an emphasis on technological and organizational rationality, the development of a modern bureaucratic administration, and a compatible social and moral order that would ensure sustainable modernization.

Social Change in Market Transition

The critical features of China's market transition since the 1978 reforms are the emerging market institutions, the rise of new organizational forms, and the building of a legal framework to regulate these new arrangements. The role of markets in China has steadily broadened since 1978. First, the agricultural sector was "privatized" by the "household responsibility system." Under this system the farm household has control over the land it uses, and it can choose what to produce and how to market its products, as is the case in a market economy (Chow 1987, 296). The success of this system can be measured by the rapid increase in rural income: from 1978 to 1988, per capita annual income rose from 134 to 520 yuan; adjusting for inflation, this represents a 192 percent increase in per capita income (Nee 1989, 664).

Following the rural reforms, urban reforms began in the early 1980s. As various reforms were initiated simultaneously, the pace of institution building accelerated. The contract system reform, the reform to increase labor, capital, and product-market mobility, and legal norms for property rights were carried out almost at the same time. The urgency to make things work was unprecedented. New laws were promulgated almost monthly. We are talking about institutional innovations at the national level. If we look at the thirty provinces, two thousand counties, and fifty thousand townships, where each government, because of its newly granted autonomy, experimented with its own institutional designs, the extent of the institution building is striking (S. Li 1998). Because of the expanding role of local governments in market transition, one commentator has called the Chinese reform a case of "privatization from below" (Naughton 1994).

Organizational changes have been similarly eye-catching. One landmark development was the 1990 establishment of two stock exchanges, one in Shanghai and the other in Shenzhen. This was important because stock and commodity exchanges are the correlates of modern large-scale commerce and indicate that a society has passed beyond the most basic stage of a subsistence economy.

The return of private firms to the Chinese economy was another historic event. The process of their legitimation was gradual and hesitant. At the beginning stage of the reform in the early 1980s, only "individual industrial and business households" were allowed to compete with state firms. These were private firms with no more than seven employees, engaging mostly in handicraft production and peddling activities. The go-ahead for the rise of individual households was an integral part of the reestablishment of a "free market" in rural China. Because of the economic scarcities in the early reform days, individual industrial and business households rapidly sprang up. By the end of 1997, there were 28.5 million of them, employing about 54 million workers (State Statistical Bureau 1998, 12).

The 1990s saw a rapid increase in the number of private enterprises. Emboldened by Deng Xiaoping's 1992 declaration that economic development is the central national policy, registered private enterprises grew from a few thousand to almost one million by the end of the decade, employing 21 million workers. Together with foreign firms, the private sector produced one-third of the national product in China.

The most interesting organizational form is the "township and village enterprise" (TVE). Due to their sheer number and their role in the economy—about 20 million TVEs, employing 130 million workers and producing one-third of China's gross domestic product—they have attracted much attention. One thesis attributes their success to the involvement of local governments and the rise of local corporatism, a process consisting of such institutional innovations as profit sharing and informal privatization (Walder 1995; Nee and Su 1997).

To promote and regulate these new organizations, as well as to contribute to the reform of the "state-owned enterprises," new laws—with legal norms and procedures borrowed from the West—were promulgated. The main direction in the building of a legal framework for the market transition has been toward a convergence with the capitalistic systems of the world rather than inventing a different system. The most important event was a 1988 constitutional amendment that legitimized private ownership. Another landmark event was the 1993 promulgation of the "company law." Other market-regulating laws promulgated over the last two decades include the "contract law," the "labor law," and the "law of succession." As Edward J. Epstein observes, "China was at the same time borrowing legal ideas to legislate a spanking new system for foreign trade and investment on a scale never before seen in China" (Epstein 1991). The reformers hoped to use the law as a tool to promote market transition.

The enormous market expansion in the reform era has had far-reaching consequences for China's modernization process. As Weber observed more than a century ago, market expansion not only promotes exchange between buyers and sellers but also sharpens competition, among buyers and among sellers (Swedberg 2000, 376). The expanding exchange and competition resulted in a much increased level of structural differentiation of the economy and society, a higher level of per capita income, a transition from scarcity and inflation to abundance and deflation, and an increase in geographical and social mobility. The rise of the market correlated with the development of a modern social system in China.

Community Development

When Yang conducted fieldwork in the 1950s for *Chinese Communist Society*, Nanching, though located in the vicinity of Guangzhou, the capital of Guangdong Province, was an agricultural community with a significant degree of self-sufficiency. Today, Nanching is a suburb of Guangzhou, earning income by renting apartments to thousands of migrant workers who have flocked to the city for jobs. The suburbanization of Nanching epitomizes the pattern of community development during the reform period. Some Chinese scholars describe the reforms as a "four-step strategy": (1) building the township and village enterprises (TVEs), (2) building small towns, (3) merging the towns and the villages, and (4) modernizing regionally. In most coastal provinces, such as Guangdong, some rural areas have already reached the third stage.

This new strategy of community development shares its organization-centered approach with its pre-reform counterpart. The difference, however, is in the organizational forms. In the pre-reform decades, especially in 1950, organizational reform centered on the community itself. It went through four stages: the first stage focused on building mutual-aid teams, in which the neighborhood communities were organized. This task was basically completed in 1955. The second stage focused on cooperative farming, when the entire natural village was organized, resulting in about one million agricultural producers' cooperatives in China by 1957. The third stage was characterized by advanced cooperatives, formed by combining several existing cooperatives and resulting in an organization as large as an administrative village. The last stage, begun in 1958, was the formation of people's communes consisting of hundreds of villages and thousands of households (China 1979; Schurmann 1969).

Throughout these stages, the purpose of organizational reform remained the same: collective farming and sharing wealth equally. In retrospect, these objectives planted the seeds of failure. Large-scale farming and the division of labor were incompatible with the small-sized Chinese plots. Collective ownership and equal sharing caused free-riding problems and low morale. The failed strategy brought rural communities to the brink of bankruptcy.

The rural reforms of the late 1970s relied on another form of organization: private enterprises. First, the farm households were granted autonomy under the "household responsibility system." This new institution solved the free-rider problem of collective farming, sparking the economic boom of the reform era.

The household responsibility system also gave rise to several new organizational innovations due to the freeing up of surplus labor from collective agriculture. As more and more peasants became involved in small businesses, "individual industrial and business households" and the private enterprise system were instituted. The unemployed labor force was attracted to the rural industries, giving birth to the TVEs. Their predecessor, the commune industries, were assigned a supporting role to increase mechanized farming. The TVEs, no longer playing a subordinate role, were more market-driven and quickly became the largest employers in China's labor market.

These new organizations were viable because of the existence of the market. The market was nonexistent in the pre-reform decades as everything was state-owned or collectivized and the economy was centrally planned. The market transition brought about by the reform provided a favorable environment where private firms and semiprivate TVEs could compete and develop. As a result of this new freedom, more and more rural residents abandoned the less profitable farming and moved to towns and cities to do business. As a consequence, the past two decades can be seen as a gigantic movement in which millions of Chinese peasants left the farms and plunged into the unpredictable market as a means of survival.

The Contemporary Family

Observing the changing structure of the Chinese family, Martin King Whyte advances the proposition that the new familism can be seen as the engine of growth in China's economic miracle (Whyte 1995, 1996). Indeed, the Chinese family today is very different from the familial system Weber described as one of the inhibiting factors in China's socioeconomic development.

Some of these changes, as Yang points out, were well underway before the Communist movement. In three respects—namely, parental control over marriage, the low status of women, and the kinship system as a center of loyalty—the institution of the family was already under attack in the pre-Communist period. Like other ideas, freedom of marriage was imported, but its effect on educated youth was infectious. It was first practiced among the modern intelligentsia in large cities during the Republican period. In most rural areas the arranged marriage system still prevailed. For the large majority of Chinese people, real change started only after the Communists came into power.

The ascendancy of women's status began with the rise of the women's movement in the early twentieth century. Women's organizations began to appear in large cities after the 1919 May Fourth Movement. Beginning in the second quarter of the last century, the principle of gender equality generally came to be accepted by the urban intelligentsia. But like freedom of marriage, the status of women still remained low prior to the Communist period. Under Communist law, women gained equal status with men for the first time in Chinese history.

The rise of individualism and the declining importance of the kinship system as the center of an individual's loyalty also began in the Republican period. Modernizing forces such as economic growth, education, and population mobility broke down the confinement of family members and opened their eyes to the outside world. The rise of voluntary associations also competed for their commitment. But the strongest force for individual identification, the state, asserted its claim only after the Communist accession to power.

The Communist regime's rise to power began the real changes in the Chinese family. The Communists used the legal system as a tool for its big push. The marriage law was promulgated on May 1, 1950. Article 1 abolished the feudal marriage system that was based on the superiority of man over woman and ignored the interests of children and replaced it with a system based on equal rights for both sexes and protection of children. The twenty-seven articles in the law attempted to remake the Chinese family in accordance with a modern model. Although it took years of mass campaigns to put the law into practice, it contained the same things contemporary Americans would consider the right family conditions, as Parsons points out in his "foreword" to Yang's *Chinese Communist Society* (Yang 1965, vii and 221–26).

When Yang wrote *Chinese Communist Society*, the Communist regime was only ten years old. Yet he was already able to discern the "modernizing" trend that was occurring in the Chinese family under the new regime. Here are the main characteristics of this trend cross-correlated with Yang's observations (Lau 1993):

Family size: The trend toward having smaller families is obvious when comparing family size over time. For instance, in 1911 the average nuclear family had 5.17 members; by 1990 it had 3.96. Yang discusses family size in connection with the contradiction between the multiple functions of the nuclear family and its small size; this gave rise to the integration of the extended kinship circle. As the kinship organization, the clan, disintegrated under Communist rule, the nuclear family could not retain all its functions, and a more differentiated community structure replaced it to fulfill the functional needs (Yang 1965, 7–10, 191–96).

Family form: The "nuclear" trend was discovered in the early 1980s by the Chinese Academy of Social Sciences during its "Family in Chinese Cities" research. About half of the families formed from 1938 to 1965 were nuclear families, compared to about two-thirds of the families formed in the 1966–1982 period. In his discussion on the "family revolution," Yang summarizes its main objective as promoting a new family institution similar to the Western pattern (Yang 1965, 17).

Family life cycle: The drastic changes in the family life cycle include the rapidly declining death rate and the increasing average life expectancy. During the half-century under Communist rule, the average national life expectancy increased from about fifty years to more than seventy years.

Marriage patterns: The family survey conducted by the Chinese Academy of Social Sciences in the 1980s found that more than one-third of marriages before 1953 had been arranged by parents, but from 1966 to 1982 less than 1 percent of them had been. Only 12 percent of the older generation had the freedom to marry whom they pleased, whereas 34 percent of the younger generation had such freedom. Yang reports a trend in the loosening of parental control and the beginning of a family revolution as early as the last quarter of the nineteenth century.

Reproductive behavior: The trend is toward later marriages, fewer births, and later births. The trend is confirmed by the declining total fertility rates: from a national average of 6.13 births per woman in 1949 to 2.25 in 1990.

Divorce: The divorce rate has been rising, particularly during the reform era. Yang makes the following observation on the "modern divorce" as a result of the marriage law: "There is the almost overwhelming proportion of divorce suits brought by women as compared to those brought by men" (Yang 1965, 71). This trend continues in reform China as well. Today, divorcees tend to be younger, the duration of marriages shorter, and more women than men initiate divorce.

Status of women: The rising status of women is most observable in their increasing labor participation, rising education levels, and growing share of professional and administrative jobs. Yang noted this trend as well.

Status of children: Whyte argues that the reformed Chinese familism resulted in an expanded role for youth because of their abilities and performance. Such changes allow the Chinese family today to be more compatible with the prerequisites of economic development. Indeed, these characteristics are similar to those William J. Goode identifies in his "World Revolution and Family Pattern" published thirty years ago (Goode 1963). As in the West, the trend in China is toward a "modern" family system.

The Moral Order

In his analysis of communism as a nontheistic "faith" Yang points out that the religious quality of the Communist ideology was based in its fusion with the two leading aspirations of the Chinese nation over the last two centuries: the quest for national strength and for material progress. These overarching quests demanded that all other concerns—economic well-being, health and life, family, aesthetic and cognitive truth, justice and humanity—be sacrificed. The Communist ideology became a faith and an effective integrative force for a nation in social transition. The unconditional nature of the demand was based on the believer's absolute certainty that the Communist ideology was the only guide to man's inevitable destiny, the only infallible road to national strength and economic improvement. This absolute certitude was proclaimed in the name of the power of "the people," whose importance transcended that of any individual thought, judgment, interest, or existence. This absolute certitude, like that of a religious doctrine, was not based on empirical evidence but on a promise that performed a function parallel to life after death. This absolute certitude based on a messianic promise was closely related to the development of Communist fanaticism, which helped bring the revolution to victory in China (Yang 1961, 381–85).

The rise of communism in Chinese society stripped the traditional social order of its sacred, awe-inspiring quality. Yang points out that the replacement of China's theistic religions by the new nontheistic faith was not complete, however. Theistic beliefs still held a strong influence over the people in spite of persistent interference and systematic control by the new faith. Yang concludes that the coexistence of both a new nontheistic faith and the old theistic traditions was a characteristic of the transitional state of Chinese society. In *Religion in Chinese Society* Yang speculates: "Will theistic religion eventually go on the path of extinction, and will new theistic symbols rise to replace the fallen gods? This will depend on the adequacy and enduring quality of secular faith, including communism, as the new stabilizing foundations for social institutions" (Yang 1961, 402). Put differently, Yang proposes that the future of religion in Chinese society depends on communism's efficacy.

Several hypotheses can be derived by testing the events of the past decades. First, we may postulate that the more the Communist regime appears to be able to attain the two national goals, the more the people will have faith in its ideology, and the less the people will be inclined toward theistic religions. Second, as Yang suggests, because the new faith is nontheistic and lacks mythical and cultic symbols, passing it on to the successor generations will be difficult. Thus we postulate that as time passes the new faith eventually may become extinct and more people may turn to theistic religions. Finally, because the Communist ideology initially acquired its religious character by identifying with the two national goals, it may lose its appeal among people who no longer aspire for national strength and material progress. We may thus postulate that among the sectors of the population who no longer share these two aspirations, the Communist ideology will lose its appeal and other religious beliefs will become more attractive.

Events in the first decade under Communist rule seemed to confirm the first hypothesis. The messianic promise of the Communist doctrine was substantiated by the new regime's numerous accomplishments, especially in the early 1950s. The suppression of other faiths was tolerated and the people's "self-remolding" (for conversion to the new faith) seemed genuine. Even the disaster of the Great Leap Forward did not alter people's belief in the Communist Party and its leadership because of their trust in the party's good intentions.

The second decade was quite different. The Cultural Revolution (1966–1976) turned the tables on the Communist Party and Mao Zedong, its chairman. The "crisis of three beliefs" (loss of faith in communism, socialism, and the Communist Party) spread as millions of Maoist Red Guards rampaged the country and brought the economy to the brink of collapse. The high tide of such disillusionment swept the country after the 1971 Lin Biao incident (Lin was killed after an attempted coup). A power struggle among the leadership showed that the Communists were not selfless fighters for a strong and wealthy

China and that the party's pursuit of personal gain was what had brought about national disaster and humiliation. The loss of faith in the Communist Party was as rapid as its earlier rise. Overnight, the moral character of the regime dissipated like the morning dew.

The reform era saw the revival of traditional religions and the rise of numerous theistic cults. The eclipse of political orthodoxy was further evident as a significant segment of the younger generation was drawn to the dissident movement. The reformers could no longer rely on the governing ideology for legitimacy. After June 4, 1989, when the regime crushed the democracy movement, Deng Xiaoping insisted that the "opening and reform" policy must be continued because economic performance had become the regime's new legitimacy.

Economic success, however, is no substitute for moral authority. The more the reformers rely on the people's material progress for legitimation, the more emphasis is put on economic construction at the expense of noneconomic matters. This creates much dissatisfaction in other realms of life. Materialism is very much to blame for the deterioration of China's health care system. The rapid rise of the Falun Gong, a sect whose members believe in the restorative power of breathing exercises, can be attributed in part to the populace's general fear of illness.

The declining authority of the governing ideology and competition among the theistic faiths have restored the former order of religious coexistence in Chinese society. The reform government is willing to tolerate theistic religions as long as its political authority is not threatened. But in cases where its authority is challenged, as the Falun Gong and dissident movements have, the Communist regime has had to resort to force to crush them since the Communist ideology has lost its attraction among these segments of the population. However, since the cost of using force is permanently damaging the legitimacy of the regime, more tolerance of theistic religions can be expected as Chinese society seeks to lay a new moral foundation for its social order.

Applying Sociological Knowledge

The value of a sociological theory rests on its ability to guide researchers to the salient aspects of social phenomena. In the case of attempting to understand the Chinese revolution, this function is particularly important. Through his life-long empirical research, C. K. Yang constructed a theory of the Chinese revolution that also served as a theory of modern social system change. He focused on the restructuring of the institutional pattern of society and the new organizational forms this process unleashed. Institutions are important because social system change essentially involves a change of rules. As rules are changed, the social game is organized differently.

To determine which rules are essential, one can profitably learn from the West. From his early research on the market and his most important study on Chinese religion, we can be certain that Yang is a student of Weber. The market is a good starting place for the study of modern change. The expansion of the market gives rise to large portions of the modern transformation. Marketization and its resultant rationalization are the most important impetuses for further modernization. Without sufficient institutional conditions, such as the rule of law and property rights, marketization cannot begin. Once the process starts, the change may happen quickly. Long before the economic miracle of the last two decades, Yang was confident that China's material construction could be expedited if the institutional system were appropriately changed.

The market cannot take the place of all social groups, however. Familial, communal, and religious groups retain their roles in modern society. Their position and function in the new social system are critical areas of research. They will acquire new organizational forms, but they will not lose their integrating functions. A significant portion of Yang's research efforts were thus devoted to the evolution of the Chinese family, village, and religion.

Yang's contribution to the sociological enterprise was his life-long pursuit of empirical evidence to prove the validity of sociological knowledge in the Chinese case. His theory of China's modern transformation adapts sociological theory to the contemporary period, and his theory continues to anticipate the recent developments in Chinese society.

4

AMBROSE Y. C. KING AND LIZHU FAN

A Sociological Paradigm in the Study of Chinese Religion

C. K. Yang's Religion in Chinese Society

PROFESSOR C. K. YANG's contribution to the world of scholarship certainly is not confined to the study of Chinese religion, but his work on this topic stands out as a remarkably distinct and masterful achievement. His book *Religion in Chinese Society*, published in 1961 by the University of California Press, has become a modern classic. Indeed, it has secured a paradigmatic status in the sociological study of Chinese religion. We still find it refreshing, relevant, rich in scholarship, and innovative in sociological theory, reading it forty years later. The problems Yang dealt with, the interpretations he presented in the book, concerned much more than simply Chinese religion. What he studied and what he wrote about was Chinese society and religion as an integrated whole. Like Weber's *Religion of China*, Yang's work must be read as a treatise on the comparative study of religions and civilizations.

What motivated Yang to write the book? "For many years," he explains in the book's preface, "I have been perplexed by the problem of the place of religion in traditional Chinese society." Further, he continues in the introduction, "This study is an attempt to answer the questions: What functions did religion perform in Chinese social life and organization so as to provide a basis for its existence and development, and through what *structural forms* were these functions carried out? Hence, the basic purpose here is functional interpretations of critical facts in order to reveal a pattern of relationship between religion and the social order." Then, why was Yang "perplexed" for many years? The main clue to this question is his own statement: "Among the three leading centers of civilization, Europe, India, and China, the place of religion in society is the least clearly recognized in the case of China" (Yang 1961). Yang wondered why this was so.

According to prevalent observations, the pervasiveness of magic practices and beliefs at the folk level largely carried no apparent ethical connotations. Western observers generally considered the Chinese people as a superstitious lot who had yet to experience an ethicoreligious life of a higher order. Because of the pervasive influence of magic, the Christian West refused to treat Chinese beliefs religious. Furthermore, there were other baffling phenomena that made the place of religion in China the least clearly understood among the world's religions. Here, Yang's account is especially worth quoting: "Instead of social and political domination by a religious doctrine and a powerful priesthood, there was the seemingly agnostic Confucian tradition of secular orthodoxy in which the leading scholar-official class was indoctrinated. There was no strong, centrally organized religion in most periods of Chinese history, and there appeared to be no protracted struggle between the church and the state. Confucian ethics dominated the system of social values, largely replacing the ethical function of religion as found in Christianity" (Yang 1961, 4). But it was not just the Christian West that failed to recognize the Chinese religion as such. Even modern Chinese cultural elites held that view while they were painstakingly identifying and examining the unique character of Chinese culture in the context of the East-West intercivilizational encounter during the late nineteenth century. According to this view, "China is a country without religion and the Chinese are a people who are not bound by religious superstitions." This statement was made by no other than Hu Shih, who was widely regarded as the leader of modem Chinese intellectuals and whose view on Chinese religion was representative of his time (Hu 1934, 78).

With a shrewd sociological eye, Yang knew well that those prevailing views were not supported by reality. As he pointed out, "There was not one corner in the vast land of China where one did not find temples, shrines, altars, and other places of worship. The temples and shrines dotting the entire landscape were a visible indication of the strong and persuasive influence of religion in

Chinese society, for they stood as symbols of a social reality" (Yang 1961, 6). It is worth mentioning that Yang's ability to refute the prevailing views on the place of religion in Chinese society on empirical ground had very much to do with his skillful use of historical data, particularly from local gazetteers (Yang 1961, table 1). Through his use of vast amounts of information from local gazetteers, Yang was in a position to grasp more comprehensively the functional relationship between religion and society.

The most challenging task Yang faced was a conceptual and theoretical one. What he set out to develop was an interpretative scheme to understand and explain China's complex and baffling socioreligious reality. For him, the obscurity of the place of religion in Chinese society was a question that needed to be convincingly answered. He argued that "An important reason for the obscurity is the lack of structural prominence of a formally organized religious system in the institutional framework of Chinese society, which leads to the frequent interpretation that the numerous popular cults are unorganized and are of little importance in the Chinese social and moral order" (Yang 1961, 20). Yang greatly admired Weber's accomplishment in the study of religion of China. Nevertheless, he concluded that "the lack of structural prominence of Chinese religion" had misled even Weber to characterize the cultic situation in China as "a chaotic mass of functional gods."

What enabled Yang to rightly attribute the "obscurity" of the place of religion in China to "the lack of structural prominence" was his insightful understanding of the functional role of religion in Chinese society. In employing the structural-functional approach, Yang, inspired by Talcott Parsons's concepts of diffuseness and specificity, innovatively broadened Joachin Wach's structural viewpoint that there are two types of religious groups: those that are identical with "natural groups" and those that are "specifically religious" organizations. For Yang, the distinction is between institutional religion and diffused religion. This conceptual innovation provided a powerful interpretative scheme under which the plural, complex, seemingly chaotic religious phenomena all became intelligible. As a result, a clear understanding of the religious order in China emerged.

Under Yang's interpretative scheme, Buddhism and Taoism are two institutional religions that are social institutions in themselves, having their own basic concepts and their own structural system. However, both Buddhism and Taoism were never the same source of ethical values for secular social relations that Christianity was in European society (Yang 1961, 280). More importantly, the structural position of the two religions was relatively weak (303), and what was dominant in the Chinese religious landscape was what Yang called diffused religion. In his view, the original indigenous religion of China—which he termed the classical religion (23)—was largely incorporated into the secular social institutions as a form of diffused religion (304). That is to say, the diffused religion had no independent and separate institutional base, and its religious functions were performed, through and by sociopolitical institutions, such as the imperial state and the kinship system.

The core of religions that attained full development in the classical period of Chou (1122–221 BC) and early Han—before the foreign influence of Buddhism and the rise of Taoism as a religion—was the worship of Heaven (*bai tian*), and its pantheon of subordinate deities, and the worship of Ancestor (*bai zhu xian*)(23). Yang, employing functional analysis, demonstrated most convincingly the place of religion in the Chinese kinship system, in extra familial social and economic groups, in the Chinese community, in the Chinese state, and in Confucianism as an institutionalized orthodoxy. Indeed, he made the best use of the structural-functional approach and put an end to the question once and for all of whether China was a country without religion. Robert Redfield viewed his work as "the first functional study of Chinese religion" and praised it as "a large achievement" (Freedman 1974).

It was not an exaggeration to say that Yang's study was a triumph of sociological interpretation over other forms of interpretations of the Chinese religion. While Maurice Freedman did not see much achievement in Yang's book in his 1962 review in the *Journal of Asian Studies*, by 1974 he had changed his mind. In an article in that year titled "On the sociological study of Chinese religion," he came to a very different reading of Yang's achievement, saying, "That book is, after all, the latest of the very few works of its kind: an attempt to characterize Chinese religion as a whole and in relation to the society within which it was thought and practiced." He placed Yang's work in the sociological tradition of Weber and Marcel Granet and wrote, "In what I have said so far I have tried to show that there is a sociological tradition, culminating for the moment in Yang's book, which takes Chinese religion to be one entity" (Freedman 1974, 36).

True enough, methodologically, Yang stood within the tradition of Durkheim and Parsons, but his theoretical interests were closer to Weber's. It can be well argued that Yang's *Religion in Chinese Society* should be understood in comparison to Weber's *Religion of China*. They are compatible and comparable in terms of interpretative power and theoretical significance. The fundamental difference between the two great books lies in the fact that while Weber's book tried to give a cultural account for the failure of the Confucian ethic (Confucianism and Taoism) to initiate any drastic change in the socioeconomic order toward capitalism, Yang's book gave a comprehensive account for the success of the Chinese religion to sustain a long-lasting ethicopolitical order of the Chinese civilization.

Indeed, Weber's *The Religion of China* was admirably appraised by Yang in his penetrating introduction to the 1964 edition of Weber's book. He wrote, "Max Weber's *The Religion of China: Confucianism and Taoism* represents the lone example of systematic characterization of Chinese society and its dominant value system by a great Western intellect of the modern age. Though half a century of rapid social science development has elapsed since its original publication, the book remains an extremely stimulating work in comparative study of complex social systems and a source of provocative ideas for the study of Chinese society and its pattern of socio-economic development" (Weber 1964, xiii). But Yang knew well that Weber, despite his amazing sociological insights, had not given Chinese religion a full treatment. It is likely that Weber's work motivated Yang to produce an analysis of his own. Indeed, his book has not only supplemented Weber's work but also engaged Weber in debate, friendly yet critical. More accurately, Yang engaged himself in debates with various prevailing views on Chinese religion. In a sense, he set a challenging task for himself to provide a new sociological interpretation of Chinese religion. By so doing, he actually created a new reading of Chinese culture, in general, and Confucianism, in particular. Whether Confucianism is a religion is, indeed, a key question to the understanding of the Chinese religious order.

Whether Confucianism is a religion depends much on one's definition. In Yang's definition, "religion may be viewed as a consortium ranging from non-theistic belief systems with an emotional intensity that borders on ultimacy, to theistic belief systems with ultimate values fully symbolized in supernatural entities and supported by patterns of worship and organization" (Yang 1961, 26). While he recognized the seemingly "agnostic character of Confucianism" (which was emphasized by Western sinologists such as James Lagge and Lionel Giles) and its rationalistic features (emphasized by modern leading intellectuals such as Hu Shih), he perceptively pointed out that, following his own definition of religion, "Confucianism did address itself to the ultimate meaning of life and death, but only in terms of moral responsibility to man, not to any supernatural power. The religious nature of Confucianism as a system of thought lies in its furtive treatment of the ideas of *Heaven* and *fate* as an answer to human problems unaccountable for by knowledge or in moral terms" (26). Yang further wrote, "The belief in Heaven and fate, the condoning of divination, the close alliance with the theory of Yin-yang and the Five Elements, the emphasis on sacrifice and ancestor worship as a basic means of social control, and the lack of a thoroughly agnostic and rationalistic attitude toward spiritual matters, all these represented major aspects of the Confucian doctrine. These religion factors were important for the functioning of Confucianism as the guiding doctrine in a society in which gods and spirits were thought to lurk in every corner" (255).

Yang concluded that Confucianism was not to be treated as a full-fledged religion in the theistic sense, but as a sociopolitical doctrine having religious qualities (26). Yang's sociological analysis dealt with the total religious system of China as such. In particular, he addressed the functional relationship between religion and society. With regard to the controversy about the "cult of Confucianism," Yang observed that, "Although the great Master was singularly not deified, the cult of Confucianism may nevertheless be regarded as what Emile Durkheim calls a commemorative cult invested with considerable religious elements. . . . As Confucianism formed the core of the traditional ethico-political order, it is important to recognize here that religious influence played its part in making this doctrine a revered institution not only among scholars but also among the illiterate population" (165).

Part II

PUBLIC INSTITUTIONS

5

ISABELLE THIREAU AND HUA LINSHAN

New Institutions in Practice:

Migrant Workers and Their Mobilization of the Labor Law

ONE MAJOR LESSON that can be drawn from C. K. Yang's studies is the necessity of adopting a dynamic, open, relational definition of institutions. Indeed, the concept of institution is a core concept in Yang's work, and although his efforts were not devoted to elaborating a theory about institutions, how they act and influence society, his writings reveal a subtle and cautious approach to such processes, an approach that anticipated many of the debates arising among sociologists in recent years. These debates have benefited from recent developments in such fields as cognitive science, anthropology, and sociology. As a consequence, new terms have been elaborated and new assumptions stated regarding the way institutions should be apprehended (Douglas 1986; Elster 1983; Favereau 1996; Salais 1999). However, many of the concerns underlying these concepts and assumptions were already present, though often as a hidden agenda, in sociological studies such as Yang's.

The first chapter of Yang's *The Chinese Family in the Communist Revolution* concerns changes in social institutions during the first half of the twentieth century (Yang 1959). In less than twenty pages, Yang observes, beyond important empirical assessments, that social innovations do not always bring about institutional change; whether institutions change depends on a complex process of legitimizing the innovations introduced. There is no mechanical influence of institutions; the primary effect of a new institution can be to limit the influence of past institutions rather than to create new patterns of behavior; and, finally, an institution cannot avoid being influenced by other institutions. All these are key themes at the forefront of academic discussions. Social scientists, facing the rapid institutional changes characterizing Chinese society today, the multiplicity of administrative and social layers bound to interpret a given institution under particular circumstances, and the discrepancies among various social and public institutions, would therefore certainly benefit from recalling Yang's work.

As a matter of fact, the reforms launched in China more than two decades ago have encouraged the emergence of a new social stratification and a diversity of interests, preferences, and values. Confronted with this new diversity and plurality, the members of Chinese society, in order to diminish uncertainties and support some degree of coordination, need to rely on the creation of new shared usages, norms, and institutions. Institutions—which can guide individuals' and groups' behavior, provide some knowledge regarding which action will be efficient under certain circumstances, and, more than anything else, establish specific rules to settle disagreements and disputes—are particularly required. Hence, one can witness an impressive institutionalization process of rules, principles, and practices anchored in a diversity of spaces and governing various forms of interaction and cooperation.

Here, we deal with a specific public institution whose objective is to govern new forms of labor relationships, the Labor Law enforced since January 1, 1995. We provide a preliminary analysis of 123 written complaints addressed, in 1996 and 1997, to the labor bureau of Shenzhen municipal government (Guangdong Province) in an attempt to understand how workers and employees invoke existing legal provisions to denounce the reality they experience as unfair or unacceptable. If institutions provide legitimate grounds to justify disagreements or dissatisfactions, such a denunciation process is affected by the way institutions are understood and used by individuals and groups. This process contributes to assigning institutions their real meaning and effectiveness in a given society at a given historical period. In other words, knowing an institution's explicit rules does not give social scientists an understanding of the part the institution played: one has to look at the way different actors, confronted with different needs and obligations, use it, talk about its meaning, confront their interpretation, and negotiate about the way its rules and norms should be applied. This chapter's core issue, therefore, is the question of the knowledge, understanding, and effective mobilization of the Labor Law by the authors of the written complaints collected, who happen to be migrant workers enjoying a provisory right of residence in the city at stake.[1]

From Social Constraint to Practice

The word "institution" betrays a multiplicity of meanings. Following Jacques Revel (1995), we distinguish three definitions assigned to the concept of institution in the sociological literature. The first considers an institution as a juridical-political reality, such as France's Supreme Court. This meaning is illustrated by the discipline called "history of institutions" as it has been performed by jurists and historians. The Chinese word *jigou* is usually used to describe this category. The second meaning is broader: it concerns any organization functioning within a society on regular terms, according to explicit or implicit rules, and presumed to answer a specific collective need. The family, the school, the army, or the hospital are examples of such institutions. A third and even wider usage that can eventually be indefinitely extended identifies "any form of social organization linking values, norms, patterns of relationships and behavior, as well as roles" as an institution (Balandier 1989). To illustrate this last meaning of the word, Mary Douglas (1986) discusses the ancestors' cult. It should be added to this very brief list of possible definitions that the term *institution* is often implicitly used to designate a "public institution." Economic sociologist Robert Salais (1999) observes, for instance, that institutions are "a collective and intentional object"; Olivier Favereau (1996) considers an institution as "a coherent system of rules, linked to a collective entity clearly identified and generally sanctioned by law." But both of them actually discuss the action of state institutions in the economic field.

A more detailed historical understanding of the transformations of this concept would be welcome to attain some sociological clarification. However, without elaborating any further on this semantic issue, one cannot but wonder what happens when the word *institution* is translated into Chinese by the word *zhidu*, making it somehow synonymous to "system," or by the word *jigou*? In other words, do the multiple possible meanings of *institution* overlap with those of *zhidu* and *jigou*? What are the implications of the differences eventually existing as far as the type of experiences these terms can express or the kind of theory they can support are concerned?

This useful, though polysemic, sociological concept of institution has become the object of debate during the last decade. While disagreements still persist, some consensus has emerged regarding the way institutions should be handled, a consensus that opens new fields of research and forces social scientists to consider as part of the study of institutions issues and phenomena they would have tended to ignore in the past.

In his previously mentioned essay published in 1995, Jacques Revel stresses the Durkheimian position as one of the most influential ones in the sociological tradition as well as the fact that, for Durkheim, institutions support the creation process of identities but moreover of constraints within a given group. Such an understanding reflects the belief that social representations anticipate and encompass individual representations: hence their fundamental influence is a constraining one. Durkheim's position has thus supported the central role assigned to institutions by sociologists during many decades but also the attention paid to their normative dimension. During the recent decades, the merits but also the limits of such assumptions have been discussed. In 1986, Douglas, although very much influenced by Durkheim, published *How Institutions Think*, in which she argues that institutions do not think, and, more than anything else, they do not think in the place of social actors. In other words, she stresses the cognitive part played by institutions: institutions provide classifications, categories, values that are the outcome of a specific historical experience. The study made by French sociologist Christian Topalov (1994) of the rise and institutionalization process of the notion of *chômage*, or "unemployment," in Europe exemplifies such a perspective.

Other authors have stressed the pragmatic dimension of institutions, that is, how institutions influence and develop social actors' capacities to judge and act but also how, on the other hand, such judgments and actions influence institutions. The concept of institution is therefore widened to include a set of rules as well as the practices affected by these rules, a dynamic relationship and a mutual dependence being established between both. John Rawls (1987) is one among those having contributed to enlarge the approach of institutions by stating that one cannot understand the effective part of an institution within a given society if one does not take into account the "common knowledge" supporting it. By common knowledge, he means the public debate centered on this institution and concerning various issues: the collective intention underlying the creation of such an institution, the choice of the most efficient or fair means to achieve this intention, the evaluation made of the unanticipated difficulties or biases emerging from the institution's actions and decisions, and, finally, the discussions focusing on the modifications that should eventually be implemented. In other words, this common knowledge that locates the institution in a given context must also be analyzed, according to Rawls, in order to anchor the understanding of institutions in a certain history and illuminate dominant practices and interpretations (Salais 1999).

Other studies have enlarged even more the scope of analysis considered to be relevant when the study of institutions is at stake by saying that one should consider institutions as practice, that is, observe the interaction process between institutions and their daily mobilization by the members of a society. The first justification brought forward to support such a shift is that the common knowledge cannot be separated from the kind of tests of validity and legitimacy that institutions undergo each time one mobilizes them to perform a given social or economic action. These tests nourish the public debate, modify the common knowledge accumulated by bringing new questions to the fore, and eventually suggest institutional changes to remedy unanticipated difficulties. The second justification is that if social actors need institutions to coordinate their actions, this means, of course, that they make use of institutions, and it is in this concrete usage that institutions are assigned a "real" meaning, a meaning that may vary according to individuals' or groups' positions, resources, trajectories, or relationships. In other words, what some have called the "real institution" is composed of norms and institutions whose effective meaning cannot be separated from the way they are understood and used by social actors wishing to seize the possibilities offered to them in a given context, as well as to devise the appropriate action in order to achieve their objective. In this sense, every norm, every institution becomes a reality during concrete moments of judgment or action which, in turn, test the validity and legitimacy of the norm or institution at stake (Salais 1999).

Such an approach seems to be quite relevant to understanding the effective consequences of the institutional innovations witnessed in China during the last two decades. Local variations in the way institutions are implemented nowadays are indeed often either ignored or considered as dysfunctions, thus blurring the dividing line between legitimate local variations and illegitimate actions, that is, the mobilization of a given institution in order to protect particular interests. The fact that a common knowledge about a given institution is elaborated in China within very limited and closed spheres appears also to be a rather neglected issue. However, such configuration, and the uncertainties it induces, actually widens the margin of freedom of local interpretation of institutions with all the positive but also negative consequences attached to it. Finally, new areas of investigation emerge as important when it is recognized that the influence of institutions is nothing but mechanical: to observe the legitimation process of rules, principles, and institutions in a variety of arenas becomes an important means to observing normative and relational transformations within a society.

Institutional Objectives of the "Letters and Visits Bureau"

> Respectful Mayor Li,
> The day you will read this letter, maybe blood will have already been shed. We are about twenty people and we went to visit all kinds of municipal administrative departments in order to try to solve our problems but to no avail. . . . Our survival is at risk, we cannot but ask the factory to bring back justice to us. . . . The enthusiasm we had when we arrived in Shenzhen has been so much trampled down that it has vanished. There is no road to go to the sky, no door to go beneath the earth. After all the steps taken during the last ten days, we trust nobody. Our Labor Law that has been given so much publicity has not crossed the doors of our factory. We are not missing words to tell things, but since we are so powerless, it is as if we have no mouth. (Letter 121)

This written complaint was addressed by workers to Shenzhen mayor and then transmitted to a specific administrative organ: the "letters and visits bureau" of the Labor Department of Shenzhen municipality. What is this administrative body, also named "the complaint bureau"?

The "letters and visits bureaus," officially responsible for handling written and oral complaints from ordinary citizens, were implemented by the Communist Party after it came to power and were formally institutionalized in 1955. They may be found today at the level of municipal governments but are also found in party organs and people's congresses. Complaints lodged can regard administrative abuses as well as all kinds of social injustices. Moreover, these bureaus may specialize in hearing grievances linked to specific issues, as is the case, for instance, when they are affiliated with municipal departments dealing with health, environmental, and educational issues, or they may be more generalized, receiving grievances related to all kinds of matters when they belong to general party organs or administrations. Such Maoist institutions were nonetheless often assigned a new role after economic reforms were launched two decades ago.

Regarding labor, for instance, state-owned enterprises and private enterprises or enterprises belonging to mixed ownership systems have supported the emergence of new labor relations, and a new labor system is being implemented in which the state is considered a third party. Laws and regulations have been promulgated and specialized bodies have been created since the end of the 1980s. Quite automatically, "letters and visits bureaus" previously linked to the labor administration have become a main component of the new labor system.

One of the first initiatives national authorities took was to create in 1986 arbitration committees to solve labor disputes. Formed by members of the labor bureau and representatives of unions and other economic organizations, these committees are theoretically located between mediation committees—whose creation is encouraged within enterprises—and people's courts.[2] From 1993, when new regulations were issued regarding labor disputes, to the end of 2001, such committees officially handled 688,000 labor disputes involving 2,368,000 workers.[3] A few years later, in 1989, Shenzhen municipality launched a system of labor inspection, an innovation that was expanded to the whole nation in 1993.[4] The local body chosen to supervise the implementation of existing labor provisions was the "letters and visits bureau" of the labor municipal administration. More pointedly, a "brigade of labor inspection" was created and divided into five departments, one of them being the "letters and visits bureau," which, through the grievances received and handled, help the brigade to identify transgressions and eventually investigate the enterprises exposed. Besides trying to prevent and solve labor disputes, two tasks were initially assigned to the brigade: to institute the labor contract system and to supervise the number of workers coming from outside the locality and hired by local entrepreneurs, a system of quotas having been established to control migration flows. In June 1994 another important institutional innovation was adopted: the Labor Law was issued, its national enforcement beginning on January 1, 1995. This new legislation, which includes 107 articles divided into thirteen paragraphs, considers workers as a whole and does not establish differences according to the type of enterprise they are working for. The main provisions address such issues as the labor contract system, working hours and leaves, salary, labor security, special protection granted to women and children, professional training, social security and welfare, resolution of labor disputes, and, finally, labor inspection (Zhang and Zhang 1995, 599–615). Since then, a new objective has therefore been assigned to the "labor inspection brigade" or letters and visits bureau, both appellations being maintained: to promote and supervise the implementation of this legislation.

In order to combine labor inspection with the prevention of social unrest, two types of action have been privileged by the Shenzhen labor brigade during recent years: conducting regular inspection tours within local enterprises and handling complaints. Every year a highly publicized major inspection is thus organized during one month to deal with all kinds of labor issues, whereas shorter and more specialized tours, concerning, for instance, the methods of calculating and paying salaries, are carried out more frequently. The members of the brigade read the letters addressed to them, receive visitors' complaints, listen to the facts exposed, and decide eventually to launch an investigation in a given enterprise. Such investigations may pursue various aims: to explain official provisions regarding labor issues, to require employers to run their enterprise in conformity with the law, to sanction them if necessary by imposing fines, and, finally, to intervene in order to reduce tensions in the working places. It can be difficult, when reading the files, to understand the criteria prompting an intervention by the brigade, but a conflict that mobilizes more than thirty workers is usually considered serious and in need of some immediate, official action.

The labor inspection brigade stands at the top of an administrative pyramid that includes some forty other offices created after 1990 and located within the hierarchy administered by the labor bureau.[5] In other words, workers and employees in Shenzhen can send written complaints to a variety of addresses linked to the labor administration and located at the level of the neighborhood, the district, or the municipality. The extension of such a network to collect information and an officially acknowledged worsening of labor relations explains the steady increase in the number of letters and visits the brigade receives, ranging from 500 letters received in 1988 to 5,360 in 1998.[6] In 1997, the year most of the corpus was addressed to the letters and visits bureau, 12,581 grievances related to labor issues were exposed through letters or visits handled by the whole administrative network of the municipal labor bureau in Shenzhen.[7] It can be stressed that most workers lacking the needed resources to refer their problems to the arbitration committees tend to turn to the labor inspection brigade not only to denounce violations of the Labor Law but also to solve labor disputes. Shenzhen municipal authorities regret indeed that the brigade is actually considered by most workers as the most efficient and legitimate means to settle conflicts even though the responsibility has officially been assigned to arbitration committees.[8]

In the 123 letters collected, workers and employees expose their grievances to the members of the labor bureau in charge of promoting official policies regarding labor issues, including the new Labor Law, and ask for their intervention. More pointedly, the authors of these letters are addressing themselves not to members of a private sphere, such as friends and relatives, nor to agencies, such as the media, but to official authorities. It is therefore from this specific arena, where private grievances are addressed to public authorities, that these complaints participate in assigning a meaning to the new institution considered here: the Labor Law.

The Transient Labor Force

Most of the claimants in the corpus at stake work for the new economic sector born out of the reforms. This sector includes private Chinese or foreign enterprises, joint ventures, mixed forms of enterprise combining Chinese and foreign investments, especially Hong Kong and Taiwan investments and arrangements known as *sanlai yibu*.[9] Only one collective enterprise is explicitly mentioned in the corpus. One state enterprise is also represented, but the practices exposed occurred in a workshop subcontracted to an individual. The economic activities involved belong to the following sectors: garments, toys, electronics, plastic and paper wraps, detergents and soaps, metallic pieces, objects made in plastic or in osier printing, decorative objects, restaurants, and mechanics.

Moreover, claimants usually enjoy only a provisory permit of residence in Shenzhen (Cheng and Selden 1994; Kam and Li 1999), such permit being renewable every year. Many letters begin indeed by a formula stating that the workers taking the floor come from all parts of China or from "the five lakes and four seas" of China. The appellants often identify themselves as *dagongzai* and *dagongmei*, the expressions used to designate migrant workers, providing sometimes information regarding the time they arrived in Shenzhen (usually running from a few months to three years). A few of them justify their claims by stressing that the purpose of their geographical mobility was to alleviate their family's burden back home, to support themselves, or to allow the development of a new domestic activity. Two authors state only that their situation is particularly unfair because they actually possess a permanent right of residence in Shenzhen and should be better treated. In other words, although the letters do not include systematic information regarding the *hukou* status of the claimants, most of them belong to the large group of migrant workers employed on a temporary basis and enjoying only a provisory right of residence in Shenzhen.

As a matter of fact, one of the outcomes of the structural reforms that began in 1978 was to diminish many of the prerogatives enjoyed since 1950 by the workers in state-owned enterprises (Solinger 1995; Rocca 1999; Lee 1998). However, another outcome was the rise of new forms of enterprises attracting mainly but not only migrants, that is, individuals who work and live in a locality that is not their official place of residence. Shenzhen municipality, established in January 1979 and which includes a special economic zone extending over four of its six districts, is by definition a city of migrants: the local population shifted from 30,000 people in 1978 to 4,051,300 people in 1999, 70 percent of them enjoying only a provisory right of residence in Shenzhen.[10] In addition, 60 percent of the labor force works in nonstate and noncollectivist enterprises. The authors of the written complaints at stake are therefore members of this large transient labor force.

To understand the specific nature of the grievances expressed by such claimants, it is necessary to note that although the Labor Law concerns all workers and employees in China, those belonging to this "floating population" are not fully recognized as part of the working class in the sense that expression acquired under Maoist state socialism. The discrimination they face can partly be grasped from the terms used to describe them: *mingong*, or "peasant-workers," although not all of them originate from rural areas; *dagongzai*, a word difficult to translate but which encompasses the idea of a young wage-earner working for short periods; *laowugong*, a more official term meaning something like "workers into service"; and, more recently, *wailai congyezhe*, or "outsiders carrying on an activity," as opposed to *shimin*, or city residents. All these appellations underline the provisory rights as well as the outsider status of the workers concerned. A sense of the discrimination they face can also be gained from reading the local regulations governing labor relations involving migrants. Such regulations often complement the Labor Law on specific issues—such as the illegality of an employer's use of violence—but they also introduce distinctions that actually limit the universal reach of the law. The regulations enacted by Shenzhen municipality and revised for the third time in 1998 mention, for instance, that migrant workers should have at least finished the first cycle of secondary school to be hired in local enterprises and that living space in the collective dormitories should be no smaller than two square meters per worker. Finally, one cannot but mention the differences existing between those enjoying a provisory permit and those with a permanent residence permit in a given locality as far as access to education, medical care, housing, and other services and benefits are concerned.

As a consequence, whatever their geographical origin, past professional activity, or educational background, the claimants of our corpus share some characteristics: the uncertainties hanging over their future encourage them to try to make the most of their stay. In other words, the urgency lent to the financial and training benefits they hope to obtain from such a stay affects their choices and expectations as well as the relations established with local companies. Among other outcomes, mobility between enterprises is high, although migrants, being unable to avail a family support between jobs, are obliged to reduce downtime as far as possible. A survey done by the labor bureau in 1997—that is, the year most of the complaints collected were written—and filled by 2,762 migrant workers illustrates, for instance, the diversity of their professional background: 28 percent had never worked before coming to Shenzhen, while 26.2 percent were farmers, 17.6 percent had worked in state-owned factories, 11 percent had worked in rural industries, 12.3 percent were former technicians, and 4.3 percent were members of local administration departments.[11] But the same survey also reveals that the length of migrants' stay in Shenzhen was often rather short: 57 percent of them had been working there for less than three years.[12] Moreover, 22 percent of the respondents had changed factory once, 21.8 percent had done so twice, and 17.6 percent had shifted firms at least three times and at most ten times. The main reasons put forward to explain such mobility were low salary (56.6 percent), bad enterprise management (46.9 percent), long working hours (44.6 percent), and bad working environment (43.5 percent).

The grievances expressed in the material reviewed appear to be very much in conformity with the findings above. As a matter of fact, although most letters mention a diversity of problems, the letters and visits bureau has labeled all complaints according to the main issues at stake and offered the following classification: salaries paid too late or only partly paid (sixty-five mentions);

overtime too long (forty); no conclusion of contract (fifteen); "other causes" (twenty); unjustified dismissals (ten); no contribution to insurance funds (three); intense collective conflict (three); request for legitimate indemnity after an injury (one); request for information on the Labor Law (one).

Likewise, resort to a labor administration body, such as the letters and visits bureau, does not represent for migrant workers the main answer to labor conflicts: withdrawal or resignation appear to be more frequent. Only a minority (3.7 percent) of the respondents to the Shenzhen survey actually stated that turning to the labor bureau would be their first means of settling a dispute. In addition, only dramatic and frequent abuses seem to justify such appeals to authorities, and the facts exposed are described by the appellants as not only unfair and illegal but also unacceptable and unbearable. Finally, migrant workers tend to denounce to the labor administration conditions that affect a whole factory or workshop rather than a few individuals. The corpus gathered reveals indeed that only twenty-one letters are written by workers describing specific events for which they seek personal redress. The remaining ninety-two complaints describe practices and abuses considered as recurrent and common in the enterprises at stake and against which migrant workers stand collectively.

Members of the transient labor force, confronted with uncertainties regarding the length of their stay in Shenzhen, turned to the labor administration when all other means of improving their conditions had failed and denounced a diversity of recurrent abuses in their work places. The elements related to the identity of the claimants and the nature of the facts exposed, although very sketchy, must be taken into account when analyzing the specific mobilization of the Labor Law observed in the corpus.

The Labor Law in Practice

Written in 1996 and 1997 and selected at random from the archives of the letters and visits bureau, the complaints analyzed are undoubtedly deeply influenced by the promulgation of the Labor Law. The authors of as many as ninety letters mention the provisions of this legal document: the Labor Law thus clearly increases the capacity of these workers to find legitimate arguments in order to criticize some of the practices observed and to request the implementation of other norms and rules. However, the claimants mobilize this new legislation in a rather dynamic and complex way.

Legal Knowledge

The degree of knowledge of the law and, therefore, the degree of accuracy with which it is invoked vary greatly from one letter to the next. This is somehow an expected situation and one pervasive regardless of the society and legislation at stake. It is even more understandable that the Labor Law was enforced just a few months before the letters collected were written. As a result, the links established between the facts exposed and the content of the law are often loose and implicit. Indeed, most letters (forty-two out of ninety) include a description of the reality encountered, simply preceded or followed by such expressions as "the legitimate rights and interests of workers should be protected" or "these problems should be solved according to the law," no relationship being clearly established between the facts narrated and specific articles of the law.

A second category of letters proceeds with the description of certain practices, adding that they do violate the provisions of the Labor Law without mentioning which provisions are at stake (twenty-eight letters). A third category exhibits an explicit comparison between the legislation and the transgressions exposed (ten letters). Such is the case, for instance, of letter 45:

> "Workers here are very much angry with their boss, but until now we have been unable to change anything. So we decided to turn to you and complain about our employer, hoping that you will be able to bring this situation to an end by using existing regulations. The Labor Law sets that the ordinary working hours should amount to eight hours per day, but here we work half an hour more every day. Moreover, we work thirty days a month—that is, we have not a day to rest, which is not in conformity with the law, and we do overtime everyday, sometimes until one or two in the morning. Not only are we not entitled to refuse such overtime, but no meal is provided to us when we finish so late."

Finally, a last category of documents (ten out of ninety) demonstrates a detailed knowledge of the law, mentioning the numbers of the specific articles of the legislation that are considered to be violated by given practices, or quoting the content of these articles to ground the description of certain facts as illegitimate.

The variations observed regarding the knowledge and understanding of the law actually confer a high diversity to the ninety letters whose authors make some reference to this legislation. At one end of the continuum—if one classifies the letters according to the degree of precision with which they mention the content of the law—stand the written complaints in which appeals to the law seem to be rather rhetorical, while at the other end are found letters in which legal provisions are clearly identified and support a detailed and systematic description of the facts experienced as illegal. As a consequence, the law does not achieve the same type of visibility and recognition in all letters. One must add that the extreme conditions workers describe in the letters also contribute to the rather loose mobilization of the law: many letters, indeed, include passages stating that, whatever the law's actual provisions, it cannot presumably tolerate or support the facts exposed.

Social Expectations

The letters reveal that the migrant workers' backgrounds influence how they mobilize the law. More pointedly, the working conditions these individuals consider to be most unfair or unacceptable depend on their past professional experience and their expectations when coming to Shenzhen. As a consequence, they tend to stress some provisions of the law and ignore others. Almost never mentioned in the letters, for instance, are paragraphs 8 and 9 of the Labor Law, which deal, respectively, with professional training and social welfare and social security.

Professional training is considered an important issue by migrant workers. However, in Shenzhen, and, moreover, in the type of enterprises the present corpus addresses, technical training is usually acquired on the job or during evening courses offered, in most cases, by private organizations and paid for by the workers.[13] Migrant workers try to increase their technical skills, and thereby their competitiveness, through all kinds of means, but they do not request that employers assume a main responsibility for their training. Furthermore, although the Labor Law has articles related to "social security" and "social welfare," the authors of the letters analyzed do not seem to see these as relevant to their own situations. One interviewee summarized the shared perception of migrant workers on this issue:

> I do not know how long I will be able to stay in Shenzhen, and I do not know where I will go from here. Maybe I will go back to my native place, or maybe I will try to see if there are some opportunities for me elsewhere. So what is the point for me to ask my employer to participate [in] some insurance funds, or to spend part of my money to enjoy some social welfare. As soon as I will leave Shenzhen, these rights will not follow me. So I would rather have the employer giving me some

more money, I would rather try to save as much as possible every month rather than invest in this kind of thing. We are actually hardly recognized as real workers today; how could we be recognized as unemployed tomorrow?[14]

If paragraphs 7 and 8 of the Labor Law are somehow considered as not relevant to their situation and therefore ignored by the workers concerned, one provision of the widely invoked paragraph 5, concerned with salary issues, is also never mentioned in the data collected: the provision concerning minimum salary, a new concept in the Chinese legislation. Migrant workers, who aim at earning as much money as possible during their stay, seem to consider this provision inapplicable to their situation even though many complain about their low salaries: "The minimum salary, it can be easily understood by the boss as the maximum salary. So, we do not like to speak too much about it. What we want are simply acceptable conditions of living and working. We also want people to give us an opportunity to work, even if means working a lot, but then we should be paid according to the work done."[15]

Migrant workers' social positions, as well as their objectives and expectations developed under all kinds of individual and institutional constraints when coming to Shenzhen, explain a tendency to neglect certain aspects of the new legislation and to overemphasize others. Eighty percent of the letters mentioning the new legislation bring up paragraphs 4 and 5, which deal, respectively, with the issues of working time and salaries. Since the primary aim of migrant workers is to accumulate resources as quickly as possible, long working hours are actually accepted if they remain within certain reasonable limits and if overtime work is paid accordingly. Moreover, wages should be paid on time and in conformity with the rates previously stated. Finally, wages should not be diminished by all kinds of fees and fines. These are the fundamental requests of the claimants for whom the decision to migrate, and the sacrifices or hardships they faced, is difficult to justify if no money is earned. For example, here are excerpts from two letters:

I am a *wailaigong* [migrant worker] coming from Sichuan, and I can seem to be lucky since I found a job in an enterprise here in Shenzhen where I have been working for more than one year. But actually I am writing to expose our working conditions. I read recently the Labor Law and now I understand that we should definitely not face such hardship. I learned the honor of working in this part of China but also the hidden side of it. . . . The best thing to do would be to quit, but it is not an easy thing to do when you have no money and no one to help you while you look for another job. We are actually working much more than the law states: we do nine ordinary hours of work per day and then we work evenings from 7 PM to 10:30 PM. We cannot refuse to do overtime, nor can we refuse to work all Sundays, otherwise we are fined 20 to 50 yuan. . . . I am telling you the truth and you just have to come and look at our working cards. . . . We really hope you can pay attention to our situation and come to save us. I am writing on behalf of all those working in our enterprise and I thank you for the help that you will bring to us. (Letter 5)

I am coming from the countryside. I left our village because we had not enough land to cultivate. I arrived here and found a job in enterprise X through an employment center, but the situation I discovered is far from being normal. I have been here for more than one month and I have not been paid yet. I heard very different things regarding how much I will be paid and I still cannot guess what my salary will be. What is sure is that I owe money to the enterprise even before I have been paid for the first time because the boss kept all my documents proving that I could stay in Shenzhen, and then he told me that members of the police station came to the enterprise and took all workers documents. I have now to pay 300 yuan to get these papers back from the police station. The foreman takes 20 percent of my salary; we have to pay for food and accommodation, electricity, and water, so according to those who arrived here before me, we are actually working for nothing. . . . I know the Labor Law does not protect such practices. . . . I beg you to come and make an investigation in our factory to improve workers' lives. (Letter 15)

Not only are specific provisions of the legislation stressed by the migrant workers; they are also referred to in a very specific way. Most letters complaining about the long working hours performed actually mention legal provisions, not to ask for their strict application but rather to illustrate the distance existing between what is imposed upon them and what can legally—that is, reasonably—be required from workers. In fact, migrants interviewed in Shenzhen often express that they dislike those months during which no overtime work is required. Since most of them have no family to care for in Shenzhen and wishing to earn as much money as possible, they consider having long periods of leisure a waste of time. Therefore, appellants do not typically complain about working longer hours than the law specifies, but they do complain about being forced to work so much that their physical and mental health is endangered. To illustrate that certain acceptable limits have been transgressed, they compare the requirements of the law—by definition, bound to be perceived as reasonable and fair—with the practices imposed upon them, and show the gap existing between them. Moreover, they expose the fact that they are not paid according to the efforts invested, mobilizing here basic principles of distributive justice.

Thus, interpretation of law varies according to the position occupied by the social actors and, more pointedly, according to the resources they possess and the institutional constraints they face. Such resources and constraints delineate here migrant workers' possibilities and encourage them to assign more value to certain aspects of their working experience than to others, leading to their selective mobilization of the Labor Law.

Worker's Experiences

In analyzing how migrant workers interpret and use legal regulations, one cannot but observe a third phenomenon: workers' propensity to refer to rules and principles that are not explicitly stated in the legislation. The experiences faced by the claimants at stake are indeed often very difficult, if not dramatic. "We cannot stand it anymore," "we will not survive if it goes on": these are some of the expressions often read in the corpus. Yet workers have difficulty grounding their grievances in the legislation because it was not intended to deal with such extreme cases.

Confronted with such problems, appellants tend to designate as components of the law facts or principles that are not stated in the legislation, addressing, instead, not the explicit content of the law but the collective intention of its promulgation, what jurists call "the spirit of the law." Such discussions were held, nonetheless, under many uncertainties regarding what really was at stake when the legislation was drafted. As a consequence, migrant workers' denunciations contribute to bringing new elements into this collective intention.

Some facts are exposed as violating the provisions of the Labor Law, even when the violation is not explicitly mentioned in the legislation, for example, an employer's refusal to answer employees' questions; lack of transparency regarding calculation of salaries; lack of clear and shared norms to coordinate each other's actions in the work place; existence of abusive internal regulations, such as requiring workers to write self criticisms; refusal to act in conformity with existing regulations regarding premiums; imposing loans on employees; lack of showers in the dormitories; and resorting to violence to force workers to comply with certain rules. The practices that are seen as violating the provisions of the law are quite numerous and diverse.

The facts the migrant workers expose in the corpus can be divided into three categories. The first category are those actions whose illegality is so much taken for granted, it is believed, that there is no need to codify them in the law—resort to violence and imposition of loans are examples. Everyone knows these actions are wrong, so the law need not explicitly address them.

A second category of facts may be condemned as illegal out of the need to assign a concrete meaning to abstract legal provisions. Such is the case, for instance, when workers refer to article 8 of the law, which addresses the right of workers to discuss and negotiate on equal footing with their employer in order to determine local norms and protect their interests. This very important but general statement can be interpreted to support a variety of claims. Calls for more transparency in wage calculation and payments, requests for employers to answer workers' questions and justify their decisions: these are some of the issues mentioned in the corpus that are grounded in article 8 and contribute to assigning a more concrete meaning to this specific part of the law.

A third category of practices relates to such issues as living conditions in dormitories, which the law does not address because its focus is on working conditions. However, employers in Shenzhen often provide housing to their workers. Dissatisfaction with living and eating conditions are thus expressed by mobilizing, for instance, the first article of the Labor Law stating the need to "protect the legitimate rights and interests of the workers." In other words, the law is here complemented, and the scope of its relevance and validity extended, in order to include situations linked to labor relations outside the workplace.

Facts identified as illegal and thus incorporated in the law may therefore violate norms that are considered as so much shared and legitimate that they do not need to have been explicitly written in the law; others are labeled as such out of the necessity to assign a concrete meaning to the general statements of the law; and others are anchored in a process of extension of the scope of the law required to fill its blanks. Whatever the process, the law is thus put to the test: while it supports the expression of a specific judgment on the facts encountered, it is interpreted in a rather selective and creative way.

Other letters in the corpus stress that the practices denounced are illegal because they violate the moral and social principles implicit in the law. The principles then stated vary from rather simple social norms, such as that no worker should enjoy privileged treatment, to more fundamental rules, such as allowing workers to fulfill their filial piety by granting them leave to participate in their parents' birthday, or employers respecting human beings' dignity. The legitimacy of these moral and social norms is thus reinforced, and they are explicitly identified as having been influential during the drafting of the law.

> My name is Zhang XX and I want to expose the facts that I witnessed in factory Y. This factory began its activities in 1993 but has applied for no authorization to hire workers. Still, our employer was able to hire people from official organizations. One of the main issues at stake is that he promised us a certain wage for each piece done, but then when the time comes that we should be paid, the wage has been diminished. In other words, he is a *xiaoren* ["small man"] because he does not live up to his word while the Labor Law asks him to do so. The Labor Law also requires employers and employees to sign a formal contract but he refuses to do so, always postponing to tomorrow the time to solve this issue.... Most of us have a wife and children at home, but it is already a few months since we have been unable to send money to our family. But the law says that one should be paid according to the work done, and that one should be given a reasonable wage or at least some means to survive until the day the salary can be fully paid (Letter 63).

One of the basic moral principles underlying the law is thus the requirement that one live up to one's word, be a trustworthy person, a requirement leading to the emphasis placed on verbal as well as written contracts. Moreover, the law is perceived as defending a variety of principles of distributive justice, such as the rule of equity according to which investments and profits should vary together, as well as the principle according to which the distribution of resources should be done according to the basic needs perceived. Other letters discuss not only the social principles considered to be directly linked to the law but also the fundamental principles of justice considered to have guided the content of the legislation:

> I am a *dagongmei* coming from Sichuan. I have been working for more than one year in factory X. I want to make public what I personally witnessed in that enterprise, what I heard and saw there. I hope by doing so that you will pay attention to us and that you will restore equity and fairness.... Because the law is not followed, we have a feeling of insecurity and our basic rights as human beings are not respected.... A Yan fell ill and her parents sent money to her through the post office, but because our boss keeps all our documents, including the identity card, she was unable to prove her identity at the post office and to get her money. As her illness was getting more serious, we launched a collection to support her way back home and she left with only her tears to cry.... The law is done to protect our security,

> our life as human beings, but some people just do not consider us as human beings. . . . We work every day contrary to what the Labor Law posits, and we work about 14 hours a day. We are actually working more than we can, we are sacrificing our youth to this place and this factory, despite the fact that the law tries to prevent some people [from being] treated like machines. (Letter 67)

In this letter it is the fundamental moral norm that each member of the society should be treated as a human being—that is, the principle that posits the equal humanity of all individuals and the necessity to respect such humanity—which is considered as being the ultimate objective of the law.

Many more examples could be found in the corpus regarding the way migrant workers tend to demonstrate the illegitimacy of the treatment imposed on them by qualifying as "illegal" practices the legal provisions do not explicitly address and by stressing moral and social principles that are not clearly stated in the law. By doing so, they interpret the Labor Law on the basis of principles of justice or reasonableness embodied for them in this context, and ultimately linked to their own capacities of judgment.

The Labor Law and Other Institutions

Finally, a fourth phenomenon can be observed in the way claimants invoke the Labor Law. At the same time they demonstrate the legitimacy of their grievances by relying on this specialized legislation, they mention other institutions that eventually encompass different principles of justice.

Of the claimants' letters examined, about forty of them mention, for instance, principles qualified as political or ideological to ground their descriptions of certain facts as unfair and illegitimate and combine them with legal principles. Indeed, many complaints associate the Labor Law with another important institutional fact: the socialist nature of the political regime. They do so by resorting to such formulations as "the law has to support the building of socialism" (Letters 3, 18, and 82)› "every effort has to be done to implement a socialist legal system" (Letters 21, 32, 65, and 91), and "no one should be able to breach the laws decided by the Chinese Communist Party" (Letters 12, 86, 33, 118, and 120). Such general and abstract statements could appear as simply reproducing a certain rhetorical form, but coming after the exposure of a diversity of facts detrimental to workers' interests, they should rather be considered as an attempt to privilege a specific interpretation the Labor Law. More pointedly, the socialist ideology relies on a certain number of principles of justice and patterns of rights distribution that are used here to stress that a specific interpretation of the law should prevail, one assigning a dominant position to members of the working class. Hence the frequent reminder in the letters that if workers are no more "the masters of the factories," they remain nonetheless "the masters of the country" (Letters 11, 26, 51, 90, and 105). Others stress that the situation of migrants should be closer to that enjoyed by workers in the state sector because all share the respected and somehow privileged appellation of "worker" (Letters 65 and 122). The meaning of the Labor Law is therefore influenced by the incorporation of such a specialized text in a wider institutional and political background, allowing the assessment of the legitimacy of migrant workers' claims.

In a second possible configuration, appellants confront the validity of local and national regulations. They simultaneously praise the achievements of Shenzhen—achievements they feel they contributed to—while questioning the limits of the exclusive status of this locality. Whatever privileges such places may enjoy, their members should indeed act in conformity with existing national laws. "We can read in the newspapers about the Labor Law, we know about it, but there is no sign of it in our factory. Why is it not applied in our city? Although Shenzhen is a special economic zone, is it so special a place that it is not concerned by the national laws of the People's Republic of China?... You really have to protect the legitimate interests of the workers and defend the dignity of our socialist legal system" (Letter 34).

Two different institutional facts—a national legislation and a local status—are thus confronted and their respective scales of validity discussed. Moreover, the hierarchy existing between them is questioned and finally reassessed in order to show the superiority of one fact on the other and to encourage, as a consequence, the mobilization of existing legal provisions to interpret the situations exposed.

From Local Interpretation to Public Debate

A multiplicity of factors influence how migrant workers use the Labor Law to ground their grievances and thus express judgments regarding the treatment they receive. The extent of their legal knowledge, the resources and expectations born out of their individual experiences, the nature of the facts encountered, and simultaneous use of a variety institutional provisions or objectives:

these are some of the issues identified as having an impact on the interpretation process of the Labor Law. As such, migrant workers offer one among the possible interpretations of the law and participate in the debate concerning the norms such institution should encompass.

However, to what extent do such private complaints, and therefore judgments, affect the common knowledge of this specific legislation? It is difficult to trace in this realm very clear links of causality and show how the claims made in letters such as those included in the corpus at stake affect the general understanding of the law: the complaints lodged are indeed legitimate because they are not addressed to a public audience. Nonetheless, it is important to note that the normative and empirical content of such grievances is explicitly mobilized by other social actors in order to identify social problems in general and, more specifically, to reveal the limits or unanticipated consequences of existing legal provisions, such as the initiatives recently taken by the official trade union organizations.

Trade-union representatives recently discussing the Labor Law in newspapers, such as *Workers Daily,* often mention that their perspectives are influenced by the complaints lodged by workers or by the disputes observed in arbitration committees.[16] Some of them reveal that their organizations have created their own letters and visits bureau in order to be informed of labor problems and offer another venue for their resolution.[17] Such bureaus regularly publish internal documents about the local labor situation that they pass along to the municipal government. Trade unions, therefore, possess the needed evidence to denounce the abuses witnessed in the state sector and particularly in the nonstate sector. Low or unpaid wages, unilateral dismissal of workers, excessive overtime, poor working conditions, no conclusion of the required contract, discrimination against migrant workers: the evidence reflects the grievances workers express in their written complaints. Moreover, efforts to defend workers in the nonstate sector—estimated at almost 70 million—are justified by appealing to arguments present in the letters: "In a socialist country like ours, it is not possible and it will not be tolerated that workers are put in the incapacity to protect their rights."[18] Migrant workers in private firms "are still working there as masters of the country; they are members of the working-class. . . . Their democratic rights to participate in their enterprise management should be protected by the law."[19]

Faced with such a situation, local trade unions are taking action: in Yucheng (Shanxi Province), a complaint hotline for migrant workers has been created;[20]

in a very interesting move in Xinyang (Henan Province), the local trade-union organization has created a mobile membership, allowing the 1.5 million workers originating from Xinyang but working elsewhere to be protected by their local organization wherever they go.[21] But the main concern among workers and trade unions is the need to revise the existing Labor Law. "With the society's development, the Labor Law has become unable to respond to workers' objective needs; to revise and complement the Labor Law is now one of the main hopes of the large masses of workers as well as of the people of our country."[22] It is pointed out that the law, which is supposed to reflect the political importance of the working class, is actually unable to support and protect such a status since "workers are put in a position of inferiority as far as labor relations are concerned." The law is denounced as too simple compared to foreign labor laws. As a consequence, many abusive situations are not dealt with, nor are they identified as such. In addition, the law is described as too general and abstract; its interpretation is so blurred that employers are able to use the law to defend their illegal actions. Regulations and sanctions are not detailed enough, making it difficult for workers, particularly migrant workers in the nonstate sector, to use the law as a weapon to defend their interests. It is also claimed that, although the law focuses on a fundamental issue, workers' rights, its drafting, unlike the drafting of the Marriage Law, for instance, was not part of a wide national debate. Finally, it is often stated that the relevance and strength of such legislation is hampered by the numerous and contradictory local and national regulations.[23]

Hence, the complaints lodged by workers, especially migrant workers, not only test and interpret the Labor Law but serve to stimulate the public debate about its merits and shortcomings.

Transforming the Institution

The corpus gathered, being composed of complaints written by a certain category of workers, does not support a comprehensive understanding of the present significance of the Labor Law within Chinese society. Such a significance is indeed the outcome of a complex process of interpretation based on the interaction of various social actors—including those in charge of applying the law—seizing the law to achieve individual or collective objectives. Nonetheless, the written complaints examined here illustrate the importance of the process of institutional creation developed by Chinese authorities in order to govern situations born out of the reforms launched two decades ago. These new institutions support the capacity of the state to influence social relationships and social order by establishing rules and punishing transgressions. In the meantime, they provide new possibilities for individuals and groups to elaborate the needed course of action in order to achieve their specific projects as well as to protect their rights.

To understand how such institutional creations affect Chinese society, however, one has to look at the "real" meaning of the newly built institutions by paying attention to the set of rules and roles they encompass as well as the way they are understood and mobilized by ordinary citizens according to their past experiences, social position, and interpretive resources. The problem at stake is actually wider than the issue of the effectiveness or the good implementation of existing institutions. It is related to the plurality of legitimate principles of justice that can be used to understand an institution, in a given society at a given time. Institutions are put to the test by social actors; they support different claims and different actions according to the norms or principles that will be privileged in various contexts. Migrant workers in China, employed in the new forms of enterprises having arisen out of the reform process, thus contribute, when using the Labor Law in order to defend their interests, to the complex process of assigning to this new institution its real meaning and effectiveness. In other words, they participate, from their very specific position, in transforming this institution into a complex reality.

Moreover, each institution is embedded in a common knowledge, that is, in discussions regarding its creation, its deficiencies and inadequacies, its required adjustments. Such discussions are nourished and stimulated by those very diverse and fragmented moments of mobilization of the institution at stake, even when, as is the case in present Chinese society, public debate still faces a diversity of constraints. As a consequence, to observe the interaction between the creation of institutions and the formation of new capacities of judgment and action—that is, to observe how institutions are effectively understood—seems to constitute a privileged means of grasping the dominant values emerging today in China within a complex historical process.

6

THOMAS G. RAWSKI

Social Capabilities and Chinese Economic Growth

DURING THE LAST four decades of the twentieth century, China's economy produced a truly remarkable sequence of events. The Great Leap Forward of 1958–1960 initiated a twenty-year interlude of widespread hunger and deprivation. Twenty years later, the reform policies of the late 1970s triggered a massive and unexpected economic boom that catapulted several hundred million people from absolute poverty. This experience raises profound questions about the links between culture, institutions, and economy, a central focus of C. K. Yang's distinguished research career.

Recent studies document the scale and impact of China's 1959–1961 famine. The persistence of hunger and undernutrition throughout the 1960s and 1970s is less widely recognized. A Fujian village leader's pithy observation effectively summarizes the rural situation: "By the fall of 1959, hunger suddenly emerged without warning. . . . For the next twenty years, the problem of hunger was part of our lives" (Huang 1989, 61). Table 6.1 substantiates this observation by showing that for twenty consecutive years the average rural diet fell short of widely recognized standards of nutritional adequacy. The Chinese government has established 2,100 calories as a dietary threshold for absolute poverty (Kang

1995, 39). Calculations summarized in Table 6.1, based on Alan Piazza's estimate of nationwide calorie availability (Piazza 1986, 92) and information about urban-rural dietary differentials, show that average rural diets fell short of this standard in every year between 1959 and 1972. Average rural calorie supply fell below Piazza's estimated standard of safe nutrition in every year from 1959 to 1977. Chinese sources describe annual consumption of less than 150 kilograms of grain as "semistarvation" and associate annual cereal consumption of under 150 kilograms (or 200 kilograms in southern rice-growing regions) with deprivation (Lardy 1983, 166). Data in Table 6.1 show that average grain consumption for rural Chinese remained below 200 kilograms throughout the period 1959–1977. These data leave no room to doubt that as of the mid-1970s, the income and consumption levels of typical Chinese farm households fit any plausible criterion for absolute impoverishment.

Chinese sources provide a rural poverty head count of 250 million for 1978; the World Bank suggests a somewhat higher figure of 260.5 million for the same year (Fu Min 1996, 35; World Bank 1992, 23). Collective distributions to rural households climbed steeply in 1978, reaching a level 16 percent higher than the average for 1970–1977 (Agricultural Yearbook 1980, 41). Since the increase in earnings from private economic activity was probably even larger, rural incomes in 1978 may have surpassed the average for 1970–1977 by 20–25 percent. If 250 million lacked basic necessities in 1978, the comparable figure for 1970, 1972, or 1975 could be as high as 400 million, or more than half of China's agricultural population.

A quarter-century later, the hunger and deprivation that formerly afflicted most villagers is effectively confined to a much smaller segment of the population. Figures for 1998 place the poverty headcount at 48 million (using the Chinese government's austere poverty line) or 106 million (based on the World Bank's considerably higher international poverty standard), that is, 5.5–12.2 percent of the rural populace.[1] Whatever the exact numbers, it is evident that several hundred million rural Chinese have escaped absolute poverty since 1975. Villagers who formerly struggled to feed their families now ride bicycles, watch television, and maintain savings accounts. Whether we focus on sheer numbers or on the share of rural people lifted from poverty, the historical record contains no precedent for the scale or the rapidity of this transformation.

Economists have learned that extricating populations from absolute poverty is an agonizingly slow process that typically requires multiple policy interventions to provide poor communities with education, information, credit, sani-

Table 6.1

Dietary Overview for China's Agricultural Population, 1952–1981

	Average per capita consumption			
Year	*Processed grain (kg/year)*	*Calories (per day)*	*Safe calorie level*	*Calorie adequacy (%)*
1952	192	n.a.	2,048	n.a.
1953	191	n.a.	2,083	n.a.
1954	190	n.a.	2,088	n.a.
1955	196	2,129	2,092	102
1956	205	2,213	2,097	106
1957	205	2,106	2,102	100
1958	201	2,122	2,107	101
1959	183	1,742	2,111	82
1960	156	1,480	2,116	70
1961	154	1,663	2,121	78
1962	161	1,772	2,126	83
1963	160	1,763	2,130	83
1964	179	1,934	2,135	91
1965	177	1,918	2,139	90
1966	187	2,046	2,142	96
1967	184	2,011	2,146	94
1968	171	1,883	2,149	88
1969	171	1,859	2,153	86
1970	185	2,090	2,156	97
1971	186	2,036	2,160	94
1972	166	1,878	2,163	87
1973	189	2,113	2,167	98
1974	185	2,157	2,179	99
1975	187	2,159	2,191	99
1976	186	2,129	2,203	97
1977	189	2,128	2,215	96
1978	194	2,297	2,227	103
1979	206	2,461	2,239	110
1980	214	2,345	2,251	104
1981	220	2,376	2,263	105

Note: n.a. = data not available.

Sources: Rural grain consumption from Chinese sources compiled in Sicular 1989, 252. Rural calorie availability is from author's calculations based on national figures from Piazza 1986, 92; and data for urban and rural consumption of grain (weighted 87 percent) and four subsidiary foods (edible oil, meat, sugar, eggs, weighted 13 percent) shown in Trade Statistics 1984, 27–31. Safe calorie level is from national figures calculated in Piazza 1986, 92.

tation, health care, tax relief, market access, and employment opportunities (World Bank 1990). China's remaining pockets of rural poverty, concentrated in a handful of northwestern and southwestern provinces, exemplify the persistence of absolute impoverishment.

This consensus underscores the remarkable achievement of China's economic reforms in liberating several hundred million villagers from absolute poverty without the policy support that is widely regarded as essential to the success of antipoverty efforts. If anything, the mass escape from rural poverty coincided with a reduction in the scope and intensity of public-sector support for poor villagers, as collective assistance deteriorated or vanished amid the rush to reinstate the household economy.

How did China's rural reform elicit such dynamism in communities that began their ascent from income levels that international agencies routinely associate with absolute impoverishment? Economic research has focused on establishing a strong correlation between the reversion to household farming and growth of farm output (Putterman 1993, chap. 7). Noneconomists emphasize the entrepreneurial leadership of local governments in promoting development.[2] Both approaches seem inadequate.

In retrospect, we know that, unlike most impoverished communities, a large proportion of Chinese villages was somehow poised to achieve sustained growth. Where did this preparation reside? Economic studies confirm the link between incentives, market access, and productivity. But why did improved incentives and expanded market access inspire a historic breakthrough to new levels of output, productivity, and income on this occasion when earlier reforms in 1949–1952 and in 1962–1965 merely delivered a gradual return toward living standards attained prior to wartime disruption (1937–1949) and the Great Leap Forward (1958–1960)? And what enabled local leaders to deliver levels of village prosperity and rates of growth unknown in Chinese history? More generally, why is it that characteristic persistence of deep poverty emerges at much lower income levels in China than in Egypt, India, or Nigeria?

My proposed answers revolve around the interaction between long-standing cultural legacies and the developmental impact of China's commune system. I believe that, dating back to the Imperial period, rural Chinese society produced individuals who, despite low levels of income and wealth, were, on average, unusually well equipped to thrive in a market economy. Furthermore, for all its costs, China's commune system enhanced both the material and the human capabilities available to support rural growth. By removing barriers to private economic activity and local entrepreneurship, the agricultural reforms of the late 1970s revealed the developmental capabilities of village economic culture, newly strengthened by the intended and unintended consequences of the commune experience. The result was an unprecedented and unexpected rural boom.

Cultural explanations of economic outcomes are rarely convincing. We cannot claim that Chinese individuals are genetically greedier, more mercenary, or quicker to grasp financial opportunity than non-Chinese. Broad appeals to "Confucian values" seem equally implausible, since the exceptional performance that we seek to understand occurs only in specific historical contexts. To be successful, a culturally linked explanation of economic outcomes must relate individual or group traits to the particular historical and institutional circumstances associated with episodes of rapid growth or structural transformation.

Economics is not devoid of ideas about the origins and economic consequences of individual traits. Beginning with the work of Theodore Schultz (1961), economists have drawn a parallel between investment in tangible assets (machines, structures, laboratories) and investment in human capabilities, or "human capital." Economists see both as governed by a search for high returns. They imagine that families decide whether to send children to work or to school, and that employers determine the amount of training to offer their workers according to the same principles that govern the allocation of pension funds among cash, stocks, and bonds.[3] Empirical studies offer considerable support for this sort of theorizing.[4]

Feminist critics attack the tendency for studies of human capital to emphasize the contribution of formal schooling and organized job training programs to the economic capability of individual workers: "Most human capital investments are given to children by parents. Yet economic theory focuses on the small amount of human capital that can be obtained by adults able to choose. Because economic theory examines adult behavior, parents' gifts of time, love, and money to infants and children are reconceptualized as 'natural endowments' and thus are hidden by a theory that focuses on how people get what they choose. These lost gifts, forgotten or ignored by economic theory, are yet another manifestation of the invisibility of women's work" (Strassmann 1993, 58).

The omissions resulting from a narrow interpretation of human capital extend far beyond the neglect of women's work. Strassmann's acute critique exposes the implicit broadening of Adam Smith's assumption of a universal human "propensity to truck, barter, and exchange" into the much broader proposition that the economic capabilities of individuals reared in different societies are unlikely to differ substantially as long as the individuals receive similar amounts of formal education and employment training.

This expansive and ahistorical interpretation of "natural endowments" seems unwarranted. The understandable pursuit of a parsimonious theoretical framework unwittingly excludes culturally rooted social practices—what Douglass North (1990, chap. 5) calls "informal constraints"—from the analysis of economic phenomena. China's recent achievements in poverty alleviation highlight the potential significance of cultural differences in the human factor, differences arising from historically embedded informal institutions, as determinants of economic outcomes.

This essay focuses on one dimension of these issues, that of cultural legacy. The following pages review evidence suggesting that what I propose to call the village economic culture of imperial and republican China produced individuals who were well prepared to make their way in modern market systems.

Economic Culture in Rural China

Japan's post-1989 stagnation and the financial crash of the late 1990s have focused world attention on Asian realities rather than Asian miracles. For East Asia, the realities include massive long-term economic gains without convergence to sociocultural patterns observed in North America or Western Europe. Recent historical experience permits us to reject the once-popular notions that Chinese family structures stifle development or that Japanese personnel management practices cannot support new technologies. We can also see that, despite the importance of opportunities to expand trade, a dynamic home economy is the basic ingredient in East Asian economic success. This is particularly clear for China, whose share of global trade has only recently surpassed comparable figures from the 1920s.

The richness of domestic entrepreneurial resources is especially striking in China, which has recently emerged from a socialist era in which, for nearly three decades, the authorities worked to eradicate opportunities for private enterprise and to vilify profit-seeking behavior. Despite this massive regulatory and propaganda effort, relaxation of controls following the agricultural reforms of the late 1970s brought an immediate and far-reaching response. What is the source of this responsiveness to market opportunities, which seems inherent even in Chinese villagers with little or no personal experience of a market economy? The following pages offer a sketch of rural China's traditional economic culture in the areas of market experience, the institutional setting of commercial activity, complex organizations, popular religion, and family and personal life. The evidence comes from studies of the Imperial period as well as the twentieth century.

Market Experience

Commerce has a long history in China. Farmers as well as urban residents encountered the opportunities and the dangers inherent in a market economy. The volume of trade was large in relation to total output and, at least since the mid-nineteenth century, growing ahead of population. We find village communities integrated into national markets for grain as far back as the eighteenth century. By the twentieth century, prices of a wide range of farm crops, handicraft products, and manufactures reflected national or even international market forces. Markets were generally competitive, with many buyers and sellers, easy entry and exit for both small and large participants, and wide circulation of commercial information. Men and women with the wit to anticipate the needs of their neighbors and the skill to act on such insights could use the market to improve their income and status starting from any position on the social ladder. Rapid downward mobility threatened the fortunes of all who failed to grasp the logic of market behavior.

Even in localities beyond the reach of interregional trade, people participated in active markets for land, labor, and funds. The market for land, the principal asset in a traditional agrarian economy, was enormously complex. Buyers and sellers included kinship groups, business partnerships, schools, temples, and voluntary associations as well as individuals. Land ownership was no simple thing. In some regions, ownership rights could be divided into two or even three separate segments, with different persons holding transferable claims to a single plot. Tenancy was equally intricate, including a variety of rental arrangements with differing degrees of responsibility and security for tenants. Land could be pledged, mortgaged, rented, and sold.

Labor markets were similarly complex, involving arrangements for short- and long-term labor service, apprenticeship, temporary or permanent servitude, and sale or exchange of persons among households, including betrothals and adoptions. Money markets existed everywhere, ranging from simple personal loans to complex transactions involving interregional remittances, spot or future currency exchanges, and mobilization of substantial sums by business groups. Bidding and auctions were common, for example, in selecting the managers of local security forces (R. Watson 1990, 253).

It is important to note that women as well as men participated in market exchanges and other aspects of economic life. We have many reports indicating the commercial acumen of women who served as managers of family enterprises nominally controlled by their husbands or sons. Women also entered the marketplace on their own behalf, using funds obtained from their natal families at the time of their marriage or from the sale of their own produce or labor.

The Institutional Setting for Market Activity

Market transactions in China's traditional economy were conducted under institutional arrangements that placed a high premium on behavior patterns that seem essential to successful functioning in a modern market economy. We briefly consider monetization, brokerage, shareholding, agency functions, business associations, and customary law.

MONETIZATION

Extensive monetization has characterized China's economy at least since the days of Marco Polo. Monetary arrangements were highly complex, with prices and wages in even the smallest markets feeling the influence of fluctuations in the exchange between copper and silver. In the twentieth century, a monetary revolution in the private sector brought banknotes and deposits to the fore, displacing metal coin and bullion as the principal medium of exchange even before the currency reform of 1935. When Communist revolutionaries set up Soviet republics during the 1930s, they found banknotes circulating in even remote and isolated localities. With government unable to support the banking system or to stabilize exchange rates between copper and silver or between the currencies prevalent in various trades and localities, participation in the money economy meant exposure to the risk of sudden shifts in the value of the particular money in which one's wealth or income was denominated.

BROKERAGE

Market participants often employed brokers who earned commissions by seeking out potential buyers and sellers, facilitating business negotiations, mediating disputes, and recruiting scribes and money changers. In addition to commodity transactions, brokers often participated in the sale or rental of land or real estate, family division of wealth, and marriage or adoption arrangements. Since integrity and diligence rather than wealth were the main requirements, brokerage offered an entry-point to the business world for men (and some women) with few tangible assets.

SHAREHOLDING

Division of ownership rights into shares was common in China's traditional economy. Kinship groups, local associations, and business partnerships apportioned property and claims to resources into shares. When shares were transferable, the passage of time, bringing with it the rise and decline in the fortunes of households or lineage branches, led to complex ownership structures. Individuals might own shares in one enterprise that in turn shared ownership of a second venture with another set of persons, families, or even corporate groups. The phenomenon of *fenjia,* or division of family assets among brothers, brought the concept of shared ownership of corporate assets into even the humblest households.

AGENCY FUNCTIONS

The prevalence of shareholding necessitated the use of agents to undertake a wide range of tasks. Family members often acted as agents for the kinship group, with one member attending to one enterprise or activity while relatives took responsibility for other tasks. Frequently, however, managerial duties were assigned to persons lacking close blood ties to the principals in an enterprise. Collection agents employed by large estates (landlord bursaries); managers of stores, workshops, or business branches; teachers in clan schools; business partners or correspondents in distant places—all might be recruited from outside the family, necessitating complex arrangements for specifying tasks, assessing candidates, formulating agreements, maintaining incentives, and evaluating performance.

BUSINESS ASSOCIATIONS

Business associations, some based on common occupations (bankers, beggars, rice merchants) others on place of origin (*Landsmannschaften*) or business location, figured prominently in Chinese commercial life. These organizations maintained public services (standard weights and measures, fire brigades), lobbied for favorable government action, entered into negotiations with representatives of other interest groups, mediated commercial disputes, maintained charitable institutions (schools, soup kitchens), and enforced business ethics. Here again we find the need to formulate rules and policies that will command the allegiance of a large group of unrelated individuals with diverse backgrounds and interests.

CUSTOMARY LAW

Even today, China has no official system of dispute resolution comparable to Western commercial law. Yet the frequency of complex economic transactions and business structures necessitated the development of viable substitutes. Decisions about such matters as liability for the destruction of goods in transit or sanctions against fraudulent business practice cannot be left to chance. Transactions in China's traditional economy took place within a framework of customary law, reflected in written contracts, deeds, and agreements, adjudicated by village elders, guild directors, and other respected individuals, and enforced by public support for the norms embodied in written agreements and accepted business practice and for the values articulated by community leaders in their quasi-judicial role. Since the justice dispensed by government officials was remote, expensive, and unpredictable, disputes were often settled informally on the basis of customary law by men who, despite their lack of official position, wielded sufficient power to levy substantial fines or even to exclude offenders from the marketplace.[5] The same tradition of informal justice prevailed in overseas Chinese communities, where disputes were settled and (often severe) punishments decreed and accepted without reference to official legal codes or procedures.

Complex Organizations

Complex organizations and institutions played a significant role in the daily life of Chinese of all social ranks. Making the best of one's circumstances required an ability to understand the structure and operation of these arrangements in order to manipulate them in directions favorable to one's own interests. The search for loopholes or ambiguities offering possible advantage or, contrarily, the framing of regulations in ways that prevent others from such maneuvers, have long been familiar to ambitious Chinese at every level of wealth, status and power. We refer briefly to family, government, village associations, and the educational system.

KINSHIP GROUPS

Chinese families range from isolated nuclear households to the multigenerational Confucian ideal. Kinship ties provided the foundation for corporate arrangements that had the potential to accumulate great wealth and extensive political power. Lineage trusts controlled substantial proportions of land in parts of South China (R. Watson 1990). In Sichuan, salt merchants "skillfully adapted the institutions of the traditional charitable estate to the needs of early modern industrial development. . . . They, in effect, turned the lineage trust into an analogue of the business corporation" (Zelin 1990, 91).

GOVERNMENT

Although the formal structure of the imperial state terminated at the county seat, where a magistrate presided over as many as several hundred thousand citizens, government regulations and systems affected the daily lives of many Chinese. Landowners, including small owner-farmers, were liable for land taxes. Tenants, though exempt from the land tax, might be obliged to deal with official personnel involved with land records or administration of justice.[6]

Government systems for mutual surveillance (*baojia*), labor service, and household records theoretically involved all families. The presence of government systems and their agents even in rural villages placed a premium on literacy and numeracy, on the possession of basic information about the regulations for the land tax and other official systems, and on the ability to counter demands by persons claiming superior knowledge of these matters.

VILLAGE ASSOCIATIONS

Rural villages often supported voluntary groups whose operations required substantial managerial, financial, and diplomatic skills. Irrigation associations offer an excellent example. Management of an irrigation network serving several hamlets or villages calls for careful allotment of rights and responsibilities among landowners whose plots will benefit from improved access to water. As Fu-mei Chang Chen and Ramon H. Myers observe, the varying fortunes of different landowners required periodic adjustments lest the imbalance of benefit and cost encourage some members to abandon their responsibilities, leading to a gradual crumbling of both physical facilities and community support (Chen and Myers 1978, 12–15). Village associations organized to promote education, security, local festivals, and other activities required similar skills. The prevalence of such undertakings in rural China, many of which were managed in turn by different households, offers eloquent testimony to the wide dispersion of talent in management, accounting, and related skills.

EDUCATION

China's traditional system of education was built on an impersonal, merit-oriented structure that attracted widespread attention and imitation in Europe. Academic advancement was possible for any male who could master widely known texts and skills. Although the highest rewards, while theoretically open to all, were in reality accessible only to candidates with both talent and financial backing, scholarship opportunities created openings for poor but bright students, and even the poorest families could aspire to academic success through several generations of human capital accumulation.

Popular Religion

It might be argued that the foregoing examples apply most particularly to elite individuals and households and tell us little about the experience of ordinary villagers. But Chinese society cohered through strong vertical ties of shared knowledge, institutions, and behavior among elite and masses. Peasant proverbs, for example, mirror the entrepreneurial values of the commercial classes (Arkush 1984). This cultural unity is nowhere more evident than in the practice of popular religion, which reveals villagers' widespread familiarity with and imitation of elite activities.

Chinese folk religion conceives of heaven as a bureaucracy in which different levels of deities maintain files containing dossiers on individual citizens, whose good and bad deeds are tallied in "ledgers of merit and demerit." Mortals submit petitions and await celestial edicts, all cast in the form of communications between the terrestrial emperor and his servants.

Ties between religion and commerce have a long history: pawnshops, mutual financing associations, auctions, and lotteries "either originated in or had close connections with Buddhist temples and monasteries" (Yang 1961, 198). With this background, it is perhaps not surprising to find that religious observance is filled with imagery of the marketplace.[7] Taoist scripture conceives of life as a financial loan that must be repaid. The practice of burning money to propitiate the gods dates back nearly fifteen hundred years. The evolution of religious currencies "has generally followed the changes of the real currencies in use," with imitations of banknotes, bank statements, letters of credit, and even foreign currency gradually spreading from the temporal to the spiritual marketplace.

These observations illustrate the pervasive influence of bureaucratic and commercial practice on the mentality of Chinese at every level of society. Even humble farmers who might never see a district magistrate or visit a market larger than a village trade fair could, through religious practice, popular literature, theater, and other forms of popular culture, acquire accurate, though stylized, information about the broader economic and political world.

Family and Personal Life

Many writers note the propensity of Chinese-run business enterprises to adopt structures based on kinship ties. I propose to stand this observation on its head by emphasizing the resemblance between the position of individual families in Chinese society and that of individual enterprises in a market economy. Like a business firm, the family seeks to expand its wealth in order to ensure its capacity to survive unexpected shocks. The practice of ancestor worship places a high value on perpetuating the descent line lest family extinction (equivalent to bankruptcy) disrupt the tending of graves and other forms of honoring one's forebears.

Just as the threat of insolvency leads to mergers in the world of business, failure to produce sons leads to adoption or uxorilocal marriage, practices that amount to mergers between families. Families, like businesses, pursue strategies of specialization or diversification. Like businesses, families may partition their assets into separate entities to obtain greater efficiency or more harmonious management. For families, as for businesses, the time horizon over which returns are maximized is influenced by technology. In China, the economics of wet-rice culture, a basic form of farming since the Han dynasty, if not earlier, encourage a long time horizon, for yields in paddy culture rise gradually from initially low levels and reach peak levels that can, with careful husbandry, be maintained and indeed increased almost indefinitely, as is evident from the historic yield curves for both China and Java.[8]

The analogy between the Chinese family and the atomistic business firm extends to encompass the insecurity surrounding the existence of family or firm. Mobility is possible in either direction. Illness, incapacity, or death of key personnel can send even a prosperous family into headlong decline. A family can expect support and assistance from friends and especially relatives, but such assistance is not without its component of self-interest. Households that appear incapable of reciprocity may find friends and even relatives melting away as a crisis deepens. Blood ties are no guarantee of mutual support, for competition among households does not stop outside the extended family.[9]

Our analogy between families and business stretches into the realm of personal relations. From an American perspective, social interaction in a Chinese setting seems to involve close calculation of favors given and received. Chinese seem keenly aware of the current balance with their acquaintances. They readily use ties of personal friendship or shared experience to request and offer favors that require extraordinary effort.

Social Capabilities and the Genesis of China's Post-Reform Economic Boom

In contrast to earlier literature portraying Chinese society as inhospitable to modern forms of economic progress, village economic culture seems well suited as a training ground for would-be participants in modern economic growth. Successful pursuit of individual and family self-interest in traditional Chinese communities requires the same attitudes and behavior patterns that lead to entrepreneurial success in industrial societies. Accumulation of varied portfolios of physical, financial, and human capital; drawing on networks of mutual support to mobilize resources for purposes of economic gain; creation and manipulation of large organizations with written regulations and complex management systems; disciplined compilation of information to search for opportunity in markets influenced by the actions of disparate interest groups and surrounded by systems of quasi-legal regulations—all these represent skills enabling individuals or households to improve their positions and bolster their defenses against insecurity in the face of vigorous competition from a larger community that is fundamentally indifferent to their fate. And all these skills seem equally relevant to the requirements of social and economic life in a Chinese farming village of the 1880s, a Chinese urban community of the 1930s, or the local or international marketplace of the 1990s.

Beginning with the specific example of rural poverty alleviation, this chapter establishes the foundations for a culturally linked explanation of China's recent economic boom. The analysis emphasizes individual capabilities that are nurtured outside the formal education system, an area that conventional economic theory tends to overlook.

Discussion of public policy in the United States has focused considerable attention on just these elements. Youngsters who lack a suitable family background are said to be unprepared for school or even "uneducable." Contrary to the predictions of economic theory, such children are thought to derive little benefit from schooling unless they receive special guidance and mentoring. Without such support, attending school may fail to enhance these children's human capital. They may emerge from the classroom as antisocial or unemployable.

My analysis emphasizes the same connection between family or community life and economic capabilities, but in the opposite direction. I suggest that China's traditional village culture harbors specific cultural legacies, behavioral routines, and social practices that take ordinary individuals endowed with no special degree of intelligence or greed and equips them with an unusual capacity to capitalize on market opportunities. The argument is a statistical one. Take two populations of children with similar distributions of intelligence and access to schooling. One population is reared in Chinese villages; the other, in some other cultural venue (medieval Europe, contemporary Bihar or Bangladesh) at a similar level of economic development. The hypothesis is that, upon maturity, the former population will display a stronger array of market skills and accomplishments than the latter.

This analysis seeks to establish the plausibility of such an argument. It focuses on concrete and specific aspects of Chinese society and avoids the romantic and mysterious imagery that often surrounds the discussion of Asian economic matters. I believe that the legacy of traditional social practice equips Chinese farm communities with a culturally based repertoire of effective responses to market opportunity that surpasses what one would expect to observe among non-Chinese villagers at comparable levels of income, productivity, and wealth.

The intended and unintended consequences of two decades of collective farming strengthened this legacy of village economic culture. As a result, the rural reforms of the late 1970s triggered an unprecedented and completely unexpected rural boom that propelled hundreds of millions of Chinese villagers from absolute poverty with astonishing rapidity. This interpretation is steeped in irony, for it attributes the initial success of China's protracted economic boom to the combined impact of collective institutions and the cultural legacy that the communes were designed to obliterate.

7

ZHANXIN ZHANG

Institutional Change and Income Inequality

SOCIOLOGISTS INTERESTED IN social transformation and stratification dynamics in post–state socialist countries are familiar with the "market transition debate."[1] This theoretical discussion was triggered by Victor Nee's formulation of "market transition theory" (Nee 1989, 1991, 1996). The central idea of Nee's theory, presented in his first work (1989), is that a market mechanism will gradually replace a state redistribution mechanism in market-oriented transitions and thus become the dominant causal force of social stratification in post-socialist societies. Following Ivan Szelenyi's logic of state socialist redistributive economy (Szelenyi 1978), Nee assumes that a market economy and a state redistributive economy are two fundamentally different social systems in terms of social stratification order. As markets emerge and develop in the reforming era, the roles of the market mechanism in resource allocation and income distribution become increasingly important, while the roles of the state redistribution are inevitably in decline. Market transition theory has derived a set of hypotheses concerning the issue of "who gains and who loses" in market-oriented transformation, among which, two are most important. One is the depreciation of the value of political capital in rewards; the other is increasing return to human capital.

Contentions against market transition theory come from a variety of angles, but more scholars concentrate on distributional privileges from administrative power and question diminishing returns to political capital. Power conversion argument (Rona-Tas 1994) claims that in market transition the redistributive power of the cadres is being converted into personal advantages or assets in market exchanges. Political market image (Parish and Michelson 1996) asserts that the growth of political markets as economic markets develop maintains the rewards to political power. Power persistence thesis (Bian and Logan 1996) argues that redistributive power should remain in privileged political groups under partial reform. Markets-politics coevolution model (Zhou 2000) has extended this theoretical debate from emphasis on political power to a broader perspective: emerging markets and interests politics coevolve because of the interaction between them. In addition to these different arguments, Andrew Walder's criticism (Walder 1996) goes into the foundation of market transition theory: though they are ideal types, "market economy" and "redistributive economy" provide no research agenda about the transition from one type to the other.

Walder's remark leads us to further examination of the framework of Nee's theory. According to this theory, marketization, which refers to the shift to market allocation of goods and resources, causes the change in stratification order. What causes marketization? In other words, what is the institutional foundation of marketization? This theory does not clearly specify this issue. Nee does use the term *institution,* viewing labor markets, subcontracting arrangements, capital markets, and business groups as examples of "market institutions" (Walder 1996, 910). These, however, are market relationships or economic players in a market economy, rather then "the rules of the game" shaping these relations and actors.[2] Therefore, Nee's theory does not mediate between institutional change and stratification dynamics in a transitional society; it merely attributes changing stratification order to emerging market coordination, which seems to be an intervening variable between institutions and stratification.

Employing an institutional approach in an inquiry of changing stratification order in post–state socialist societies is still an open avenue;[3] more important, it is promising. Economic transitions in such societies are led by redefining the fundamental institutional rules conducted by the central authority. Reformation in the legal framework and social norms alters the patterns of human interaction. Institutional change thereby is a key to explaining social transformation. Therefore, it is reasonable to resort to institutional theories, especially theories on regulative aspects of institution,[4] to construct convincing arguments about the reshuffling of social strata. My aim here is to address the significant sociological issue of stratification dynamics in transforming societies by focusing on income inequality in reforming urban China.

Institutional Change in Reforming China

Institutions as the rules of the game in a society determine and limit the choices individuals can make, and hence shape social relationships (North 1990; Nee 1998). While economists develop institutional theories to explain economic efficiency of organizations and long-term economic performance of social systems (Eggertssion 1990; Williamson 1981, 1991; North 1990), sociologists suggest the decisive impact of economic institutions on income distribution and social stratification (Nee 1996; Walder 1992). Central to economic institutions are property rights. "Property rights are the rights individuals appropriate over their own labor and the goods and the services they possess" (North 1990, 33). A complete bundle of property rights in general comprises three typical rights: the right to use an asset (user right), the right to earn income from the asset (income right), and the right to sell or rent the asset (transfer right). Elementary sets of property rights in a society are rights over basic productive resources —labor, land, and capital—which are, in North's terms, property rights in labor, in land, and in capital (1981). The system of property rights in a society results in the differences between social groups in terms of their rights and the relationships between them; such rights networks, under the influence of economic and technical conditions, determine the allocation of power (de jure or de facto) over income stream and, ultimately, generates inequality.

The proposition that the structure of property rights shapes the framework of social strata is corroborated by the human history of stratification. The principal arrangement of property rights in a slavery society was that the slave owner possessed the entire property rights in the labor of the slave (North and Thomas 1973; North 1981). This means "alienation of labor": a slave physically held the labor in his body but did not legally own it. This arrangement maintained the power of the slaver owner over economic surplus and hence resulted in the two major strata: masters and slaves. The situation of Western feudalism was analogous with that of slavery: "the distinctive feature of feudalism was that the nobility not only owned large estates or manors but also held legal title to the labor power of its serfs. . . . The statuses of serf and slave differ only

Table 7.1
Property Rights Perspective on Stratification History

Type of society	*Basic structure of property rights*	*Allocation of power over income*	*Dominant strata or classes*
Slavery	Rights of slave owners over labor	Full legal power of slave owner	Slave owners and slaves
Feudalism	Partial rights of nobility over the labor of the serf	Partial legal power of the nobility	Nobilities and serfs
Industrialism	Private and alienable rights over labor in one's own; private and alienable rights over capital	Bargaining power of the capitalist	Capitalists and workers
"Advanced" industrialism	Private and alienable rights over labor in one's own; private and alienable rights over capital	Relatively balanced power among different groups	Upper class, professions and managerial elite, and working class

in degree" (Grusky 1994, 10). Compared with these two preindustrial social systems in history with the feature of coerced labor, a characteristic of capitalist industrial societies is that the complete set of property rights over labor resides in the laborer. Corresponding to such private rights in labor is private property right in capital—capital freed from regulations from guilds and other institutional constrains under feudalism. Private capital employs free labor via mutual voluntary contracting. This arrangement had ever resulted in an unbalanced power structure. In the early phase of industrial societies, the group with a controlling power over the central means of production—capital—was able to capture a large share of income and wealth, resulting in new inequality between two major social classes: capitalists and workers. In post or "advanced" industrial societies, although the framework of property rights in labor and capital is not altered much, the labor force is extensively diversified, the power structure is considerably more balanced than before, and human capital becomes the key factor for stratification (Grusky 1994). Table 7.1 summarizes these observations.

This historical review highlights two important points. First, labor is a fundamental factor of social stratification. In any society, the precondition of production is the economic organization that combines labor with other resources. Property rights in labor and relevant to labor are devised and improved to define right-liability structure in order to shape the organization. This institutional matrix gives rise to the power in employing labor and over income and, therefore, is ultimately responsible for the formation of inequality. Second, there is a watershed between agricultural (slavery/feudalism) societies and industrialism in terms of labor. In agricultural societies, laborers, deprived of ownership rights in their own labor, were forced to work and depended on the land and the ruling classes, whereas free labor institutions and private capital systems under industrialism yield an independent and mobile labor force and facilitate mutual voluntary combinations of capital and labor, resulting in the capitalist firm.

An important suggestion of this institutional and historical viewpoint for the research of social stratification under state socialism is that labor institutions should be taken into account. The idea that the inequality structure in state socialist societies is relevant to the institutional arrangements concerning labor is not new. When investigating the pattern of stratification under state socialism, Szelenyi (1978) has noted that the essential disparity between capitalism and state socialism lay in their labor institutions.[5] This insight, however, has for the most part been ignored as attention has predominantly focused on his conceptions of "market economy" and "state redistributive economy." Close inspection of the linkage between labor institutions and social stratification in state socialist societies provides a number of propositions. First, private property rights in labor were entirely denied and deprived, and the state had control over labor (Bian 1994; Szelenyi 1978). Second, state capital was bureaucratically tied up with state governed labor. State or government ownership over capital is not a unique phenomenon existing in pre-reforming state socialist countries. In Western capitalist economies, there are various forms of state ownership over capital and different types of government-managed enterprises. A remarkable distinction between socialist state capital and capitalist state capital is that under the former system state capital was combined with labor through bureaucratic labor allocation, whereas under the latter system state capital employs free labor by contracting. Third, the bureaucratic labor organization of state socialism was the result of the labor institutions and relevant rules. Finally, these institutional and organizational arrangements underlay the regime of state redistribution. Without private labor rights, individuals were unable to claim income—to bargain wages and other welfare treatments. The state, by controlling all economic surpluses, defined the status of different social groups and distributed income and wealth accord-

Table 7.2
Comparison of Property Rights and Related Aspects under Capitalism and State Socialism

	Capitalism	*State socialism*
Property rights in labor	Private and alienable rights in one's own labor	State ownership; bureaucratic labor management
Property rights in capital	Private and alienable rights; employing free labor	State ownership; associated with state governed labor
Labor organizations	Contractual employment	Bureaucratic arrangement
Distribution of labor income	Labor market mechanism	State redistribution mechanism

ing to its interests and purposes. The consequences of state redistribution on social stratification under pre-reform socialism were a "redistributive class" versus a working class (Szelenyi 1978) and inequality based on hierarchical work organizations (Bian 1994; Lin and Bian 1991; Walder 1986). In addition, Mao's China in particular resulted in a considerable income gap between rural peasants and urban citizens (Whyte 1975). Table 7.2 compares the characteristics of labor institutions and stratification under state socialism and capitalism. These characteristics together comprise an alternative image of state socialist society that emphasizes formal rules and inequality.

Conceptual Model of the Rights-Power Interaction Perspective

In post-socialist societies undergoing market-oriented reforms, institutional change in labor alters the rights, power, and opportunities of the laborers, causing the transformation from state-governed labor to free labor with alienable rights. One of the most significant issues of this transformation is the increasing value of human capital.[6] Nevertheless, reforms give rise to new bourgeois. But the growth of a professional and managerial elite nourished by changes in labor institutions to a large extent contains the size and power of the new bourgeois. The rise of private and alienable property rights in labor, therefore, is the decisive factor for the changes in the pattern of inequality. China's case seems to provide more support to this proposition. Mao's China was a state-socialist country where the state control over labor was sterner than that of her comrade countries (Walder 1986). While China during reform has not yet conducted large-scale privatization of state-owned enterprises, privatization in labor has been a very important result of the reform, though it has not drawn much attention (Cheung 1989). The growth of alienable private property rights in labor—driven either by the revision of the legal rules concerned or by the institutional competition between old and new arrangements—is a basic causal force for stratification dynamics. The impact of alienable private rights in labor, however, is not overwhelming; the transforming state power is involved substantively in the determination of inequality. The above reasoning proposes the central argument of the rights-power interaction perspective: The development of alienable private property rights in labor, under the influence of transforming state power, determines the basic changing pattern of social stratification in a transitional post-socialist society.

China's economic transition over the past twenty years is a historical process of emerging and growing private property rights in labor. The crucial steps have been the actions of the state that have redefined "the rules of the game" with regard to the relevant rights of individuals and organizations. The breakthrough took place in the countryside. The implementation of a contract system in the rural areas allowed farmers to work for themselves rather than for the collectives, signifying the beginning of privatization of labor. The contract system, however, still maintained peasants' ties to the land, which means the restored private rights were restricted only to user rights and income rights at that moment. The liberalization of rural labor evolved later, from long distance transportation to diversified business. The implication of the rise of township and village enterprises (TVEs) for private rights in labor has been profound. Industrial capital emerging in the countryside during the 1980s was the capital that came out of the state planning system and was irrelevant to state-governed labor. As the result of combining such capital and free labor, rural contractual labor organizations, TVEs, came into existence, though they were not private ownership in the normal sense.[7]

China's urban areas have also experienced weakening state control over labor, resulting in new forms of enterprise. Self-employment, foreign enterprises, and urban private firms grew in the 1980s, and growth accelerated in the 1990s. The bureaucratic coordination of labor in state-owned enterprises (SOEs) had gradually declined, and workers have been able to change jobs. However, constrained by the existing formal rules, SOEs have until recently maintained the obligation of offering secure have carried out a "contractual employment system" for all staff and workers.[8] This means SOEs have been transformed from bureaucratic labor organizations to semibureaucratic ones. While new forms of enterprise characterized by contractual employment—such as TVEs, foreign corporations, and private firms—have facilitated the diffusion of alienable private labor rights, SOEs have preserved some legacies of state control over and state redistribution among the urban laboring population.

Paralleling constitutional reforms has been the expansion of alienable private property rights in labor and contractual employment organizations by means of institutional competition.[9] The partial reform has resulted in a dual framework of labor institutions: rules defining alienable private property rights in labor and rules concerning job security and welfare benefits of employees in state and urban collective sectors. New enterprises with contractual employment are the organizational agent of the former set of rules, and SOEs and urban collective enterprises as semibureaucratic labor teams are the organizational agent of the latter set.[10] This dual framework has not been stable; rather, institutional competition has driven the expansion of rules specifying private rights in labor. This institutional competition occurs in two ways: through organizational competition between the two institutional agents and through penetration of private rights in labor through semibureaucratic labor organizations. Due to the relative advantages of contractual labor in terms of labor input and incentive-disincentive structure, such organizational competition has contributed to reduced profits for semibureaucratic labor organizations and even driving some into bankruptcy. Meanwhile, new enterprises have been able to grow rapidly. Apparent differences in growth rates between TVEs and SOEs exemplify the effects of such organizational competition. However, semibureaucratic organizations have imitated the behavior of contractual organizations, resulting in the penetration of the rules prevailing in contractual organizations. Internal reforms of SOEs in employment and income distribution reflect this penetration.

Institutional change and institutional competition, as two basic sources for the growth of alienable private rights in labor, are interrelated. The introduction of new rules that specify, enforce, and protect private rights gives rise to the dual framework of labor institutions and results in institutional competition. Institutional competition, in turn, exhibits the advantages of new institutions and resultant organizations, creates entrepreneurs, and hence induces further institutional innovation. Although it is the state that establishes the new legal framework, institutional competition plays a key role in institutional change (North 1995). In a transitional society where reforms are relatively moderate, like China, institutional competition is more important.

The development of alienable private property rights in labor through institutional reformation and institutional competition has a decisive impact on social stratification. It undermines the institutional foundation of state redistribution, provides new power structures, and changes the framework of inequality. Under the assumption that stratification dynamics are absolutely dominated by the rising of alienable private rights in labor, it is predictable that the value of human capital will rise or fall according to market signals, and privileged income advantages, such as the extra rewards to cadre position and organizational status, will be reduced and eliminated at the end. However, a crucial question is, is this assumption credible? The answer is no, because state power—that is, the state's economic power—substantively influences the effects of institutional competition.

The influence of state power on institutional competition can be divided into two aspects: the effect of preexisting state redistributive power and the effect of emerging state intervention power. In the economic transition, the state is also in transformation: its economic roles and power structure are changing. On the one hand, as the state planning mechanism is shrinking, state redistributive power, which was fully exerted before reforms, is inevitably weakened. On the other hand, the emergence of markets requires the development of state intervention, enabling the governments to provide regulatory services, supply public/semipublic goods, and perform other necessary functions for market exchanges.

State redistributive power and state intervention power favor competitive state enterprises and monopolistic state organizations, respectively.[11] On the one hand, the state redistributes financial resources to competitive state enterprises and hence lessens the impact of competition on them. In China a variety of state redistribution forms—different from traditional planning mechanisms—prevailed in the 1980s and continued in the early and even later 1990s. The state retained a large amount of profits in state enterprises in the latter 1980s (Wong 1992). The state provided financial subsidies to state enterprises (Lardy 1998). Bank loans to state enterprises were given priority over loans to private enterprises (Cheng 1996; Lardy 1998). In addition, tax reduction or remittance for state enterprises has been a popular practice since the beginning of the reform. All these measures have to certain degrees protected state enterprises from severe market competition and maintained their viability. Consequently, the impact of organizational competitiveness on semibureaucratic organizations has been varied: urban collective enterprises and small state enterprises with little support from state redistributive power have suffered more from competition than big state enterprises.

On the other hand, the state furnishes secure monopolies and exclusive power to state organizations with functions relevant to state intervention, which may engender more privileges for them. The functional intervention power of monopolistic state organizations allocated by the state guarantees that they are free of organizational competition and with less penetration of the principles of private labor rights; moreover, this functional power may become the privileges of monopolistic state organizations in capturing gains, when such organizations are able to misuse the public power for their own interests, rather than for public interests expected by the state and the public. This has been particularly true in China (Lin and Zhang 1999; Zhang 1997). State intervention power has thus enhanced the already advantaged position of monopolistic organizations relative to competitive state organizations.

The characteristics of the rights-power interaction perspective can be further illustrated by comparing it with two other frameworks—the market transition theory and the markets-politics coevolution model. Different from these two, at first the rights-power interaction perspective brings about an institutional approach to stratification dynamics with an emphasis on "the rules of the game" regarding labor. More important, the logic of the rights-power interaction perspective differs from the others. While Nee emphasizes the overwhelming effect of market forces, the rights-power interaction perspective points to the limitation of emerging markets as the state restricts competition. Meanwhile, because the interplay between market forces and political forces is a common phenomenon in the development of capitalist societies and the transition of post-state socialist societies, it can be difficult for the markets-politics coevolution model to generate clear and creditable corollaries, at least the one about the privileges of "redistributors."[12]

The Dynamics of Income Inequality

The crucial implications of the rights-power interaction perspective for the dynamics of income inequality in the urban areas of China lie in the redesign of labor institutions and transformation of state power. From the 1980s to the mid-1990s fundamental changes were taking place in labor institutions and state power. Five basic factors relevant to the changing pattern of inequality in this period can be identified:

- An institutional change was occurring in labor and contractual employment organizations, encouraging alienable private property rights. Gradual reforms in the legal framework regarding labor employment facilitated the legitimatization of alienable private property rights in labor and contractual employment organizations.[13]
- Some changes occurred in labor institutions for state organizations and urban collective enterprises after the 1980s, but changes in the formal arrangements of secure employment and vested welfare interests did not take place until the mid-1990s (Solinger 1999).
- There was severe institutional competition between the contractual employment sector and the semibureaucratic sector. This competition intensified from the 1980s to the 1990s, during which time marketization was substantively advancing.
- State redistributive power was declining due to diminished financing capacity, but it continued functioning to a certain degree.
- Market expansion gave rise to state intervention power.

These factors constitute a foundation for generating hypotheses about the dimensions of changing income inequality from the 1980s to the mid-1990s. The discussion focuses first on the organizational aspects of income inequality.

Contractual Employment versus Semibureaucratic Labor Organizations

Intensified institutional competition tends to considerably reduce the profit-making capacity and even threaten the survival of competitive state enterprises and urban collective enterprises and therefore diminishes the funds available for distribution among employees with guaranteed jobs. Urban collective enterprises without redistributive financial supports from the state are in the most disadvantaged position under such competition; as the state's redistributive power shrinks, competitive state enterprises become more disadvantaged. As a result, the income levels of employees in such enterprises continue to drop, even reaching the point of absolute income disadvantage.

Hypothesis 1: In a competitive market, income levels will tend to be higher in contractual labor organizations than in semibureaucratic labor organizations.

State Organizations Versus Urban Collective Enterprises

Urban collective enterprises have almost no access to state power. On the contrary, state redistributive power favors competitive state enterprises, and monopolistic state organizations capitalize on state intervention power in seeking gains. The inequality between the state sector and the urban collective sector, traceable to Mao's China, will continue.

Hypothesis 2: State ownership will continue to have income advantages over urban collective ownership.

Hierarchy within the State Sector

Redistribution of financial resources is top down from the central government; allocation of functional state intervention power is also top down from the central government. This hierarchy, based on bureaucratic rankings, also a legacy of the traditional planning system, maintains the income inequality among state organizations.

Hypothesis 3: A state organization's bureaucratic rank will have a lasting influence on its employees' income.

Competitive State Enterprises Versus Monopolistic State Organizations

While the state redistributive power that competitive state enterprises rely on is declining, state intervention power that monopolistic state organizations resort to is increasing. This implies the emergence of income inequality between employees in competitive state enterprises and those in monopolistic state organizations.

Hypothesis 4: Monopolistic state organizations will have an increasing advantage over competitive state enterprises regarding employees' incomes.

Education

The next question concerns the returns to education. The returns to human capital in terms of rewards to education must have been promoted by the development of alienable private property rights in labor. Contractual labor teams, of course, are the major agent of this improvement. Even within labor organizations with semibureaucratic arrangements, the rewards to education tend to increase, due to the penetration of the principles of alienable private labor rights through such organizations. As a result, there must be an overall trend of increasing rewards to education.

Hypothesis 5: There will be a lasting general tendency of enlarging returns to higher education (college or beyond) over time.

Increasing returns to education in semibureaucratic organizations, however, tend to be uneven among economic organizations. Although under the pressure of market competition semibureaucratic organizations have to increase returns to human capital, the institutional constraints on them to a large extent retain the egalitarian feature of income and welfare distribution. Accordingly, returns to higher education in such organizations stay lower than the returns in contractual organizations, in which income distribution is closely associated with individual performance.

Hypothesis 6: Returns to education have remained high in contractual labor organizations compared with semibureaucratic labor organizations over time.

Most of these hypotheses are relevant to the current concerns of research. The first three hypotheses deal with the changing patterns of organizational inequality, addressed in studies on urban China (Bian and Logan 1996; Walder 1992; Zhou 2000). Return to education is a common focus. The study here proposes a new hypothesis about the rising income privilege of monopolistic state organizations—hypothesis 4. Hypothesis 6 about unequal returns to education in two forms of economic organization is also new, for it considers alternative definitions and interpretation of organizations and consequential distributional issues.

Research Design

Data for the study are derived from two nationwide income surveys: the 1988 and 1995 Chinese Household Income Project (CHIP) (Khan and Riskin 1998). I use the two urban portions of CHIP data sets to conduct an individual-level analysis. The sizes, coverage, and qualities of the two portions are reported by the designers (Khan and Riskin 1998). Individuals not belonging to the urban employment population are dropped from the analysis.[14] After these exclusions, the sample from the 1988 data set contains 17,930 individuals from ten provinces; the 1995 data set contains 12,326 individuals from eleven provinces (one province was added in 1995).

Measuring Variables

Earnings as the Dependent Variables

I focus on income from the workplace, or work earnings. Total earnings consist of the basic wage and any extra earnings. In the state and urban collective sector, the state controls and regulates the basic wage, the main component of work earnings, called "standard salary" or "base salary" (Bian and Logan 1996). Extra earnings refers to a variety of earnings from the workplace, such as bonuses, subsidies, allowances, that are in addition to the basic wages (salary).

Independent Variables

Work organizations are usually classified on the basis of ownership and bureaucratic rank. The competitive versus monopolistic attributes of state organizations are taken into consideration. Table 7.3 shows the outcome of calculating the ratios of employment in state work units to employment in two forms of nonstate enterprises rising in the transition: (1) rural enterprises and urban private firms and (2) individual businesses. Table 7.3 shows two types of industries: one with ratios ranging from 0.52 to 3.48; the other with ratios ranging from 0.11 to zero. These ratios suggest that the first type of industry is quite open to nonstate enterprises and that the second is highly restricted to state units operation.

On the basis of the results in table 7.3, table 7.4 assigns features of industries from the 1995 CHIP data, classifying the thirteen industries into "open," "mixed," and "restricted" categories. According to table 7.4, a state organization or work unit can be defined as competitive when it is in an open industry and as monopolistic when it is in a restricted or mixed industry.

The division of competitive/monopolistic state organizations brings about the following categories of work organizations. Eight variables are used to signify the characteristics of work organizations:

1. High rank competitive state organization: a competitive state organization with provincial or central bureaucratic rank.
2. High rank monopolistic state organization: a monopolistic state organization with provincial or central bureaucratic rank.

Table 7.3

Employment by Industry, Form of Enterprise, and Ratios, 1995

Industry	*Number of employees (x 10,000)*			*Ratio*
	I *State units*	*II* *Rural enterprises*[a]	*III* *Urban private firms and individuals*	*II + III*
Farming, forestry, animal husbandry, and fishery	633.6	313.5	13.4[b]	0.52
Manufacturing	3,326	6,694.5[c]	339	2.11
Electricity, gas, and water production and supply	237.3	22.6[c]	0	0.10
Mining and quarrying	833.8	847.2[c]	10.2	1.03
Geological prospecting and water conservancy	131.7	0	0	0
Construction	604.7	1,932.5	28.1	3.24
Railways	221.3	0	0	0
Air transportation	10.3	0	0	0
Highways, waterways, and other transportation	305.3	952	111	3.48
Postal and telecommunication	106.5	0	0	0
Wholesale and retail trade, restaurants, and storage	1,221.8	1,677.4	1,265.8[d]	2.41
Real estate activities	61.3	0	0	0
Public facilities services	163.9	0	18.3[e]	0.11
Residential services and other services	151.2	225.2	223.6[e]	2.97
Health care, sporting, and social welfare	378.6	0	8.4[f]	0.02
Education, culture and arts, radio, film, and television	1,264.5	0	10[f]	0.01
Scientific research and polytechnical services	167.3	0	14[f]	0.08
Financial intermediation and insurance	202.6	0	0	0
Government agencies, party agencies, and social organizations	1,018.9	0	0	0

Notes: [a]TVEs (township- and village-owned enterprises) and other rural firms, such as those owned by rural individuals.

[b]Excludes individual farmers in the countryside.

[c]Number of employees in rural enterprises in "manufacturing," "electricity, and so on," and "mining, and so on" is cautiously estimated. The total number of employees in rural enterprises in the three industries (together called "industry") in 1995 was 75,647,000. Total employees in TVEs in the three industries in 1995 was 39,027,000 (manufacturing), 226,000 (electricity), and 4,935,000 (mining); employees in "mining" were 11.2 percent of the total. If this proportion remained in total employees in rural enterprises, and rural enterprises in "electricity . . ." were all TVEs, then one would obtain the estimated figures in col. 3 in the three industries.

[d]Some employees in rural enterprises who work in storage workplaces are not counted in the industry of "wholesale and retail trade, restaurants, and storage." So employment in this industry is somewhat underreported; these "excluded" employees are counted in the industry of "highways, waterways, and other transportation," so employment in this industry is somewhat overreported.

[e]This figure is cautiously estimated. Official statistics shows that there are 2,419,000 employees in social services, which consists of two subindustries: "public facilities services" and "residential services, and so on." Assuming 10 percent (183,000) are employed in "public facilities services," then 2,236,000 are employed in "residential services." The first category may be overestimated, since this industry is basically operated by government bodies at different levels.

[f]This category is not reported in official statistics in 1995 but was reported in some preceding years. Numbers are estimated by doubling the highest figures previously reported to take possible increases into account; they tend to be overestimated.

Sources: Zhongguo Tongji Nianjian [China Statistics Yearbook] 1996; *Zhongguo Xiangzhen Qiye Nianjian* [China Township and Village Enterprise Yearbook] 1996.

Table 7.4
Categorization of Industries into Open and Restricted Sectors

INDUSTRY		Feature based on table 7.4	Industry assignment (1995 CHIP data)
1995 CHIP code	*State statistics codes (1995)*		
Industry 1	Farming, forestry, animal husbandry, and fishery	Open	Open
Industry 2	Manufacturing	Open	Open
	Electricity, gas, and water production and supply	Restricted	
Industry 3	Mining and quarrying	Open	Open
	Geological prospecting and water conservancy	Restricted	
Industry 4	Construction	Open	Open
Industry 5	Railways	Restricted	Mixed
	Air transportation	Restricted	
	Highways, waterways, and other transportation	Open	
	Postal and telecommunication	Restricted	
Industry 6	Wholesale and retail trade, restaurants, and storage	Open	Open
Industry 7	Real estate activities	Restricted	Mixed
	Public facilities services	Restricted	
	Residential services and other services	Open	
Industry 8	Health care, sporting, and social welfare	Restricted	Restricted
Industry 9	Education, culture and arts, radio, film, and television	Restricted	Restricted
Industry 10	Scientific research and polytechnical services	Restricted	Restricted
Industry 11	Financial intermediation and insurance	Restricted	Restricted
Industry 12	Government agencies, party agencies, and social organizations	Restricted	Restricted
Industry 13	Others	Unknown	Unknown

Note: CHIP = Chinese Household Income Project. Industry 2 is defined as an open industry because "manufacturing" is much bigger than "electricity, gas, and water production and supply"; the case is similar in industry 3. Industries 5 and 7 are defined as mixed industries because their "open" and "restricted" subindustries are comparable in size.

3. Unidentified high rank state organization: a state organizations with provincial or higher rank, in mixed industries or "other industries."
4. Local competitive state organization: a competitive state organization with bureaucratic rank below the provincial level.
5. Local monopolistic state organization: monopolistic state organization with bureaucratic rank below the provincial level.
6. Unidentified local state organizations: state organizations with rank below the provincial level, in mixed industries or "other industries."
7. Urban collective enterprise.
8. New organization: work organizations with contractual labor arrangements.

The following variables represent individual characteristics:

1. Occupational status, which contains four categories: "technician" refers to a professional job in terms of technology, "cadre" refers to a head or middle-level head in a state or collective organization, "clerk" refers to jobs of ordinary staff, and "worker and other" refers to worker and other occupations.
2. Gender, which is a dummy variable (male = 1).
3. Age and age squared (age × age) is measured by year of living.
4. Party membership, which is a dummy variable (party membership = 1).
5. Education, which is a dummy variable for high education (college or above = 1).

Note that this study does not present and test hypotheses about the income advantage of "redistributor"—that is, government officials or elite administrators. The main reason is that the available data does not provide systematic information about this group, though there is a general term called "head of *danwei*" (work unit) in the data sets. "Cadre," like the other occupational variables—"age and age square," "gender," and "party membership"—is regarded as a control variable in the statistical analysis.

Findings

I use two linear regression models to estimate determinants of earnings in logarithm form. Table 7.5 shows the results. Significant differences and directions of change in coefficients between 1988 and 1995 are also noted. The effects of new economic organizations on total earnings with reference to local competitive state enterprises were increasing significantly from 1988 to 1995. The coefficient of foreign enterprise shows that other things being equal, total earning in new firms was on average 10.8 percent lower than in local competitive enterprises in 1988, and was 5.3 percent higher in 1995, achieving an increase of 16.1 percentage points. Relative to local competitive state enterprises, the increase of average total earnings in high rank state enterprises from 1988 to 1995 was only 13.1 percentage points, whereas the total earnings in collective enterprises decreased. These findings strongly support hypothesis 1, reflecting the increasing income advantages of contractual organizations.

The results demonstrate that the intersector inequality between state organizations and collective enterprises had been enlarged from 1988 to 1995. Relative to local competitive state enterprises, while the incomes in all other state organizations had increased from 1988 to 1995, the income level of urban collective enterprises had been lower during this period. This evidence is consistent with the expectation of hypothesis 2.

The reshuffle within the state sector is worth noting. On the one hand, the inequality between organizations with different ranks is obvious in both 1988 and 1995. The income advantage of high rank competitive state organizations over their local counterparts grew from 2.6 percent to 15.7 percent. Meanwhile, the average income in high rank state monopolistic organizations in 1995 was 19.7 percent higher than in local state competitive organizations, whereas the average income in local state monopolistic organizations in 1995 was only 9.7 percent higher than in local state competitive organizations. Therefore, income benefits to employees were larger in high rank state organizations than in local state organizations. This is just the tendency predicted by hypothesis 3.

On the other hand, the income advantage of monopolistic organizations emerged. In 1988, at all levels, total earnings in monopolistic state organizations was on average lower than in local competitive state organizations, which is indicated by the negative values of the coefficients. Up to 1995, however, the entire situation was just the opposite: total earnings in monopolistic state organizations at the two levels all grew higher than their counterparts in the competitive sector. At the local level, average earnings in monopolistic organizations were 9.7 percent higher than those in competitive state enterprises in 1995; at the provincial and central level, the incomes in all state organizations were higher than in local competitive state units, but monopolistic state units showed a 5 percent advantage over the other: 19.7 percent higher versus 15.7 percent higher. The overall income privilege of monopolistic organizations is consistent with hypothesis 4. The new organizational inequality in the state

Table 7.5

Unstandardized OLS Coefficients from the Regression of Yearly Earning (Log Form) on Selected Independent Variables: Urban China, 1988–1995

Independent variables	*Total earnings*	
	1988	*1995*
Workplace characteristic[a]		
High rank competitive state unit	0.026**	0.157***>
High rank monopolistic state unit	−0.027*	0.197***>
High rank unidentified state unit	0.085***	0.200***>
Local monopolistic state unit	−0.043**	0.097***>
Local unidentified state unit	0.023$^{\phi}$	0.076***>
Urban collective enterprise	−0.105***	−0.157***<
New organization	−0.108***	0.053$^{\phi}$>
Occupational status[b]		
Professional/Technical	0.108***	0.187***>
Cadre	0.106***	0.174***>
Clerk	0.050***	0.093***>
Individual characteristic		
Age	0.081***	0.084***
Square of age	−0.001***	−0.001***
Gender (male = 1)	0.113***	0.126***
Party membership	0.057***	0.089***>
Education (college or higher = 1)	0.047$^{\phi}$	0.129***>
Interaction term		
High rank competitive state unit × education	−0.018	−0.088*
High rank monopolistic state unit × education	0.014	−0.066
High rank unidentified state unit × education	−0.025	0.038
Local monopolistic state unit × education	0.019	−0.037
Local unidentified state unit × education	−0.050	−0.002
Urban collective enterprise × education	0.041	0.104$^{\phi}$
New organization × education	0.221**	0.195**
Constant	5.612***	6.467***
R^2	0.307	0.238
Number of cases	17,931	12,327

Notes: Significant differences in coefficients across years are indicated by "<" for significantly less than the corresponding items in 1988 and ">" for significantly greater than the corresponding item in 1988 (one-tailed tests at the $p < .025$ level).

[a] Omitted category is "urban collective firm."

[b] Omitted category is "worker and other occupations."

$^{\phi}p < .10$; $^{*}p < .05$; $^{**}p < .01$; $^{***}p < .001$ (two-tailed tests) sector between monopolistic organizations and competitive enterprises is thus being confirmed, and this shows the increasing significance of state intervention power in social stratification.

Increasing returns to education was demonstrated by significant increases in coefficients of college and higher education from 1988 to 1995: from 4.7 percent higher to 12.9 percent higher than the average return to lower educational attainments in those years. These results are predicted by hypothesis 5. Because most urban employment was in state and collective sectors in the 1980s and 1990s, this finding suggests that all work organizations, including state organizations and urban collective enterprises, had enhanced rewards to education.

In spite of this overall trend, the gap between new economic organizations with contractual labor employment and old organizations with bureaucratic legacies of employment and distribution remained stable from 1988 to 1995 with regard to the return to education, as shown in table 7.5. The interaction terms of state and urban collective organizations do not differ significantly, and they are all lower than the interaction term of new organizations. This general pattern of interaction effects has not changed with statistical significance in the 1995 model, though the interaction term of collective enterprise has increased a little and that of high rank competitive enterprise has decreased compared with local competitive enterprise. These findings suggest that the additional return to higher education in new organizations had been about 20 percent from the late 1980s to the mid-1990s. Human capital was better valued in new firms than in danwei.

Privileged Inequality

This empirical study guided by the rights-power interaction perspective has provided evidence that the impact of rising alienable private property rights in labor is significant. The development of alienable private labor rights, through its agent, contractual labor organization, substantively undermines the two basic aspects of stratification order under Mao's redistributive regime: privileged income advantages among organizations and egalitarian income distribution within organizations. First, by means of institutional competition, contractual organizations in product markets weaken and even defeat urban collective enterprises and local competitive state enterprises, lowering their income levels. Meanwhile, the principles of alienable private labor rights in terms of employment and income distribution are diffusing among semibureaucratic organizations, enhancing the value of human capital in the entire economy. This reduces the egalitarian pattern of internal distribution. In this sense, the rising of private rights in labor is a major causal force for the redefining of social strata.

This study also demonstrates the influence of state power on inequality dynamics. State redistributive power resists organizational competition in product markets, protecting competitive state enterprises with high bureaucratic ranks. State intervention power, on the other hand, has been capitalized on for its own interests by state organizations producing public goods or supplying regulatory services, yielding a new inequality structure. This discovery is significant, for it explains the huge income gap among state organizations that emerged in the 1990s. More important, this finding suggests a new source of officials' "corruption" that is contrary to the traditional source: state redistribution. This privileged administrative group, composed of individuals in public organizations holding functional state intervention power, can hardly be specified through income surveys, because a considerable part of their incomes is illegal and therefore hidden. Their gains, however, are reflected in frequent reports in the mass media about the "economic crimes" of government officials.

State intervention is a common practice in market-dominant economies. Why is misusing state intervention power, such as "rent-seeking" activities, moderate in most advanced capitalist countries but serious in some Third World countries that have adopted market economies? In particular, why has the rising state intervention power in China's transition become the major new source of privileged inequality? These are important questions, though beyond the scope of this analysis. However, political democracy, political markets, and freedom of mass media appear to be important factors in checking misusage of public power. What is crucial to emphasize here is that market forces will not automatically eliminate the rising privileged groups basing their power on state intervention; reducing their influence will require redesigning the entire political and social system. If this proposition is credible, it reflects an imperfection of Victor Nee's market transition theory: he expects too much from market mechanisms. Identification of state intervention power and its impact on social stratification may improve our knowledge about "coevolution" of market forces and political forces in transforming societies toward the market-oriented model.

8

WANG FENG AND TIANFU WANG

Categorical Sources of Income Inequality in Urban China

As RECENTLY AS the early 1980s, China, as well as the Eastern European socialist societies, were among the world's most equal societies in terms of economic equality.[1] Yet in slightly more than a decade's time China had transformed, by most measures of income distribution, from one of the most egalitarian to one of the more unequal societies in the world. By the mid-1990s, after less than two decades of reforms in its economic and political systems, China was believed to have joined Bangladesh, Indonesia, the Philippines, and the United States as among the countries with the highest levels of income inequality.[2] In the process, China gained its membership in this club more quickly than any other country has ever done so.

Such a spectacular rise in income inequality in such a short time is no doubt one of the most, if not the most, salient social outcomes of a society's transitioning away from socialism. At the same time, the fact that rising income inequality in China has not resulted in widespread poverty, as it has in the former Soviet bloc countries, defies a simple characterization of the effect of market reforms on inequality.[3] Rather, to understand the transformation requires investigating the sources and structures of the increased inequality.

While studies of China and formerly socialist societies elsewhere comprise a rich body of literature on the nature of a new social stratification order, there are few analyses that directly address the overall inequality structure. Much existing research on income inequality in China and other formerly socialist countries has been subsumed under a debate of winners versus losers in the process of social reconfiguration and restratification (Nee 1989, 1991, 1996; Bian and Logan 1996; Rona-Tas 1994; Gerber and Hout 1998; Cao and Nee 2000; Zhou 2000; Wu 2002). Much research has concerned the types of *individual* characteristics rewarded more often during the transition period than during the socialist redistributive regime. Debates as such, however, are inadequate for directly addressing the institutional changes in these societies (Parish and Michelson 1996; Walder 1996). Moreover, they are unable to address directly and satisfactorily questions such as why income inequality in places like China has increased sharply, and what the sources are of the increased inequality.

The case presented here, that of urban China, highlights a central theoretical perspective in studies of social inequality: that categories, not individual characteristics, form the most important and persistent source of inequality. Categories that were created as integral parts of the planned economy system, not only defined patterns of inequality under socialism but also formed an important political-economic basis for the emerging patterns of inequality in the reform era.

Categories and Social Inequality

It has been long known to sociologists that social inequalities are fundamentally outcomes of social structure, created and maintained by various categories or groups in a society. To the extent that individuals are active agents in the process of generating and maintaining inequality, they do so by forming or joining groups (Tilly 1998). Studies of social inequality over the past two decades, in particular, have increasingly focused on analytical units above and beyond the individual income earner. Using capitalist market economies as their analytical settings, Baron and Bielby (1980) called for conceptualizing the structural organization of work at the firm level. Their work, along with many others', pioneered a research line that has bridged organization and stratification (e.g., Baron and Bielby 1984; Hedstrom 1991; Spilerman and Lunde 1991; DiPrete 1993; also see Baron 1984 and Kalleberg 1988 for reviews). A shared understanding among these researchers is that structure and institutions are both "more important than and logically prior to" individual resources in determining individual attainment. By the 1990s, this sustained if not dominant voice in analyzing institution-based inequalities had become the most distinctive feature of a "fourth generation" of comparative stratification research (Treiman and Ganzeboom 2000).

Social category is a term that has a ubiquitous presence in the sociology literature, but it is also a term often vaguely defined and used interchangeably with others, such as *social group* and *organization*. An organization, in the words of Tilly in his synthesis of a framework analyzing various forms of inequality, in the broad sense "encompasses all sorts of well-bounded clusters of social relations in which occupants of at least one position have the right to commit collective resources to activities reaching across the boundary." Examples include "corporate kin groups, households, religious sects, bands of mercenaries, and many local communities" (Tilly 1998, 9–10). Social categories so defined, therefore, are broader than the class concept commonly used in the analysis of inequality. They can be composed of individuals as long as the individuals share a certain type of social relation and have a similar claim to common collective resources. Social categories, in other words, are simply social groups with "unequal access to and unequal distribution of resources and social opportunities" (Lamont and Molnár 2002).

For social categories to exist and to function, boundaries need to be drawn so that insiders can be separated from outsiders. To facilitate the boundary-drawing process, members of the society often resort to, or employ, existing markers. Such markers can be either geographic, such as a common residence area, work place, or place of origin; or biological, such as kinship, sex, skin color, and age. It is through the process of social construction that these and other markers are used to serve a social function of collective identity, and of closure and exclusion (Parkin 1979). Boundaries can be further differentiated into two types: the physical location and the membership of a social category. There are boundaries that coincide with easily identifiable physical boundaries where members of a social category share a common physical space, such as households, local communities, and workplaces. There are also boundaries that transcend local physical space and permeate the whole society. Members in such social categories share a characteristic that allows them to have access to resources and opportunities but is not confined to a common local physical space (e.g., gender, ethnicity, and citizenship).

Social categories, or "empty places," engender and sustain inequalities through a number of mechanisms. Whereas exploitation is clearly the mechanism that best associated with the class analysis approach to inequality, the focus here is on another main mechanism of inequality, that of opportunity hoarding, or rent-seeking. Inequality is generated by such a mechanism when members of one social category derive benefits based on the resources they have access to and by blocking others' access to such resources, a notion long understood by sociologists (Sørensen 1996; Tilly 1998). Inequalities associated with gender, age, households, and kin groups are mostly maintained by such a mechanism. Moreover, inequalities arise when social relations and models of inequality are copied or transplanted from one setting to the other, by emulation, and they spread and persist because we allow ourselves to adapt our daily routines according to categorically unequal structures (Tilly 1998).

Categorical Sources of Inequality under Socialism

Formerly socialist states are perhaps among the most explicit examples to illustrate the pivotal roles of categories in structuring inequality. Socialist regimes of the twentieth century, China and elsewhere, were constantly plagued by a fundamental dilemma embedded within their systems. On the one hand, the economic goal of rapid industrialization required unequal allocation of resources according to the priorities of the centrally controlled economic plan. On the other hand, the ideological promise of egalitarianism central to the political legitimacy of this system demanded equal treatment of the population. Driven by such dual goals, a salient characteristic of the socialist states was that they redistributed resources *unequally* to different groups according to their importance to the goal of industrialization and to the redistributive regime, while maintaining distribution as *equally* as possible within each category to fulfill the ideological promise.

In addition to social and political categories such as class background, gender, and Communist Party affiliation that differentiated the population, new and employment-based categories were created as the basis of economic organization and social control. Four categories—locales, industries, ownership types, and work organizations—stood out in the case of urban China. Under the socialist planned economy system, these categories were either transformed or created as primary inequality generating sources. Moreover, the differential endowment received by these categories in capital, technology, and the product market positioned them at different starting points in the race toward economic security and prosperity in the reform era. Accordingly, members of these categories derived their income based on their social positions, which in turn defines the contour of social inequality in urban China. These durable categories continue stratifying individuals, and they constitute an important structural basis for the rising inequality and the emerging pattern of inequality after the 1980s.

Locales

Locale, what seems to be a simple and largely geographic construct, was transformed into a prominent political economy unit under socialism. The planned economy system made locales, either at the provincial or the city level in the case of urban China, into integral parts of a vertically controlled bureaucratic planned economy system. Not only did the centrally planned economy system rely on local governments to function as monitors or executors of the plan; the relationship between central and local levels of governments was also recognized from the very beginning of the planned economy period as a central relationship to be dealt with (Wu and Zheng 1995). Regional inequalities were created or redefined by deliberate state policies, often through investment decisions. Driven by the political and economic goals of a redistributive regime, state-sponsored investment was directed to specific regions at different times, either for the purpose of regional balance or for national defense (Riskin 1987). This unbalanced regional development has continued as the central government hands out favorable economic policies to the southern and eastern coastal areas in the reform era.

A salient feature of China's economic system following the reforms is the strengthening of local government's power as well as responsibilities to manage the local economy. Two institutional arrangements are critical for understanding the rise of the local government's power: the nature of China's property rights regime and the fiscal reforms carried out by the central Chinese government in the mid-1980s (Granick 1990; Wong 1992; Walder 1992, 1995; Wang 1995; Oi and Walder 1999). The more localized economies have reshaped income distribution in the reform era.

Unlike the former USSR or countries of the East European Bloc, China has not had a wholesale privatization of public assets. Rather, what happened is mostly either decentralization of control or limited experiments in workers' ownership. Over the past two decades, while the central government or its ministries relinquished their direct control over most enterprises, many of these enterprises were increasingly under the jurisdiction of various levels of local governments. As a result, the ties between enterprises and local governments strengthened in an unprecedented way (Granick 1990; Hammer 1990). Up to the mid-1990s, Chinese reforms in the state finance and taxation systems also tilted clearly the balance of economic power from the central state to local governments. Enterprises, instead of submitting all their income to the state for redistribution, were allowed to keep their incomes after paying for state taxes and a certain portion of their profits (Xiang 1999). Local governments were allowed to keep not only taxes under their jurisdiction but also a portion of other local revenue (Oi 1993; Xiang 1999). Local investment rose accordingly, with its share in total investment rising from 46 percent in 1990 to over 60 percent by 1994 (NBS 1996, 33). Starting in the mid-1980s, local government's share of total government expenditures also rose to an unprecedented high level and stayed that way. By the early 1990s, local governments' expenditures accounted for over 70 percent of all government expenditures. To augment revenue, local governments, against repeated warnings from the central government, levied many different kinds of local fees and taxes against enterprises under their jurisdiction.[4]

Industrial Sector and Ownership Type

Compared with locales, which were transformed into integrals parts of the planned economy system based on preexisting geographic boundaries, industrial sectors and especially ownership types were two categories that were more direct products of the planned economy system. The socialist planned economy proceeded with a clear list of priorities: industry was favored over agriculture, heavy industry over light industry, state-owned enterprises over collectively owned, and production of producer goods over consumer goods. As a result, under a façade of egalitarian goals and slogans, even during the socialist era, a wide range of differentials in wages and benefits existed within the urban Chinese labor force, differentiated by industrial sector and ownership type (Walder 1986; Bian 1994; Naughton 1997).

Economic reforms in the past decades have also injected new meanings to the roles of industrial sectors and ownership types in income distribution. The changes are both political and economic. Politically, an ideological shift has allowed the rapid growth of economic sectors outside of state ownership and control. The nonpublic sectors include not only individuals working for private employers or those who are self-employed but also those working in foreign-owned or joint-venture firms. Income distribution in these sectors is not subject to the same stipulations as that in the state-owned sectors. Unable or unwilling to match the welfare benefits provided with employment in the publicly owned sectors, firms in the private sectors also used higher pay to compensate for the lack of benefits, especially housing. Within the state-owned sector, while some firms have further prospered with the backing of the state, others have sunk due to their loss of state support.

Economically, rapid economic growth inevitably meant a reordering of the ranking of industrial sectors. Industries deemed essential under the planned economy system, such as mining, geological survey, construction, and heavy industry, lost their old glory, as new sectors, such as electricity, telecommunication, banking, and real estate, rose to become new stars. As it did during the early days of the planned economy, the state also played an important role in the shift of economic sectors. A priority investment program in the early 1980s, for instance, allocated 96 percent of total investment in three sectors: energy, transportation, and materials industries (Naughton 1997, 134).

Work Organizations

A greater source of income stratification in urban China originates from an organizational level lower than the city or industries. This is the urban Chinese work organization, or *danwei.* Even after more than two decades of reforms, as of 1999, only 15 percent of all urban laborers worked outside a danwei or organizations as self-employed, and nearly three-quarters of all urban employees still worked in publicly owned organizations (NBS 2000, 118).

A key to understanding the increased role of work organizations is again the nature of the property rights regime in transitional China. The public ownership under socialism was effectively a collective ownership, segmented into different regions, sectors, and work organizations. Even before recent reforms, the unequal status of the danwei in the Chinese economic and political hierarchies formed a basis of intergroup inequality.[5] The Chinese urban work units are therefore "minor public" structures, as compared with the state, the "major public." It was this segmented property right regime under the socialist planned economy that served as the key institutional basis for the redistributive economy (Walder 1992).

Since the start of economic reforms, the most important changes in the property rights regime have been a downward reassignment of use and appropriation rights (to lower levels of the government hierarchy, to firms, and to households), with the state retaining its control over transfer right (Walder 1994; Walder and Oi 1999). With such a change in the property rights regime, urban Chinese work organizations have gained an increased role in economic organization and welfare provision, largely because they have been liberated from the hands of the state. Whereas under socialism better work organizations meant better welfare provisions and higher prestige, in the era of reforms the role of the danwei has become more crucial to many urban residents, often serving as a lifeboat. Workers and their family members become urban poor when their enterprises go broke. At the same time, those working in profitable work organizations continue to enjoy a wide range of benefits, from better pay, jobs for children, to virtually free apartments. It is widely known that all organizations have their own "little coffers" (*xiao jinku*), or secret/semisecret accounts, evading auditing from the government. Funds deposited in these accounts are used not only for entertainment by officials but also to accumulate and distribute bonuses and welfare to employees. Many work organizations also create their own subsidiary enterprises to employ children of their employees.

Together, these four categories—locale, industrial sector, ownership type, and work organization—represent important legacies of the socialist planned economy system. At the same time, they also constitute some of the most important institutional sources that directly explain the rise and structure of income inequality during China's transition from socialism.

Research Design, Methods, and Data Sources

Guided by a theoretical formulation that treats categories as important sources of social inequality, we examine the roles of institutional categories, especially locales, ownership types, industrial sectors, and work organizations, in the overall rise in income inequality in urban China. We do so by modeling group and individual effects in income determination through both descriptive and multivariate approaches.

Modeling Group Effects

To examine the separate roles of categorical and individual characteristics, we employ three sets of methods. First, we construct the Theil index, which allows decomposing sources of income inequality, to describe income inequality between and within categories.[6] Second, we rely on analyses of variance, which allow us to attribute the variance in income to individual characteristics, as well as to categorical variables such as city, ownership type, and industry. Third, we use the hierarchical linear model (HLM), which allows explicit modeling of group and individual effects separately, to estimate simultaneously equations at both the group and the individual levels (Bryk and Raudenbush 1992; Raudenbush and Bryk 2002). At the micro, or individual, level, we model income as an outcome of individual characteristics as the following:

$$INCOME_{ij} = \beta_{0j} + \sum_{q=1}^{Q} \beta_{qj} X_{qij} + \varepsilon_{ij}$$

where β_{qj} ($q = 0, 1, \ldots, Q$) are level-1, or individual level, coefficients, X_{qij} are level-1 predictors for case i in unit j, and ε_{ij} is level-1 random effect of each individual, and is assumed to be independent and normally distributed with a variance σ^2. At this level, we use group-centered values. Thus, β_{0j} becomes the group mean income for individuals in the jth organization. At level-2, or the level of work organizations, we treat level-1 coefficients as outcomes of level-2 variables. Specifically, here we only treat the intercept of level 1 equation, β_{0j}, as an outcome of level-2 variables. Such a simplification is based on two considerations. First, finding out what organizational characteristics account for differences in the mean income of a work organization is in itself a first step in identifying categorical effects. Second, results of exploratory data analyses did not reveal major effects of level-2 variables on the coefficients of level-1 variables. This simplification leads us to postulate that the group mean of individual income (the intercept at level-1) is influenced by attributes of work organizations. The level-1 intercepts therefore become:

$$\beta_{0j} = \gamma_{00} + \sum_{s=1}^{S} \gamma_{qs} G_{sj} + \mu_{qj}$$

where γ_{qs} ($q = 1, \ldots, S_q$) are level-2 coefficients, G_{sj} are level-2 predictors or group-level variables (e.g., rank or size of the work organization) and μ_{qj} is the level-2 random effect, which is assumed to be normally distributed across unit organizations with a variance τ.

Data Sources

There are two main data sources used in this study. First, we use a sample from China's Urban Household Income and Expenditure Survey data for the decade 1986–1995. Our sample survey data cover three provinces, close to thirty cities of various sizes, and over 2,000 households annually over the one-decade period under study.[7] These three provinces, while not representative of all China, are nevertheless appropriate cases because they represent different parts of China that have undergone different changes during economic reforms. Guangdong Province was the first province to enjoy a policy relaxation from the central government with more freedom to carry out economic reforms from the early 1980s. Liaoning Province, having served as an important industrial center under the socialist planned economy, has suffered the most from this legacy. Its heavy concentration of large state-owned enterprises has made the economic transition much harder. Sichuan, the largest Chinese province until the mid-1990s, is situated economically somewhere in between the other two. The annualized individual level data from these surveys provide the basic source for constructing indexes of inequality trend as well as for conducting statistical analyses of income determination patterns in urban China. The second data source comes from the Survey of Chinese Work Organizations.[8] The most noticeable advantage of this data set is that its research design generated a sample of individuals that are nested within work organizations. This survey simultaneously collected data on characteristics of both individual employees and work organizations.[9]

Our data sources contain several limitations that have implications for our analyses. First, neither of our samples includes rural immigrants who resided in cities at the time of the surveys.[10] Second, similar to most household income surveys, our samples are likely to exclude high-income individuals due to their unwillingness to be interviewed. These two data limitations may well result in an underestimate of income variation and also income inequality. At the same time, for both samples, the income variable does not include most in-kind income from work organizations. Since in-kind income is more likely to be equally distributed within work organizations, omission of in-kind incomes may result in a bias in the other direction, namely, to overestimate income variation. Lastly, although our samples cover more than forty cities with various characteristics, they are not nationally representative surveys. The relatively large number of cases included in these two surveys, nevertheless, makes our results at least suggestive of the overall income distribution dynamics in urban China.

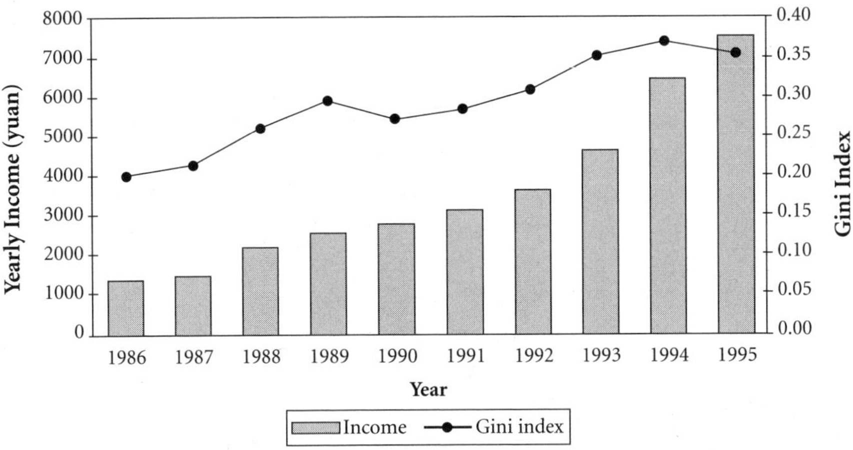

Figure 8.1. Growth with inequality: Income and inequality among urban Chinese employees, 1986–1995

Decomposing Income Inequality

Rising Income and Rising Inequality

Between 1986 and 1995, urban Chinese experienced both an unprecedented income increase and an escalation in income inequality. Using China's Urban Household Income and Expenditure Survey data, we calculate both income increase and income inequality measures for the decade 1986–1995. As shown in figure 8.1, the nominal mean yearly income of urban employees included in our sample increased by more than fivefold in a decade, from 1,329 yuan in 1986 to 7,491 yuan in 1995. Adjusting for the rampant inflation during most of the decade, real income over this period rose by about 70 percent, an impressive record for China's recent history. Income inequality rose by a magnitude almost equal to that in real income increase, about 70 percent. In the mid-1980s, urban income inequality was at an extremely low level, only 0.2 measured by the Gini index. By the mid-1990s, it rose to over 0.35. It is during this decade that urban China transformed from an egalitarian to an unequal society.

The contour of inequality increase, as shown in figure 8.1, also mirrored the different phases of urban economic reforms. The decade-long increase in income inequality is characterized by two periods of rapid increase, separated by a noticeable reversal in between. The first period of rising inequality occurred in the late 1980s, when the Chinese price reforms took place and when

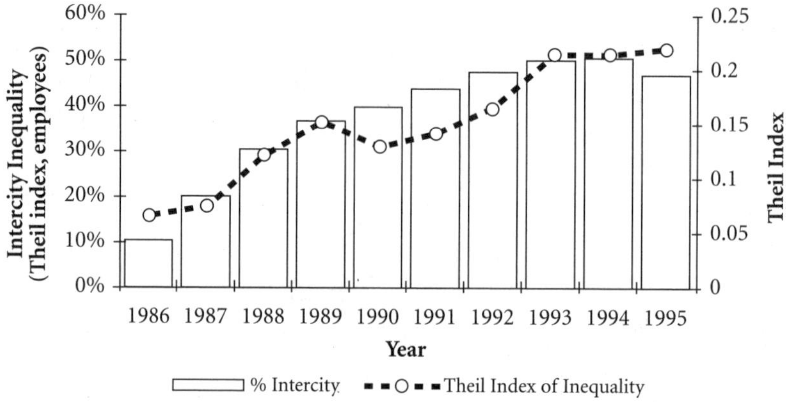

Figure 8.2. Rising intercity inequality, urban China, 1986–1995

inflation swept urban China in double digits. Rampant inflation, widely perceived corruption, and drastically increasing inequality, as shown here, no doubt all contributed to the urban unrest and massive demonstrations seen in Chinese cities in the spring of 1989. The crackdown in 1989 not only put a hold on economic reforms and inflation but also on the rising inequality trend. Rising inequality picked up its speed again in the early 1990s, following a call for deepening reforms by Deng Xiaoping, who feared that the 1989 crackdown might derail the Chinese economic reforms.

Categories versus Individuals

LOCALES

A major contributing factor to the rapid increase in income inequality is the growing gaps between categories, first among different locales. Among the three provinces included in the sample of Urban Household Income and Expenditure Survey data, the share of interprovincial urban income inequality as overall urban income inequality (measured by the Theil index) rose from less than 2 percent in 1986 and 1987, to close to 25 percent in 1989, and to over 40 percent in the early 1990s. One main reason for this rapid increase is the inclusion of the province of Guangdong in our sample.[11]

At the city level, a level of locale that makes more direct political economic sense, a similar, if not more pronounced, trend also emerged. As shown in figure 8.2, at the same time when the overall inequality (the Theil index) in-

Table 8.1
Shares of Income Inequality (Percentage of Theil index) by Ownership Type and Industrial Sector, Urban China, 1986–1995

	Ownership type (%)				*Industry (%)*			
Year	*Liaoning*	*Sichuan*	*Guangdong*	*Combined*	*Liaoning*	*Sichuan*	*Guangdong*	*Combined*
1986	11.3	5.4	6.8	6.3	13.4	7.6	6.8	6.4
1987	5.3	13.3	4.1	6.3	3.0	7.6	6.6	4.5
1988	13.0	11.0	3.0	5.6	4.9	2.9	4.8	1.8
1989	8.6	11.0	2.8	3.4	2.2	6.3	4.4	3.4
1990	9.8	14.6	2.8	3.6	2.2	7.1	4.9	3.4
1991	7.5	10.5	1.5	3.6	2.8	3.9	3.5	2.5
1992	10.4	16.7	2.7	5.2	4.3	5.0	3.8	4.6
1993	12.2	14.3	3.5	7.1	3.1	5.5	4.5	4.3
1994	9.9	14.0	6.0	7.1	5.4	12.1	9.2	6.7
1995	8.7	12.5	5.1	6.8	3.4	10.2	7.4	4.6

creased by threefold, from less than 0.07 to over 0.21, the share of the inequality that is intercity rose fivefold, from 10 percent in 1986 to 50 percent in 1993 and 1994.[12] By the mid-1990s, half of all urban income inequality could be accounted for by the city level geographic location alone.

INTEROWNERSHIP TYPE AND INTERINDUSTRY INEQUALITY

Two other categories in urban China, ownership type and industrial sector, also play important roles in shaping the pattern of urban income inequality. Table 8.1 presents the share of income inequality (Theil index) by these two categories.

Ownership type accounted for a significant share of urban income inequality. For the three provinces in our sample combined, the share of income inequality index accounted for by ownership type was about 6 percent in the mid-1980s. It dropped to below 4 percent by the end of the 1980s, and edged back to over 7 percent by the mid-1990s. The importance of this category variable varied in the three provinces. In both Liaoning and Sichuan, ownership type played a more important role than in Guangdong. In these two provinces, ownership type alone accounted for around 10 percent or more of income inequality.

Similar to the role of ownership types, interindustry inequality also first declined and then increased in the decade after 1985. The share of interindustry inequality as total income inequality dropped from around 8 percent in the mid-1980s, to around 4 percent throughout most of the decade, then rose to the 5–6 percent level around the mid-1990s. Similar to interownership type inequality, urban Sichuan Province again appears to be the most segregated across different industries.

Interownership and interindustry income inequalities, combined, accounted for over 10 percent of the overall income inequality in urban China by the mid-1990s. Their effects also varied from province to province, as they accounted for over 20 percent of overall income inequality in the province of Sichuan.

Categories versus Individual Characteristics in Income Determination

The effects of these and other categorical factors on income inequality, however, are not independent of one another, as the categories overlap in their effects (e.g., higher income industries tend to be state owned and located in certain regions). Moreover, income inequality among individuals is a result not only of the categorical differences delineated above but also of factors at the individual level, including a person's educational attainment and work experience or skills (e.g., higher income regions or industries may also have a higher-than-average concentration of highly educated individuals). To disentangle the independent effect of each main category and to distinguish the role of categories from those of individual characteristics, we turn to multivariate analysis.

Locale, Ownership Type, and Industrial Sector

To examine the relative importance of individual and group membership characteristics in income determination, we follow Xie and Hannum (1996) and use a relatively simple method, analysis of variance (ANOVA).[13] The dependent variables in this part of the multivariate analysis include total yearly income of currently employed individuals, as well as incomes separated by base salary or wages and other labor incomes (all transformed into their log form).[14] Independent variables used in the analyses include those commonly used in studying income determination, such as gender, educational attainment, seniority (indicated by the length of employment), and occupation, as well as variables indicating broad categories. The analyses are carried out both for 1988, the first year we have individual data by income sources, and for 1995, the

Table 8.2
Categories as Explanatory Variables: Urban Income Inequality, China, 1988 and 1995

	1988			1995		
Model	R^2	*df*	*f*-test	R^2	*df*	*f*-test
Base: "education, gender, employment length, and occupation"	0.3529	69	—	0.1908	66	—
Model 1, plus "ownership type" and "industry"	0.3722	87	1.34	0.2559	84	3.67
Model 2, plus "province"	0.475	89	17.43	0.447	86	29.72
Model 2, plus "city"	0.5471	117	45.18	0.5091	107	55.19

end of the study period. The results are summarized in two tables. Table 8.2 presents results comparing models with only individualistic level variables versus models with category variables. Only total income is used in comparisons. Table 8.3, by contrast, presents more detailed information on the relative importance of each and every variable in determining urban employees' incomes.

In table 8.2, the comparison of different models is carried out by an *f*-test. This test statistic is based on the difference in the R^2 of successive models. For instance, in 1988, the "base" model, which includes only an employee's educational attainment, gender, length of employment, and occupation, has an R^2 of 0.35. In model 2, two group membership variables are added: "ownership type of the work organization" and "industry." Adding these variables increases the R^2 from 0.35 to 0.37. The *f*-statistic resulting from the comparison of these two models, 1.34, suggests that there is no statistically significant difference between the explanatory power of the two models. In other words, in 1988, "ownership type" and "industry" did not make a significant difference in income, once the four variables at the individual level are controlled for. This is not the case, however, for the other two category variables, "province" and "city." Adding them (models 3 and 4) increases the explanatory power of the model significantly. The most striking observation one makes from these results in table 8.2 is that over time, the combined importance of individual characteristics in determining income declined drastically (as seen in the large

Table 8.3

Relative Importance of the Determinants of Income in Urban China, 1988 and 1995

	1988								
	Total income			*Base salary*			*Other labor income*		
Source	Partial SS	*df*	MS	Partial SS	*df*	MS	Partial SS	*df*	MS
Gender	6.67	1	6.67	2.16	1	2.16	15.67	1	15.67
Education	1.82	5	0.36	2.03	5	0.41	16.12	5	3.22
Length of employment	223.14	45	4.96	254.62	44	5.79	230.05	45	5.11
Occupation	16.13	18	0.9	10.51	18	0.58	24.72	18	1.37
Ownership type	15.62	5	3.12	9.63	4	2.41	92.03	4	23.01
Industry	1.6	13	0.12	2.298	13	0.18	8.066	13	0.62
City	221.76	30	7.39	68.27	30	2.28	680.38	30	22.68
Model	693.79	117		537.72	115		1,371.41	116	
Residual	574.38	4,217		400.2	4,049		1,901.73	4,186	
Total	1,268.18	4,334		937.92	4,164		3,273.13	4,302	
Adjusted R^2	53.45%			56.12%			40.29%		

Table 8.3 *(cont.)*

Relative Importance of the Determinants of Income in Urban China, 1988 and 1995

	1995								
	Total income			*Base salary*			*Other labor income*		
Source	Partial SS	*df*	MS	Partial SS	*df*	MS	Partial SS	*df*	MS
Gender	16.61	1	16.61	13.62	1	13.62	12.87	1	12.87
Education	15.09	6	2.52	14.70	6	2.45	22.98	6	3.83
Length of employment	178.69	47	3.80	140.88	47	3.00	160.55	47	3.42
Occupation	8.96	12	0.75	9.98	12	0.83	15.20	12	1.27
Ownership type	40.29	6	6.72	110.64	2	55.32	59.19	6	9.87
Industry	29.27	12	2.44	9.32	12	0.78	74.48	12	6.21
City	670.38	23	29.15	292.70	23	12.73	1,357.62	23	59.03
Model	1,348.12	107		874.39	103		2,068.02	107	
Residual	1,300.16	4,886		1,555.05	4,693		3,893.70	4,724	
Total	2,648.28	4,993		2,429.45	4,796		5,961.73	4,831	
Adjusted R^2	49.83%			34.59%			33.21%		

Notes: SS = sum of squares, the variance in income that can be accounted for by a particular source/variable; *df* = degrees of freedom, an indicator of how many categories a particular variable possesses; MS = mean sum of squares, the sum of squares divided by the degrees of freedom. MS can be viewed as the mean variance explained by each independent variable, and it is more suitable for comparison than simply the sum of squares, since a large number of categories tend to result in a large amount of variance, other things being equal. With the exception of the effect of "industry" in 1988 for total and other labor income, all MS are statistically significant at the ≥ .05 level. R^2 gives the percentage of total variance in the dependent variable explained by all independent variables included in a particular analysis.

reduction in R^2 for model 1), whereas the importance of categorical variables increased substantially (as seen both in the relative increment in R^2 when category variables are added and in the larger *f*-statistics).

Results in table 8.3 allow for a more detailed examination of the changing relative importance of income-determining factors, not only for total income but also for income broken down into "base salary" and "other labor incomes." Two sets of comparisons can be made, one within each year across different categories of income, and the other across time, between 1988 and 1995. First, for each year, the variable "city" not only plays the most significant role in income determination, as the variable with the largest mean sum of squares; its role is also found to be much more important in determining other labor income than are base salary and wages. The difference in the mean sum of squares between the variable "city" and the next most important variable is much larger in the other labor income model than in the base salary model.[15] In other words, local city plays a much larger role in determining the portion of income less subject to control from the state. Second, the role of city became more important in 1995 than in 1988. For total income, in 1988, the ratio between the most important variable, "city," and the second most important, "gender," was only 1.11 (7.39:6.67). Even for other labor income, the ratio between "city" and "gender" was only 1.45. In 1995, the ratios were 1.75 and 4.59, respectively. Clearly, whereas the total variance in income that is accounted for by all these variables decreased somewhat, the role of geographic location increased substantially. These results are consistent with the earlier decomposition of the overall inequality change.

Also worth noting is the role of the other two category variables, ownership type and industry. Ownership type is an important factor in determining income, but its role relative to other factors is much greater in the base salary and wage income than for other labor-based incomes. The role of the industrial sector in income determination rose during the decade under study. In 1988, similar to what table 8.2 reveals, the variable "industry" was hardly an important factor at all when other factors affecting income are taken into consideration. In 1995, "industry" not only became significant but also rose to be one of the most important factors. It ranks fourth, after "city," "gender," and "ownership type," among the seven variables in affecting nonbase salary income. It is more important than education, occupation, and seniority, all of which have been shown to be highly important income determinants in most settings.

Another important change in the determinants of income distribution is the role of gender, a categorical variable that is often incorrectly assigned as an individual trait. As shown in table 8.3, the role of gender in income determination increased drastically between 1988 and 1995 when total income is used as the dependent variable (the measure mean sum of square rose from 6.67 to 16.61). A further scrutiny of results in table 8.3 reveals that the most drastic change occurred in the determination of "base salary," where the magnitude of the effect increased by nearly sevenfold. Whereas the results in table 8.3 do not reflect the direction of change, our other analyses of these data show clearly that the increase is due to a greater income penalty for female workers. Such a pattern of worsening gender income inequality lends support to the criticism that the Chinese state's withdrawal from its commitment to gender equity has contributed directly to the increased gender inequality in Chinese workplaces (Bian, Logan, and Shu 2000; Parish and Busse 2000).

Work Organization as a Source of Inequality

To examine the effects of work organization on income inequality, we turn to analyses of the data from the Survey of Work Organizations. We use logged yearly income as our dependent variable. Our independent variables include both individual characteristics and organizational attributes. At the individual level, we include variables that have been widely used in previous studies.[16] At the organizational level, we rely on a number of variables that characterize a Chinese urban work unit.[17] Moreover, we also include city as a control variable since, as we have already shown, income differences across cities are pronounced. The descriptive statistics of variables used are in table 8.4.

We begin our analysis by partitioning the variance of individual incomes into within-organization and between-organization components. In table 8.5 we present results of variance partitioning and reliability estimation. Nearly half of all income variance among individual employees was accounted for by interorganizational sources. Among urban employees in our sample, 53 percent of the total variance in income is at the individual level, and 47 percent at the organizational level. Our reliability index of 0.96 also suggests that the sample means of income are reliable estimates of the true group means of individual income across organizations.[18]

In table 8.6 we present results of multilevel models. Specifically, we present two types of models, with the first (model 1) including only predictors at the

Table 8.4
Descriptive Statistics of Work Organization Data Set

	Level-1 descriptive statistics				
Variable	N	*Mean*	*SD*	*Min.*	*Max.*
Logged income	2,404	7.95	0.39	6.40	9.62
Gender	2,404	0.53	0.50	0.00	1.00
Age	2,404	33.74	9.38	19.00	59.00
Party membership	2,404	0.33	0.47	0.00	1.00
Junior high	2,404	0.15	0.36	0.00	1.00
Senior high	2,404	0.35	0.48	0.00	1.00
College	2,404	0.49	0.50	0.00	1.00
Age^2/100	2,404	12.26	7.04	3.61	34.81
Size					
≤ 300	81	0.19	0.39	0.00	1.00
300–500	81	0.44	0.42	0.00	1.00
500 or above	81	0.37	0.49	0.00	1.00
Ownership					
Private	81	0.05	0.22	0.00	1.00
Public	81	0.75	0.26	0.00	1.00
Collective	81	0.20	0.23	0.00	1.00
Rank					
Low	81	0.30	0.46	0.00	1.00
High	81	0.58	0.50	0.00	1.00
Performance					
Low	81	0.41	0.49	0.00	1.00
High	81	0.19	0.39	0.00	1.00
Gov't agencies	81	0.41	0.49	0.00	1.00
City					
Beijing	81	0.06	0.24	0.00	1.00
Shenyang	81	0.10	0.30	0.00	1.00
Shijiazhuang	81	0.12	0.33	0.00	1.00
Baoding	81	0.09	0.28	0.00	1.00
Lanzhou	81	0.12	0.33	0.00	1.00
Wuhan	81	0.11	0.32	0.00	1.00
Guangzhou	81	0.05	0.22	0.00	1.00
Chendu	81	0.12	0.33	0.00	1.00
Suzhou	81	0.10	0.30	0.00	1.00
Luoyang	81	0.12	0.33	0.00	1.00

Table 8.5
Decomposition of Variance and Organization Reliability of Income in Urban China, 1993

		% total variance
Within-unit organization variance σ^2	0.081	53
Between-unit organization variance τ_{00}	0.071	47
Unit organization reliability	0.961	—

individual level, and the second (models 2 and 3) introducing some characteristics of work organizations by adding variables into the equation of the intercept (group mean income) at the organizational level. The results in model 1 show that among employees in our sample, an older male employee who was a Communist Party member and has a college education was the most highly rewarded in terms of income. We learn further that our variables explain more than one-fourth of the income variance at the individual level (13 percent of the total variance), not too dissimilar to what we have learned from other studies. While education, an indicator of human capital and usually rewarded in a market economy, plays a significant role in determining individual income, other individual resources such as party membership and seniority (here manifested by the variable of age) continue to remain important as well.

In the next model, we introduce organizational size, ownership type, rank, and profitability into the level-2 equation that predicts the intercept (group mean income). Size, ownership type, and rank are important indicators of a work organization's position in the redistributive economy (Bian 1994; Zhou 2000; Wu 2002). Together with profitability, these factors are expected to explain a significant portion of the average income of an organization's employees. This is indeed the case. Adjusting for variables at the individual level, our results in table 8.6 show that medium-sized work units (versus small-sized organizations), state as well as private ownership (versus collective ownership), higher rank in the bureaucratic hierarchy, and higher economic performance all contribute significantly to individual income differences. Overall, these variables explain about 18 percent of the variance at level-2.

In model 3, we add the variable "city" to the list of variables used in model 2. The effects of work organization size and rank disappear, while ownership type and profitability remain as important organizational traits. Organizational size and rank are sensitive to the city effect because large-sized and high-ranked organizations also tend to be located in large cities. Similarly, more private

Table 8.6

Hierarchical Linear Model Coefficients of Income (Logged) in Urban China, 1993

Independent variables	*Model I*	*Model II*	*Model III*
Mean income	7.962	7.456	8.232
	(0.030)***	(0.120)***	(0.113)***
Individual			
Male	0.035	0.035	0.036
	(0.011)**	(0.011)**	(0.011)**
Age	0.039	0.039	0.039
	(0.005)***	(0.005)***	(0.005)***
Age^2/100	–0.032	–0.033	–0.032
	(0.007)***	(0.007)***	(0.007)***
Party member	0.058	0.057	0.057
	(0.013)***	(0.013)***	(0.013)***
Education (vs. junior high or below)			
Senior high school graduate	0.003	0.003	0.003
	(0.022)	(0.022)	(0.022)
College or above	0.052	0.052	0.052
	(0.022)*	(0.022)*	(0.022)*
Work organization			
Size (vs. < 300)			
300–500		0.192	–0.018
		(0.072)**	(0.059)
500+		0.083	0.019
		(0.066)	(0.045)
Ownership (vs. collective)			
Public		0.287	0.163
		(0.109)**	(0.070)*
Private		0.506	0.277
		(0.123)***	(0.081)***
High rank (vs. low rank)		0.121	0.071
		(0.073)+	(0.052)
Performance (tax handed up) (vs. low)			
Nonprofit agencies		0.105	0.178
		(0.078)	(0.055)**
High		0.189	0.208
		(0.079)*	(0.051)***

Table 8.6 (cont.)
Hierarchical Linear Model Coefficients of Income (Logged) in Urban China, 1993

Independent variables	*Model I*	*Model II*	*Model III*
City (vs. Guangzhou)			
Beijing			–0.416 (0.157)**
Shenyang			–0.647 (0.095)***
Shijiazhuang			–0.775 (0.090)***
Baoding			–0.724 (0.093)***
Lanzhou			–0.715 (0.093)***
Wuhan			–0.670 (0.090)***
Chengdu			–0.606 (0.098)***
Suzhou			–0.212 (0.118)+
Luoyang			–0.701 (0.095)***
Percentage of variance explained by model			
Within unit organization	27	27	27
Between unit organization	—	18	69

Notes: Numbers in parentheses are standard errors; N = 2,404 for the individual-level variables; N = 81 for the unit organization-level variables.

+p < .10; *p < .05; **p < .01; ***p < .001

firms are located in southern coastal cities than elsewhere. Compared with individuals in Guangzhou, individuals in other cities earn one-fifth to three-quarters less. Private firms and public work organizations add, respectively, 28 percent and 16 percent premiums for their employees. Individuals in low-performance firms earn not only 21 percent less than those in high-profit firms, but also 18 percent less than those in nonprofit agencies (government-funded). The fact that these nonprofit public organizations (*shiye* danwei) do almost as well as the high-performance production work organizations highlights an important feature of transitional Chinese society, namely, that organizations close to the political power that possess unique resources benefit equally if not more than organizations that have market advantages.

Compared with model 2, the proportion of between-organization variance explained in model 3 also increases from 18 percent to 69 percent, leaving 31 percent of the total variance at the organization level unexplained. Given that we have controlled for these conventionally used organizational characteristics, the residual portion of the variance is due to the unobserved factors that are unique to each of these work organizations.

What we learn from the analyses is that in addition to different individual attributes, a large portion of income inequality in urban China is explained by work units and their locations. Just as cities themselves differentiate individuals' income after controlling for the characteristics of the individuals, work organizations play a similar role. By bringing to their members either a premium or a penalty, groups or categories contribute to income determination at least as equally as individual characteristics. Given the magnitude of the income variance these categories explain, our results further suggest that organizations also play an equalizing role in maintaining a certain degree of equality within their boundaries.

Restructuring Inequality in Post-Socialist China

To account for the spectacular rise in income inequality in post-socialist urban China, we have focused on the roles of inequality-generating categories that are crucially important but have been largely neglected in past studies of inequality in transitional societies. By considering categories and boundaries, we redirect the institutional stratification research in China and explicitly spell out the "specificity" of institutional settings (Walder 1996). These settings include locales, ownership types, industrial sectors, and work organizations that were created during the high socialism period and that have continued to exert profound influence on individual economic attainment. By distinguishing between-group and within-group stratification processes, we also offer an institutional explanation of the sharply increased inequality in urban China and contribute to the understanding of the overall inequality structure. The unprecedented increase in overall inequality in urban China lies in two juxtapositional dimensions: the sharply climbing inequality between groups and the relative equality maintained within groups. In China, perhaps more so than elsewhere, group membership plays an important role in determining income inequality. Whereas vast inequality exists between groups, equality is maintained to some extent within groups.

The categories we have identified—locale, industry, ownership type, and work organizations—are not simply geographic or workplace constructs within which urban Chinese happen to live or to work. Rather, these are meaningful political economy units with clear boundaries, institutional histories, and income-generating capabilities. Categories created by socialist practices prior to the reforms have functioned as the institutional settings that define the contours of social inequality in the post-reform era. As the central government's control loosened in an emerging market economy, members of various categories began to adopt new strategies to maintain group boundaries and pursue collective benefits. For the majority of urban Chinese who are still affiliated with work organizations, their geographic location, employment sector, and work units have all become so much more important in determining their livelihood and status in the society than they were in the past.

Exclusion and opportunity hoarding are clearly the mechanisms that are responsible for the pattern of income inequality analyzed here. Take locale as an example. Local governments are not only major players in promoting economic growth within their boundaries; they also serve as agents to reinforce boundaries and to exclude nonmembers. One recent example is how Chinese cities have designed their own regulations to exclude migrants from certain jobs (Solinger 1999; Wang, Zuo, and Ruan 2002). While migrants, mostly from rural areas, have been welcomed to cities to provide needed services, cities, including the capital city of Beijing and the largest metropolis Shanghai, issued formal regulations to exclude migrants from certain jobs that appeared more attractive to urban unemployed people. These regulations not only specify job categories reserved for urban residents but also make explicit suggestions that urban residents not be underpaid compared with "outsiders." Employers violating these restrictions may face stiff fines.[19]

As active agents engineering growth and regulating distribution, local officials in urban China have clear motivations to act as gatekeepers. First, economic growth and improved standards of living are the primary sources of political legitimacy. This is the case at every level of the Chinese Communist bureaucracy. Bureaucratic establishments use economic growth as a central criterion to determine the appointment and promotion or demotion of officials at lower levels. Second, as pointed out by Oi (1995), the Chinese government is a bureaucracy that has a long tradition of engineering economic growth. Last but not the least, local officials' personal welfare, from salary, bonuses, and housing, to sedans, banquets, cellular phone bills, and overseas trips, also depend on the local fiscal coffer, which is increasingly intimately linked to the local economy (Walder 1995; Lin 2001).

The sharply increased intercity inequality, therefore, cannot be labeled simply as an outcome of uneven regional development. In other words, the rising intercity inequality is not just a function of divergent economic development and different costs of living across cities. In the United States, for example, where cost of living varies vastly from places like New York City to Wichita Falls, Texas, the share of income inequality that can be accounted for by intercity inequality was only 4 percent among employees in 1989, in contrast to the nearly 50 percent we find in urban China in the mid-1990s.[20] Different levels of average wage and costs of living do not necessarily lead to a high level of intercity inequality as in the urban Chinese case. Moreover, intercity inequality, as well as other intercategory inequalities, is not simply an outcome of a sorting process, by which individuals of higher earning capabilities concentrate in certain categories. As the multivariate analyses reveal, the prominent roles of categories remain when individual level attributes are controlled for.

Similarly, the shift in the hierarchy of industrial sectors is more than an outcome of technological change. It reflects both the socialist history and the policy priorities set by the leadership during the reforms. Employees in industries that have monopoly power, such as electrical power generation, telecommunication, and banking, enjoyed collectively an income level and welfare provisions far exceeding those in other sectors. In 1995, for example, the average wage of employees in the real estate industry was 22 percent higher than the national average, in banking it was 35 percent higher, and in the electricity industry it was 37 percent higher (NBS 2000, 142–43).

For urban Chinese work organizations, gaps in average income levels have enlarged, and a countervailing trend of maintaining within-group equality has also been documented. As late as the mid-1990s, in many urban Chinese work organizations, the "tacit alliance" between managers and workers that Walder (1986) observed a decade earlier remained, and an egalitarian distribution of income continued. Several recent studies have reported that the income ratio between the highest paid employees (top managers) and average workers is no more than three or four to one (Lin and Zhang 1999; Lu 2002). Such an egalitarian practice in income distribution is found in urban public work organizations and in nonpublic enterprises, where managers supposedly have greater powers to decide the pay scale (Kung 1999). In the publicly owned work organizations, a sense of community persisted, as the organization used to be state owned and all workers were employed in the same factory for a long time and made contributions. Such a common identity contributed to the need for sustaining a "collusive collection action" (Lin and Zhang 1999).[21]

The pattern of within-group equalization can also be observed from our analysis and from Xie and Hannum's (1996) careful analysis of a 1988 survey data set. Our results show that membership variables such as industry and city play a larger role in affecting other labor income than basic wages or salaries, revealing not only the sources of income growth but also of income inequality. Similarly, Xie and Hannum's study reported that most of the positive regional economic growth effect on individual income was through the bonus share of the income rather than regular salary or wages (1996, 969). Moreover, they also reported that the distribution of bonuses was *not* strongly associated with individual characteristics such as years of schooling, experience, party membership, and gender (1996, 961–62; for a similar argument, also see Wu 2002). In other words, while income level differed in different cities in China, distribution of income within these cities tended to be rather equal, as least according to the characteristics included in their study.[22]

The categorical nature revealed in this study, as seen in the pattern of income inequality, bears political implications for class formation and social stability in contemporary China. While some observers have asserted that the sharp increase in inequality in China would lead to social unrest and formation of a "new" working class, our results suggest a possibly different scenario. The maintenance of local (within-group) equality may dampen social discontent associated with the global (overall) increase in inequality, while segmentations by locale, industry, ownership type, and work organizations may cut across class lines and impede efforts of class mobilization and formation. A survey conducted in Beijing in 2000, for example, found that while an overwhelming majority of respondents (more than 95 percent) believed that the degree of inequality for China *as a whole* was too large or somewhat too large, and only less than 3 percent thought it was "about right," 42 percent also reported that the level of inequality was "about right" *within* their work organizations (Wang 2003).

Our results also directly shed light on the market transition debate. The continuing large impact of categories and boundaries on individual income reflects the marks of the redistributive reward system in an emerging market. Not only do these "old" categorizations not die out in the new market, but members in these groups adopt various measures to maintain boundaries and to exploit their advantageous positions in pursuit of collective benefits. Clearly, old institutions created under state socialism have exhibited a vibrant new life in the new market. In this sense, we provide cautions to the overemphasis of "newness" in studying the restratification process and echo the path-dependence perspective (Stark 1994, 1996; Rona-Tas 1998).

How durable will these categories be in shaping future inequalities in China? On the one hand, one is tempted to believe that the categories we identify here are legacies of socialism and are transitional in nature. One may predict that inequality may lessen if a more genuine labor market is established. Free movements of labor across regions, industries, and work organizations may serve to remove much of the inequality we now see across categories. On the other hand, categorical inequalities everywhere suggest caution in not underestimating the durability of the categories and the rigidity of the boundaries. A stratification process like the one shown here by no means unique for China or only for post-socialist societies. Labor markets are segregated not only in emerging market economies but also in existing mature market economies. Our study in fact joins the body of emerging studies of social inequality that bring macro-structure into institutional analysis of social stratification (DiPrete and Grusky 1990; DiPrete et al. 1997; Tilly 1998). Studies have shown, for example, that the recent rapid increase of rural migrants in Chinese cities has not brought about a corresponding desegregation between urban and rural Chinese. Instead, invisible boundaries have been erected to prevent rural migrants from settling in cities and have contributed to the formation of migrant villages within Chinese cities (Chan 1997; Solinger 1999; Wang, Zuo, and Ruan, 2002). Therefore, income inequality structured according to the categories we have identified may rise or fall, and the relative importance of these particular categories may change in the future, but the persisting role of categories in structuring inequality is unlikely to fade away.

9

KA-HO MOK

Local Response to a Global Agenda

Changing State-Education Relations in Mainland China

SOME GLOBALISTS HAVE stressed the limitations of a state-centered approach in analyzing socioeconomic developments, thereby pointing out that the external constraints on states have significantly reduced the state's capacity to respond to the changing and far more complicated socio-political-economic environments. For those radical globalists, the increasing interdependence and connectedness of nation-states have made the state less of an autonomous decision-making body, and local policies are increasingly shaped by global trends (O'Brien 1992; Ohmae 1995). Nonetheless, recent comparative studies on education policy show that even though there seem to be similar patterns and trends in education development in East Asian societies, recently initiated education reforms have had diverse agendas (Mok 2000; Green 1999a). Thus, the considerable convergence of policy rhetoric and general policy objectives may not satisfactorily explain the complicated processes of changes and the dynamic interactions among global, regional, and local forces that shape education policy making in individual countries (Dale 1999; Green 1999b; Dale and Robertson 2000).

This chapter reflects on the impact of globalization on national policy, with particular reference to the question of how the government of the People's Republic of China (PRC) has responded to the global tide of marketization and decentralization. Changes in China's higher education system have much in common with those elsewhere, suggesting that China's higher education system has been affected by similar trends. But before jumping to this conclusion, we should also bear in mind an alternative hypothesis, that local events are crucial and determining factors for change.[1]

Globalization and Socioeconomic Changes

Over the past decade or so, people have begun to talk about the impact of globalization on economic, social, political, and cultural fronts (see, for example, Giddens 1990, 1999; Fukuyama 1989, 1992; Sklair 1995; Robertson 1995; Rodrik 1997; Hirst and Thompson 1999). Although *globalization* has no generally agreed on definition, an ever-increasing number of books and articles have been written about different aspects of globalization and their effects on human history (Robertson 1992; Waters 1995; Albrow 1996; Held et al. 1999). Seeing globalization as complicated and complex processes of economic transactions and worldwide telecommunications, sociologists generally believe that its effects are profound since it is restructuring the ways in which we live (Giddens 1999; Sklair 1999) and creating a new hybridity of cultural styles and mixes (Fukuyama 1992; Robertson 1995; Giddens 1999). Central to the debate about globalization is to describe, recognize, investigate, and explain the accelerated and worldwide increase in the interconnectivity and interdependence among economies, polities, societies, and cultures in different parts of the globe, examining also the impact of globalization on human development (Ohmae 1990; Fukuyama 1992; Giddens 1999).

There are three major schools of thought in the current globalization debate: hyperglobalists, skeptics, and transformationalists (Held et al. 1999). Hyperglobalists argue that the increasing connections and interactions among different nation-states and the freer and quicker interchanges and movements of capital, goods, services, people, technologies, information, and ideas have inevitably transcended national borders, thus suggesting an inevitable convergence of human activities and a receding role of the nation. They also believe economic liberalization inevitably brings about a "denationalization" of economies and a "borderless economy," whereby nation-states or national governments are superseded by world market forces. The rise of the global economy, together with the growth of institutions of global governance, and the hybridization of culture have created a borderless global village (Held et al. 1999, 3–5). Nonetheless, it is clear that not all those who accept economic globalization as a reality would agree with the hyperglobalist argument on the inevitability of convergence (see, for example, Ekong and Cloete 1997; Ratinoff 1995; Veseth 1998; Hirst and Thompson 1999).

Scholars who oppose the convergence thesis criticize the globalists for overstating and overgeneralizing or even overselling the convergence tenets of globalization. Instead, they point out the importance of nation-states and heterogenization in terms of national or local responses to global processes or imperatives (Krasner 1999; Sassen 1999; Weiss 1998). For skeptics, globalization is merely a myth. Unlike the globalists, the skeptics believe that national governments are still the main architects and players in internationalization. They even argue that the power and authority of nation-states are enhanced because they stipulate more centralized regulation over cross-border economic activities. With regard to cultural homogenization, the skeptics point out the danger of the "clash of civilizations," especially when the management of the world order is dominated by the Western states. In view of the increasing pressures for internationalization, the skeptics believe national governments are not passive victims and immobilized because they are active in response to external pressures (Held et al. 1999, 5–7).

The transformationalists, like the hyperglobalists, perceive globalization as an unprecedented driving force for rapid political, economic, and social changes in modern societies. Nonetheless, they reject the thesis of global convergence because the transformationalists believe that globalization would result in "global stratification," since some states, societies, and communities are enmeshed in the global order at the expense of other countries, thus marginalizing some so-called less competitive economies in the process of globalization. In addition, they argue that nation-states still retain the ultimate claim of legal legitimacy within their territories even though they have to respond to external pressures generated from international laws and authorities. Seen in this light, national governments are far from diminished but are reconstituted and restructured in the growing complexity of processes of governance in the context of globalization (Held et al. 1999, 7–9).

In short, although hyperglobalists, skeptics, and transformations differ on globalization's causes, characteristics, and impacts, they all recognize its growing effect on political, economic, social, and cultural developments. In the context of globalization, modern states have begun to transform the ways they manage themselves. Notions such as "reinventing government" (Osborne and Gaebler 1992) and "entrepreneurial government" (Ferlie et al. 1996) have become fashionable, and the concomitant consequence is the initiation of reforms in public sector management. To improve the efficiency and effectiveness of public service delivery, new ways to maximize productivity and effectiveness comparable to that of the private sector are sought (Dale 1997).

Challenges to Modern States and Changing Governance

The challenges globalization poses to modern states have changed the philosophy of governance and the way the public sector is managed (Baltodano 1997; Rhodes 1997; Flynn 1997). Turning to the political aspect of globalization, Cerny observes that, "Globalization as a political phenomenon basically means that the shaping of the playing field of politics is increasingly determined within insulated units, i.e., relatively autonomous and hierarchically organized structures called states; rather, it derives from a complex congeries of multilevel games played on multi-layered institutional playing fields, above and across . . . state boundaries" (1996, 253).

The growth in the global economy has inevitably forced individual states to change both their roles and their constitutions in order to accommodate, and not just adapt to, the demands and pressures generated from the external environment. According to Viven A. Schmidt (1995, 85), the rise of the global economy has led to the decline of the nation-state: "The unwritten story behind the internationalization of trade lies not so much in how international and trade associations are diminishing the autonomy of the nation-state, or in how multinationals are escaping the control of the nation-state, but in how nation-states have been altering their own policies to function in the new international arena, and in how these have in turn affected their policymaking processes. These changes have, in most instances, undermined the nation-state's particular kind of democracy by strengthening executive power vis-à-vis societal interests and freeing business from its traditional constraints." The growing impact of globalization has unquestionably drawn a number of people to believe that there are many aspects of globalization that are beyond the control of states. When talking about the impacts of globalization on nation-states, Roger Dale (2000, 94) suggests:

> The world is in the process of becoming wholly commodified, both through the recommendation of those elements of public provision that the welfare state decommodified and much more by the extension of the commodity form into all those areas of the world that were previously concealed from it. Alongside this goes the destruction of the very environment that is being commodified, creating problems that are truly global and transnational—indeed, anational—and beyond the power of any individual nation to solve. What particularly distinguishes globalization from what has gone before is that it is throughgoingly supranational.

According to radical globalists, multinational corporations have replaced the modern state as the key actor in globalization. Similar to neoliberal doctrines, the "minimal state" position argues that modern states are responsible for maintaining internal order and providing protection from invasion by hostile states, but economic affairs are left nearly exclusively to the market (Faulks 2000). When neoliberal doctrines are put into practice, two core principles are honored:

- The superiority of markets over politics in providing for human need, generating prosperity and enhancing personal freedom.
- The need to defend individuals' market rights, including property rights, the right to assert one's inequality, and the right to choose from a diversity of goods and services in the marketplace (cited in Faulks 2000, 75).

In response to a more "globalized" context, modern states have taken two broad forms: individually, they have taken on what Cerny (1996) calls a "competitive state" form, and, collectively, they have tried to set up a framework of international organizations—what James N. Rosenau (1992) refers to as "governance without government"—to cope with those far more complicated matters and issues in the context of an increasingly globalizing economy (Dale 1999) or the idea of the "evaluative state," which attaches importance to effectiveness, efficiency, and economy in recent public management literature (Henkel 1998; Kogan and Hanney 2000).

Governance, under the rubric of globalization, has been equated with the minimal state, whereby the form of state intervention is redefined and the principles and practices of the market are adopted in managing the public sector. In addition, the role of the government/nation-state has had a fundamental change from a "provider of welfare benefits" to "builder of markets" (Sebagia 2000).

Decentralization and Marketization in Education: A Global Trend

Higher education, of major importance in public policy, is not immune to the change in governance modes. To promote effectiveness, efficiency, and economy in the delivery of higher education, the World Bank has shown its support for a "managerial approach" in reforming higher education. Its dominant rationale for education, addressed in *Priorities and Strategies for Education* and *Higher Education: The Lessons of Experience*, is economic (World Bank 1994, 1995). According to Keith Watson (1996, 49), "It is largely concerned with finance, economic returns, human resource development, efficiency, effectiveness, costings, private funding, and the like." Despite the fact that in recent annual reports (World Bank 1997, 1998) the bank substantially rethought the import of the state's role in education, the impetus for change the bank initiated a few years ago has undoubtedly shaped educational restructuring along the lines of a managerial approach.

The increasingly popular tide of "managerialism" has affected not only the public sector management discourse in general but also the higher education development in particular. Amidst the pressure for management efficiency in the face of widened access and reduced resources, the use of market, or economic, principles is seen as a disciplinary mechanism to make the higher education sector and its people work harder, more efficiently and effectively. The global practices of corporatization, privatization, and marketization have undoubtedly affected the governance of universities (Currie and Newson 1998). By "corporatization," we refer to the running of higher educational institutions as businesses or corporations. As for "privatization," we mean that the state has reduced its subsidy to higher education, while other nonstate sectors/actors are becoming more prominent in the higher education sector. By "marketization," we refer to the adoption of market principles and practices to run higher education institutions. All these practices can be understood as the strategies to make higher education more effective and efficient. It is particularly true when ideas and practices of managerialism gain popularity in running the public sector.

Universities and schools now experience pressures from governments, the main providers of education, to demonstrate maximum outputs from the financial inputs they are given. At a time of economic constraints, people begin to ask for better use of limited public money, thus more attention is given to the issue of "value for money" and how the investment in higher education can really facilitate social and economic development (Lucas 1996; Jones 1998; Ball 1998). In response to calls for "cost-effectiveness" and "value for money," new managerial doctrines have been adopted and management-dominated decision making has become common practice in the university sector. A culture of entrepreneurial competitiveness has emerged and become the new ethos in the university sector. In order to become more competitive, universities have changed the ways they manage themselves. "Terms of new discourse" have emerged, such as mission statements, system outputs, appraisal, audit, strategic plans, cost centers, and public relations (Duke 1992).

The economic rhetoric of individual rights and ideologies of "efficiency" are gaining momentum not only in industrialized countries like the United Kingdom, the United States, and Australia (see, for example, Bridges and McLaughlin 1994; Brown 1995; Currie and Newson 1998) but also in less developed countries (Bray 1996). Other scholars have also noted that different countries (regardless of their levels of development) have a mixture of public and private services (James 1992; Tilak 1991; Bray 1997). Many empirical studies reveal that the private sector is playing a more important role in education (e.g., Mok 1999; Yee and Lim 1995; World Bank 1996). Mark Bray's (1996) work on the financing of education in East Asia also points out that in some settings parents and local communities have played a more important role than government in the financing of education, while the state has gradually withdrawn from the frontier of educational provision. Similar experiences have been reported in Vietnam, the Philippines, and Malaysia, leading to a new definition of the public-private boundaries (Cheng 1995a; Bray 1996; Mok and Welch 2001). Increasing critical attention is now being paid to the application of this ideology and processes to schools, and more recently to the academic profession (Hartley 1995; Mok 2000b; Lo 1997). In short, unlike the traditional notion of education, which was dominated by the public sector, the emergence of "internal markets" and the prominence of "economic rationalism" in the educational sphere seem to be a feature of the globalization agenda.

Policy Context of Marketization of Education in China

In the Mao era, education was regarded as an instrument to spread the official ideology of communism, thus the Communist state exerted a strict control over education. After founding the PRC in the 1950s, the Communist state adopted a centralization policy in managing the education sector, thereby establishing an educational system characterized by unified planning, administration, syllabuses, curricula, textbooks, enrollment, and allocation. In addition, all schools and higher education institutions were under the direct and strict control of the party-state. Under such a policy framework, the state assumed the responsibilities for formulating education policies, allocating education resources, exerting management control, recruiting teaching staff, and determining curricula and textbooks. In short, the party-state monopolized three major aspects of education services: providing, financing, and managing.

Since the launch of economic reforms and the adoption of the "open-door" policy in the late 1970s, Chinese leaders began to realize the importance of education in the modernization project started in the post-Mao era. In the early 1980s, Deng Xiaoping already proposed a fundamental redirection of education and claimed that education should meet the needs of modernization of the world and of the future. He also emphasized that education and the development of the Chinese economy could not be separated. By pointing out that education was a foundation for economic development and scientific improvement, Deng also confirmed the strategic role that education should play in the economic reform and modernization of China (Chen 1999, 8).

In view of its limited capacity and scarce resources, the central government realized that the state alone was unable to assume responsibility for satisfying people's increasing demand for education. The poor development of education in the Mao era made the party-state acknowledge that overcentralization and stringent regulation would kill the initiatives and enthusiasm of local governments and educational institutions. Under such circumstances, the party-state took initiatives to relax state control over education and deliberately reduced its role in the education sphere (Mok 1997a).

With the promulgation of the "Decision of the Central Committee of the Chinese Communist Party on the Reform of the Educational System" in 1985, the CCP outlined the blueprint for restructuring China's educational systems. This called for resolute steps to streamline administration, devolve powers to units at lower levels so as to extend the schools' decision-making power in administrating school affairs, and thus reducing controls over schools. The state started to diversify educational services, allowing and encouraging the establishment of schools run by the nonstate sector. In 1993, the CCP and State Council issued the "Program for Education Reform and Development in China," which reinforced the policy of decentralization and diversification of education services. The document declared that "the national policy is to actively encourage and fully support social institutions and citizens to establish schools according to laws and to provide right guidelines and strengthen administration" (CCPCC 1993). In this way, the central government had changed its policy from direct control to managing schools through legislation, funding, planning, advice on policies, and other necessary means (SEC 1993, 6).

By 1995, the education law had further revitalized local community and informal sector support for education, and, hence, decentralization of management and financing was further stressed (SEC 1995). Undoubtedly, the ideas and practices of the "socialist market economy" have had decisive impacts on educational development in the mainland. Concepts like "efficiency," "effectiveness," and "competition" have become far more popular in management and governance of the educational sector, while the law of supply and demand in the labor market has started to play a more significant role than did the "manpower-planning" approach to education.

By the 1990s, Chinese leaders promulgated the basic national policy of developing education and science to build a strong and rich nation and stressed that carrying out the policy was a fundamental aspect of cultural construction (Chen 1999, 5). To do so the Ministry of Education proposed an "Action Plan to Vitalize Education into the Twenty-First Century" in December 1998. The aim was to establish a new educational system and a lifelong learning system to cater to the needs emerging from further economic development of society in the coming century. On June 13, 1999, the Central Committee of the CCP and the State Council convened the Third National Education Working Meeting and promulgated the "Resolution on the Further Development of Educational Reform and Quality Education," which reinforced the firm will of the Chinese government to support education (*People's Daily*, June 14, 1999).

Decentralization and Marketization in Higher Education

Financing Higher Education

In line with the 1985 programmatic document "Decision of the Central Committee of the Communist Party of China on the Reform of the Educational Structure" and "The Outline of Education Reform and Development in China" promulgated by the CCP Central Committee and the State Council, local governments and educational practitioners searched for "multiple channels" to finance education (Cheng 1990). Instead of relying solely on the state's financial support, educational institutions have diversified by seeking other resources, such as overseas donations, financial support levied from local government taxes and subsidies, and tuition fees (Mok 1996).

In the 1990s, the CCP shifted the responsibility for financing education further from the state to individuals and families by introducing a "fee-paying" principle—that is, student tuition fees.[2] Early in the 1980s, the plan to charge students fees was regarded as an "ultra-plan," implying that the in-take of these "self-supporting" students was beyond the state plan (K. M. Cheng 1996). But after the endorsement of a socialist market economy in the CCP's Fourteenth Congress, the State Education Commission officially approved allowing institutions of higher education to admit up to 25 percent of their students from the "commissioned training" or "fee-paying" categories in 1992. In 1993, thirty institutions of higher learning were selected for a pilot study known as "merging the rails," whereby students were admitted on the basis of their public examination scores or a willingness to pay a fee even though their scores were below the required minimum. In 1994, more institutions entered the scheme, and the fee-charging principle was thus legitimatized (K. M. Cheng 1996).

The structural change in the financing of education in China is most obvious in higher education. Before the 1990s, the number of fee-paying students was small, but it has been increasing since the "user charge" principle was adopted. The percentage of fee-paying students attending higher educational institutions in Shanghai increased from 7.5 percent in 1988 to 32.1 percent in 1994 (Yuan and Wakabayashi 1996). Although the number of self-financing students dropped from 25,800 in 1989 to 11,300 in 1992 for political reasons,[3] the number rose again after the formal endorsement of the socialist market economy in 1992 when the role of the nonstate sector (including the market) received due recognition. Since 1997, all students have paid tuition fees. Students from poor families can apply for scholarships or subsidies from their universities/institutions.

During my field visits to Guangdong, a laboratory for economic reforms and China's most prosperous province, I learned that all students (from primary to tertiary levels) pay tuition fees. In the higher education sector, Zhongshan University, for instance, began merging the tracks in 1995, indicating that differences no longer exist between "publicly funded students," "self-paying students," and "commissioned students." Professor Cai He, head of the Department of Sociology, and Professor Zhang Minqiang, director of the Institute of Higher

Education of Zhongshan University, stated that students had begun to accept the fee-paying principle. The range of tuition fees students pay varies among courses, typically, 2,500 to 3,500 yuan per year (while the average per capita monthly salary in Guangzhou was around 1,000 yuan in 1997). Wu Yechun, deputy director of the Office of Administration, South China University of Technology, told me that in his view students have had far more incentives to study hard since the universities have adopted the fee-charging principle. He said,

> In the past, university education was entirely supported by the state, and students seemed to take higher education for granted and thus their motivation was low once they were admitted. But the situation has changed since the adoption of "self-paying" principle in the university sector. Students are strongly motivated to study because they have to pay for the courses and they are eager to learn a wider range of subjects to broaden their knowledge base. Despite the fact that some students, particularly those who are from poor families, may have difficulties paying for tuition fees, many of them are able to secure financial support to obtain higher education. . . . More fundamentally, people are generally supportive of the "fee-paying" principle in higher education because they believe that higher education is an investment. With higher qualifications university graduates would find it easier to get jobs in the open labor market, "value" is thus added to the students after university training.[4] (Field interview, March 1998, Guangzhou)

Similar observations were made during my various field visits to other parts of the mainland. Students in Shenzhen, Wenzhou, Shanghai, and Beijing have all had to pay tuition fees since 1997. Higher education is no longer free on the mainland.

Emergence of Private Higher Education in China

The Fourteenth Congress of the CCP, held in 1992, endorsed the principle of a socialist market economy, creating a favorable environment for the emergence of private education (Mok 1996). To foster further economic development in China, the State Education Commission issued the document "Points Regarding How to Expedite Reforms and Vigorously Develop Ordinary Higher Education," which presented guidelines for adapting higher education to the socialist market economy (Yin and White 1994). The development of private education was supported by "Provisional Regulations for the Establishment of

People-Run Schools of Higher Education" promulgated in 1993 by the State Education Commission. In late 1993, "The Program for Reform and the Development of China's Education" stipulated that the national policy was to actively encourage and fully support social institutions and citizens to establish schools according to laws and to provide right guidelines and strengthen administration (CCPCC 1993). In June 1999, during the Third National Meeting for Education Practitioners, Jiang Zemin, the general secretary of the CCP, openly confirmed the role of nonstate-run universities and colleges and encouraged more "social forces," "nongovernmental organizations," and individuals to engage in establishing *minban* (private) higher education to create more learning opportunities (*People's Daily*, June 16, 1999).

Under such a legal framework, different types of school systems have flourished, and privately run educational institutions have become popular in China's big cities (Mok and Chan 1996). Realizing the importance of education, Chinese citizens believe that achieving a high educational level may enable them to earn more money, and many surveys report that people are of the view that education is vital to their career development. A survey in Shanghai, for example, found that more than 60 percent of parents hoped their children would receive higher education (Zhang 1996). Another survey carried out by the Central Education Science Institute in Guangzhou in 1993 showed that 73 percent of five hundred respondents favored establishing nongovernmental schools at the basic education level (Zhang 1996). Under this favorable policy environment, nonstate-run educational institutions are developing rapidly in China, from kindergartens to higher learning institutions.

The past few years has seen a resurgence and development of *minban* higher education institutions in Guangdong, Shanghai, Wenzhou, and Beijing (see Mok and Chan 1996; Mok 1997a,b, 1998, 1999). By 1994, there were more than 800 nonstate higher educational institutions across the nation, of which 18 were fully recognized by the State Education Commission and had authority to grant their own diplomas (China National Institute of Educational Research 1995, 11). By 1996 the number of *minban* higher education institutions had increased to 1,230 (K. M. Cheng 1997). As a part of the formal education system, these *minban* higher education institutions have undoubtedly increased because of their recognition by the state (field interviews and observations, 1998, 1999, and 2000, Shanghai, Guangzhou, and Wenzhou).

In 1998 alone, there were three nongovernmental *(minban)* higher education institutions in the Guangdong area, and they have adopted different strategies to run their colleges. Hualian Private College, the first privately owned higher education institution in Guangdong, primarily relies on students' tuition fees to run the institution, while Minban Nanhua Industrial and Business is financed partially by students' tuition fees and partly supported by the Trade Union of Guangdong Province. Another newly established private college, Pei Zheng Business College, adopts a *minban gongzhu* model (i.e., people-run and publicly assisted) to run the college. The college is financially supported by the local government (Hua Du City) by subsidizing the price of land for college buildings and paying teachers' salaries. In addition to the local government's support, Pei Zheng alumni also raise funds to run the college (Mok 1997a; Wu 1996).

Realizing the pressing demand for higher education, these nongovernmental institutions take advantage of this relatively liberal sociopolitical environment to develop courses and programs catering to market needs. For instance, Nanhua Industrial and Business College offers programs in four major areas: law, catering and tourism, business management, and administrative management. In order to be competitive in the "education market," the college adopts a "five gears strategy." First, courses are geared to the market. Second, courses are geared to availability. Third, English courses are geared to international needs. Fourth, education is geared to students' needs. And, finally, the college is geared toward becoming a renowned school to attract more students (Niu 1997). Professor Niu Xianmin, president of the college, observed that students are the "life-blood of the college," and the market has actually guided the development of nongovernmental colleges (field interview, July 1995; Mok 1997b).

Knowing that they would face immense difficulties in competing with their state-funded counterparts, *minban* colleges are eager to differentiate themselves by specializing in courses geared to newly emerging market needs. They are also committed to serving the local communities in which they are located. For example, Pei Zheng Business College seeks to produce educated people for Hua Du City and has established a close link with local enterprises to create more opportunities for its students through internships and job placements. Following a similar path, other nongovernmental colleges are in the process of formation; private Chaoshan College and private Nanling College, for example, have already secured financial support from local governments and are ready to launch in the Guangdong area in the near future (Wu 1996).

Private education is also popular in Shanghai where a *minban gongzhu* (people-run, publicly assisted) model has been adopted to create more educational opportunities. I visited several colleges of this kind in 1997 and 1998. Shanghai Guang Qi College, for example, was established in 1996 by Professor Chen Quanfu, Dean of Adult Education of Shanghai Jiao Tong University. When asked about the nature of *minban gongzhu,* Chen stated: "*Minban gongzhu* means that the college is not entirely funded by the nonstate sector but partially supported by the government in terms of financial support of school buildings."

Seeing a gap between demand and supply in formal higher education, a group of formerly retired professors from Shanghai Jiaotong University and Fudan University secured local government support and have committed to running a *minban* college to create additional quality educational opportunities. Chen proudly told me that Guang Qi College was a "community-based" higher educational institution. To make the college better known to the local community, Guang Qi has identified several selected areas for teaching, offering programs that emphasize practical knowledge, computing skills, foreign languages, and advanced technology. Sharing the facilities and libraries of Shanghai Jiao Tong University, coupled with a stable teaching team of experienced educators from Fudan and Jiaoda, Guang Qi College has proved itself a success in its students' public examination. Its good record attracted 9,000 applicants for only 250 places in the 1997–1998 academic year (Field Interview, April 1998).

The formation of Hua Xia College, another *minban gongzhu* college in Shanghai, was initiated by the East China Normal University to create more learning opportunities for Shanghai citizens. Like Guang Qi College, Hua Xia College is a community-based college. The central government has not formally recognized Hua Xia, but the Shanghai municipal government has approved it, and its has received support from the local community and East China Normal University. It derives its funding from tuition fees, overseas donations, and the local community. Its affiliation with East China Normal University enables Hua Xia students to share library and laboratory facilities with the university. Professor Zheng Hong, president of the college, said that Hua Xia had a degree of autonomy that her formally recognized counterparts did not enjoy.

Realizing that the state alone can never meet the pressing demands for higher education on the mainland, Professor Zheng strongly believes that *minban* colleges have a role to play, particularly to fill the gap between the existing supply and demand left over by the formal university sector. Zheng feels the central government should allow more autonomy to local educators and intellectuals to run *minban* colleges. Moreover, he also urges the state to formally recognize *minban* colleges. He told me, "There is no harm at all to have *minban* colleges in China. First, we can create additional learning opportunities for students.

Second, we can make use of the expertise, knowledge, and experience of retired professors and they are very keen to serve and teach in the higher educational sector. Third, it is a better utilization of existing facilities and space from formal public universities. Calculating all these advantages together, I think the state must support and recognize the development of *minban* colleges" (field interview, May 1997).

The state has not formally granted *minban* colleges university status but has gradually accepted their existence. In the education law promulgated in 1995 and 1998, the role of *minban* education was formally recognized, and proper systems and mechanisms are being worked out to monitor the qualifications awarded by and academic standards of these colleges. No matter how the state perceives the role of *minban* higher educational institutions, they have become a crucial component of the educational system in Shanghai (field visits and interviews, 1998, 1999, and 2000, Shanghai).

Field visits to Wenzhou have enabled me to learn that the role of the "market" has become far more significant in higher education development. The Wenzhou government has encouraged different social forces to invest and engage in higher education development. Wenzhou University, for example, originally a public university, is going through a fundamental restructuring to become a *minban* university, and it is attracting donations and investments from the market. The newly inaugurated *minban* Wenzhou University plans to admit around 100,000 students by 2010. The Wenzhou government, instead of directly running the university, has assumed the role of "builder of markets," allowing more flexibility and offering a policy framework to make use of market forces to run higher education (field visits and interviews, September 2000, Wenzhou).

This discussion has focused on only a few major models of private education. There are other approaches and models of nonstate-run schools throughout the country, however.[5] All of these developments indicate that educational services have become diversified, and the emergence of different types of schools is a response to market-generated demands.

Competition among Educational Institutions

Drawing comparative insights from observing leading universities in other countries, the CCP has begun to realize the importance of bringing about substantial improvements in its university education. In order to enhance quality education at the tertiary level, the CCP introduced "Project 211," an initiative to select one hundred institutions of higher education to promote development in selected disciplines. The state is attaching a new financial and strategic importance to these universities and disciplines in an effort to promote the development of world class institutions in the early twenty-first century. Central to the scheme is a plan to introduce "competition" among universities. Universities are assessed by quantifiable, objective criteria on staffing, buildings, libraries, laboratories, research, funds, and so on, to determine whether they are "qualified" to be included as top institutions. Most important, the selected universities will receive more funding from the central government. To be ranked near the top, many universities have merged with other universities to improve their research and academic profiles (Christiansen 1996; Rosen 1997). For instance, old Shanghai University announced a plan to merge with other local colleges to become a more comprehensive university. After the "merger" the new Shanghai University proved itself a more competitive university and was selected as one of the "211" universities. More significantly, the 211 program formalized competition among universities.

Since the introduction of competition in the university sector, the resources and funding of individual universities have been determined by their research output and proportion of graduates gaining employment. According to Ruth Hayhoe (1996), university authorities have a general expectation that staff in research institutions should spend two-thirds of their time on research and one-third on teaching, while the reverse expectation is commonly held in teaching institutions. Inevitably, when competition is introduced among higher educational institutions, rewarding winners and pointing out losers, faculty members experience intensified work pressure to improve their research profile.

In 1997, the State Education Committee (SEC) (now the Education Bureau) issued a new direction for higher education. Universities are encouraged to share resources and facilities, to merge universities to enhance research and teaching quality, to consolidate and strengthen existing good work, and to establish new universities in collaboration with local governments (Wu 1997). Under such a policy direction, different local universities in Guangzhou (the provincial capital of Guangdong) have attempted to merge with others to consolidate their common strengths, hoping the undertaking will enable them to be selected into the "top one hundred." In order to upgrade the Guangzhou city-run higher education institutions, Guangzhou Normal University, Guangzhou Institute of Education, and Guangzhou Teacher College will merge and form a new Guangzhou Normal University. At the same time, Guangzhou Medical College, South China Construction College and Guangzhou University are committed to improving their research and teaching, establishing closer links with local industries and businesses to make their courses more attractive and competitive in the market (Wu 1997).

Another growth area will be the establishment of a "university city" in Guangzhou. Realizing the limitations faced by Guangzhou's city-run higher education institutions (particularly small student population, limited space for school buildings, and inadequate resources and faculty members), local governments in Guangdong proposed that a university city be developed encompassing various local institutions of higher learning such as Jiaotong College, Vocational College, Industrial and Business College, College of Arts and Law, and College of Finance. The merging of these institutions will bring together these institutions' resources and strengths. Students would benefit from this resource sharing, as well as from better facilities, well-qualified faculty members, and enhanced research and teaching (Wu 1997). Most recently, the Ministry of Education, a newly established administrative body replacing the SEC, announced that the central government will allocate additional funding to develop Beijing University and Qinghua University, while other universities must search for alternatives to generate educational funds. In order to upgrade the academic position of local universities and make them more competitive in the "national academic market," Shanghai has allocated additional financial support to establish Jiaotung University and Fudan University, hoping that these universities could be developed as world-class universities comparable to Beijing and Qinghua in Beijing. Acknowledging the importance of higher education to future economic development in Wenzhou, the local government has tried to establish a university city in Wenzhou to upgrade and offer more higher education opportunities for local residents (field visits and observations, September 2000, Shanghai and Wenzhou).

Consumer Choice in Education

Considering students' choice as a very prominent factor affecting course design, educational institutions in China have adopted a "customer-oriented" approach to running their educational services. For instance, the department of teaching, People's University of China (Renda), conducted a survey on teaching matters among faculty and concluded that new teaching materials must be introduced to prepare students for the needs of newly emerging markets. Thereafter, a "textbook revolution" was initiated throughout the university in 1993. New teaching materials were developed, and a special "teaching materials working committee" was set up to coordinate a comprehensive reform in teaching (Wei 1996).[6] In addition to these reforms, another major action Renda took was to reshuffle the disciplines and specializations. Programs such as international commerce, international enterprise management, marketing, taxation, national economic management, real estate business, and management have been introduced and are attracting more students.

One striking example of a reform to meet market needs was initiated by Zhongshan University's department of history, which faced declining enrollments. To attract more students, the department began repackaging courses to make them more "marketable." Courses such as "culture and history" and "tourism and history" have been introduced, with similar practices also adopted by other departments of pure academic studies. Applicability is also emphasized in such courses as applied mathematics, applied physics, and applied chemistry to attract students. Similar cases can easily be observed elsewhere in China's schools, especially when computer literacy, spoken English, diversified subjects, and practical value are stressed in course design and curriculum development.

Quality control systems have been introduced to attract consumers. For instance, Hading Chemical Industry Institute proposed a reform measure called "teachers hanging up their shingles and students choosing their own courses." This means that, for the same course, classes of different specializations, requiring different amounts of study time, providing different amounts of credits, and using a diversity of teaching methods, are employed. These are taught by teachers with varied teaching styles, each of whom "hangs out" his or her "shingle"; students may choose whichever teacher they like best and compete fiercely for the opportunity to be taught by the best teachers (Wei 1996). Since the implementation of this system, teachers have acquired control over students' examinations and grading, and students have gained control of teachers' standards and the amount of wages and bonuses they receive. More importantly, the scheme is seen as a means of raising teachers' sense of responsibility toward teaching. This reform is also used to inspire excellence and to encourage everyone to focus their energies on teaching and research. Hading Chemical Industry Institute also introduced "competition" among its faculty, rewarding hard-working researchers with monetary prizes, which induces other faculty members to follow suit (Wei 1996, 84–88).

The price of and access to educational services depend on consumers' perceptions of prices and abilities to pay. All in all, refocusing curricula to meet emerging market needs, emphasizing vocational training, and responsiveness to student and market demands are strong indicators that China's educational system has gone through a marketization process (Yin and White 1994; Mok 1997a).

A Mandate to Generate Revenue

Unlike during the Mao era when educational development was entirely directed by the central government, there has been a strong tide of diversification and decentralization of education in post-reform China. From the mid-1980s onward, senior leaders of the CCP began to encourage administrators, principals, and presidents of schools and universities to search for additional funding to run educational services (Mok and Wat 1998). Zhao Ziyang, the former party secretary, openly admitted that the state had insufficient funds to meet the pressing demands for education. He therefore encouraged educational institutions to join in the nationwide proliferation of commercial activities in 1985. Similarly, Li Peng, the former commissioner of education in 1987, urged local governments to multiply financial sources to support educational development. It is in such a policy context that *chuan shou* (income-generating activity) was initiated and officially endorsed (Kwong 1996).

To generate income to support educational development, school principals and university administrators have ventured into business and commerce. Educational institutions have opened business firms and enterprises *(xiaoban qiye)*, run commissioned courses, offered adult education and evening courses to attract more students, and charged consulting fees for services. They have also rented out their premises, run cafeterias and bars, and even turned their assembly halls into discos and other places for entertainment (Kwong 1996; Mok 1997a, 1998).

Many of China's most renowned universities—Beijing University, for instance—have created business firms to generate income. This new mode of funding education—"integrate the school and business units, support the schools with factories"—has gained momentum among other schools and colleges in China. Ren Yanshen, vice-secretary of the party committee of Beijing University, believes that universities' ventures into the commercial and business activities could support their scholastic and research activities. He openly said that "the financial income obtained [from doing business] will be used to improve teaching conditions, provide teachers and staff with opportunities to exercise their professional skills, and relieve them of any anxieties about their livelihood" (Y. M. Ren, cited in Wei 1996, 72–73). Qinghua University, another key-point university, has run factories and business firms for years, and many faculty and staff have established close links with the industrial sector, playing a consultant or managerial role in some enterprises (Mok 1999; Zhou 1995).

According to a study of fifty higher educational institutions, among them were 238 companies, 144 factories, 43 three-tier enterprises *(sanzi qiyi),* and about 40 percent of the profit from these enterprises was diverted to support scholastic activities (Zhou 1995). Other activities included "holding international conferences and charging registration fees to foreign participants, conducting training courses for local industry workers, organizing tours to Chinese archaeological sites, assisting in computerization activities [for] businesses, offering preparatory courses for individuals who may wish to pursue advanced degrees" have been organized (Julius 1997, 148). With the additional income gained from ventures in the "commercial sea," educational institutions can allocate more money to raise the salaries of teachers and improve teaching and research facilities (*China News Analysis,* October 15, 1993; X. Cheng 1996).

Responding to Local Needs

A close scrutiny of the higher education sector in mainland China reveals that the central government and local governments have engaged in creating educational opportunities in response to pressing needs for quality education and well-qualified workers. The policy of decentralization and the methods governments at various levels have adopted to diversify education services are internally driven by local needs rather than merely a response to exogenous forces. For instance, by repeatedly emphasizing the importance of making Shanghai an international player in the global marketplace, the Shanghai government has participated in improving Shanghai's educational standards and raising its technology level. Realizing that the average educational level of Chinese citizens still lags behind other developed economies, the Chinese government has repeatedly emphasized the important role of higher education and lifelong learning. The drive to create more educational opportunities could be understood as China's response to both the internal and external environments rather than merely a reaction to the globalization impact.

In addition, recent changes in China's educational system clearly reflect the central government's reduced role in providing, regulating, and subsidizing education. The boom of the nonstate sector, particularly the rise of different types of *minban* schools in Shanghai, and the increasing number of self-financed students suggest that a quasi-market is evolving. Despite privatization and quasi-marketization, however, internal markets in Chinese education have not yet fully evolved. The split of purchaser and provider in the education market, if any, is unclear. The strategy of privatization or marketization adopted by the Shanghai municipal government is *highly instrumental*, intended to improve administrative efficiency and effectiveness rather than to make a fundamental shift in value orientation. One crucial point that deserves attention here is that the PRC government has never committed itself theoretically and ideologically to public choice theory, the philosophical basis of marketization and privatization. The adoption of market principles and practices to improve the efficiency of the higher education system and the search for multiple channels to finance higher education through the nonstate sector reveal that the CCP adheres to *pragmatic instrumentalism* to run its higher education.

The State's Changing Role in Education

China's implementing a policy of decentralization in the education sector does not mean that the state has really *deregulated* its control over schools. The flexibility and freedom that *minban* schools now enjoy should not be understood as reflecting the entire withdrawal of state and local governments from the education arena. Allowing different types of schools and various governance models to flourish in the mainland is to fulfill the policy objective of creating more education opportunities. Realizing that the central government alone could never meet the increasing demands for high quality education, local governments adopted a decentralization policy and made use of the market to fill education gaps. One major indicator of the persistence of government control is the existence of mixed public-*minban* schools in Shanghai. For example, the government provides the school building or land, while nonstate bodies or organizations take care of operations and secure financing (field observations, June 1999 and September 2000, Shanghai).

The changing nature of education is also reflected in the transformation of the state's role in it, from being the sole provider or reliable guarantor of educational services to becoming a regulator or service purchaser. China has moved in a direction similar to that of some Western countries where their policies "amount to a 'hollowing out' of the state (Jessop 1993) with the loss of some activities 'upwards' to supranational bodies and the loss of others 'downwards' to subnational or nonstate bodies" (Dale 1997, 274). More importantly, the shift from direct state control to governance has caused fundamental changes in the state's role in education. Like the West's establishment of differentiated markets in the welfare sector and similar to the move toward a post-Fordist mode of economy, which "places a lower value on mass individual and collective consumption and creates pressures for a more differentiated production and distribution of health, education, transport, and housing" (Whitty 1997, 300), China's central government has gradually retreated from governance activities of funding, provision, and delivery. At the same time, different coordinating institutions other than the state (that is, the market and the community) have taken a far more active role in governance of education.

Nonetheless, although the state has realized that its own capacity to provide people with sufficient higher educational opportunities is severely limited in the present social and economic context, it is wrong to say that the CCP has entirely withdrawn from the educational arena. Broadly speaking, the nature of the work it does has changed from directly coordinating and administering education to determining where the work will be done and by whom. The strong tide of "marketization" affecting China's higher education does however suggest the mode of governance in education has changed from one of "state control" to one of "state supervision."

Important to note is that there are different levels of government in China. Undoubtedly, the central government (the state) has changed its governance model from a sole service provider to a facilitator and supervisor, and the role local governments play has become increasingly important, particularly when the policy of decentralization is implemented. Alternatively, we may conceptualize the recent transformations of the government's role in light of the shift from "provider of benefit" to "builder of markets," as Seragia (2000) suggested. Since welfare and social policy provision is now carried out by state actors different from those involved in the provision of social benefits and the evolution of the welfare state in the past few decades, different types of state actors may emerge. The power of public authority has also changed especially when policies of decentralization and marketization are introduced. Therefore, when analyzing the changing roles of the state/government in China's education, we must pay due attention to which levels of government we are examining and their respective roles and functions in terms of educational financing, policy-making, management, and other aspects of governance.

This discussion has reflected globalization's effects on local policy making. The measures and policies the CCP has adopted to improve the quality of education for its citizens is closely related to the needs of the people. Instead of being a mere response to the external environment, the policies made and reform measures taken by the PRC reveal how a nation-state reacts to the growing impacts of globalization. Local governments or individual nation-states are still the most important agents in local policy formulation. This is particularly true when we connect the recent changes that have taken place in higher education with the wider social policy context of "demonopolization" of state provision in social services in China. We can better understand the changing relationship between the state and education by seeing it as part of the transformation that has taken place in the public domain of China rather than as externally driven by the effects of globalization (Mok 2000a). Well aware of the globalization pressures, many governments have attempted to make use of the globalization discourse to legitimate their policy measures or to justify their inaction. Therefore, we must contextualize our policy analysis, paying heed to the complicated tensions between global, regional, and local policy environments.

10

RANCE P. L. LEE

Chinese Diffused and Institutional Health Care and Global Change

THE HEALTH CARE system of a society can be broadly defined as a set of ideas, practices, and organizations developed to deal with problems of health and illness. Numerous studies by medical historians and social scientists have shown that although the content of health care systems vary from one society to another, their structures appears to have at least one feature in common, that is, the availability of more than one form of medical care for use by the population (Kleinman et al. 1975; Leslie 1976; Fulder 1996; Cant and Sharma 1999; Goldstein 2000). This is the case in both industrialized and developing countries. The concept of medical pluralism has generally been used to describe this global phenomenon: the coexistence of multiple forms of healing in society.

A distinctive feature of medical pluralism in world perspective is the preeminence of scientific biomedicine that originated in the West. Nevertheless, medical pluralism could be observed in many Western societies not only before but also after scientific biomedicine emerged as the dominant form of medical care in the middle of the nineteenth century (Fulder 1996). Over the last one and a half centuries, scientific biomedicine has spread from the West to many other parts of the world, but medical pluralism was and still is the situation in many non-Western societies (Leslie 1980). Apparently, medical pluralism has been a normal, rather than abnormal or unusual, state of affairs in human societies over many centuries. The various forms of healing do not blend into a unified system of health care, despite claims that they perform similar functions for the society, including preventing disease, treating illness, and enhancing health.

Since medical pluralism has been a global phenomenon in the history of mankind, it is important for sociologists to study how the different forms of healing interact with one another and how they are viewed and supported by the state and the public. I use the health care situation in Hong Kong as an example to show how C. K. Yang's classification of institutional and diffused religions can be applied to understanding the dynamics of medical pluralism, especially the changing relationship between biomedicine and other forms of health care.

Yang's Typology of Chinese Religion

C. K. Yang's book *Religion in Chinese Society,* published in 1961 by the University of California Press, is generally regarded as a masterpiece both for the understanding of religious life in Chinese society and for the advancement of the sociology of religion as an academic field. Yang formulated a conceptual scheme by classifying Chinese religious behavior and organizations into diffused and institutional religions. It appears that such a scheme is applicable to the study of health behavior and organizations.

According to Yang (1961, chap. 12), institutional religion refers to a system of religious life consisting of three major elements: (1) an independent theology or cosmic interpretation of the universe and human events, (2) an independent form of worship consisting of symbols (gods, spirits, and their images) and rituals, and (3) an independent organization of personnel to facilitate the interpretation of theological views and to pursue cultic worship. In other words, institutional religion has its independent existence in society and is separable from secular social institutions. It has separate concepts, rituals, and organizations and can thus function independently. In China, institutional religion was represented by Buddhism and Taoism and by religious or sectarian societies, including the cults of professional magicians and sorcerers.

As regards diffused religion, Yang conceived it as a religion having its theology, cultus, and personnel so intimately diffused into one or more secular social institutions that they become a part of the concept, rituals, and structure of those institutions. In other words, diffused religion is inseparable from secular social institutions; it does not exist independently. In China, diffused religion could be illustrated by ancestor worship in the family, the worship of patron gods in the trade guilds, the worship of deities in the local community, as well as the ethicopolitical worship in the secular institution of government. Yang argued that although diffused religion does not appear as a separate factor, it may serve importantly as an undergirding force for secular institutions and the general social order as a whole.

In view of Yang's typology, I venture to propose that the various forms of healing in a society can be classified into two types: diffused medicine and institutional medicine. Institutional medicine refers to a system of healing that has (1) an independent theory of disease and its causation, (2) an independent body of technical skills and work procedures, and (3) an independent organization of trained personnel and special agencies for dealing with health and illness in society. In other words, it has a set of distinct concepts, skills, and organizations and can thus assume the nature of a separate social institution. On the contrary, diffused medicine does not function independently. Its theory, skills, personnel, and organizations are so intimately associated with family, religion, and other nonmedical institutions in society that they become an integral part of those institutions. Institutional medicine functions as a separable and independent system, while the role of diffused medicine depends very much on the functioning of the nonmedical institutions of which it is a part. This classification of the various forms of healing in terms of institutional medicine and diffused medicine can help us to understand the structure and functioning of each medical tradition, the dynamic interaction among different forms of healing, and the relationship between medical and nonmedical institutions. In this chapter, I use this conceptual scheme to analyze the pluralistic health care structure in Hong Kong.

Hong Kong and Its Health Care

Hong Kong was a British Colony for over 150 years. Its sovereignty was reclaimed by China in July 1997. Because of China's "one country, two systems" policy, Hong Kong is able to maintain a high degree of social and political autonomy after reunification (So 1999). The territory has been designed by China as Hong Kong Special Administrative Region.

According to the 2001 census, Hong Kong's total population was over 6.7 million living in a total land area of about 1,100 square kilometers. Hong Kong is a densely populated and highly urbanized Chinese society. Its economy has experienced a phenomenal growth over the last several decades. It has been recognized as a major industrial, commercial, and financial city-state in the global economy (Chiu, Ho, and Lui 1997).

The health care sector in Hong Kong has been performing quite well, although the rise of medical cost has become an issue of mounting concern in recent years (Hay 1992). In 2001, the crude death rate was 5.0 per thousand population. The infant mortality rate was 2.7 per thousand live births. Life expectation at birth was about 77 years for men and 82 years for women. About 11.2 percent of the population were aged 65 and above. For many years, the objective health indicators of Hong Kong compared favorably with those of most developed countries (Gauld 1998). Health problems in Hong Kong are mostly due to chronic degenerative diseases, especially cancers, heart diseases, and cerebrovascular diseases, though in early 2003 the territory was badly hit by the global outbreak of atypical pneumonia—SARS (severe acute respiratory syndrome).

The subjective indicators of health in Hong Kong are also favorable. A territory-wide sample survey of over four thousand adult residents in the summer of 2001 (Wan 2003) found that 46.7 percent of the respondents were generally satisfied with their lives, while only 14.3 percent were dissatisfied. Moreover, nearly six out of ten people under study were satisfied with their state of health, while only one out of ten showed dissatisfaction. These findings reveal that most people in Hong Kong felt that they were healthy. The survey also found more people generally satisfied (54.3 percent) with Hong Kong's health care services than dissatisfied (14.0 percent).

The health care services in Hong Kong are quite diversified. As in many other contemporary societies, scientific biomedicine is the predominant form of health care in Hong Kong, but it has been coexisting with a wide range of traditional Chinese health beliefs and practices. Biomedicine and the various traditions of Chinese healing that are widely utilized by the Hong Kong Chinese can be, in my opinion, categorized in terms of diffused and institutional medicine. It should be explained that in Hong Kong there are other forms of healing imported from other countries, such as Ayurveda, aromatherapy, yoga, chiropractic, and Christian Science. To delimit the scope of discussion, these forms of healing will not be dealt with here.

Diffused Medicine

In Hong Kong, a number of health beliefs and practices are diffused into and have thus become an integral part of family, religious, and community life. Medicine was very much a part of religion in primitive or traditional societies (Landy 1977). Nowadays, it is still closely tied to religion in many complex industrial societies. A poll conducted by TIME/CNN in 1996, for instance, estimated that more than 82 percent of the adults in America believe in the healing power of personal prayer, 77 percent believe that God can sometimes help cure a serious illness, and 77 percent trust the healing effects of praying for someone else (Wallis 1996). The United States is a highly industrialized and modernized society, but religion still plays an extensive role in its health care system. Hong Kong and many other contemporary societies are no exception. Despite the rapid growth of modern science and technology, Chinese people in Hong Kong continue to adhere to traditional religious concepts and practices in dealing with health and illness (Lee 1980). For instance, it is believed by some segments of the population that mental illness, especially hysterical disorder, is due to possession by evil spirits or malevolent foxes. The patient's family, therefore, have to pray in a Chinese temple and obtain amulets for getting rid of the demons (Yap 1967). Another example is the "injury by fright," which has been taken by some Hong Kong Chinese as a common problem among children, especially in the first one hundred days after birth. A popular preventive measure is to have children wear jade bangles, as it is believed that jade is harmony-inducing and can thus help settle fear. When a child is found to be suffering from fear, the help of a Taoist priest may be required (Topley 1970).

Anthropological studies have shown that there are spirit-mediums in both urban and rural areas of Hong Kong and that one of their major duties is to call on a spirit to cure illnesses (Potter 1974; Myers 1981). For instance, in a study of a Chinese spirit-medium temple in an urban district, John T. Myers (1981) found that the petitions were mostly for the curing of disease, followed by security in the future, solving of problems, and acquiring of wealth. It was also observed that the spirit-mediums often used herbs in combination with religious rituals.

There are now more than six hundred Buddhist or Taoist temples in Hong Kong, many of which are often crowded at festivals with worshippers, both young and old, coming from all walks of life. Many shops and residential units also have their own ancestral shrines and deity shelves. Curing of disease has been a very popular request by the worshippers at home or in temples. No less important, Hua-t'o, the patron god of medicine who was a famed surgeon in the third century AD, has been worshipped by numerous health care seekers in Hong Kong and other Chinese societies.

In early 2003, the outbreak of SARS posed a big threat to the entire community of Hong Kong. Many leaders and followers of major religions, including Buddhism, Taoism, Confucianism, Christianity, the Orthodox Church, Islam, Hinduism, Sikhism, and the Baha'i faith, responded by organizing prayer sessions not only in their own temples, monasteries, and churches, but also in public parks, shopping malls, city halls, and squares, praying for an end to the spread of the disease, for recovery of SARS patients, and for good health to the people. Most sessions held in public places were well attended by worshippers and well covered by the media (see, for instance, *South China Morning Post,* April 28 and May 9, 2003). Some functions were joined by the chief executive of the Hong Kong Special Administrative Region and by some high-ranking government officials such as the secretary for home affairs (see *South China Morning Post,* June 3, 2003).

I conducted a sample survey in 1972 and another survey in 1993 in the urban areas of Hong Kong (Lee 1980; Lee and Cheung 1995). I found that in the early 1970s, about 23 percent of the Chinese adult residents under study tended to believe that the worship of deities or ancestors could help cure diseases. In the early 1990s, the figure increased to 43 percent. It seems that the change in the social and economic environment is a key factor in the increasing proportion of people believing in the use of religious methods for dealing with health and illness. Over the last twenty some years, Hong Kong has become a highly competitive and increasingly stressful society. More and more people may be turning to religion for emotional support. As a result, religion has emerged as an increasingly important institution for daily life in Hong Kong (Lee 1985). This is also the case in Taiwan and many other parts of China (Li 1992).

The rise of Falun Gong in Chinese and other societies in recent years may serve as another example, illustrating the diffusion of medicine into religion. It was originally supposed to be a set of teachings plus some physical and spiritual exercises for improving health. Increasingly, however, it has turned into a religious movement. Li Hongzhi, the founder of Falun Dafa, is being treated by thousands of followers as a godlike master. To many of the followers, the benefit of practicing Falun Gong as a part of their daily life goes beyond the pursuit of health; it helps to acquire wisdom and brings enlightenment and meaningful living.

Besides its diffusion into religious institution, medicine has also been part of the family institution in Chinese society for many centuries. It is a common practice for Hong Kong families to keep at home a variety of Chinese and Western medicinal materials for possible self-medication. It has been estimated that about 80 percent of families follow this practice (Lee 1980). Also common is the use of food or diet manipulation for treating disease and promoting health, such as using ginger juice for treating a baby's sweating, taking fresh-water goby soup to stop bleeding after injury or surgery, eating snake's gall bladder to cure arthritis, and drinking black fungus and beef soup for treating hypertension (Anderson and Anderson 1975; Topley 1970; Koo 1984; Ho 1985). From a randomized telephone survey conducted from October 1989 to April 1990, Cindy Lam and her associates (1994) estimated that the overall prevalence of self-medication within a two-week period was 32.5 percent and that those who reported illness were more likely to use self-medication (65 percent) than those who did not report illness in the preceding two weeks (18 percent). Similarly, a territory-wide sample survey in 1993 showed that among the adult respondents who had a worrying illness in the past year, over 62 percent had actually practiced self-medication (Lee and Cheung 1995). Moreover, among these self-medicated respondents, 65 percent used Western drugs, 15 percent had Chinese remedies, and 20 percent used both types of medicine. In general, the less educated were more likely to use Chinese remedies than Western pharmaceuticals for self-medication. There was, however, no age or gender difference. It should be reported that self-care practices are also common in the Western world (DeFriece et al. 1989). A notable feature of the Chinese self-care behavior is the continual reliance on traditional Chinese remedies.

Preparing meals with Chinese medicinal materials has been a salient characteristic of the Hong Kong family tradition for many generations. The food selection and preparation are often based on the traditional Chinese concepts of maintaining yin-yang or cold-hot balance inside the body. This observation was confirmed by a sample survey in the early 1970s (Lee 1980). It was found that for daily meals, over 90 percent of the families would prepare such soups as wax gourd or leaf mustard soup during summer in order to prevent the excess of hot over cold elements in the body constitution. In the dry autumn season, nearly 95 percent of the families would make their daily meals to include watercress or sun-dried Chinese white cabbage soup for the purpose of purifying the liver and strengthening the lungs. When winter cames, about 65 percent of the families would take such foods as long-boiled chicken or mutton with certain Chinese herbs in order to combat the cold wind and to strengthen the body. Among families with members working as barbers, street cleaners or teachers, pig's blood is often cooked in daily meals presumably for helping to dissolve many kinds of poison and to clean dust and dirt from the lungs.

Among all kinds of home recipes, Hong Kong Chinese (especially the Cantonese) are most particular about soup. A salient criterion of being a good wife is to be able to prepare soups with the right kinds of Chinese medicinal materials at the right time for the purpose of preventing disease, treating illness, or enhancing health. After a day of hard work, many husbands would be happy to go home to enjoy the healthy and caring soup prepared by their wives. A territory-wide survey in recent years (Lee and Cheung 1995) indicated that over 90 percent of the families sometimes or often prepared tonic soups as part of their daily meals. There are also chain restaurants by the name of "Wife's Superb Soup" and "Mistress's Superb Soup" throughout the city. These various examples suggest that medicine is diffused into family institutions and it can be a source of family integration in Hong Kong.

Besides religion and the family, medicine has also been diffused into the media institution and community life. In Hong Kong, there are regular television and radio programs for health information and education, and nearly all the daily newspapers and popular magazines have special sections introducing medicinal materials and methods for preventing disease, treating illness, and promoting health. Owning to the public's rising concern with health and their increasing demand for health information, medicine appears to have become an inseparable part of the media institution. It has helped to increase the circulation of print media and broaden the audience of broadcast networks. It should be reported that media conglomerates in America and other Western countries have also recognized health and medical information as a highly sought after and profitable commodity (Goldstein 2000).

The diffusion of medicine into community life can be illustrated by the increasing variety of Chinese medicinal materials and Western biomedical drugs available for sale in regular supermarkets, countless Chinese herbal tea shops in commercial districts, and a growing number of physical fitness centers and programs in town, and by the rising popularity of medicinal soft drinks, wines, and liquor in the community (Lee 1980). In recent years, a number of restaurants have emerged specializing in Chinese medicinal cuisine. The diffusion of medicine into media, family, and community life can be taken as a form of medicalization (Gallagher 1995). It has made people's daily life increasingly inseparable from health beliefs and medical practices, and it has made health increasingly a supreme value in society. A community survey of more than four thousand adults aged 18 and over in 2001 confirmed that nowadays health is most valued by the Hong Kong Chinese (Wan 2003). Over half of the respondents (52.8 percent) regarded good health as the most important ingredient for personal happiness, and this was followed quite far behind by peace of mind (9.8 percent), having dutiful children (9.6 percent), money (9.4 percent), love, marriage, and family (6.5 percent), personal freedom (4.4 percent), career (4.4 percent), material enjoyment (0.7 percent), serving society (0.6 percent), and others (1.9 percent).

We have seen that in Hong Kong many health beliefs and practices are diffused into nonmedical social institutions and become an integral part of the latter. Let us now turn to institutional medicine.

Institutional Medicine

Both scientific biomedicine and traditional Chinese medicine are major forms of institutional medicine in Hong Kong. It should be explained that biomedicine was introduced from the West to the Chinese mainland in the mid-nineteenth century. To distinguish it from local medical traditions, Chinese people generally regard biomedicine as modern Western medicine and take their own indigenous medicine as traditional Chinese medicine (Croizier 1968).

Scientific biomedicine was introduced by British colonial officers and missionaries to Hong Kong in the late nineteenth century. Although traditional Chinese medicine was more widely utilized by the common people in the early history of Hong Kong, scientific biomedicine has established itself as the most dominant force in the health care market ever since the early twentieth century (Lee 2000). Biomedicine is typically an institutional medicine, for it has developed an independent body of theoretical knowledge and technical skills based on biological, chemical, and physical sciences. It also has formed specialized organizations with specially trained personnel for performing the various medical tasks. It has a well-developed self-regulatory system, and its wide range of services have been well accepted throughout the population. For many decades, biomedical doctors in Hong Kong have achieved a high degree of professionalism and are in close alliance with both political and academic elites for the control of health and illness in the community. The biomedical profession is indisputably a very powerful, highly prestigious, and well-paid group in Hong Kong (Lee 1982) as well as in other societies (Freidson 1970; Gallagher 1995).

In 2001, Hong Kong had about 10,412 registered biomedical doctors to serve its 6.7 million inhabitants, that is, roughly one doctor to 643 people. About 45 percent of these doctors were engaged in public service. There were 5.2 hospital beds per thousand population; nearly 90 percent of the beds were provided by the government, which charged relatively low fees. Apparently, the government has been playing a crucial role in the development of biomedical care services. It should be stressed that up until the eve of the resumption of sovereignty of Hong Kong by China in 1997, the British colonial administration supported only biomedical care. All the government-funded hospitals and clinics and all the University medical schools are exclusively engaged in biomedicine. This government policy, however, has not driven out traditional Chinese medicine in Hong Kong. Chinese remedies are still widely used by the local population (Lee 2000).

Like scientific biomedicine, traditional Chinese medicine is a form of institutional medicine. It is based on Chinese cosmological ideologies, of which the primary ones are the balance between yin (dark, feminine) and yang (bright, masculine) forces of the universe, the interplay among five elements (metal, wood, water, fire, and earth), and the close interdependence between the macrocosm and the microcosm. Chinese medicine is not scientific in the strict sense, but its formulation is based on naturalistic and rationalistic principles. It has an abstract theoretical framework, an elaborate system of diagnosis, and a detailed classification of diseases and medicaments. This body of knowledge was well documented by scholars and was refined and expanded through empirical observations for several thousand years (Croizier 1968).

An organizational framework for education and practice of Chinese medicine has been developed over many centuries. As Rance P. L. Lee (1982) has shown in his historical-comparative analysis of mainland China, Hong Kong, and Taiwan, a commonly shared ethic among practitioners of Chinese medicine is to serve people without self-interest. Moreover, to become a practitioner, one has to spend several years studying the literature and acquiring clinical experience. The collective orientation and the prolonged specialized training have thus been two of the core characteristics of the profession of Chinese medicine.

An official survey estimated that as of January 1, 1995, there were 6,890 practitioners of Chinese medicine in Hong Kong (*Report of the Preparatory Committee on Chinese Medicine,* March 1999). About 60 percent of these practitioners were engaged in general practice, 20 percent in bone-setting, and less than 10 percent in acupuncture. The rest included specialists in Qigong, massage, and dermatology. All of them were in private practice, and they had organized more than ten professional associations. There were sixteen schools offering a total of fifty-five courses for training practitioners of Chinese medicine, and a total of eleven courses for training dispensers of Chinese medicinal materials. However, the professional associations were loosely organized. There was no licensing or registration system, and there was no uniform standard of training or practice. For more than one and a half centuries, the British colonial administration was tolerant but not supportive of Chinese medicine. Without political and legal support, Chinese medicine could hardly be as institutionalized or uniformly controlled as biomedicine. Its social-economic status in the community was significantly lower than that of biomedicine. It was less powerful, less prestigious, and less resourceful than its counterpart (Lee 1982). Chinese medicine practitioners and traders repeatedly made efforts to gain official recognition during the colonial period, but they met with little success (Ko 2002).

The lack of government support has resulted in Chinese medical care services being less accessible to the public, since people have to pay a higher fee, on the one hand, and are less certain of the quality of care, on the other. A territory-wide sample survey of Chinese adults in 1993 found that in the year preceding the survey 84 percent had seen biomedical doctors while only 24 percent had visited practitioners of Chinese medicine, 11 percent had consulted bone-setters, and as few as 2 percent had seen acupuncturists (Lee and Cheung 1995). Although people were much more likely to use biomedicine than Chinese medicine, a significant number of them tended to follow a "dual model of health care." From the above survey, nearly six out of ten respondents (59 percent) agreed that both types of medical services should be used simultaneously for dealing with health and illness. Recently, the Institute of Asia-Pacific Studies of the Chinese University of Hong Kong formed a research team, of which I was a member, to study the social response to the SARS crisis in Hong Kong in early 2003. A random sample of 1,018 residents aged 18 and above were telephone interviewed from May 27 to May 30, 2003. It was found that when asked what was the best way to treat SARS patients, 64.9 percent went for combining both Western biomedicine and Chinese medicine, 14.1 percent for Western biomedicine only, 1.8 percent for Chinese medicine only, and 19.2 percent had no opinion.

Indeed, it has been a common practice for Chinese patients to resort to traditional Chinese medicine before seeking scientific biomedicine, especially when they are suffering from chronic or terminal illnesses, such as cancers, heart diseases, diabetes, back pain, and arthritis (Lee 1980; Wong, Wong, and Donnan 1993). This pattern of health behavior exists not only in Hong Kong but also in other Chinese and Asian societies (Kleinman et al. 1975; Leslie 1976; Lee 1982). The dual model of medical care has also become increasingly popular in the United States, Great Britain, and other Western nations (Fisher and Ward 1994; Fulder 1996; Weiss and Lonnquist 1997; Eisenberg et al. 1998; Cant and Sharma 1999; Goldstein 2000). More and more people in the West, particularly those who are chronically ill or at risk for such conditions, tend to use both biomedicine and some forms of complementary and alternative medicine, such as chiropractic, homeopathy, acupuncture, herbalism, and spiritual healing, for treating disease or enhancing health.

Both biomedicine and Chinese medicine are institutional forms of medicine. They have been coexisting in Hong Kong for one and a half centuries. Because of the political and academic support, biomedicine has come to be highly institutionalized and has gained a great deal of power and autonomy (Lee 1982, 2000). It has been dominating the health care market since the early twentieth century. However, political changes took place in the mid-1990s, providing opportunities for the resurgence of Chinese medicine. In the few years before China's 1997 recovery of the sovereignty of Hong Kong, both the general public and social and political elites appeared to be increasingly nationalistic and also increasingly conscious of their Chinese cultural heritage. Many of them worked closely with and lent support to the Chinese medicine practitioners and traders in their collective movements for gaining official recognition and subvention (for details, see Ko 2002). The Chinese government on the mainland got the message while the British colonial administration in Hong Kong was under mounting pressure.

A big success of the Chinese medicine movement was the stipulation of Chinese medicine in the Basic Law governing Hong Kong after reunification with China in 1997. Article 138 of the Basic Law stipulates: "The Government of the Hong Kong Special Administrative Region shall, on its own, formulate polices to develop Western and traditional Chinese medicine and to improve medical and health services. Community organizations and individuals may provide various medical and health services in accordance with law." The article provides a constitutional basis for the development of Chinese medicine in Hong Kong. Soon after the political transition in 1997, the new government of the Hong Kong Special Administrative Region (HKSAR) ventured to establish a statutory system regulating the practice of Chinese medicine and the use, manufacturing, and trading of Chinese medicines in order to ensure the professional standard of health care by Chinese medicine (see *Report of the Preparatory Committee on Chinese Medicine*, 1997, 1999). In 1998, the government laboratory added a Chinese medicine section, while the department of health set up a Chinese medicine division.

A significant event shortly after the political transition was the call by the new political leadership for developing Chinese medicine not only for the purpose of protecting people's health but also for the sake of sustaining Hong Kong's economic growth in the global context. In his policy addresses in both 1997 and 1998, the chief executive of the Hong Kong Special Administrative Region Government forcefully and repeatedly asserted that the city should be made a world center for research and development of Chinese medicine. In his first policy speech in 1997, the chief executive said he strongly believed that Hong Kong has the potential to develop over time into an international center for the manufacture and trading for Chinese medicine; for research, information, and training in the use of Chinese medicine; and for the promotion of this approach to medical care. In his second policy address in 1998, the chief executive added that Chinese medicine was an industry that, through the application of innovation and technology, could enhance Hong Kong's economic growth and give Hong Kong a competitive edge on a global scale.

The chief executive's policy speeches in two consecutive years heated up a great deal of discussion and debate in the community, resulting in a number of changes conducive to the advancement of Chinese medicine in Hong Kong (see Ko 2002). The public and business circles generally shared the government's view that the development of the Chinese medicine industry would substantially strengthen the city's health care system and, no less important, it would enhance the city's economic competitiveness in this age of globalization. Chinese medicine was for the first time publicly portrayed not only as a health care issue but also as an economic issue. It appears that the commodification of Chinese medicines can provide ample business opportunities for Hong Kong people in the global health care market. To follow up the call of the chief executive, the trade and industry department announced in 1999 a ten-year plan for the development of a Chinese medicine–based industry and, meanwhile, established the innovation and technology commission to support projects related to research and development of Chinese medicine. In 2001, the government helped to establish the Institute of Chinese Medicine to promote the industry by strengthening and coordinating various efforts—education, scientific research, manufacturing, and quality control—for the development of Chinese medicine in Hong Kong (Tse 2001). The institute was funded substantially by the Hong Kong Jockey Club.

The government's initiatives succeeded in attracting more local and overseas investments in the Chinese medicine industry, though none as sizable and significant as expected. According to the *Hong Kong Monthly Digest of Statistics* (April 2003), the number of establishments manufacturing Chinese medicine in 2001 was 179, an increase of 11.2 percent compared with 2000. And the total number of persons engaged in this industry was 1,567, an increase of 4.2 percent compared with 2000. Regarding the distribution of Chinese medicines, the value of gross outputs in 2001 was about US$25.6 million in the wholesale industry, US$166.7 million in the retail industry, and US$102.6 million in the import-export industry. When compared with 2000, these figures represent an increase of 2.7 percent in wholesale, an increase of 1.4 percent in retail, and a decrease of 13.8 percent in import-export.

A major landmark in Hong Kong's Chinese medicine movement was the passing of the Chinese medicine ordinance by the legislative council in July 1999, putting the development of Chinese medicine on firm legal footing. The Chinese Medicine Council of Hong Kong was then established in September 1999, serving as a statutory body for implementing regulatory measures for Chinese medicine practitioners, manufacturers, and traders. The council takes up the major tasks of making transitional registration arrangements for the numerous Chinese medicine practitioners in Hong Kong, preparing a universal registration examination to ensure public credibility, and compiling the code of practice for disciplinary action (Tse 2001).

At the end of 2000, the Chinese Medicine Council of Hong Kong received a total of 8,051 applications for registration as Chinese medicine practitioners. After vetting by the council's Chinese Medicine Practitioners Board and Registration Committee, a total of 7,707 applicants were allowed to practice as "listed" practitioners of Chinese medicine. This was taken as a transitional arrangement. Listed practitioners may become registered practitioners through direct registration, registration assessment or licensing examination. In November 2002, the council announced that a total of 2,384 listed practitioners were permitted to directly become the first batch of registered Chinese medicine practitioners in Hong Kong. These practitioners were found to have been practicing Chinese medicine in Hong Kong for a continuous period of (1) not less than fifteen years, or (2) not less than ten years and had obtained a qualification acceptable to the council. Other listed practitioners would have to go through registration assessment or licensing examination in the months to come (for details, see *Hong Kong Monthly Digest of Statistics,* April 2003). Plans are also being made to enforce in phases the licensing system for Chinese medicine traders and the registration system for proprietary Chinese medicines.

With the support of the government, three local universities (Hong Kong Baptist University, Chinese University of Hong Kong, and University of Hong Kong) have in recent years introduced bachelor's, master's, and doctoral degree program in Chinese medicine and have launched a number of scientific studies and international collaboration projects on Chinese medicines. There have been numerous conferences, workshops, and exhibitions on Chinese medicine both inside and outside academic circles. The government plans to start providing Chinese medicine outpatient clinics in 2003 and, in due course, to set up public hospitals in Chinese medicine. Its policy is to gradually incorporate Chinese medicine into the official system of health care. The government has claimed that all the eighteen districts of Hong Kong will be provided with Chinese medicine clinics by 2005, but it is not clear when the government will fulfill its promise of establishing Chinese medicine hospitals.

Nowadays, biomedicine remains the dominant form of medical care in Hong Kong, but Chinese medicine is resurging (Lee 2000; Ko 2002). The revival of Chinese medicine, however, has taken on a new institutional form. As shown by the above-reported changes during the political transition period, Chinese medicine in Hong Kong increasingly follows standard, objective, and scientific procedures in education and research, while its social organization follows rationalistic, self-regulatory principles. It also strives to strengthen alliances with the government, enterprises, and universities. In effect, what the Chinese medicine movement has done is to model itself after biomedicine in both technical content of work and social organization. Its work organizations and its relationships with political, economic, and academic sectors of the society are being reinstitutionalized for the sake of upgrading its public legitimacy vis-à-vis biomedicine and thus expanding its share in the health care market.

Community surveys in recent years have generally indicated an upward trend in the local population's use of Chinese medical care. The territory-wide household surveys conducted by the government's census and statistics department (1983, 1992, 1996, 2000, 2002) estimated that of those persons who had consulted medical practitioners during the fourteen days before enumeration, 6.7 percent consulted practitioners of Chinese medicine (including general practitioners, acupuncturists, and bone-setters) in 1989, 6.3 percent in 1992, and 7.5 percent in 1996. After China's recovery of the sovereignty of Hong Kong in 1997, the utilization rate of Chinese medicine practitioners increased considerably; it was 19.9 percent in 1999 and 16.9 percent in 2001. Nevertheless, these figures imply that in all these years, there were consistently many more people resorting to biomedical doctors—93.3 percent in 1989, 93.7 percent in 1992, 92.5 percent in 1996, 86.5 percent in 1999, and 89 percent in 2001—than to Chinese medicine practitioners.

Medical Pluralism and Institutional Reform

Since the mid-nineteenth century, biomedicine emerged as the dominant form of medical care initially in the West and then in the East. It is often referred to as "modern," "scientific," "Western," "conventional," "orthodox," and "cosmopolitan" medicine. All these terms signify its emphasis on standard procedures and scientific research, its origin in the West, its general acceptance by the public, its recognition by state power, and its widespread existence in many parts of the world. It cannot be overstated that the request for science-based modernity has been an important force in the advancement of biomedicine both in the West and the East (Croizier 1970; Leslie 1976; Lee 1982). Biomedical transcendence has made other forms of health care often referred to as "traditional," "complementary," "alternative," "unconventional," "unorthodox," "folk," or "local" medicine. Indeed, biomedicine has come to be so powerful and so pervasive in contemporary society that, as Adele Clarke and her associates (2003) have suggested, a historical shift from medicalization to biomedicalization has emerged. While medicalization refers to an emergent force that extends the medical jurisdiction and magnifies the importance of biomedical care for human welfare (Gallagher 1995), the concept of biomedicalization highlights the increasingly complex, multisited, and multidimensional processes of medicalization, both extended and reconstituted through the new social forms and practices of a highly technoscientific biomedicine. As Clark and her associates (2003) have explained, such technoscientific innovations as molecular biology, biotechnologies, genomization, transplant medicine, and new medical technologies, coupled with the advancement of computer and information technologies, have led to a sizable growth and a from-the-inside-out reorganization of the biomedical service complex in the West. No less important, Western biomedicine has become a distinctive sociocultural world, ubiquitously webbed throughout mass culture. It has become a potent lens through which people culturally interpret, understand, and seek to transform bodies and lives.

Despite biomedical transcendence, recent decades have seen the resurgence of other forms of medical care, such as Chinese medicine, Ayurveda, chiropractic, and homeopathy. These other forms of health care have come to be increasingly recognized by the government, developed by academia, and utilized by different segments of the population, including men and women and people in all age categories and socioeconomic groups (Leslie 1980; Fisher and Ward 1994; Goldstein 2000). They exist side by side with biomedicine, making medical pluralism a normal state of affairs in many contemporary societies. The question is, Why and how do these other forms of healing resurge in the modern era that is dominated by biomedicine?

There are a multitude of reasons for the growing acceptance of complementary and alternative medicine both in the West (Weiss and Lonnquist 1997; Cant and Sharma 1999; Goldstein 2000) and in the East (Kleinman et al. 1975; Leslie 1976; Lee 2000). I have highlighted the importance of political opportunity and globalization. Let me recapitulate some of the arguments.

The British colonial administration of Hong Kong had long been cynical of Chinese medicine. The reclaiming of the sovereignty of Hong Kong by China in 1997 provided a new political context conducive to the rise of nationalism and the emergence of cultural consciousness, thus leading to the success of the Chinese medicine movement in Hong Kong (Chiu, Ko, and Lee 2005). The policy and related institutional changes in support of Chinese medicine, however, are not entirely a result of political change. The city's role in the global economy is also an important matter under consideration. In recent years, political leaders, economic elites, and academic researchers have come to recognize the growing demands in the global market for Chinese health foods and medicinal materials. It is generally believed that the commodification of Chinese medicine can make a significant contribution to Hong Kong's economic growth in the global context.

In this connection, it should be explained that globalization over the last two centuries has led to the spread of scientific biomedicine from the West to many other parts of the world. In recent decades, it has also led to the rapid diffusion of alternative forms of medical care, through population movements and electronic media, from non-Western societies to the Western world. In the United States, for example, there are alternative medicines that originated in the West, such as osteopathy, chiropractic, homeopathy, and Christian Science, but there are also other types of alternative healing, such as acupuncture, Chinese herbal medicine, Ayurveda, and yoga therapy, that originated outside the Western world and are gaining increasing popularity (Goldstein 2000). In view of the globalization of Chinese medicine and the resulting growth in demand for Chinese-style health care, Hong Kong's policy makers decided to make the city become a world center for research and development of health foods and pharmaceuticals based on traditional Chinese remedies. It is envisaged that the commodification of Chinese medicine is a big business; it could greatly enhance the city's economic competitiveness in the global economy. The government has declared a policy to make Hong Kong an international center of Chinese medicine. Recent years have seen some growth in the acceptability, manufacturing, and distribution of Chinese medicines. Universities have also introduced training programs and established research centers of Chinese medicine.

As the globalization process is bound to progress in the twentieth century, the various forms of alternative medicine will most likely continue to spread from one place to another, and many of them will also seek opportunities for revival. Decision makers and administrators should be aware of this worldwide trend, that is, the globalization of alternative medicine and its revival. The planning of health care services in society should take into consideration the organization and development of both scientific biomedicine and the various forms of alternative healing. Medical pluralism as a normal state of affairs in this age of globalization cannot and should not be ignored.

The story of the Chinese medicine movement in Hong Kong indicates that political changes and forces of globalization are important factors conducive to the success of an alternative medicine in the struggle for power and autonomy. The story also shows that another key factor in the resurgence of alternative medicine is institutional transformation: dumping the old institutional form and moving toward a new form that, in effect, models itself after the dominant biomedicine in its technical content and social organization of work.

However, the various forms of alternative medicine in society do not have an equal capability for such an institutional transformation. Those with a long-standing institutional heritage should be more capable of mobilizing political and economic resources for institutional transformation in the struggle for power and social legitimacy. Let me explain.

I have ventured to propose a conceptual scheme to classify the different forms of healing in society in terms of diffused medicine and institutional medicine. This classification is based on the late Professor C. K. Yang's typology of diffused and institutional religions. Diffused medicine (such as home remedies or magical-religious healing) does not have independent existence; it is built into one or more nonmedical social institutions, such as the family, religion, mass media, and community life. The health care patterns in Hong Kong suggest that the prevalence and strength of diffused medicine are dependent upon the functioning of the nonmedical social institutions of which it is a part. The rise of religion in recent decades, for instance, has increased the popularity of magical-religious remedies in Hong Kong and elsewhere. On the other hand, the functioning of diffused medicine may help to sustain the nonmedical social institutions of which it is a part. Food therapy, for instance, has been an integrating force in many Chinese families. The preparation of daily meals in accordance with Chinese medical concepts has been a long-standing practice of the Chinese to show their concern about and their care for family members. As mentioned in the beginning of this chapter, the late Professor Yang made a similar observation about the role of diffused religion in Chinese society.

In this connection, I should point out that the selection and preparation of food by Chinese families for dealing with health and illness indicate the close relationship of diffused medicine with institutional medicine. These two types of medicine are not independent of each other. Several studies (Topley 1970; Anderson and Anderson 1975; Koo 1984) have shown that in Hong Kong the food prescriptions and proscriptions are based on the traditional Chinese medical concepts of cold and hot or yin and yang, and are also derived from some classical medicinal literature such as the *General Compendium of Materia Medica (Pen-ts'ao Kang-mu).* It should be reported that C. K. Yang (1961) made a similar observation about the relationship between diffused and institutional religions. He argued that in many situations institutional and diffused religions are interdependent. Diffused religion, for instance, relied on institutional religion for the development of mythical or theological concepts, for the device of symbols and rituals, and for services of trained personnel (the priests).

Diffused medicine may be widely utilized by the population. It could be functionally strong, but its being part and parcel of a nonmedical social institution means that structurally it is unlikely to develop a collective struggle for power and autonomy. It does not have independent theories and skills, nor does it have a set of specially trained personnel and special organizations for launching collective actions. Its fate depends on the nonmedical institution of which it is a part, not on its independent existence.

Unlike diffused medicine, institutional medicine is separable from other social institutions. It has an independent body of theories, skills, and organizations of personnel specifically for dealing with health and illness in society. The interaction between scientific biomedicine and traditional Chinese medicine in Hong Kong shows that the different forms of institutional medicine tend to compete and conflict with each other in acquiring resources from society, including power, prestige, and wealth. However, as they differ in patterns of institutionalization (Powell and DiMaggio 1991), they also differ in dominance over the health market. The revival of a subordinate institutional medicine (such as Chinese medicine) may take reinstitutionalization as a major strategy of development, trying to model itself after the dominant institutional medicine (such as scientific biomedicine) in terms of both technical contents and organizational forms. The adoption of scientific research and test procedures, the standardization of education and training, the alliance with the state, enterprises, and academics, the rise of professionalism, and the development of a statutory system for self-regulation are some of the central features of the reinstitutionalization of Chinese medicine in Hong Kong. It is these processes that would have allowed Chinese medicine to gain greater acceptance by the general public, to be incorporated into the official system of health care delivery, and to make a greater contribution to the city's social and economic development. It is noted that in other countries, an increasing number of alternative forms of healing, such as Ayurvedic medicine in South Asia, chiropractic in North America, and ethnomedicine in Africa, have also undertaken a similar course of change (Leslie 1976; Last and Chavunduka 1986; Good 1987; Cant and Sharma 1999; Goldstein 2000). A global phenomenon in the twenty-first century appears to be the reinstitutionalization of alternative medicine, that is, moving from its old institutional patterns to a new institutional form organized around rules and principles of the dominant biomedicine.

Part III

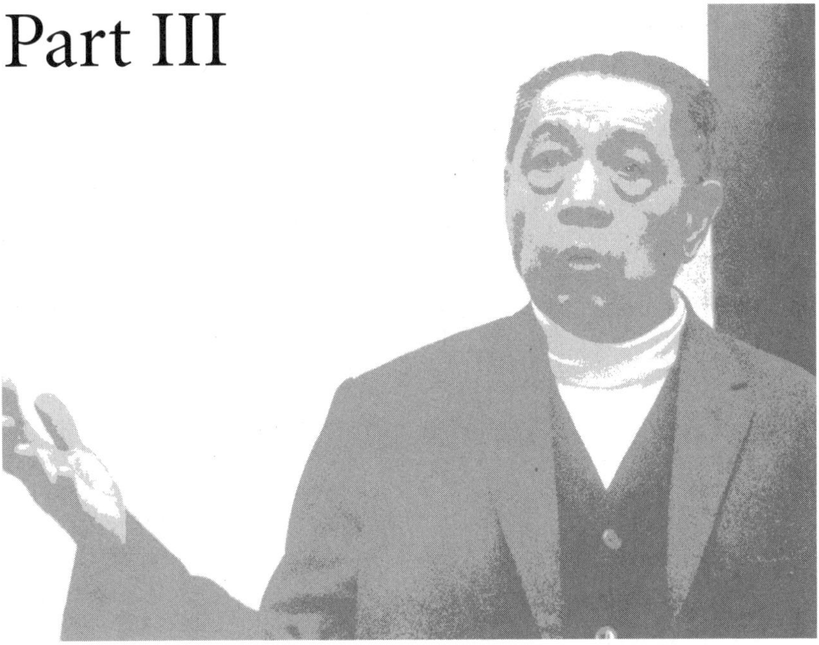

FAMILY AND COMMUNITY

11

DEBORAH S. DAVIS

When a House Becomes His Home

In December 1978, twenty years after Mao's Great Leap Forward, Deng Xiaoping took the first steps to dismantle the people's communes and recommodify property relations throughout China. In the first decade of reform, privatization of urban real estate was not a major objective, and even after twenty years of market reform, only a third of urban homes were owner occupied.[1] Nevertheless, the nationwide experiments to sell existing housing stock to sitting tenants begun in the mid-1980s, and the subsequent expansion of a private housing industry to stimulate the economy and attract foreign investment had a profound impact on contemporary urban society.[2]

Under Mao, private ownership had been stigmatized as antisocialist. In the final years of Deng's leadership, the central government would look to private real estate development as an engine of economic growth, and among the general population homeownership would come to signify social and financial success (Fraser 2000). In this environment, whether or not a family purchased their home, the new legitimacy of individual property rights granted all urban residents permission to dream of homeownership and to view their homes as a private space where they could display family and individual prestige.

Previously, when historians of Western societies analyzed the role of the home during eras of rapid commercialization, they observed a marked "feminization" of domestic space as urban men ceded the home to wives and concentrated their own energies on the expanded opportunities for sociability in the public sphere of clubs and politics. Leora Auslander even argues that as France built the republic in the second half of the nineteenth century there was an explicit dichotomy where "bourgeois men were [encouraged] to represent the family through the vote, and women to represent the family in their bodies and their homes" (Auslander 1996). In the United States Thorsten Veblen also saw the home as the quintessential location where wives reworked the economic success of their husbands into a heightened social prestige for all family members. Randall Collins described a similar feminization of domestic property among upper middle-class American men after World War II (Collins 1991).

Yet it is not obvious that domestic space must be primarily the domain of women. In fact, the feminization observed in Europe and the United States is more likely the exception than the rule. Throughout the world, wives' claims to property are generally weaker than those of husbands. Also of note is the larger political environment in which citizens or subjects nurture unofficial sociability and associational life. In societies with longer traditions of democratic governments there is less control and censorship over public sociability and therefore less need for men to use the privacy of the home to socialize or nurture nonofficial social ties. By contrast in societies where leaders routinely censored public sociability, the home became a primary site for unofficial male associational life, and females were often restricted to certain locations within their own homes and denied control over the use or disposal of domestic property.[3]

In the case of imperial and even republican China, wives were identified as *neiren* (the person within), and to those unfamiliar with the history of China this designation may suggest that the Chinese home was traditionally a female domain while space outside the home was the domain of men. But as anyone familiar with Chinese history can attest, the *nei-wai* distinction, rather than validating female claims over domestic property or space, indicated the subordinate and excluded position of married women. Thus, for example, when Susan Mann wrote about the Jiangnan elite in "China's Long 18th Century" she not only rejected the equation of *nei* as female space and *wai* as male space, but concluded that the women's chambers *(guige)* were actually "willed by men to be a refuge for men" (Mann 1997, 75).

My own earlier work on interior space and urban family life in Shanghai during the 1980s, however, found a clear departure from pre-Communist patterns as described by Mann for Ming-Qing China or by C. K. Yang for the Republican era. When I interviewed one hundred women living in one residential estate north of Suzhou Creek in 1987 it appeared that wives' claims were equal to, or even greater than, those of their husbands or coresident married sons (Davis 1989). Because the neighborhood where I interviewed had been constructed with a uniform architecture, all flats had two rooms; and because my sample required that each household have at least one woman born between 1925 and 1935, the families were all at a stage in the life course when adult children were launching careers and marrying. Among the interviewees the most typical household was a patrilocal home with a middle-aged couple, one married son, his wife, and one grandchild.[4] Typically, the husband's employer had arranged the rental, and the apartment was registered in the man's name. However, because the collectivization of urban real estate had transformed housing into a welfare benefit, husbands legally had had no greater claims of ownership than did their wives, and sons had as weak inheritance rights as the daughters to the parental home. Although predominantly patrilocal in structure, for these families tenancy claims did not privilege men. Rather, the situation followed the logic of C. K. Yang when he noted "that the weight of private property rights as a factor in (determining) the status of women . . . [has been] drastically reduced by the socialization of the Chinese economy" (Yang 1959, 143).

In fact, when I looked closely at the way interior space was decorated and asked respondents about daily routines, I discovered a gender "tilt" in accord with the Western European experience of feminization of domestic space. Because each room had multiple functions—bedroom, living room, dining room, study, and workspace—the apartments were crowded with things and furnished in the most utilitarian fashion. The possessions of women in their roles as housekeepers and mothers—sewing baskets, candy dishes, utensils for cleaning and cooking—filled the cabinets and covered the tables. Walls were painted a dull green, florescent strips supplied the lighting, and kitchens were nothing more than a table with a gas burner vented to the alley. Typically, decorations were limited to a wall clock, a calendar, and family photos displayed under a glass tabletop. Awards from the workplace, souvenirs of business trips, chess sets, or artifacts of the masculine "scholars studio," such as calligraphy brushes, ink stones, or ceramic bowls, were generally invisible. Thus I hypothesized that collectivization of domestic property and transformation of housing into a welfare benefit had feminized or more specifically "maternalized" urban domestic space. Chinese urban homes of the 1980s were best described as "my mother's house" rather than "my father's house" (Davis 1989, 88). Or to use the vocabulary of Mihaly Csikszentmihalyi and Eugene Rochberg-Halton, Shanghai men had apparently "cooled out their relationship to the home" (Csikszentmihalyi and Rochberg-Halton 1981, 129).

Young and middle-aged Shanghainese whom I met that summer also seemed to emphasize the female character of city residences and routinely referred to their parents' homes, whether their fathers were alive or not, as their "mother's house" *(wo muqin de jia).* Subsequently, male friends from Shanghai have told me they would probably more often refer to their natal home as *wo laojia,* and colleagues from northern China have reported that they never used nor heard other men use *wo muqin de jia,* thereby suggesting that feminization of domestic space may be restricted to southern China, or even to Shanghai in particular.[5] Historian of Shanghai Hanchao Lu has also questioned my interpretation, but in a different way. Rather than denying that men might also call their parents home "my mother's house," Lu notes that because in pre-Communist years women used mother's house *(niangjia)* not father's house to describe their natal home, it is not obvious that the use of *wo muqin de jia* is anything more than a modern translation of a traditional phrase. Therefore, what is most intriguing to Lu about my respondents' language in 1987 is not a break from the past but a revealing continuity (pers. comm., January 31, 2000). Let me now turn to a discussion of materials I have gathered on the recommercialization of Shanghai real estate and the growth of homeownership in the late 1990s to explore the possibility that reprivatization of homeownership has favored male over female claims to domestic space and property.

Marketing the Dream of Homeownership

On June 4, 1999, a twenty-foot high balloon soared above the reflecting pool of the Shanghai Exhibition Center to announce the opening of the seventh Shanghai Real Estate Exhibition. Inside, 189 development companies had rented space to showcase their commercial offerings. According to the evening newspaper of that day the apartments featured at the exhibition represented 60 percent of all available properties in greater Shanghai,[6] and, indeed, vendors featured a wide selection of apartments and villas in all districts of the city and surrounding counties.

In 1995, I had attended an auto show at the same venue. Admission was by ticket only, and the prices of the gleaming Porches, Mercedes, and BMWs made individual purchase impossible. My colleague's husband, who was the vice head of a then profitable instrument factory, was actually in the market for a second-hand motorcycle. After we left the exhibit we posed in front of the reflecting pool to commemorate our outing and then pushed our way back to the street where scalpers hawked tickets and the crowd spilled into the street blocking traffic.

In 1999, anyone could enter the exhibition hall, and the sponsors were actually promoting a lottery to boost attendance. Inside the main entrance employees of two local banks distributed application materials for individual loans for home purchase, home renovation, or real estate investment. I arrived at 10 AM, one hour after the doors had opened, and already the long corridors were packed. That summer there was a glut of unsold space. Developers therefore courted customers, and the socialist economy of shortage, where would-be tenants were "supplicants of the state" (Davis 1993), seemed a distant memory. Of course, it was impossible to gauge the actual intentions or financial resources of the milling crowds. Were they simply gawking at inaccessible luxury in the same way we had gazed at the sports cars? Or were they serious buyers? Certainly, the brochures from the banks documented practical steps for securing ownership. Equally incontrovertible was the professionalism of the exhibitors. They may have been marketing a dream, but these purveyors of a dream aggressively touted their good prices and methodically pushed the visitor-voyeurs to sign up for an afternoon van tour.

When historian David Fraser compared Shanghai housing advertisements in 1994 to those in 1997, he found that over these three years developers increasingly sought customers through promises of exclusive lifestyle rather than simply the prospect of ownership. In Fraser's words, the ideal of the home as a private "oasis [had] moved into the foreground" (Fraser 2000). In 1999, the advertisers continued to market luxury and exclusivity, but property values and affordability shared the foreground.

In their brochures and videos the developers advertising at the June 4th exhibition addressed an ungendered but upwardly mobile customer.[7] On the Friday morning when I visited, males slightly outnumbered females, but in the illustrated material from the Bank of Industry and Commerce the prototypical customer was more often a woman than a man. Generally the video clips of newly completed interiors excluded any resident, and illustrations of the exteriors featured anonymous pedestrians of both sexes. To the extent that they had a targeted buyer, it appeared that marketers wanted men and women of all ages to imagine themselves as potential owners.

Promotional materials from two of the most expensive complexes, however, did have explicitly gendered messages. In the brochure for Joffre Gardens *(Dongfang Bali)* under construction in the heart of the old French Settlement, the featured customer was a glamorous man in his thirties who carried a small boy on his shoulders as he strolled through a field of flowers. The large caption described him as "the new age man who loves his family/home" *(xinshidai aijia de nanren),* and then in the subsequent, smaller type the prospective customer reads that this "new age man" was "the good father who is the first to send his child off to school, the good leader who is the first to arrive in the office, and the good husband who is the first to return home" *(diyige songhaizi de hao baba, diyige dao gongsi de hao lingdao, diyige huijia de haojiangfu).* In none of the other flyers for upscale developments was there a comparable profile of an ideal female customer. However, Kathleen Erwin, who has analyzed the speech in Shanghai radio shows (Erwin 2000), has asked me whether the target here is an affluent woman for whom the new age man is the ideal husband or a financially successful man eager to identify himself as the good leader (pers. comm., February 10, 2000). In one housing advertisement that Fraser found, would-be buyers are enticed to "buy a home and become a boss!"[8] I would suggest that the agents for Joffre Gardens want to entice both men and women to buy a flat through identification with success, but not incidentally the graphic image of the success of the late 1990s is a handsome, young businessman.

Advertisements for Hua'an apartments in the fashionable Jingan District in the old International Settlement made the most explicit pitch to a male buyer, designating a male as the targeted customer and the home as the female object. In this advertisement—which proclaimed in English "I love Jingan"—there were no male persona, but the Chinese text explicitly described the housing complex as the beloved female whom the buyer loves for her incomparable taste. Also of note, the word for taste is *weidao,* which connotes something tasty to eat, rather than *pinwei,* which would denote refinement.[9] Not surprisingly I found no example in these promotional brochures where a home was presented as the male object of female desire.

Overall, however, the exhibitors relied on a conjugal vocabulary that spoke simultaneously to husbands and wives. And in the materials from the Shanghai branch of the Bank of Industry and Commerce the message was explicit. Above the bank's logo was a photo of a heavy golden door swinging open to a vista of three modern apartment towers. Printed over the photo was a list of eight types of personal loans, and below the photo the title "A Compass to Mortgage Loans for Individual Purchase of a Home" *(geren goufang anjie daikuan)*. To the left of the photo, the English phrase "Our Home" ran the entire length of the pamphlet. Here the bank represented the residential property of the 1990s not only as privatized and commodified but also as overtly centered around a couple strategizing to create a home of their own.

A Survey of the Conjugal Home

A conjugal profile also emerged during home interviews conducted in Shanghai in December 1998 as part of a project I designed with Yanjie Bian and Shaoguang Wang on urban consumption patterns. As part of this project our team interviewed one hundred Shanghai couples about their current household situation and their plans for the near future.[10] Although each member of the couple was interviewed separately, husbands and wives rarely disagreed about issues related to their home. For example, when asked about the necessity of homeownership, in only five cases did one spouse say homeownership was essential while the other said it was not.[11] They also gave almost identical answers when asked about the value of the home, its size, and the amount they had spent refurbishing. These high levels of agreement about the need for homeownership and the financial details of their current home confirmed the general impression that homes of the 1990s were a shared marital property. Equally noteworthy, when asked to identify the names of all family members listed on a rental agreement, mortgage, or deed, less than 10 percent of couples listed a parent or in-law as a co-owner or householder.[12] In terms of property claims, these were homes of married men and women, not coresident sons or daughters or members of an extended family.

However, joint ownership or tenancy was exceptional, and men were by far the most likely to be the sole name on the deed or rental agreement.[13] But would it be accurate to conclude that "my mother's house" *(wo muqin de jia)* of the 1980s had become "my husband's home" *(wo zhangfu de jia)*? During the interviews and casual conversations, I never heard this phrase. Rather like the bank brochure, the more commonly used phrases were "our home" *(women de jia)* and "my home" *(wo de jia)*. Nevertheless, discussions about home renovation among our December 1998 survey respondents did suggest a tendency for the house to become *his* home when real estate property became the focus of major investment.

Furnishing and Renovating the Conjugal Home

During the first decade of economic reform, urban families enthusiastically spent their savings on their first color television, refrigerator, and washing machine.[14] Some families repainted walls, installed tile flooring, or bought a new suite of bedroom furniture, but the main improvements were consumer durables that eased the drudgery of housework and retained their financial value. During my 1987 visits, it also seemed that pre-reform attitudes about appropriate display—as much as concerns about economizing—curbed expenditures and kept decorative improvements modest. Many people seemed to worry that neighbors would be critical, even hostile, if they discovered a family other than a recently married couple spending lavishly to make a home more comfortable than others in their community. Wall paper and curtains were exceptional and wooden floors so extravagant—perhaps even decadent—that I remember one respondent going out of her way to hide the wooden blocks her son was using to lay a parquet floor to keep them from her neighbor's view. Over coffee one night with a university teacher who had just recently returned as a legal tenant to her family's house, the three guests marveled at the small English creamer, the only remaining piece of what had been a complete set of China from her marriage in 1956.

By the late 1990s, however, there had been a paradigm shift, and men and women of all ages felt free to use their homes to display economic success or cultural refinement. Mass-produced decorating magazines urged readers to leave behind the old simple styles and strive to furnish their homes in richer cultural taste *(genfuyou wenhua pinwei)*. (Zhang 1998, 3). Even the educational television channel controlled by the municipal government sponsored an evening show on home renovation where the male decorator who hosted the show prefaced his first demonstration by noting "that as soon as one enters an apartment, you know immediately whether the residents' have taste *(ruguo zhuren you pinwei)*."[15]

Throughout the city, neighborhood shops sold the supplies to install parquet floors, recessed lighting, and upscale bathroom fixtures. Bookstores devoted entire sections to home improvement publications. New Web sites and television programs instructed viewers how best to decorate their new homes or renovate the old.[16] In 1987, household furnishings had been minimal and utilitarian; by the late 1990s merchandise was plentiful and styles were often indistinguishable from those found in North American and European magazines. Ikea was a popular destination of both young and middle-aged Shanghai residents, and Toto, American Standard, and Simmons advertised heavily on billboards throughout the city.

One can also trace the impact of the new global styles in the decorator magazines sold in state-run bookstores, small kiosks, and even the newly opened Shanghai library.[17] In these magazines the home is a happy nest, a warm and cozy place. It is also the place where residents *(zhuren)* are encouraged to display *(tixian)* their cultivation *(xiuyang)*, personality *(xingge)*, and economic power *(jingji shili)* (Zhang 1999, 5; 1998, 5). As in the developers' brochures, the interior-decorating magazines addressed a gender-neutral *zhuren* or *fangzhu*, and as in the real estate videos, illustrations omitted residents of either sex. In bookstores when I observed those reading decorating magazines, men were at least as numerous as women and the targets of promotional materials seemed androgynous.

However, when in December 1998 we asked the Shanghai couples in our consumer study who had renovated their apartment to identify those individuals who had participated in the process, husbands played the central role.[18] In all aspects more husbands than wives had been active, and in regard to finalizing plans, buying materials, supervising labor, and managing the finances, men's greater involvement was statistically significant (see table 11.1). Only in choosing furniture and interior decoration were wives as likely to be involved as husbands.

When I designed a pilot study in 1997 about home renovation in Shanghai and Shenzhen, I found that husbands were knowledgeable about the renovation and in many cases claimed to have taken the lead. When we did observations in furniture stores that summer, men outnumbered women in the sections devoted to the sale of couches, desks, and dining room tables. And when we took simple inventories of wall decorations in the living rooms, the husband's possessions and signs of distinction were more numerous than those of the wife. Moreover, it appeared that the higher the income and the greater the authority of the husband in the workplace, the more clearly had the house become

Table 11.1
Participation in Decisions about Home Renovation

Action	*Husbands*	*Wives*
Raised the issue of renovation	79%	70%
Discussed initial renovation plan	79%	71%
Decided final renovation plan	76%	63%*
Bought materials	72%	41%***
Hired workers	79%	26%***
Supervised workers	54%	29%***
Chose furniture and decorations	83%	80%
Managed renovation budget	74%	57%**
Personally did some renovation work	26%	19%

Source: Consumer Project December 1998
$^{*}p \leq .1$; $^{**}p \leq .05$; $^{***}p \leq .01$

his home.[19] What emerged in the subsequent interviews with both working-class and professional men in 1998 and 1999 was how important it was for men to be able to claim a space distinct from the bedroom where they could entertain friends or enjoy their hobbies. The following home interviews illustrate this pattern. They also document the remarkable improvement in the quality of residential conditions since the Mao years as well as the impact of home-ownership on investments in a family home.

Teacher Chen's Mao Button Collection

When I visited Teacher Chen in June 1999, he entertained us enthusiastically in his bedroom/sitting room. He was a generous host and had prepared coffee and a rich array of cookies and chocolates purchased to celebrate his daughter's recent wedding. The room of twelve square meters was stuffed with furniture and memorabilia. A large double bed occupied one third of the floor while two chairs and a small table created a sitting space in front of the veranda that faced the street. In one corner, as remote from the kitchen as physically possible, stood a small refrigerator on which they had placed several dolls and an inflated plastic replica of a roll of Charms lifesavers. All the remaining wall space was filled with bookshelves, cabinets, and tables piled high with suitcases and boxes.

In many ways the room reminded me of the "mother's homes" I had visited in 1987. One entered the five-story, unpainted cement-block building from a dark, dirty stairwell, and each apartment opened onto a narrow corridor jammed with old wicker baskets, rusted bikes, and wet mops. Inside the apartment the walls were green, the floors scuffed, and the furniture a mixture of a few simple wooden stools, screened kitchen cupboards, and assorted pieces of a bedroom suite. Over Teacher Chen's bed was a colorized, formal photo of the couple standing shoulder to shoulder in their 1961 wedding attire. Beneath the photo was a calendar with a red racing car, and on the back of the door another calendar with a traditional Chinese landscape painting.

In many ways, though, the apartment was not at all like those "mother's houses" I had visited in 1987. First, the Chens were homeowners, not renters. In 1995 they had purchased the home through the wife's work unit for 9,000 yuan, and Teacher Chen now holds title, in his name alone, to a valuable property in central Shanghai worth more than 200,000 yuan. Even before they bought the flat, they had invested 5,000 yuan to redecorate, and he proclaims he would never move no matter how much money he was offered. In fact he told us later that he and his wife had offered the home to their daughter and new son-in-law and made a plan to move to another larger flat that they had bought for 65,000 yuan in eastern Pudong with help from his old unit. But the son-in-law preferred to move to an apartment that his mother had arranged in Hong Qiao District.

Other ways that the commercialization and affluence of the 1990s distinguished this apartment included the furnishings and decoration. Above the head of the Chen's bed and on the opposite wall were two framed, color photographs of their daughter posing as if for a fashion magazine. The English words "Happy to you" had been embossed across a diaphanous yellow scarf she held under her chin. Across from the foot of the bed was a large-screen color television, a VCR, and a karaoke microphone.

Finally, the apartment reflected the ways in which Teacher Chen wanted to relax and entertain his guests. The shelves displayed many different wine bottles to which he drew attention when he discussed how much he enjoyed socializing. Also, when I asked what room he would add if he could have another room, he promptly answered, "I would add a big living room. We can sleep in any old small room, but if we had a big living room I would read, watch TV, and sing karaoke there. I like to drink wine and would like to invite guests here to have a good time." And then Teacher Chen stood up from the folding chair on which he had been sitting opposite me and started to pull out twenty battered boxes from the drawers of a cabinet under his TV. For the next forty minutes we listened as he told with relish and pride how he had acquired his nearly seven thousand Mao buttons. The display was dazzling. He had them organized by size and then by material. In each box there were five or six layers of treasures, each pin carefully sewn onto a cloth or paper sheet. In one box there were only plastic circles of less than an inch in diameter, in another only ceramic ovals with the Great Helmsman gazing into the mountains or over the sea. He said that he had been offered hundreds of yuan for certain pins, but he never sells. He still is building his collection, visiting markets to look for rare finds and occasionally trading with other collectors. In 1987 he had already begun the button collection, and perhaps if I had asked then about his leisure time or hobbies I might have been treated to the same lavish display and hospitality. But in the homes I visited in 1987, husbands usually expressed no interest in joining the interview, and no one—male or female—offered to display or show me treasures that they had hidden away.

Auntie Li's Dropped Ceiling

I first met Auntie Li in 1990 when she was a neighborhood cadre. We worked together on a daily basis for six weeks during one of Shanghai's worst heat waves, and I was forever grateful that I had been assigned a colleague of such unflagging good will. When I returned in 1995 to do a third follow-up study, she officially became part of the neighborhood sample and I began to learn more about her family history. In 1997, I missed a chance to visit because she was traveling, but in June 1999 I was able to spend a Saturday afternoon chatting with her husband, son, daughter-in-law, and grandson.

Again, the recommodification of real estate and the keen interest in renovation had made an imprint on their home. Like Teacher Chen and perhaps the majority of Shanghainese now in their early sixties, Auntie Li had been born in the countryside. In 1947 at age nine she came to Shanghai for primary school, and after her father was disabled she took his place as a shift worker in a large textile mill. When I asked her to tell me about her memories of her earliest homes in the village and then in Shanghai, she uncharacteristically said she could remember nothing: "We, my mom and us three kids, just slept in a series of little rooms. My dad worked shifts; he only came home a few times each month."

In 1956, when she became a full-time worker, she too moved into a dorm at the mill. Four years later she married a man through an introduction of her sister's friend. Again when I asked about the size and neighborhood of her home after marriage, she refused to give details, saying that at first they had a small room of their own, and then in 1962 after the birth of her daughter, her mother-in-law came from the countryside. Between 1962 and 1970 they moved from one small room to another. I asked if it wasn't inconvenient to keep moving all the furniture and possessions. She replied, "What furniture? We had very little, we had my mother-in-law, two kids, and no money. So we really had nothing to move."

In 1970, as part of Mao's policy to build a third industrial front in remote areas, Auntie Li was transferred to work in a mountainous area of Fujian Province. Her family stayed behind, and for the next fourteen years she only saw them once a year until she took retirement at age forty-six. In 1987 after her daughter married she moved to their current apartment on the top floor of a six-story walk-up with her husband and son. The interior space is divided into two bedrooms/sitting rooms, a kitchen alcove, a toilet room, and a small balcony. Since 1989, when their son married, he and his wife have taken over the smaller bedroom as their own, while Auntie Li and her husband claimed the larger room with its veranda as their bedroom/sitting room and the family living room and dining room.

Again, a visitor can see the impact of the economic changes of the 1990s on the home interior and the family's claims on the space. In 1994 they bought the apartment from the husband's steel factory for under 10,000 yuan, and today it is worth ten times as much. Like Teacher Chen, they do not expect to sell or move. They are happy with the location, and neither they nor their son and his wife have the resources to buy anything better. When I discussed her apartment in 1995, Auntie Li was singularly unenthusiastic and complained about the leaking roof and the drafty windows, saying to refurnish was really a waste of money. But four years later her husband had solved these problems by installing a dropped ceiling that allowed them to replace any section stained by mildew or rust. And on the dreary rainy day I visited, it was surprisingly bright and airy.

They had also modified the entry and reconfigured the space outside the bedroom/sitting room. Just inside the front door they had laid a checkerboard of black and white tiles that echoed the squares of their bedroom/sitting room and defined a small dining area. They also had enclosed the kitchen sink and gas burners so that the kitchen could be closed off from the rest of the apartment. However, they could not afford to create a separate living room. Their large, wooden bed still took up a third of the floor space, and the rest of the room was crowded with the sofa, a large chiffonier without a mirror, and the old screened kitchen cabinet, which they had brought from their first apartment. Yet they had made some effort to refurbish. In front of the sofa, they placed a low table that the husband had built and painted to match the white ceiling panels, and a new large-screen television stood opposite. On the veranda the husband kept a large cage for his homing pigeons, but there appeared to be nothing as large and visible that was exclusively the focus of Auntie Li's hobbies.

When asked what room she would add if they had the money to relocate, she answered immediately: a room *(fangzi)* of our own. Both her son and husband nodded in agreement:

> Ideally we would like our own *fangzi* with our own toilet and kitchen, and then my son and his family could have this apartment for themselves. Right now they have moved back to live with my daughter-in-law's mother because officially the household registration *(hukou)* of my daughter-in-law and my grandson is still with her mother, and that is where he can go to primary school without paying extra fees. So during the week they live there, and then on the weekend they come back and stay with us. But probably we will all stay here forever, because to move costs a lot of money (which we don't have). My son and daughter-in-law do not have good jobs, and there is talk of layoffs.

Auntie Li's daughter has always lived in one small room with her mother-in-law. Now, in addition to her husband, her mother-in-law, and her son, there is also a young niece. But Auntie Li is actually somewhat optimistic that her daughter—unlike her son or herself—will eventually have a home of her own because the mother-in-law's building has been scheduled for demolition and then each adult generation will be rehoused in separate apartments. If they can afford to purchase ownership, they will become homeowners. But in any case the government guarantees that they will be able to rent a self-contained apartment in a new building.

Ownership and Gender

In the early 1990s the central leadership resolved to accelerate privatization of urban real estate. At the 1991 March Work Conference, Li Peng pushed leaders to design local initiatives to popularize ownership, and the State Council announced that homeownership should become the norm among the nonmigrant urban population.[20] Over the next two years, municipal leaders all over China took steps to further monetize—if not necessarily privatize—residency claims on new real estate by recalculating rents to reflect market demand and require large deposits among new renters. Shanghai, under the leadership of Zhu Rongji, led the way by establishing the first provident fund for individual home purchases in May 1991. Guangzhou followed in April 1992 (K. Lau 1994, 16). In February 1995 the State Council launched the *Anju Gongcheng* program to establish provident funds as the primary means to promote homeownership among low- and middle-income families.[21] Subsequent banking reforms enabled an increasing number of families to take out home mortgages, with particular gains in fall 1996 and spring 1997.[22]

At the end of 1994, 30 percent of nonmigrant households held some type of ownership claim. Three years later ownership rates reached 33 percent. [23] Moreover, surveys between 1997 and 1999 suggested that the desire for homeownership remained strong even after the slowdown in economic growth.[24] Overall, housing reforms of the 1990s launched a sustained recommercialization of urban real estate and popularized the ideal homeownership.

In our Shanghai interviews, an overwhelming majority of men and women responded that homeownership was now a necessity for families and that ownership generally improved the quality of housing.[25] However, when we compared attitudes of homeowners with those who were still renting, there were some noticeable and statistically significant differences between husbands and wives. First, in response to a global question about rating their overall life satisfaction, homeowners of both sexes were more likely than renters to say they were satisfied, but only among men was the difference statistically significant.[26] Second, ownership increased the likelihood that respondents reported that they had private space *(siren kongjian)* in their homes, but among husbands the gain by owners over renters was larger than among wives.[27] Third, ownership increased the likelihood that respondents said that their name appeared on the title to the house; and again, gains of male owners were greater than those of females. Moreover, because men were far more likely than women to hold the title whether the home was owned or rented, ownership appeared to have intensified male control over family property.[28]

Clearly, there is an interaction here with class. Ownership levels are highest among the best-educated managerial and professional ranks, and thus we may primarily be seeing that high status men are more likely than lower status men to assert dominance in the home. Wealthier men also have larger homes, and it may be that it is only in larger homes that men are able to claim space exclusively for their own use. Tellingly, however, in these larger homes, wives were no more likely to claim space of their own than were wives in the smaller rented apartments. A final case study of a middle-aged couple who for years had relied on the wife's employer to solve their housing problems illustrates how homeownership may strengthen male claims over domestic property and private space.

The Calligrapher Cadre

The Yang's and their fifteen-year-old daughter live in a two-bedroom flat of eighty-five square meters purchased in 1996 through his unit and now registered exclusively in his name. Although both Mr. and Mrs. Yang said they were unsure *(bu haoshuo)* if homeownership was definitely necessary for all families, it has been extremely important to Mr. Yang.

Like most Shanghai couples who married in the early 1980s, they began their married life in the household of his parents. It was a small single room in Yang Pu District where he had grown up with his two siblings; and after the birth of their daughter, they became a household of six adults and a baby. Shortly thereafter Mrs. Yang's employer arranged for them to rent a tiny room near the old railroad station on grounds of hardship. Three years later, her unit again helped the family by finding a four-room apartment in Hong Qiao where they moved with his parents and (then) unmarried brother. The next year the brother married, and by 1990 they were a joint household of eight. Again, Mrs. Yang's unit tried to solve their housing problem by renting them a second apartment for the exclusive use of the Yangs and their daughter. However, it was designed so that one walked through the first room to get to the second, which meant the daughter slept on a folding bed next to her father's calligraphy table.

Finally, in 1996 the hotel where Mr. Yang worked as a manager arranged for them to buy a 300,000 yuan apartment for 40,000 yuan. The house is furnished simply, and like most new owners who previously lived in very cramped apartments, the Yangs purchased almost all new furniture. The walls are white, and the floors are gleaming light woods. The only decorations on the walls are paintings and calligraphy done by the husband. The second bedroom is set up as a calligrapher's studio. The daughter still sleeps on a folding cot and she and her belongings seem to have left almost no impression on the house. The kitchen is as installed by the builder; the bathroom was renovated to resemble those in the husband's hotel.

Like Auntie Li, the Yangs would like to buy again. However, Mrs. Yang, who is a well-paid accountant, is clear that the apartment is worth considerably less than when they bought it. Although both of them told a previous interviewer that neither had personal space of their own, during my visit Mrs. Yang said that "for sure, he has personal space." Mr. Yang was not only less willing to accept that the apartment had lost value but also disputed his wife's claim that he had personal space. He said, "I don't have enough space, and I still must share it when I am doing calligraphy. I really want my own space." When his wife asked him to compare the situation with their last rented place, however, he agreed that he did have space of his own. Moreover, as Mr. Yang volunteered at the end of the visit, "my daughter will move out when she marries, so in any case I will be able to use that room exclusively for my calligraphy."

When a House Becomes His Home

The economic reforms launched by Deng Xiaoping created the most sustained urban housing boom in Chinese history. By 1995 more than half of all residential units were less than sixteen years old (see table 11.2), and average per capita living space was more than twice that of 1979.[29] Shanghai followed these national trends. In the late 1970s most of Shanghai's six million urban residents lived in crowded apartments with few amenities. A majority shared bathrooms and kitchens with neighbors, and many used public latrines. Three-generation households were typical, and even when a married couple lived independently of their parents or in-laws, they rarely had the luxury of a bedroom separate from that of their children. In the entire metropolis only five buildings exceeded twenty floors.[30]

The changes to this built environment after 1978 were mind-boggling. Between 1979 and 1989, 830,000 households occupied new or renovated apartments,[31] and between 1992 and 1996, another 800,000 moved.[32] More than 4.5 million people changed address, average space per capita doubled, and in most cases a move guaranteed a higher material standard of living.[33] By the late 1990s the norm for new construction was a three-room apartment *(liangshi yiting)* with its own kitchen and bathroom looking out over a skyline punctuated with high-rise towers in diverse, international styles.[34]

Table 11.2

Age of Urban Housing Stock (by Percentage of Units Built in Each Decade)

	Before 1949	*1950s*	*1960s*	*1970s*	*1980s*	*1990–1995*
Nationally	7%	4%	6%	16%	46%	20%
Beijing	7%	13%	12%	14%	43%	15%
Shanghai	24%	5%	3%	11%	44%	13%
Tianjin	13%	5%	5%	13%	52%	12%

Source: Quanguo renkou chouyang diaocha ziliao, 1995 [Survey Results from National Census, 1995] (Beijing: Chinese Demography Publishing House, 1997, 630–32).

Just as dramatic as the transformation of the physical conditions were the changes in popular expectations. One 1997 Xinhua article reported that 37.5 percent of city residents expected to buy an apartment through their unit, and another 26 percent expected to buy on the market.[35] A 1998 Gallup poll in Chengdu, Beijing, Guangzhou, and Shanghai found that between 15 percent and 18 percent planned to buy a home within the next twelve months, and a follow-up survey in Guangzhou, Xian, and Wuhan indicated that 25 percent expected to purchase an apartment in 1999.[36]

New affluence and growing marketization of the urban economy have obliterated most Communist certainties. In the prereform years, the claims of the collective trumped those of the individual, and the public was always morally superior to the private. By the late 1990s, however, individual and personal preferences had gained a new legitimacy. Central to this cultural shift was the disappearance of the juxtaposition of proletariat and bourgeois that had structured everyday behavior for two decades. In the 1970s the ambitious as well as the prudent person stood on the side of the proletariat not only in political discussions but even when selecting an appropriate hairstyle or ordering food at the market. Complaining in public about the lack of fresh fish could signal dangerous decadence.

The decision of Deng Xiaoping to eschew class struggle and foster the hybrid of market-socialism silenced the most vocal advocacy of proletariat fashion. Growing affluence and ever greater openness to the world outside of China went so far as to rehabilitate the previously odious lifestyle of the international bourgeoisie, but this time in the more politically correct form of the modern middle classes. China remained a Communist polity throughout the 1990s. But when one observes the material culture of the late 1990s, particularly within the confines of newly privatized residential settings, socialist lifestyles have been replaced by a transnational, global reference group that at first glance looks suspiciously "bourgeois." Equally noteworthy is that with the decline of proletariat style and the increase of homeownership, one observes a strong male investment in the domestic sphere.

In 1987 I relied on interviews with women in their fifties and early sixties to understand one strand of urban popular culture. In the 1990s I interviewed a more diverse group of residents. Therefore, the greater emphasis on the husband's role may simply reflect the fact that I no longer listened so exclusively to older mothers seated in their bedrooms. But in 1998 and 1999 my Shanghai colleagues and I also spent more than four hundred hours interviewing women, and a third of the interviews took place in the single room that was the bedroom—as well as the living room, dining room, and study—of that family. Thus the strong imprint of male investments and the strong views of male respondents was not because I no longer could hear the voices or see the rooms of women. Rather, there was a stronger emphasis on conjugal and male voices because the property regime had changed.

In the late 1990s city residents of all economic strata wanted to become property owners, and the official endorsements to strive ambitiously for personal success spilled over to legitimize a more general desire to strive for distinction. In this new political economy both men and women saw their homes as an important place where they could legitimately compete for social recognition. In the mid-1980s homes had also been an important social terrain, but during the 1980s utilitarian necessity dominated home life and homes were not viewed as private property. Greater affluence, reduced state censorship, and the popularization of homeownership—as an ideal and a reality—altered the equation and increased the individual and societal significance of domestic investments.

The possibility of property ownership and the increased legitimacy for indulging personal comfort and displaying social distinctions refocused the energies of both men and women on domestic space. But when husbands have higher earnings than wives and there is a long tradition of patrilineal inheritance, as is the case in contemporary China, increased investments in urban residences are unlikely to be gender neutral or favor women. We need only look at contemporary Taiwan to see how high-capitalism accommodates exclusive male property claims. To some extent, as C. K. Yang wrote in 1959, collectivization and proletarian culture made unequal claims to family property moot

(Yang 1959, 143). Under the conditions of collective ownership and criminalization of private business and investment, household headship carried little power outside the home and Chinese families could cede domestic space to women and avoid the difficult task of putting legal equality into practice. However, once property was recapitalized for individuals and men could openly compete for status through conspicuous consumption as well as through party membership and occupational rank, men's attachments and investments in domestic space intensified. One observed a domestic space configured around the interests of a married couple who relished the opportunity to create a more comfortable and tasteful home. For these individuals "my mother's house" had been succeeded by "a home of our own," and when one observes how ownership was frequently concentrated in the husband's name, it appears that privatization may have also favored the claims of men and, by extension, reversed the earlier tendency of collectivization to neutralize male advantage and feminize domestic space.

12

YANJIE BIAN, DEBORAH S. DAVIS,
AND SHAOGUANG WANG

Family Social Capital in Urban China

A Social Network Approach

To MEASURE THE Chinese family's *guanxi* networks and their embedded social capital, we present an approach that stresses the role of event-based positions. Our approach is in contrast to approaches that define networks in terms of content-based name generators; previous applications of this approach to discussions of networks among Chinese urban residents have concluded that ties to kin and family were insignificant. Using an event-based position-generator approach to measure Chinese *guanxi* networks and embedded social capital among 386 households during spring festival, we dispute these other conclusions and find kinship ties to be powerful assets in accumulating social capital. We also find substantial variation among households by occupation of the male head, a finding that argues for greater attention to class differences in future studies of social capital and social networks.

The Name-Generator Approach and Measurement of Social Capital

For more than twenty years, sociologists have relied on name generators to identify the people (alters) who constitute the core of an individual's social world and represent one dimension of an individual's store of social capital.

In the earliest studies (Laumann 1973; Wellman 1979), respondents were asked to name a few "closest friends." Later, Claude S. Fischer (1982) asked respondents to identify those with whom the respondents discussed "personal worries." In both cases, social capital was an implicit concept. A modified version of Fischer's instrument has become a standard device of the General Social Survey (GSS) in the United States (Burt 1984; Marsden 1987); in the International Social Survey Program, European scholars have relied on multiple name generators to identify the various core parts of an individual's social support system (International Social Survey Program 1986; van der Poel 1993).[1]

During the 1980s and early 1990s, Danching Ruan and her colleagues applied this name-generator model to measure the core networks of Chinese individuals in Tianjin, an industrial city in north China (Ruan 1993, 1998; Ruan et al. 1997; Freeman and Ruan 1997). In light of past research that documented the centrality of family ties in Chinese societies before and after 1949 (Fried [1953] 1969; Yang [1959] 1965; Bian 1994, 1997; M. M. Yang 1994; Yan 1996), they initially anticipated a greater representation of kin ties than nonkin ties in discussion networks. However, Ruan and her colleagues found that kin ties were significantly less represented among the generated alters for the Chinese than for Americans and Europeans. While it is certainly possible to hypothesize that the socialist transformation of the urban economy and fifty years of Communist rule transformed the role of kin networks, other work on contemporary urban China suggests that the name-generator approach might have a particular bias favoring the nonkin alters and especially colleagues that are instrumental to one's work life. Almost certainly, name generators about discussion alters would not adequately capture the key social ties that constitute social capital in contemporary urban China.

To address these possibilities, we use a study of the pattern of New Year's socializing for 386 households through an event-based position-generator approach to identify the strength and reach of networks. We, therefore, argue that the GSS name generator may not be an adequate device for measuring the core networks in a society where an individual's core network is a highly relational *guanxi* network that originates in, and centers upon, the family and kinship and that over the life course is extended and elaborated through exchanges among a wide variety of kin and nonkin alters (Liang 1949; Fei [1949] 1992; M. M. Yang 1994). Thus, what is important to the Chinese is not with whom they discuss matters, but who is willing and able to serve as a bridge through which to reach the persons having the ability to solve problems for them (Bian 1997). Because "important matters" vary tremendously in content among individuals, we need a device that can help us generate the *guanxi* networks cutting across specific "important matters" for the Chinese.

An Event-based Position-Generator Approach

In a relational society such as China, social gatherings are important occasions used to cultivate, maintain, develop, and terminate *guanxi* ties. Who gets invited to someone's wedding, funeral, birthday party, or any gathering of personal significance, for example, is a sign about who is in this person's *guanxi* network. While gatherings of these kinds may be awash in family and kinship ties, the idea is that we may use an event-oriented approach to measure a Chinese individual's *guanxi* network.

With attention to events of cultural significance, we measure a Chinese person's *guanxi* network by examining the greeters during the celebration of the lunar New Year. The lunar New Year is the most important traditional holiday in China. Traditionally, the entire month prior to the New Year would be spent preparing for the celebration. Starting on New Year's eve, this celebration lasts for fifteen days, each day reserved for a culturally significant event or meal. Under Communist rule since 1949, urban workers were given a week-long official holiday to celebrate the New Year. During this period, people of the same *guanxi* networks are expected and obligated to greet one another by visiting one another's homes. In recent years telephone greetings have become popular, but exchanges of greetings and gifts at one another's homes continue to be among the core *guanxi* ties that are most significant to the parties linked by these ties. Although not every greeter is necessarily a core *guanxi* tie for someone, all core ties must be among the greeters; there is no good excuse for a close relative or friend not to greet each other during the New Year's celebration. Thus, a measure of exchanges during the celebration is an especially good indicator of membership, strength, and reach of network ties among the Chinese.

With this event-based approach, we also can calibrate social capital. To meet this objective, we must measure the kinds of resources possessed by the greeters. The name-generator approach would create scales that sum social-demographic characteristics of alters (Burt 1984; Marsden 1987). But a position-generator approach, as first developed by Nan Lin and Mary Dumin (1986), would allow us to capture the range and volume of the social resources and thus social capital accessible and mobilizable through social positions in society. Lin and Dumin's models focus on job positions of alters and assume that having a contact in a particular job position indicates that the individual can access that position and thus the embedded resources. For our analytic purpose, this position-generator approach can apply to the study of social capital of Chinese families: When families have greeters from many different positions, they have the potential to access many different positional resources and therefore have a high volume of social capital.

By *social capital,* we refer to valuable resources that are accessed and mobilized through the social networks of an actor—an individual, a family, or a formal organization. This definition is consistent with the social-network approach pioneered by Nan Lin (1982, 1999, 2001) but differs from the social-structure approach that has been made popular through the works of James S. Coleman (1988), Francis Fukuyama (1995), and Robert D. Putnam (2000). While the social network approach treats social capital as a network resource of actors, the social-structure approach defines social capital as the aggregate attribute and asset of the community of which actors are members (see a detailed comparison in Lin 2001). Our research task here is to measure the kinds of resources that may be mobilized by urban Chinese families through their New Year's greeter networks. The social-network approach is adequate for our analytic objective.

The 1998 Urban Consumer Project

We draw our data from the 1998 Urban Consumer Project conducted in four Chinese cities: Shanghai, Tianjin, Wuhan, and Shenzhen. Shanghai (population 13 million) and Tianjin (population 9 million) are the first- and third-largest cities, respectively, of China, and both cities are under the direct jurisdiction of the central government. Wuhan (population 7 million), the capital of Hubei Province, is the transportation and military hub of central China. Shenzhen (population 3.5 million) is a new frontier city created along the border of Hong Kong in 1978 to attract investments from Hong Kong and elsewhere. Under the jurisdiction of Guangdong Province, Shenzhen is a city primarily of immigrants from other parts of the country. Although the four cities do not represent all of urban China, they do provide substantial regional variation in population size, position in China's geo-administrative hierarchy, and pace of market reforms.

In each city we interviewed husbands and wives from one hundred households. After an extensive effort in checking the characteristics of neighborhoods and households, we selected four neighborhoods that on the whole presented diverse socioeconomic profiles. According to household heads' occupations, we classified households into nine groups and randomly selected households within each group.[2] One core interest throughout the project was to assess the impact of class differences among the households in their economic, social, and cultural life, and in all six waves of data collection, we compared the interaction of class with attitudes and behaviors.

The material we use here was gathered from daily logs where all members of the sampled household recorded (1) the number of greeters the participating household received through telephone or home visit, (2) the relational types of the greeters, (3) the number of people/families that the participating household greeted through telephone or home visit, and (4) the relational types of the people/families greeted by the participating household.[3] The total number of greeters received and people/families greeted is simplified as number of greeters. In addition, at the end of the six-day recording period, we provided a list of twenty occupations and twelve work sectors and asked the participating households to indicate, to the best of their knowledge, in which of the occupations and work sectors their greeters' jobs were located. The measures of *guanxi* networks and social capital used in this study are based on these data.

Measures of *Guanxi* Networks and Social Capital

Our unit of analysis is households. New Year's greetings are oriented to the family as a whole rather than to specific members of the family. Although members of the family may develop their *guanxi* ties separately, they by and large share these ties and the social capital embedded. Therefore, we propose to treat a family's New Year's greeters as the *guanxi* ties of the family. Tables 12.1 and 12.2 summarize the overall character of respondents' networks in terms of composition, size, density, range, and a scale of social-capital volume calculated through a factor analysis.

Network size is measured by the total number of greeters, counting both inflow and outflow greetings. The average number of greeters is 37.3 (SD = 32.1).

Table 12.1
Scores of Occupations and Work-Unit Sectors as Rated by Respondents

	Rating score (%)[a]	Greeters working in job or sector (%)
Occupation		
Scientist and researcher	95	19.8
College professor	91	18.7
Engineer	86	33.5
Legal professional/staff	86	13.7
Physician	86	30.9
High school teacher	81	29.3
Governmental official	80	26.6
Elementary school teacher	73	16.4
Party and mass organization official	73	15.8
Corporate and nonprofit organization managers	71	47.0
Economic and business professional/staff	64	35.1
Accountant	58	34.3
Administrator and clerical staff	53	44.6
Police officer	52	16.4
Nurse	48	13.2
Chauffeur/driver	25	39.6
Chef/cook	24	12.9
Industrial worker	20	52.0
Waiter/waitress	11	8.4
Nanny/domestic worker	6	6.1
Work-unit sector		
Party and government organization	86	38.0
State nonprofit organization	75	60.9
Foreign firm	73	17.7
Foreign-Chinese joint venture	66	25.1
Shareholding company	45	19.3
Private nonprofit organization	41	5.5
State enterprise	41	67.3
Private enterprise	39	22.4
Domestic joint venture	30	4.2
Collective nonprofit organization	30	15.0
Household business/self-employment	29	39.1
Collective enterprise	24	31.7

Note: [a]Respondents who gave the job or sector a rating of "good" or "very good."

Table 12.2
Structure and Embedded Social Capital of New Year's Greeter Network

	Descriptive statistics		Factor analysis	
Factor or variable	*Mean or %*	*SD*	*Factor loading*	*Explained variance*
Network size				
Total greeters (chosen variable)	37.3	32.1		
Percentage of home-visit greeters	45.5%	26.0		
Composition of relational types				
Kin (chosen "kin density" variable)	44.1%	21.5		
Friend	24.8%	15.9		
Work colleague	20.2%	16.7		
Neighbor	8.2%	12.2		
Other	2.6%	6.0		
Network range				
Total positional range (chosen variable)	57.7	25.7		72.3%
Occupational range	49.1	24.3	0.85	
Work-unit sector range	37.8	20.9	0.85	
Status ceiling				
Total positional ceiling (chosen variable)	75.3	20.4		75.0%
Occupational ceiling	79.5	18.3	0.87	
Work-unit sector ceiling	71.5	18.1	0.87	
Social-capital volume	27.9	17.4		84.0%
Number of occupations accessed	5.1	3.0	0.92	
Rating scores of occupations accessed	310.5	203.3	0.92	
Number of work-unit sectors accessed	3.5	1.9	0.91	
Rating scores of work-unit sectors accessed	181.4	102.9	0.92	

Double counting is possible but not substantial. New Year's greetings by telephone or in ways other than home visits, which accounted for more than 54.5 percent of all greetings among our participating households, are initiated by either the participating household or their *guanxi* household, and mutual exchange of greetings is considered complete with one call; no return call is necessary. Greetings through home visits may, however, involve double counting, because inflow and outflow greetings between families A and B are separate courses of action. In practice, mutual visits are likely to occur among close neighbors but highly unlikely to occur among relatives or friends who live at a distance. In these latter cases, home visits among equals are normally alternated from year to year in order to reduce "double burdens," otherwise people with a lower status would always pay home visits to their superiors (married sons and daughters visit parents, juniors visit their brothers/sisters or senior colleagues/friends, and so on). *Guanxi* ties are predominantly ties between unequals.

Kin density is measured by the percentage of kin ties among the greeters. In our 1998 Urban Consumer Project, we asked the participating households to specify the relational types of their greeters (kin, friends, colleagues, neighbors, or other relations). This measure gives us a direct test of whether or not kin relations are represented more highly in the core network of a family. Our data show that kin relations had the highest representation among the New Year's greeters (44.1 percent), followed by friends (24.8 percent), work colleagues (20.2 percent), neighbors (8.2 percent), and an insignificant proportion of unspecified, other relations (2.6 percent). This distribution is similar to those found through name-generated networks in the United States and Europe (Freeman and Ruan 1997).

Our next three measures are status ceiling, network range, and social-capital volume. These measures are based on position-generator data. The participating households were provided with a list of twenty occupations and twelve work sectors and were asked to indicate whether their greeters were incumbents of these occupations and work sectors. The occupations and work sectors were used to represent a whole range of structural positions that are of significance to Chinese stratification. In the later waves of our project, we asked our respondents to rate these positions on a five-point scale (very good, good, so-so, bad, very bad). Using the percentages of the evaluations of "very good" and "good," we obtained a rating score for each of the occupations and work sectors and ranked them accordingly, as shown in table 12.1.

The rating scores may be interpreted to indicate the prestige of occupations and work sectors. But the long tradition of occupational prestige studies makes it explicit that prestige is a function of the socioeconomic resources embedded in occupations (Nakao and Treas 1994). In China, both occupation and work sector are important resources for an individual's socioeconomic standing in society (Lin and Bian 1991; Bian 1994). For these reasons, we believe that the rating scores of occupations and work sectors can be interpreted as the quality and quantity of the embedded resources. Through a factor analysis, we combine the twenty occupations and twelve work sectors and obtain a ranking list of thirty-two structural positions, with each position assigned a factor-adjusted rating score. Because the higher the rating score, the higher the quality and quantity of the embedded resources, we can measure status ceiling with the greeter who has the highest rating, and measure network range with the distance between the greeters of the highest and lowest positions. Social-capital volume is measured by a factor score generated from four measures: (1) number of occupations accessed, (2) total scores of occupations accessed, (3) number of work sectors accessed, and (4) sum of scores of work sectors accessed.

As table 12.2 shows, on a maximum range of 1 to 100, the average network range among the 386 families is 57.7 (SD = 25.7), and the average status ceiling is 75.3 (SD = 20.4). The inequality is much higher for network range (25.7/57.7 = 0.45) than for status ceiling (20.4/75.3 = 0.27). The average of social-capital volume is 27.9 (SD = 17.4), and its inequality is even higher (17.4/27.9 = .62). How is social capital related to network structures? In other words, how is social-capital volume generated through network size, kin density, network range, and status ceiling?

The Network Structures of Social Capital

The structural parameters of a social network include its size, kin density, status ceiling, and range. Most network analysts also consider whether a network is homogeneous or heterogeneous—that is, are actors in a network similar or dissimilar to one another? The question for us is: What kinds of network structures are likely to generate more social capital for urban Chinese families? For example, is a large and sparse (or less dense) network more likely to generate social capital than a small and dense network? Between two families whose New Year's greeters come from different ranges of occupations or work-unit sectors, which is likely to have a great volume of social capital?

Following previous researchers (Marsden 1987; Lin and Dumin 1986), we expect positive size effects and negative density effects on social-capital volume. Specifically, a larger network implies higher social-capital volume than does a smaller network, and a dense network contains lower social-capital volume than does a sparse network. Because density is an inverse of size, the size and density effects are not independent of one another. As table 12.3 shows, the effect of network size is positive and statistically significant, whereas kin density, though negatively correlated with social-capital volume, does not generate a net effect independent of network size.

Table 12.3
Regression of Social-Capital Volume on Measures of Network Structure

Predictors	*Unstandardized coefficients*	*Standard error*	*Standardized coefficients*
Network size	0.14***	0.019	0.25
Kin density (% kin)	−0.03	0.027	−0.04
Network range	0.35***	0.031	0.51
Status ceiling	0.16***	0.039	0.19
(Constant)	−7.942**	2.71	
Adjusted R^2	0.644		
Sample size	386		

*$p < .1$; **$p < .05$; ***$p < .01$

We expect positive effects of network range and status ceiling on social-capital volume. When a network has a large range of structural positions, it implies different kinds of positional resources embedded in the network. In contrast, a network that has a small range of structural positions is expected to have fewer positional resources. Further, when network range is fixed, the higher the status ceiling, the higher the social-capital volume, simply because positions toward the top of a social structure imply more resources than do positions lower down in the social structure. These two hypotheses are supported: as shown in table 12.3, network range and status ceiling have strong effects on social-capital volume. The four-variable model has an explained variance of 64.4 percent (adjusted R^2), indicating that the development of social capital among the Chinese is largely due to the structures or composition of their *guanxi* networks.

Social Class, Network Structure, and Social Capital

Which families have advantageous *guanxi* networks and accumulate more social capital than other families? Table 12.4 presents the results of regression analyses designed to seek answers to these questions. Our primary interest here is to distinguish the impact of occupational and class position from such traditional measures of economic and human capitals as income, education, and job seniority.

Table 12.4
Regression for Network Structure and Social Capital (Unstandardized Coefficients)

Predictors	*Network size*	*Kin density*	*Network range*	*Status ceiling*	*Total volume of social capital*	
					Model 1	*Model 2*
City (Shanghai omitted)						
Tianjin	8.40	−11.39***	3.47	1.34	−1.23	−4.34*
Wuhan	2.12	−4.95	−2.18	−2.28	−3.30	−2.74
Shenzhen	8.68	−5.70	−3.77	?0.48	−5.26*	−5.21**
Husband's class (industrial blue-collar omitted)						
Private entrepreneur	15.12	−0.10	25.62*	14.22	16.95*	3.76
Family business owner	−9.12	−0.46	−9.02	−8.82*	−3.71	1.85
Government/party official	25.64***	−13.33**	12.21*	14.03**	11.00**	0.80
Enterprise manager	18.46**	−2.23	10.82*	8.11*	11.32***	3.83
Administrative staff	1.81	−0.40	3.51	2.10	5.04	3.23
Professional	10.42	−2.26	5.34	7.01*	5.24	0.96
Service worker	−1.92	0.44	4.26	2.41	1.91	0.31
Log-transformed household yearly income	3.16	−7.21***	−1.53	−0.83	−0.27	−0.38
Household human capital	0.49	−1.55	1.57	6.33***	2.69	1.22
Spouses' total age	−0.54	−0.03	1.58**	0.38	0.14	−0.43
Spouses' total age squared	0.00	0.00	−0.01**	0.00	0.00	0.00
Network						
Network size						0.13***
Kin density (% kin)						−0.05
Network range						0.37***
Status ceiling						0.12**
Constant	18.34	129.8***	−0.64	53.46*	18.90	17.05
Adjusted R^2	0.098	0.104	0.080	0.216	0.116	0.660
N	359	359	359	359	359	359

*$p < .1$; **$p < .05$; ***$p < .01$ (two-tailed test)

Social Class Effects

Sociologists have used multiple means to identify the social class positions of households, but in past research of married couples researchers have relied on occupational status of husbands rather than wives or a composite of both spouses. In our analysis we evaluated the impact of each spouse separately (analysis available on request), but when we found that the wife's job did not have net effects independent of the husband's, we restricted subsequent analysis to that of the husband's primary job status. Drawing on Eric O. Wright's (1997) comparative work, we categorized job according to the three criteria of ownership, managerial power, and professional qualifications and created eight class categories: private entrepreneurs, household business owners (or *geti*), government and party officials, enterprise managers, administrative staffers, professionals, workers in commercial and service sectors, and blue-collar workers in industry.

The two ownership classes—private entrepreneurs and household business owners—differ both from non-owners and from each other. Household business owners, on the one hand, do not have any advantage over blue-collar workers in industry in any of the dependent variables considered, and in fact their status ceiling is much lower. These household business owners do not differ from blue-collar workers in the kinds of networks they develop and in the total volume of social capital they maintain. On the other hand, private entrepreneurs stand out in network range, status ceiling, and social-capital volume. Being equal in household income, spousal education, and spousal age, private entrepreneurs can reach a much higher level and a much broader range within the social hierarchy than any other class considered.

Network structures also vary along the dimension of workplace authority among the non-owners. Compared to families of blue-collar workers in industry (the omitted reference group in the model), official and manager families have networks with a larger size, wider range, and higher ceiling, and their social-capital volume is significantly higher even after controlling for household yearly income, human capital, and spouses' ages. Manager families have fewer kin in their networks than do blue-collar worker families (known from an initial analysis that is not shown). These results suggest that official and managerial power is a source of network advantage and social capital in China.

Households headed by professionals as opposed to managers have modest advantages over those headed by manual workers in network size, status ceiling, and consequently social-capital volume. But, everything being equal, professional families are less advantaged than official and managerial families, a sign that we interpret to indicate a lower return on expertise than official and managerial power or entrepreneurial property. Workers in commerce and service sectors present no differences from blue-collar workers. These two classes, joined by self-employed artisans, have disadvantageous networks and low social capital.

The Effects of Household Variables

Although we included a large number of household variables in our initial analysis (not presented), three variables show significant effects, as shown in the reduced model presented in table 12.4. Household income, a variable we interpret as the family's economic capital, is the log-transformed sum of household yearly income. It exerts a significant negative effect on the reliance on kin; households with higher incomes tend to have a lower percentage of kin in their networks because their family networks contain a lot of friends, colleagues, and neighbors and a relatively smaller proportion of kin ties. Such variation implies that the exchange nature of *guanxi* networks at this time in Chinese history now requires financial resources to socialize with a large number of nonrelatives from whom to expect and generate social capital.

We use spouses' total schooling as an indicator of household human capital. Its positive effect on status ceiling and social capital indicates that human capital helps a family to develop advantageous networks and accumulate social capital. Finally, we use spouses' total age and age squared to explore the effects of life cycle on the accumulation of social capital. The results show some curve linear age effect on network range; older spouses tend to have wider networks because they know more people as they age, but aging does not affect status ceiling or social-capital volume. This is understandable, because older spouses have many more contacts than younger spouses, lowering the reliance on kin and widening network range but not necessarily creating contacts of higher status.

The Network Approach to Social Capital

Network researchers have successfully measured individuals' core networks with name generators, which require a content-sensitive context in which respondents can think of people (alters) who are significant to them in that context. When applied to urban China, however, this approach has generated alters among whom kin ties are less significant than those with work colleagues. Although this finding may be explained in terms of the instrumental importance of work organizations in life chances among the Chinese, it does not accord with the known centrality of family and kinship in current Chinese social life and *guanxi* networks, past and present.

To reevaluate this earlier research, we relied on an alternative measure of Chinese *guanxi* networks—the event-based position generator. We found that kin ties are most highly represented among the greeters, and the proportional share of work colleagues is slightly more than 20 percent of total number of greeters, between friends and neighbors. This distribution is comparable to that of the alters generated through name generators in Western societies (Freeman and Ruan 1997).

To assess the character of networks we relied on a method unavailable in most surveys: detailed daily logs that recorded the number and relational types of greeters among the families we surveyed. Therefore, if the New Year's greeter network proves to be a standard device for measuring Chinese *guanxi* networks, two survey questions can be used to carry out the measurement tasks: "How many people have greeted your family during the New Year's celebration?" and "Roughly, how many relatives are among them?"

The second aspect of our event-based approach is to use position generators to measure the status range, ceiling, and embedded social capital among the New Year's greeters. In modifying a Lin-Dumin occupational generator, for China we have used two-position generators, occupation and work sector, both of which are significant to Chinese stratification. When these two systems of positions are merged through a factor analysis, composite measures of network range, status ceiling, and social-capital volume (or positional resources accessed) are obtained. Among the families under study, we found large variations in these measures, and our analysis shows that some of these variations can be accounted for by the class and socioeconomic backgrounds of the families.

In sum, our study documents that events of cultural significance do not merely provide descriptive background material but rather effectively operationalize the compositions of social networks among individuals and families. We recommend, therefore, that measurements of sociability be routinely included in subsequent studies of networks and social capital in China and elsewhere.

13

JIEMING CHEN

When to Give and Why:

Intergenerational Transfer of Resources in Urban Chinese Families

DESPITE RAPID ECONOMIC development and tremendous cultural and social upheaval in China during the last half century, the level of economic solidarity between Chinese parents and their adult children remains remarkably high. For example, while it is usually the case that economic intergenerational exchange takes place within the multigenerational households on an almost daily basis, adult children who live in separate household also continue to maintain frequent contact and extensive exchange of resources with their parents (Bian, Logan, and Bian 1998; Davis and Harrell 1993; Unger 1993). Indeed, in terms of intergenerational support, new research evidence suggests that adult daughters now have become as supportive, if not more so, than sons, thus expanding the network of intergenerational support (Chen 1996; Liang, Gu, and Krause 1992). The uncoupling of economic interdependence from multigenerational coresidence and the inclusion of adult daughters into the familial old age support system point to a family system that is "converging" in some aspects to that in the West, while preserving in other aspects its own "Chinese characteristics" (see Goode 1963; Hajnal 1982; Macfarlane 1996; Spitze and Logan 1990). While many studies on Chinese families have noted such features, few have directly taken up the question of how intergenerational relations, the embodiment of which typically takes the form of intergenerational support, are maintained. In this chapter, I use data collected from a midsized city in northern China to examine how intergenerational transfer of resources is conducted. Adopting the concepts of continued group affiliation and expanded family boundary, I argue that despite tumultuous social and political changes, Chinese parents and children continue to view their families as a corporate group, around which they combine their resources either to get by or to get ahead in life. And, as the jointly held perception of the family continues to encompass multiple family units, one of the outcomes of the redistribution of resources between parental family and a child's own family unit is the equalization of family resources between the two.

The Decline of Parental Power

Viewed from a historical perspective, two important institutional changes in urban China's family life stand out as the most dramatic: one is the separation of production from economic activities in households; the other is the transformation of marriage from arranged to free choice. Both have significantly altered the image of the Chinese family; and both are indicative of, or conducive to, a general weakening of the power of elders in the Chinese family.

That the power of family elders has been weakened lies, in substantial part, in the fact that the family household as a production unit no longer occupies the central position in urban economy that it used to hold (Davis and Harrell 1993). Furthermore, filial piety, "once the most emphatically stressed value in the traditional social order for over 2000 years" (Yang 1959, 91), has been publicly dismissed by the socialist state as mere feudalistic remnant (Sher 1984). Within individual families, grown children no longer have to listen to the order of their parents about whom they should marry. Instead, they are encouraged by the state to make their own choices (Whyte 1990). All these changes point in the direction that family elders no longer have sufficient material resources, moral authority, and political support to hold sway over their oftentimes disobedient children.

The decline of parental power seriously limits parents' ability to manage intergenerational relations in the ways of their liking (Cowgil 1972; Hareven 1994). Without legal or any other effective coercive means to help enforce the realization of old age support from children, Chinese parents are forced to interact with their children on a more equal basis. With few economic or cultural devices left for parents to use to have their will forced upon their children, the willingness on the part of children becomes crucial to ensure old age support.

The Family as a Corporate Group

Yean-Ju Lee, William L. Parish, and Robert J. Willis (1994) suggest that three strategies are available to parents. In what is labeled the power/bargain approach, parents lure children to their side with prospective economic benefit, such as inheritance of family property. Using a short-term exchange approach, parents give their children immediate services, such as child care and housing, in exchange for old age support. The last strategy is to appeal to the commonality of interests between generations by offering unreserved devotion to their children.

In the context of contemporary Chinese urban society, the power/bargain approach is impracticable because most older parents simply do not possess enough economic power to induce support from their grown children. The short-term exchange approach is unattractive to older parents because the quid pro quo nature of the exchange requires that the upward flow of resources from children is contingent on parents' ability to reciprocate. The third approach, which is built upon the common perception of the permanence of the parent-child bond, and hence the mutual obligations attached, is within the reach of ordinary people of limited resources and, therefore, offers better assurance for old age security (Chen 1998).

Correspondingly, adult children may provide support because of expected long-term profit, or because of short-term benefits, or because of their sense of duty. Since the third strategy is likely to be one that most parents are inclined to choose, the question then becomes how intergenerational relations are formed so that grown children are willing to support their aged parents, even in the absence of immediate compensation or formal control. This is a crucial question, because the efficacy of this strategy hinges entirely on children's willingness to support.[1] A plausible explanation rests on the assumptions that a family is a corporate group (see Murdock 1949; Goode 1982), and that grown children can continue to identify in varying degrees with their parental families even after they have formed their own nuclear units (see Simmel [1922] 1955).

That Chinese families in the past exhibit features of corporate groups—that is, groups in which members put their collective interests above those of individual members and work in concert to pursue their collective ends—is well recognized among scholars (Fei 1939, [1947] 1992; Hajnal 1982; Macfarlane 1986; Lee and Wang 1999; M. C. Yang 1945; Yang 1959). Studies of contemporary Chinese families suggest that such corporate features remain largely intact. Paradoxically, the new economic system that the socialist state engineered, with the aim of undermining the old order of family system, in the end helped to strengthen the traditional Chinese familism (Davis and Harrell 1993). For example, in discussing the issue of stability of families in contemporary urban China, Martin K. Whyte and William L. Parish argue that the intrusive nature of the Chinese bureaucracy has an unintended effect of increasing family solidarity:

> While the highly bureaucratized nature of the urban system might be expected to destabilize family life by depriving families of the resources and authority they once enjoyed, paradoxically the effect is quite the opposite. Because families have lost resources and power, they confront a bureaucratic machine that controls their destinies. Success in life requires being able to cope with this machine, and that necessitates that family members subordinate individual interests and desires to the struggle on behalf of the entire family. . . . The continued importance of a strong sense of corporate family interests and obligations is one important respect in which Chinese urban families do not yet appear all that "conjugal," and at least in part this family solidarity is sustained by the bureaucratic nature of the urban system. (1984, 193–94)

Two implications can be drawn here. First, since the bureaucratic urban system has a pervasive presence in all localities, especially cities, the subordination of individual interests to family interests is likely to be a general family strategy that all have opted for or can choose if they wish, and as such the family as a corporate group is likely to be a general characteristic of contemporary China. Second, given that members can still rally around their families to cope with difficulties they face even when the family is no longer the powerful and resourceful group that it used to be, then it follows that the nature of a family as corporate unit does not necessarily decrease in degree with the shrinkage of family resources and the decline of parental power and authority. A small family with fewer resources and a smaller kinship network can still function like a corporate unit, which has been usually attributed to larger domestic groups such as lineage or clan in traditional China (Goody 1990).

Children's Continued Membership in the Parental Family

Young children's membership in their parental family is unambiguous. Correspondingly, their loyalty to the family is undivided.[2] However, such undivided loyalty faces a serious challenge with changes in the life course, especially in the transition into adulthood. Traditionally, while children's life course transition did not automatically sever the economic ties between generations, economic separation, typically in the form of family division *(fenjia)*, did take place after the marriage of children (Cohen 1976). In contemporary urban China, it appears that marriage continues to be an important life event that signals a reduced degree of economic interdependence between generations. In general, married children are less likely to live with their parents, and when living with parents are less likely to pool their income in the household budget (Treas and Chen 2000). Then, does the economic separation also signal the end of children's membership in the family of their parents? Remarkably frequent interhousehold exchange between parents and their adult children suggests otherwise (Bian, Logan, and Bian 1998; Davis 1993).

Analytically, children's continued group membership in their parents' family is likely to be enhanced with different mechanisms. At the structural level, a number of external constraints, notably urban housing shortages, restrictions on migration, and lack of affordable child care facilities, greatly increase children's reliance on their parents, and their frequent contact with them (Whyte and Parish 1984). Furthermore, improved public health and living standards create a demographic condition that the parent-child relations can be long-lasting (Lavely and Ren 1992; Zeng 1991).

At the organizational level, given that the family household is viewed as a corporate group for both generations, it becomes a common enterprise that each member has a vested interest in maintaining its existence. In other words, a family household as a corporate group not only represents an important organizational resource for each individual, but also an end in itself. As such, it is more likely that the marriage of children signifies the inclusion of new members into the collective, and thereby its expansion, rather than the complete withdrawal from the common enterprise.

At the interpersonal level, children's sense of continued membership in the parental family is likely to be nourished by parents' unreserved devotion to the children. From the viewpoint of parents, in the absence of reliable alternative, intrafamilial support continues to be a worthwhile choice to ensure old age security. Assuming that there is an implicit contract between parents and their children about old age support, over time the enforcement of such contract can only be accomplished by making the parent-child relations intimate and enduring, and the provision of the support to children can only be guided by the principle of "generalized reciprocity" (Sahlin 1972; see also H. Yang 1996). In other words, provided that parents continue to view old age support from children as an important source for old age security, the efforts on the part of parents are likely to compel children to maintain their membership within the parental family.

Redistribution of Resources

Financial and instrumental old age support by grown children entails transfer of resources across individual family units. The issue of children providing support, set into motion in response to the needs of parents, and also being constrained by their capacity, can therefore be understood as a process in which redistribution of family resources, which takes place in daily life in each individual family, is also being realized within the greater boundaries of the parental family and grown children's own nuclear family units combined (see Lee 1994; Lee and Miller 1994). Indeed, as the intensity of economic exchange between these two reaches a certain point, they can also be viewed as one expanded corporate family *(jia)* (see Cohen 1976; Greenhalgh 1982).

The distribution of resources within a family unit may shed light on how old age support is actualized. Gary S. Becker's altruism model provides a most explicit account of the mechanism of family income distribution (1991). According to this model, the altruism of a family head is defined as his or her own well-being (utility) being positively linked with that of his or her beneficiary. As such, the head diverts part of his or her income to the beneficiary without any compensation. Further, the head will distribute family income Pareto-efficiently. In other words, distribution is made in such a way that the total utility of all family members is maximal, conditional on family budget. Finally, as long as the head remains altruistic, any change in family income or members' utility (illness, for instance) will prompt the head to redistribute the income so that total utility of all family members remains optimal (see Becker 1991, 277–306).[3]

The story of family income distribution described by this model apparently fits well with ample empirical evidence. For our purpose, the insight that can be drawn from this model is its implications regarding resource flow between generations. Although in a philosophical sense whether parents are altruists in regard to their children may still be an open question, as long as parents are assumed to be motivated to support their offspring, much of the depiction of family income distribution still holds when the assumption of altruism is replaced by other similar but milder ones, such as a sense of duty or affective ties. Then, regardless of whether it is because the family head is altruistic or expects long-term benefits for the deed, the head of a family, usually a parent, supplies resources to the children for the sake of their well-being, as well as his or her own satisfaction. As the flow of resources within a family is from those who have extra resources to offer to those who are in need of them, resources are equalized between parents, the benefactor, and their young children, the beneficiary.

Thus, the way the head of a family allocates resources renders a family a place where resources are shared and joint security provided. Moreover, as has been contended before and implied in Becker's model, the way that parents redistribute also transforms a family into a place where the commonality of interests is recognized, not only by parents but also by children. Then, it follows that when adult and married children remain strongly affiliated with their parents, as posited to be so for many families in urban China, the rationale for exchange of resources between parents and children so that maximum total utility is achieved remains, whether or not they physically live under the same roof, and whether or not the children have established their own units. Thus, as parents grow older and become more vulnerable both in physical health and economic conditions, and their children are still in their prime both physically and financially, there is a tendency on the part of children to divert part of their resources, in the form of service, money, or goods, to their parents.[4]

Hypotheses About Transfer of Resources

Hence, given a certain degree of children's identification with the parental family, the higher their own economic capacity is, net of their local obligations, the more likely the children are to provide economic support to their aging parents. Likewise, other things being equal, a relatively lower economic situation of their parents, expressed either as their needs or lack of resources, is more likely to prompt a grown child to provide assistance. Thus, the whole process connotes a sharing experience. However, the degree to which parents and grown children share, in that resources are equalized, is conditioned by the extent to which children identify with their parents. Hence, the more strongly the children identify with their parents, the higher the degree of equalization.

In a nutshell, the above propositions can be expressed as follows:

$$S = f(N, C; A)$$

$$\frac{\partial S}{\partial N} > 0, \quad \frac{\partial S}{\partial C} > 0, \quad \frac{\partial S}{\partial A} > 0,$$

where *S* denotes old age support; *f* is the support function; and *N*, *C*, and *A* denote the needs of parents, the capacity of children, and children's affiliation to their parental family, respectively. The positive relationships between support and the other three variables are shown by the positive first-order partial derivatives. The exact form of the support function is difficult to ascertain, or, rather, it cannot be derived from the theoretical model without more strenuous assumptions.

Support in service by children basically can be interpreted in the same fashion. As older parents grow older and become frailer physically, as compared with their children, children increasingly provide service type support to their parents. Since in general grown children are in their physical prime, given the same degree of identification with the parental family, the instrumental support they provide to parents is largely dictated by the needs of parents, thus making it more likely "need-centered."[5]

Data, Analytic Approach, and Measures

The data used for empirical analysis come from both the child and parent samples of the 1994 Survey of Aging and Intergenerational Relations in Baoding. In the two-stage survey based on a multistage equal probability design, 1,002 parents of age fifty or older were first interviewed. In the second stage, the adult children (age eighteen or older) of each selected parent respondent were randomly sampled, and one of them was chosen for interviewing. In all, 753 such adult children were interviewed in the homes of their parents. The number of cases in which we have complete information about both the parent and child respondents is 731. Analyses presented here are based mainly on the results of interviewing these 731 parent-child pairs, with an emphasis on that of the child sample.

Two clusters of analyses were conducted to examine the questions of how strongly grown children identify with their parental family and how resources are redistributed by the act of old age support. On the first question, children's attitudes, frequency of contact, and other activities, which are assumed to reveal the degree of association with their parents, were analyzed. First, child respondents' answers to a set of statements purportedly measuring people's value orientations in regard to intergenerational relations were compared pair-wise with those of the same statements made by their parents. The purpose is to see whether there are significant attitudinal differences between children and their parents in that children view the issue of old age support less favorably than their parents do. Second, the frequency of contact of those children with their noncoresiding parents was explored, with an implicit assumption that the frequency of children's contact with their noncoresiding parents is indicative of their membership in their parental family. Finally, other types of social contact of those children with their noncoresiding parents were compared with those of coresiding children. Having the pattern of interactions between children and their coresiding parents serve as a baseline, the comparison is posited to show the extent to which noncoresiding children continue to identify with their parental family.

The second set of analyses focused on actualization of old age support as a process in which resources between generations are redistributed. Two dichotomous dependent variables measuring whether instrumental support (personal care and household chores) the child respondents have provided were regressed on functional limitations of parents, availability of spousal support, child's health, living arrangement, all operationalized as reflecting the needs of parents and the capacity of children, and a set of other variables. In the same fashion, logistic regressions of economic support (money and gifts) on incomes of parents and children, among others, were performed. Finally, using the technique of regression of censored dependent variables, the relationships between amount of economic support and the needs of parents and the capacity of children were analyzed.

A large number of questions were addressed both to parents and children respondents during the interview. Among them were a set of statements constructed specifically to gauge attitudes toward intergenerational relations and support. An English rendering of these statements is as follows:

> "If they are economically better off, parents should help their children financially, even if the children are married and live in a separate household."

"An older person who is widowed should not live alone."

"As long as health permits, an older person should live independently, and not depend on (his/her) children."

"When married children have a steady income and live with their parents, they should use most of their income for the well-being of the whole family."

"Married children who live in a separate household should not ask their parents for financial help."

"Even when a child is married and lives in a separate household, he or she should still do as much as possible to make sure that (his/her) parents have a comfortable life."

"People should be more concerned about caring for their children than about caring for their parents or parents-in-law."

"An old person can live in an old age home and still have a happy life."

Clearly, all these statements show normative judgment on various aspects of mutual obligations between older parents and their grown children, and expressed approval or disapproval of them reflects one's attitudinal disposition toward the relations between older parents and their grown children. Answers by the respondents to these statements constitute the attitudinal variables to be used for children's identification with their parental family. The coding scheme for each item is as follows: 1 = strongly disagree, 2 = disagree, 3 = agree, 4 = strongly agree. Therefore, a high value means that the respondent agrees strongly with the statement. The descriptive statistics of these variables are given in table 13.1. For those child respondents not coresiding with any of their parents, they were asked during the interview how often they saw their mothers and fathers. The distribution of the answers is presented in table 13.2.

Other variables that measure children's continued identification with their parental family include a set of variables measuring married child respondents' association with their parents: (1) the affective ties between their spouses and their parents, (2) perceived change in economic and emotional support to their parents after marriage, (3) parents' involvement in mediating conflicts between children and their spouses, and (4) the extent to which married children continued to consult their parents for advice. During the interview, the child respondent was asked to rate the warmth of the relationship between his or her spouse with his or her parents. In addition, respondents were also asked to evaluate the change of economic and economic support after marriage, and whether their parents were asked to mediate possible marital conflicts between children and their spouses, and how often parents were consulted for advice. The frequency distributions of these variables are given in table 13.3.

Table 13.1
Correlations, Means, and Mean Differences of Attitudes of Parents and Children in Intergenerational Relations

Statements concerning intergenerational relations	*Pair-corr.*	*Mean*		*t-test of mean difference*		
		Parent	*Child*	*Mean difference*	*t-value*	*two-tail sig.*
1. Parents should help children even when they do not live together.	0.067	2.77 (0.54)	2.36 (0.61)	0.414	13.9	0.00
2. A widowed elderly person should not live alone.	0.063	2.82 (0.57)	3.00 (0.55)	−0.180	−6.2	0.00
3. When health permits, an elderly person should live independently.	0.019	2.76 (0.63)	2.40 (0.58)	0.358	11.2	0.00
4. When living together, children should pool their money with their parents'.	0.052	2.53 (0.58)	2.66 (0.52)	−0.127	−4.3	0.00
5. Married children not coresident should not ask parents for money.	0.027	2.82 (0.58)	2.96 (0.52)	−0.145	−5.0	0.00
6. Children should do best to make parents' life life comfortable.	0.186	3.35 (0.51)	3.41 (0.55)	−0.060	−2.4	0.02
7. People should care more about their children than their parents.	0.085	2.45 (0.62)	2.29 (0.56)	0.163	5.40	0.00
8. An elderly person can still have a good life in nursing home.	0.124	2.47 (0.63)	2.25 (0.59)	0.225	7.37	0.00

Notes: The coding scheme for each item is as follows: 1 = strongly disagree, 2 = disagree, 3 = agree, 4 = strongly agree. Numbers in parentheses are standard deviations.

Source: 1994 Baoding parent-child paired sample (n = 731).

The dependent variables in our regression analyses, instrumental and economic old age support provided by children, are derived from a set of questions that ask about various kinds of assistance they have provided or continue to provide to their parents. They include assistance in personal care, household chores, cash giving, and gifts. For personal care, respondents were asked whether they were providing such support to their parents. For household chores, including shopping, cooking, taking buses, and household finance management, the question was whether such support was given to parents.

Table 13.2
Frequency of Children's Contact with Parents

	Contact with	
	Father (%)	*Mother (%)*
Coresiding with parents	44.0	44.0
Living in separate households		
(Almost) daily	28.3 (54.5)	28.7 (54.3)
Several times a week	16.1 (31.6)	16.7 (32.1)
Several times a month	7.0 (13.4)	7.0 (13.1)
Several times a year	0.3 (0.5)	0.3 (0.5)
Frequency unknown	4.2	3.3

Note: Numbers in parentheses are percentages among those who do not coreside with their parents and who have provided valid answers.

Source: 1994 Baoding child sample (*n*=731).

Child respondents were also asked whether they were providing financial support. Lastly, they were asked whether they had provided in-kind support in the previous year. All four variables are dummy coded, with 1 denoting a particular kind of support provided, and 0 otherwise. For the last two kinds of support, respondents were asked to give an estimate of average monthly amount in cash giving or total money worth of the gifts they had provided to their parents in the previous year. The descriptive statistics of these measures are provided in table 13.4.

In the regression analysis of instrumental support, the age of parent interviewed, again dummy coded into three binary categorical variables, was used as one of the proxy variables of parents' need for support. Functional limitation indicates the physical strength of the parent interviewed, and thereby the need for support in personal care and household chores. Marital status of parent interviewed (currently married versus widowed or divorced) measures whether spousal support is available. Inclusion of living arrangement of the parent interviewed, coded into three dummy variables (living with spouse or alone versus others; with other grown children versus others; with the child respondent versus others) would give us a clue about whether coresidence with a grown child increases the likelihood of receiving support from children in general and from that child in particular. Child's marital status (married versus not married) measures the child's local obligation. The variable of child's self-rated health, ranging from 1, very poor, to 5, very good, was used as an index of the child's own health condition. The variable of whether having own

Table 13.3
Percentage Distribution of Children's Associations with Parents by Living Arrangement

	Living arrangement (%)				
	Live with parents	*Do not live with parents*	*Chi square*	*Prob.*	*Total sample*
Spouse's relationship with father-in-law:					
Very warm	31.7	34.9			33.9
Fairly warm	67.1	62.3			63.7
Fairly cold	1.2	2.8			2.4
Very cold	0.0	0.0	1.95	0.38	0.0
Spouse's relationship with mother-in-law:					
Very warm	33.5	32.6			32.9
Fairly warm	62.8	62.6			62.7
Fairly cold	3.7	4.6			4.3
Very cold	0.0	0.3	0.68	0.88	0.2
Change in child's economic support to parents after marriage:					
Much less	6.4	12.2			10.5
Less	21.1	33.6			29.8
No change	56.7	46.8			49.7
More	15.8	7.5	20.86	0.00	9.9
Change in child's emotional support to parents after marriage:					
Much less	1.8	2.0			1.9
Less	11.1	22.8			19.3
No change	65.5	60.5			62.0
More	21.6	14.6	12.55	0.01	16.7
Parents ever asked to mediate conflict between children and their spouses:					
Yes	41.1	34.4			37.0
No	58.9	65.6	2.76	0.10	63.0
Frequency child asks parents for advice:					
Always	57.7	40.7			48.0
Sometimes	36.1	39.5			38.0
Occasionally	2.6	9.1			6.3
Never	3.6	10.8	34.21	0.00	7.7

Source: 1994 Baoding child sample.

Table 13.4
Old Age Support Provided by Children (Means and Percentages)

	Age of parent interviewed			Total sample
	50–59	60–70	70+	
Assistance given to parents				
Personal care	18.5%	29.4%	42.6%	25.9%
Household chores	57.6%	55.0%	72.2%	58.6%
Financial support	37.8%	43.7%	53.1%	42.1%
Monthly amount of money given (in yuan)	109.92 (91.89)	67.67 (68.70)	56.20 (47.11)	84.83 (80.55)
In-kind support given in previous year	54.2%	71.8%	73.3%	63.3%
Value of in-kind support (in yuan)	337.44 (327.45)	399.18 (428.99)	391.72 (492.82)	372.74 (402.22)
Number of observations	358	269	104	731

Note: Numbers in parentheses are standard deviations.

Source: 1994 Baoding child sample.

children or not is another proxy of the local obligation of the child respondent (see table 13.5).

In the regression analysis of economic support, the family income of the parent interviewed, the index of housing amenities of the parent interviewed, and the personal income of the child were used to replace the variable of parent's functional limitation and the child self-rated health.

Membership in the Parental Family as a Social Fact

The membership of a grown child in his or her parental family is inherently ambiguous. Although a grown child's nest-leaving or marriage signifies the beginning of newly gained independence, habitually or purposely, whether this also amounts to an announcement of total exit from the parental family is unclear. Unlike the husband-wife relationship, intergenerational relationships exist in a more "natural" state in that little aid of legal contract is needed to proclaim the beginning of the biologically originated parent-child link, and correspondingly no disavowal is necessary when grown children leave their primary "nests." Hence, emotionally or otherwise parents and their noncoresiding grown children, not to mention the coresiding ones, remain attached to each other, and this linkage may blur the boundaries between one's own family and his or her parental one and provide an emotional basis for one to maintain his or her membership in multiple families.[6]

By referring to grown children's continued membership in their parental family as a social fact, I am contending that their affiliations with their family of orientation in a subjective sense have influenced their conduct of family life to such an extent that a pattern of social behavior emerges in which the family of a child's own and that of his or her parents become closely interconnected. The enabling and constraining property of social relationships lie in that there exists a probability of action in some definite way appropriate to the subjective meanings given by both parties (Weber 1978a, 26–28). However, when subjective meanings have given rise to the observable human conduct, the probable becomes a fact.

Table 13.1 contains pair-wise correlation coefficients, means, and mean differences of the answers made by parents and their grown children to eight different attitudinal questions. When children's attitudes toward mutual obligations between generations are compared with those of their parents, several important features emerge. First, for question 6, high mean scores (3.35 and 3.41)—close to 4, strongly agree—for both parent and child respondents suggest that there is a general agreement that it is children's duty to make the life of their parents comfortable, and this idea is held across both the older and younger generations. Also, the fairly high mean scores on item 2—2.82 for parents and 3.00 for children—indicate that both generations would frown on the idea of a widowed elderly person living alone. Hence, the old conviction that parents have the right to demand support from their children for old age security and correspondingly children are duty bound to do so appears to be a still widely accepted social doctrine.

Second, except for items 6 and 8, pair-wise correlations for all other questions are very weak, suggesting that how children think of the mutual obligations between generations is by and large unrelated with how their parents think of them. It is unclear why this is the case. In any case, the weak correlation appears to suggest that grown children's opinions on mutual obligations between generations and old age support in particular are not influenced decidedly by those of their parents.

A plausible explanation to the puzzle of weak correlation between opinions between parents and children may be found in the third feature revealed in table 13.1. Although the *t*-test results for all questions suggest that significant differences exist between older parents and their children in regard to their attitudes toward mutual obligations, the attitudinal differences reveal a striking pattern that can be termed "family altruism." For all questions the older parents stress more strongly than their grown children their own independence and the duty of continuing support to children. Conversely, the grown children value more highly than their parents their duty in old age support. All these answers suggest a pattern that each generation wishes to be less a burden and at the same time be more supportive to the other generation. For instance, on the first statement that, when needed, parents should provide financial assistance to their noncoresiding children, parent respondents are more likely to agree with it than their children are. Similarly, on the third statement, which stresses the importance of independence on the part of older parents, more parent respondents than their children think it is important they maintain their independence. Also, it is interesting to note that on the last item older parents are more likely than their children to think that it is possible to have a good life in an old age home. This amounts to declaring that living in an old age home can be a practical and proper choice.

The pattern of family altruism, suggested by our results, provides a revealing glimpse of the ideational system that accompanies the current pattern of old age support. The results provide empirical evidence that in spite of the rapid social change in China in the past half century, the old belief that old age support is a family business remains largely unchanged. To be sure, this kind of altruistic attitude in no way represents the actual process of social exchange between generations, the hard bargaining under the table or behind the door, but the idea of intergenerational support being a foremost important family obligation moralizes between generations the emotional bond, the very fabric of family solidarity, and therefore presents an effective moral as well as emotional barrier to any easy breakup of this obligation.

Corresponding to the general tendency of viewing care for the old as one of family obligations, grown children, when not living with their older parents, continue to maintain frequent contact (see table 13.2).[7] Forty-four percent of child respondents lived with their parents. Another 44 percent (28 percent plus 16 percent), though not coresiding with parents, saw their parents at least once a week. In other words, about 90 percent of grown children interacted continually with their parents. And, of those living in separate households, close to 90 percent of them saw their noncoresiding parents frequently.

Assuming that married children who live with their parents identify with their parental family, the fact that those who were living with parents and those who did not differ very little in terms of association indicates noncoresiding children's continued affiliation. According to the results in table 13.3, over 90 percent of married child respondents claimed that their spouses had "fairly warm" to "very warm" relations with their parents, and this is so for both coresident and noncoresident children. Compared with those who lived with parents, a higher percentage of noncoresident children began to provide less economic support to their parents after marriage, and this difference is statistically significant. Nevertheless, over 50 percent of them claimed their marriage did not hinder their capacity to give economic support to parents. Similarly, proportion-wise, more noncoresident children than coresident ones (23.8 percent versus 12.9 percent) admitted giving parents less emotional support after their marriage. However, the other side of the coin is that about three-fourths of them continued to give emotional support.[8]

Furthermore, 37 percent of all married children said they (or their married siblings) would seek their parents' help to mediate possible conflicts between them and their spouses. For noncoresiding children, those who acknowledged that they would do so were some 34 percent, slightly lower than that of coresident children. With regard to consultation with parents, again, those who live with their parents are more likely than those who do not to seek advice from their parents. However, some 80 percent of noncoresident children consult their parents "sometimes" or "always."

In sum, there is clear empirical evidence that in contemporary urban China the overwhelming majority of grown children, whether coresiding with parents or living in separate households, whether married or unmarried, still consider old age support part of their family obligations, maintain frequent contact, and associate with their parents in various ways. While there exists a difference in degree between coresident and noncoresident children in their association with parents, overall the evidence points to the conclusion that children not living with parents are almost as much affiliated with their parents as those living with their parents.

Determinants of the Flows of Resources

Service-type Old Age Support

Results of logistic regression of instrumental old age support (personal care and household chores) on parental needs and children's capacity are reported in table 13.5. Model 1 is a baseline model without other control variables present. Model 2 contains three control variables representing parental investment:

current assistance parents were giving currently to their children in child care, household chores, and money. An additional control variable is gender of the child respondent.

Age and functional limitation of parents are the only two significant predictors of old age support in personal care. The odds of parents of sixty to sixty-nine years of age receiving support in personal care is 63 percent ($e^{0.49} = 1.63$) higher than that of parents in a younger age group (fifty to fifty-nine), and the odds ratio of parents of seventy years or older receiving support versus those in the reference group is even higher ($e^{1.001} = 2.72$). Thus, the pattern appears to be that the older the parents, the more likely that they receive support in personal care, other things being equal. Similarly, frail health of parents, especially in terms of their functional status, is likely to induce support in personal care from children. The effects of the two factors remain largely unchanged after other control variables have been introduced in the model. However, marital status becomes marginally significant ($p < .10$). Surprisingly, the widowed and divorced are less likely to receive support than the currently married. However, it is possible that the effect is spurious, in that the positive coefficient may simply mean that for a child whose parents interviewed were still married, he or she has two parents to care for, and therefore the chance that one of them has become physically frail is higher than is the case when the child has only one parent still alive. In addition, the variable of gender is significantly related to likelihood of support in personal care: daughters are more likely than sons to give such support.

In terms of support in household chores, the basic pattern is quite similar to support in personal care: age and functional limitations are two deciding predictors for support in household work. In addition, those children who coreside with their parents are more likely than those who do not to provide such support, and this is so especially when compared with those whose parents are living with other children (0.567 versus -0.150). Living alone, though implying stronger needs on the part of parents, does not induce more support. One plausible explanation is that those who live alone (or with spouse only) are usually in better physical condition. In the full model, the effects of all three factors remain significant. Additionally, two control variables have significant effects: daughters are more likely than sons to give support in household chores, and those who currently are receiving economic assistance from their parents tend to be more ready to support parents in household chores.

Further, children's capacity, measured by their health, marital status, and whether having their own children, has no statistically significant effect on the

Table 13.5

Effects of Parental Needs and Children's Capacity on Instrumental Old Age Support

	Personal care		Household chores	
	Model 1	*Model 2*	*Model 1*	*Model 2*
Variables measuring parental needs				
Age of parent interviewed				
(50–59)				
60–69	0.494*	0.487*	–0.081	–0.053
70+	1.001**	1.059**	0.559*	0.679*
Functional limitations	0.384**	0.355*	0.333*	0.340*
Marital status				
(Divorced or widowed)				
Currently married	0.463	0.597+	0.065	0.075
Living arrangement				
(Living with spouse or alone)				
With other children	–0.298	–0.361	–0.150	–0.189
With child respondent	–0.009	0.110	0.567*	0.725**
Child's capacity				
Marital status:				
(Not married)				
Currently married	–0.109	–0.006	0.294	0.404
Self-rated health	0.026	0.060	–0.040	0.006
Having own children				
(No children)				
One or more children	0.149	0.312	–0.261	–0.243
Assistance currently given by parents				
Care for grandchildren				
(No)				
Yes		–0.365		0.020
Help with household chores				
(No)				
Yes		0.272		0.010
Economic assistance				
(No)				
Yes		0.158		0.585*
Gender of child				
(Female)				
Male		–0.638**		–0.680**
Intercept	–2.389**	–2.489**	–0.277	–0.352
Log likelihood	–395	–387	–470	–458

Notes: Results are generated by logistic regression. Items in parentheses are reference categories.

+$p < .10$; *$p < .05$; **$p < .01$

likelihood of old age support in both personal care and household chores. In other words, whether children provide services to their parents has little to do with whether they are in good or bad health, married or single, have their own children or not.

In sum, by and large old age support of service type is determined by the health condition of parents and the fact that parents are getting old. As a rule, grown children enjoy better health than their aged parents. When parents of advanced age and/or frail health are in need of service-type support, a child's own capacity, measured by own health condition and local obligations, does not seem to have any consequential effect on whether such assistance is to be given. Hence, instrumental old age support can be viewed as being largely "need centered" (see Lee and Xiao 1994).

Economic Old Age Support

Results of logistic regressions of economic old age support are given in table 13.6. The dichotomous variables of cash giving and in-kind gifts are regressed, separately, on family income of parent interviewed, index of household amenities (which is the total count of material possessions of the household of the parent interviewed and therefore is a measure of living standard), child's personal income, and several others. Clearly, the processes of cash giving and in-kind gifts operate with somewhat different mechanisms. In terms of cash giving, the significant negative coefficient of parents' family income (-0.404) and positive one of child's personal income (0.384) suggest that the higher the parents' family income, and the lower the personal income of the child, the less likely that parents will receive economic support in monetary terms. By the same token, the negative coefficient of index of household amenities (-0.115) means that the more material possessions there are in parents' household, the less likely that parents will receive cash from their children. Further, parents' coresidence with a grown child increases the chance that the child gives money to the parents (0.744); and having own children reduces the likelihood that a child provides monetary old age support (-0.472). Thus, the basic pattern of cash flow from children to parents is precisely as expected: the likelihood of money support to parents is largely dictated by the quantity of material resources possessed by both parents and their children, in that the more that children have vis-à-vis their parents, the more likely they send money to their parents.

Table 13.6
Effects of Parental Needs and Children's Capacity on Economic Old Age Support

	Cash giving		In-kind gifts	
	Model 1	*Model 2*	*Model 1*	*Model 2*
Variables measuring parental needs				
Age of parent-interviewed				
(50–59)				
60–69	0.199	0.241	0.573**	0.590**
70+	0.404	0.526+	0.461	0.566+
Log of parent's household income	–0.404*	–0.387*	0.081	0.090
Index of housing amenities	–0.115*	–0.116*	–0.035	–0.041
Marital status				
(Divorced or widowed)				
Currently married	0.203	0.148	–0.338	–0.347
Living arrangement				
(Living with spouse or alone)				
With other children	0.172	0.195	–0.241	–0.255
With child respondent	0.744**	0.700**	–0.340	–0.252
Child's capacity				
Marital status				
(Not married)				
Currently married	0.443	0.393	0.264	0.265
Log of child personal income	0.384**	0.368**	0.137**	0.155**
Having own children				
(No children)				
One or more children	–0.472+	–0.686*	0.095	0.084
Assistance currently given by parents				
Care for grandchildren				
(No)				
Yes		0.443*		0.000
Help with household chores				
(No)				
Yes		0.088		0.398
Economic assistance				
(No)				
Yes		–0.410		–0.138
Gender of child				
(Female)				
Male		–0.046		–0.616**
Intercept	0.343	0.496	–0.539	–0.374
Log likelihood	–408	–405	–396	–389

Notes: Results are generated by logistic regression. Items in parentheses are reference categories.

+$p < .10$; *$p < .05$; **$p < .01$

Introducing control variables into the model does not change the basic pattern much (see model 2 in table 13.6). The dummy age variable of parents being seventy or older becomes marginally significant (0.526, $p < 0.10$), suggesting that those seventy years of age or older are more likely than those in their fifties to receive support, other things, including incomes of both parents and children, being equal. Hence, the variable of old age in this context may be interpreted as one that captures the effect of token value of giving money simply as a show of respect.[9] Further, if parents are currently providing assistance in child care for their children, they may also receive money in return, as the positive effect of care for grandchildren indicates (0.443).

The significant predictors of in-kind economic support are few: Those parents in their sixties are more likely than those younger to receive gifts from their children, and the likelihood that children send gifts to their parents is positively related to their personal income. Further, since the coefficient of the dummy variable indicating parents seventy years of age or older is nonsignificant and smaller than that indicating people in their sixties (0.461 versus 0.573), the effect of age of parents on in-kind support is probably nonlinear, in that it is not always the case that the older the parents, the more likely they receive gifts. Further, notice that the effects of family income, index of household amenities, and living arrangement are all nonsignificant statistically, and it can be inferred that at least a large portion of gift giving serves the purpose of showing deference to the old or maintaining parent-child relations, rather than that of meeting material needs of the older parents. Again, inclusion of the control variables in the model changes little of the basic pattern. A negative coefficient of the variable of gender (-0.616) suggests that daughters are more likely than sons to send gifts to their parents.

The results of Tobit regression of economic support are presented in table 13.7. Comparing the results presented in both tables 13.6 and 13.7, it appears that the amount of economic support (money and gifts) is influenced by the same set of variables that determines the likelihood of economic support. Parents' family income, number of material possessions, and coresidence with the child who gives support, as well as the child's personal income, affect the amount of money giving in a similar way as they do the likelihood of such support. The same can be said about determinants of total worth of gifts that children give to parents. Again, much of this pattern holds after the effects of control variables have been accounted for.

One particular feature worth commenting on in the models of monetary support is the change of the effect of children having their own children. In

Table 13.7
Effects of Parental Needs and Children's Capacity on Amount of Economic Old Age Support (Tobit Regression)

	Monthly money support[a]		*Total worth of in-kind gifts*[a]	
	Model 1	*Model 2*	*Model 1*	*Model 2*
Variables measuring parental needs				
Age of parent interviewed				
(50–59)				
60–69	0.328	0.456	1.243**	1.253**
70+	0.699	1.022	0.949	1.114+
Log of parent's household income	–0.473*	–0.460*	0.175	0.191
Index of housing amenities	–0.262*	–0.262*	0.020	–0.029
Marital status				
(Divorced or widowed)				
Currently married	0.432	0.267	–0.571	–0.558
Living arrangement				
(Living with spouse or alone)				
With other children	0.100	0.183	–0.381	–0.389
With child respondent	1.824**	1.695**	–0.618	–0.441
Child's capacity				
Marital status				
(Not married)				
Currently married	0.584	0.459	0.671	0.667
Log of child personal income	0.826**	0.794**	0.383**	0.418**
Having own children				
(No children)				
One or more children	–0.950	–1.575*	0.346	0.347
Assistance currently given by parents				
Care for grandchildren				
(No)				
Yes		1.254*		–0.054
Help with household chores				
(No)				
Yes		0.180		0.669
Economic assistance				
(No)				
Yes		–0.876		–0.212
Gender of child				
(Female)				
Male		–0.034		–1.117**
σ	4.138**	4.101**	4.091**	4.055**
Intercept	–1.094	–0.592	–1.178	–0.948
Log likelihood	–978	–974	–1298	–1292

Notes: Items in parentheses are reference categories.
[a]Both monthly cash support and total worth of gifts have been transformed into logged values.
$^{+}p < .10$; $^{*}p < .05$; $^{**}p < .01$

the initial model, the variable of whether the child respondent has his or her own children is statistically nonsignificant. However, in the full model, such effect becomes stronger and statistically significant. The probable candidate variable that plays the role of "suppressant" is parents' current assistance in child care. When the variable is introduced into the equation, the "suppressed" effect is released. In substantive terms, the results suggest that a grown child's having his or her own children may trigger two reactions. On the one hand, having own children may prevent a grown child from sparing too much of his or her resources for parents. On the other hand, the child may have to seek assistance from parents to look after the grandchildren and may therefore feel obliged to send money to parents in return. When the effect of parents' aid in child care is unaccounted for, the two opposing forces may make the effect of having own children inconclusive.

To summarize, several points can be drawn from our analyses: First, in a model where we are concerned mainly with the relative importance of the needs parents and the capacity of children, the major determinants of instrumental support (personal care and household chores) are the age and functional health of parents. Children's health conditions and their local obligations have little effect on predicting the likelihood of instrumental support. Therefore, instrumental support can be viewed as mainly "needs centered," in that given that there exists a willingness on the part of children to provide support, whether a child actually gives support of an instrumental type is decided primarily by the needs of parents for such support.

Second, parents' coresidence with a supporting child increases the chance that the child provides support in household chores, but is largely irrelevant in whether the child gives support in personal care. The difference suggests that old age support in personal care is more "needs centered" than that in household chores. The explanation probably lies in the fact that support in personal care, when needed, is more pressing than assistance in housework, and if not needed, there is little utility in providing such support. Demand for support in household chores, on the other hand, is more "elastic."

Third, in comparison with support of service type, economic old age support in cash is more "balanced," in that the material conditions of both parents and children play important roles in deciding whether and how much such support is given. The basic pattern appears to be that the lower the income of parents and the higher the income of children, the more likely that children send cash to their parents. Conversely, the higher the income of parents and the lower the income of children, the smaller the chance that parents receive cash support from their children.

Fourth, for in-kind support, the age of parents and the income of children are the only two significant determinants. Old age, on the part of parents, and prospering economic condition, on the part of children, increase the probability that parents receive in-kind support. The effects of parents' material conditions (reflected by family income and index of household amenities) are indeterminate. Hence, the proclivity of a supporting child in sending gifts to parents is dampened mainly by his or her own financial capacity. Further, that the effect of old age is statistically significant, given that the material conditions of parents have been controlled, suggests that gift giving, perhaps more so than cash giving, also serves to express children's deference to parents of advanced age, rather than to satisfy their real economic needs.

A Commitment to Intergenerational Support

The pervasive instrumental and economic intergenerational support that we have noted in urban China attests to a pattern of continued association between older parents and their grown children, not only in terms of social contact but also of exchange of resources. For grown children in today's urban China, as the economic rationale for being deferential to older generations is no longer as pressing and imperative as it was in the past, and the cultural norms that favors the "rule of elders" (Fei [1947] 1992) are no longer being upheld and guarded with such vigor and fervor as they were in the past, there are fewer powerful external forces that push or compel grown children into the preordained mode of human conduct of complete obedience to the wishes and whims of the older parents. Yet, despite a dramatic decline of parental power, it appears that the old institution of intrafamilial support has been kept largely intact, not in the sense that older parents continue to be wholly dependent upon their children, but in that the tradition of old age security of parents being mainly the duty of children, both as an idea and as a way of life, has been by and large maintained. The question, then, of what roles grown children have played in the formation and maintenance of the pattern of old age support in contemporary urban China becomes an interesting and sociologically meaningful one. The focus of this chapter was set to investigate, from the standpoint of grown children, how old age support is realized. In general, the results from our analysis support the argument that children's identification with their parental family is a prerequisite for their providing support, the way resources flow from the children to their parents is influenced by both the perceived needs of parents and their own capacity, and, finally, the redistribution of resources resulted from the act of old age support tends to have an equalizing effect.

More specifically, the main findings in this chapter may be summarized as follows: First, the overwhelming majority of grown children in our Baoding sample, regardless of their marital status or living arrangement, continue to be strongly affiliated with their older parents, and this is shown not only in their attitudes but also in the actual conduct of their daily lives. In terms of value orientation concerning intergenerational relations and support, grown children are just as committed as their parents, if not more so, to the idea of the moral importance of intergenerational support. Indeed, our results suggest that children more so than their older parents consider it a child's duty to provide support to their parents (table 13.1). While it is important to bear in mind that ideals and reality never correspond perfectly, the expressed willingness in supporting aged parents is at least indicative of children's group affiliation with their parents in a subjective sense.

Children's subjective identification with their parental family is mirrored by their close association with parents in everyday life. Again, the overwhelming majority of those who live in separate households maintain frequent contact with their noncoresiding parents. For married children, by a variety of measures (see table 13.3), those who do not live with parents differ very little from those who do live with them.

Second, in terms of instrumental support, important factors that predict actualization of support are old age and functional limitation of parents. As parents grow older and their functional health begins to deteriorate, children are motivated to provide services in personal care or household chores. The statistical nonsignificance of variables measuring children's conditions, such as their own health, marital status, and whether they have their own children, suggests that the likelihood that children provide instrumental support to their older parents is dictated primarily by parents' becoming very old and physically frail. In this regard, instrumental support, especially personal care, can be viewed as centered on the needs of parents, or, more precisely, the needs of parents as perceived by their supportive children (see Hermalin, Ofstedal, and Chang 1992).

Third, in economic old age support, children's capacity, measured by their income, marital status, and whether having own children, begins to play an important part in deciding whether and how much to give, in that the more economic resources a child has to spare, the likelier he or she is to give, and give more, to his or her older parents. Further, for cash giving, the economic conditions of parents play an opposite role: that is, the better the economic situation of parents, the less likely that a child would give. Hence, that the material conditions of parents and children have opposing effects on cash giving, in likelihood and amount, suggests a process of redistribution of resources reminiscent of equalizing the resources between the family of a child and that of his or her parents.

Fourth, for in-kind economic support, however, the effect of parents' economic conditions is indeterminate. In addition to the income of children, the effect of age of parents becomes significant. Parents of advanced age are likely to receive support from children who are relatively well to do. An apparent inference that can be drawn from this is that children, under their budget constraints, provide in-kind support to their parents, not simply for the betterment of the economic conditions of their parents, but also because of its token value of courtesy and good will, which is often attached in any gift giving. In other words, the in-kind support children provide to their older parents may carry more symbolic meaning, be it simply a show of respect or a way to maintain close contact, than economic support in cash.

Fifth, although our results have shown clearly that old age support by children can hardly be characterized as being guided by the principle of quid pro quo, a certain degree of short-term exchange does exist. Consistent with the summaries just made, parents who are giving economic assistance to a child are more likely, other things being equal, to receive old age support in household chores from the child (see table 13.5). Likewise, those parents who are providing assistance in child care for their children are more likely to receive support in cash (see tabs. 13.6 and 13.7).

Yet we must be cautious in our interpretation of such short-term exchanges in terms of cause and effect. Given the structure of the data, it is difficult to ascertain which one takes place first, therefore subject to being understood as a cause. It may well be possible that older parents give economic assistance because of the aid they receive from children in household chores or help to care for grandchildren because of the money they receive from children. However they may be causally related, a most certain interpretation is that there exists some form of short-term exchange, even though, as has been argued repeatedly, it is not the major underlying mechanism of old age support.

Therefore, our results suggest that, from the perspective of children, concerns for the well-being of their parents (the perceived needs of parents) and their own ability in setting aside part of their resources for use for their parents (capacity) are each important in their decision regarding when and how much they provide assistance to their parents. While these factors clearly carry somewhat different weights for different kinds of old age support in children's judgment of whether to provide a helping hand, it is clear that the basic pattern is that when children offer to assist, they do so mainly out of concerns for the welfare of their parents. Within the constraints of their limited resources, a sense of responsibility is the main motivational force that compels children to provide support.

14

CHO-YUN HSU

Local Community and Communal Solidarity in Rural China

In 1933, C. K. Yang took part in the Zouping Project, one of the earliest sociological fieldwork studies conducted in China. A report of this study was published in Chinese during the war years of the Japanese invasion of China; unfortunately, this version is not available for us to use. However, an English version summarized the longer Chinese report and was published in 1944 by the Institute of Pacific Relations in cooperation with the Yenching-Yunnan Station for Sociological Research (Yang 1944).

The report focused on rural marketing activities, which knit a cluster of local fairs into a network. In this network, fairs were held every five days or so in villages strategically located at crossroads and rotated from village to village in a five-day cycle, following a roughly circular motion. Several such circles of rotating fairs formed satellites around a marketing town, from which the peddlers acquired their supplies and to which dealers deposited staple products bought from the farmers in the surrounding farmsteads. Thus, several groups of villages, about ten apiece, would form a community. Above such a community was a local network surrounding a town, and at an even higher level of the hierarchy was a city, which often was the seat of the county administration. In

Yang's words, this was a hierarchical network of these types of periodic markets, basic, intermediate and centrally formed.

In his surveys, Yang described in detail the distance a person needed to walk to and from the market grounds, which then delineated the size and boundaries of the area or cluster of villages that formed these markets. He also recorded the commodity items exchanged, the professional categories of the traders, and even the magnitude of trade that took place in a day of periodic transactions in the market. He provided several maps to show the distribution of these three levels of marketing places and centers, with roads clearly marked. Though he paid most attention to the economic functions of the network, he nevertheless also suggested that information exchange and the formation of opinions were noticeable functions as well. On one occasion, Yang specifically mentioned an annual fair lasting twelve days, held once a year at the foot of Yellow Hill. This gathering, in the nature of pilgrimage activity, was nominally a ceremony to celebrate the birthday of Yu-huang (the Jade Emperor, chief of all deities), whose temple was on the top of Yellow Hill. This annual affair probably was the crowning piece of the periodic markets in Zouping. Herewith, he probably took notes on the multiple functions that the marketing network provided. Therefore, in a postscript, he proposed that communities organized in a periodic marketing network actually should be recognized as basic "cells" of Chinese society, and that such communities had the potential to be developed to serve modern social functions, such as postal service.

Here, Yang essentially described a model very similar to what William Skinner later presented in published form almost a quarter century later in his renowned works on rural marketing systems in the Chengdu basin (Skinner 1964). The concept of a rural marketing system is widely accepted by colleagues in Chinese studies now. Especially interesting is Yang's observation that a temple served as the center of a marketing network. This particular characteristic of Chinese rural marketing activities deserves further explanation.

Indeed, anthropologists in Taiwan, in their field survey, take notice of a phenomenon that local networks are organized around activities of local deities. Activities such as pilgrimages and routine "inspection tours" of such deities help to institutionalize networking of a number of villages; a local communal solidarity is developed in the form of a ritual circle of cults, known as *Jishi quan* (ritual circle), as reported by Taiwanese anthropologists working on folk cults in Taiwan (Hsu 1978; M. Lin 1988, 1990, 1996, 1999). Such an organization is a network hierarchically consisting of three or four levels: the hamlet, which is the basic entity of settlement, then the village, then the inter-village group, which often surrounds a leading village, and then the county-level community. Thus, this communal network represents a grassroots-level structure of Taiwanese society. Field surveys find that even in present times such structures can still be mobilized to influence voters during elections. It means that the strength of this communal network is surviving a stage of folk society and remains viable in establishing local solidarity in an era when the state has forced its way into the society.

The center of the communal worship circle is a temple where a folk deity is worshipped. The most popular ones among numerous gods and goddesses are Mazu, a mother goddess, and the Tudi, a communal guardian depicted in the image of a white-bearded neighborhood grandfather. A powerful temple may be multiplied into branches by means of establishing other temples where duplicate statues of the principal deities are worshipped. Likewise, subbranches can be established as extensions of the secondary temples. Each temple of these branches and subbranches individually represents a communal center while collectively forming a network. Communal activities are organized and overseen by temple managers. In contemporary Taiwan, continuing a practice that began in the Japanese occupation days, a temple is incorporated into a legal entity, which is entitled to own property and to act as a responsible body similar to that of a natural person. Thus, a temple, in its name, is embodied with the power to organize and to operate a broad range of communal activities, such as sponsoring public works and conducting religious ceremonies for community peace and prosperity.

However, the most pertinent characteristics of this kind of temple are demonstrated in the ritual aspects of its activities rather than in its legal aspects in modern civil law. The temples, by means of branching out, are fabricated into a network, the hierarchy of which is represented in its ritual activities. Pilgrimages symbolize tributary visits to the principal temple; and the "inspection" ceremony, in which the deity of a principal temple is carried on a tour around its territory, serves to pronounce its superior status over the branch temples while confirming the territorial boundaries of the temple domain. Within its domain, the community's well-being is identical to and, therefore, manifested by, the well-being of the temple and the worshipped deity therein. For illustration, the good or bad geophysiognomic condition (or *feng-shui*) of the temple is a public concern because people believe that the fortune of the community is directly affected by such conditions. Hence, a collective identity of the community is established by the very existence of the temple.

The hierarchical structure of the principal temple and its branches and subbranches are described as the relationship between parent, children, and grandchildren. It is a direct application of the Chinese kinship structure of lineage organization under patriarchy (or matriarchy if the deity is the mother goddess Mazu), a general principle which dominated the ancient feudalism of the Zhou dynasty. On the other hand, the responsibility of organizing various communal activities is rotated among members of the temple network, providing each locality with a sense of participation that is crucial in periodically reinforcing the communal solidarity of the ritual circle (M. Lin 1988).

To discern fully the ritual circle phenomenon, it would be useful to consider some real cases. Lin Mei-rong has conducted field surveys on this phenomenon at several places in Taiwan. Her investigation of Mazu worship in Zhanghua (Changhua), which she termed a ritual community, is a thorough study on the organization of such a ritual circle. The principal temple of Mazu worship is Nanyao Gong, which is organized into ten branches known as *jiao* (corners), scattered in the alluvial plain of the Dajia and Zhuoshui Rivers. Each *jiao* is led by a headman and consists of several hundred to several thousand members. Naturally, these branch temples also worship Mazu, and it is said that the "incense" of the branches is divided from the central Nanyao Gong. These ten communal associations and the *jiao* headmen are responsible for holding ritual meetings, annual inspecting tours of the main statue, and pilgrimages to the principal temple. The association staff and the *jiao* headmen are usually important members of the dominant local lineages. The entire Mazu ritual circle is in the territory of the Zhangzhou ethnic group and the lesser Hakka group, who are friendly to the former. Meanwhile the villages of the Quanzhou are excluded from participating in the alliance of ritual association because of a long-standing hostility between the Zhangzhou and the Quanzhou peoples dating back to the pioneers' arrival in the nineteenth century. Feuds between the Zhangzhou and the Quanzhou were quite frequent in earlier days when they competed to establish settlements in the fertile land. Even today, ceremonies of the Zhanghua Mazu cult still include combat formations in the processions. It is clear, therefore, that this social entity is comprised of both ethnic and kinship organizations. Other activities include community services to pray for peace and prosperity and collective projects to maintain local irrigation networks (M. Lin 1988, 1990).

Nowadays, leaders of the associations and the branches are either elected to local or state legislatures and administrations or play the roles of power brokers, whose influence at the grassroots level no politician can afford to ignore. Religious organizations of such kind and their leaders are routinely instrumental in demanding government allocation of funds for local public construction. Meanwhile, these leaders collect contributions from the local population in the name of Mazu worship to carry out various kinds of ceremonies as well as to maintain the temples. The associations, as well as their branches, *Jiao*, constitute local power machines, establishing a certain extent of community autonomy within a defined territory. Local resources are mobilized and managed by such a machine.

The same mechanism also represents the community in negotiations and bargaining with the state power for local interest. In the terminology proposed by Lin Nan, the ritual circle described above demonstrates a case of a social network that gathers, nurtures, generates, and circulates social resources within the community and manages its social capital to negotiate with the state. In other words, within the community, the leader builds his social resources into social capital, such as his reputation. Meanwhile, the general members contribute their economic capital, that is, their donations of money, time, and labor, which formed a sizable social resource. Then by means of ritualistic activities, a community solidarity is formed so that these collective social resources can carry sufficient weight to bargain for the benefit of the community in its dealings with other communities or with the state, which can be regarded as an entity on a higher level of the hierarchy of the complex system of state-society structure (N. Lin 2001, 143–64).

So far, different scholars have coined various terms to describe the phenomenon of ritual circles in Taiwan. The general conditions are well discerned now after several empirical studies in Taiwan. What invites attention are these features: (1) There is a definite space with boundaries to define this community, (2) the social organization in the community is a complex network with a hierarchy of multiple tiers spread in the said space, (3) people in this community hold common identity and solidarity, and (4) numerous functions are served in the community for whose sake social resources are mobilized and ritually institutionalized to confirm community solidarity. Such functions include exchange and circulation of materials, talent, and other social capital.

Comparing the ritual circle in Taiwan and the rural marketing system in mainland China as reported by Yang and Skinner, the similarity between the two is striking; almost all the above-listed features of ritual circles are present in the rural marketing system. It is tantalizing for scholars, therefore, to adopt the marketing system as a conceptual tool to explain the phenomenon of Taiwanese ritual circle (Crissman 1972). However, compared to the spatial model of rural marketing networks, the ritual circle organization seems to be more structured, with more clearly defined territory and more manifested symbols binding membership together to establish a communal sense of identity.

Both Yang and Skinner noted that the economic function of commodity exchange was the primary function, while the flow of information and human talents were also available. The crucial distinction is that the ceremonial and institutional boundaries of the model of the rural marketing system are not defined. Furthermore, once new transportation and communication routes (such as railroads and highways) cut into the traditional network, the foundations of a marketing system for the exchange of resources was seriously and sometimes permanently effected, a phenomenon that Yang discussed in his work (Yang 1944). The Taiwanese ritual circle first organized in the days of early settlements seems to have survived economic changes taking place in the past century in which easy access to the city by modern transportation routes replaced the function of the rotating fairs and marketing centers. Nevertheless, other activities that required collective actions continue to function well. It appears, therefore, that there is a level of local community that groups people together into basic unit cells within the gigantic Chinese society, as Yang proposed (Yang 1944). These cells might be organized along kinship groups, such as the powerful local lineages in the countryside of medieval China, or they might be organized as ethnic and dialect groups whenever migrants settled in new lands. The ritual circle in Taiwan built on the foundation of kinship and dialect groups, as in the case of the Zhanghua Mazu cult organization, finally took root to become a specially organized community. The rural marketing network may possibly be just one of such local cells with its economic functions manifestly noticed.

Temples serving as community centers also can be found in other parts of mainland China. For instance, temples of the Dragon King are very common worship centers in north China. In other areas, temples worshipping Guanyin, the Buddhist mercy goddess, and Guan Yu, a martial god, are scattered here and there in many places. Pilgrimages organized by villages to visit major temples, inspection tours of major deities circled through a cluster of villages, and stage performances of folk opera to coincide with the birthdays of certain deities, or simply as offerings to please the deities, were collectively sponsored by raising contributions from neighborhoods. All these activities were commonplace in China until the Communist revolution. Hence, it is most plausible that in traditional China, the local community cells were organized around local religious centers, in a manner similar to the Taiwanese Mazu ritual circles in Zhanghua.

A comparison between characteristics of principal communities before the Communist revolution and thereafter would be helpful to discover what the fundamental features are of rural organization in China. A recent survey conducted in South Fujian by Kenneth Dean shows great resemblance to the phenomenon of local community solidarity, as compared with the Taiwan ritual circle (Dean 2003). Dean surveyed communal activities in over six hundred villages in the Puxian region during the 1990s. In a period after the high tide of the Maoist Revolution was over, much of the traditional pattern of local communal organization reemerged. He notices that at least 27 percent of people living in these villages shared a single surname, while the average villages had three to four surnames. However, lineage organizations, although revived, do not appear as dominant as they might have been in the past, as ostensibly in communities of such concentration of few surnamed kingship groups. Marketing activities, probably due to the availability of modern transportation, facilitate exchange of commodities within an area far more extensive than the traditional marketing network suggested by Skinner's hierarchical market network.

Dean observes the prominent role of religious activities that have pulled villages together to form "ritual alliances." One hundred twenty-three such "alliances" are found among these six hundred villages wherein there are 6,960 temples, with one thousand deities being served. Nevertheless, the most important and popular ones are Guanyin, Shegong (Tu de gung), and Mazu, the same ones as found in Taiwanese ritual circles (Dean 2003).

Religious activities mainly consist of services conducted by Daoist priests on various occasions. The lunar New Year procession of each village is joined by neighboring villages' processions. Finally, a very large joint procession marched around the territory usually based within irrigation systems. The network of local temple alliances has taken on local administration work, while some retired party members participated in temple committees. Dean takes note that such a process of merging local governance with religious activities may indicate a gradual development toward a certain degree of autonomy at the local level. Yang argued that Chinese local religion may be "diffused" rather than "institutional." Such a phenomenon as reported by Dean may reflect a complexity of functional diffusion of both secular and "sacred" ritual powers to shape a local communal solidarity: Dean may be quite right to argue that other than the Skinner vertical linkage in a hierarchical network, horizontal religious and communal networks and the complexity involved thereof should be noticed (Dean 2003).

What is reported by Dean definitely bears a great deal of compatibility with the local organizational and functional pattern in Taiwanese religious ceremonial circles. Such a parallel is not surprising since southern Fujian is the homeland of many early migrants who settled in Taiwan throughout the eighteenth and nineteenth centuries. Local solidarity has always been strong in the southern coastal provinces, which seem so remote from the government seat in the north. Another set of data collected in the north in the 1990s may provide us with another test of local communal solidarity. A field survey conducted in 1996 in a few eastern counties of the Henan province provides insightful information (J. Q. Cao 2000). Cao's survey takes note of the relatively recent developments in one of the most inland rural areas. By this time, the impact of the Maoist dramatic collectivization of communes had faded, while rapid urbanization in the coastal areas had started to reach Henan as rural interposition gradually appeared in some villages. In other words, village life in rural China, casting aside much of the structure arbitrarily imposed by the central government, has now returned to the fundamental solidarity of rural communities, as embodied in the old structure and its functions.

As Cao reported, a typical Henan administrative village (Xing Zheng Cun) consists of a handful of settlements (each of which is made up of about one or two hundred households, with a population of about one thousand people). Such an administrative unit forms a basic community in which villages share common economic interests (J. Q. Cao 2000, 34). Above them is an administrative subcounty unit, or *xiang-zhen*, whose officials supervise village commercial operations. In the days when Maoist commerce still prevailed, a *xiang-zhen* often was a large commune with several tens of thousands of people. The *xiang-zhen* in a rural inland province, such as Henan, coincides with the area that was covered by a rural market network as Yang observed (J. Q. Cao 2000, 430). The Taiwan ritual circle may be much larger than a simple *xiang-zhen*, probably due to better transportation conditions today. Anyway, a Henan administrative village, as reported by Cao, is the very primary community of solidarity. Residents of a settlement, more often than not, are members of a kinship group of the same surname. The extent of kinship solidarity may vary, however, as reflected in the lineage record *(zu-pu)*, which is being recompiled recently after the government relaxed the prohibition of compilations. In some villages, a most senior member of the clan is recognized as clan chief to assume patriarchal authority as old Chinese clans did. It seems that China is gradually returning to its long-held tradition of having kinship structures dominate the rural community (J. Q. Cao 2000, 98, 532–34).

Cao does not include observations of rural marketing activities in his report. Nevertheless, in the annual financial balance of incomes and expenditures of the Henan family households, the nonagricultural income often amounts to at least 35–40 percent of their total income, which is earned by female members in the household through producing fabric work and other handicraft works as well as by male members who pick up a variety of labor jobs. For some households that had less land, the proportion of nonagricultural income in the total revenue to sustain daily livelihood can be even higher (J. Q. Cao 2000, 41–98). Such a phenomenon appears quite consistent with my own findings of the distribution of farming and nonfarming income made by a farm's household in the Han period when the Chinese agrarian economy was just taking shape. The nonagricultural activities can only possibly be conducted in markets where the cottage industry products are sold to exchange for commodities produced elsewhere. Likewise, labor jobs, such as shipping services, are often available in markets as well (Cho-yun Hsu 1980). In the days of the communes, the *xiang-zhen* was the administrative center from which resources assigned by the government were received and then distributed to villages. Meanwhile, local resources were collected and submitted to the government. Such a function is one of a hub for the exchange of resources. After the communes dissolved, *xiang-zhen* sites once again served as marketing centers with the same function of resource exchanges between villages and the outside world.

In Cao's report, religious activities are not systematically discussed. It should be noticed that in Mao's rural revolutionary days, religious activities were forcibly suppressed. In recent times, cults of folk-faith began resurging in many parts of China; Henan's countryside is one of the hubs. In Cao's report, nevertheless, temples in the Henan communities are also casually mentioned. The kitchen god is commonly served in the corner of a household kitchen; the community protector *(tudi)* has his small shrine in any village. Guangong (Guang Yu) and Guanyin (avalokitesvara Bodhisattva) are popularly worshipped deities. In addition, there are other deities, such as the Dragon King, the Lord of Fire, and the Lady of Good-Sight. In a village, sometimes, at the four corners of the crossroad, there may be three or four small shrines for such deities where the village residents go to pray for all sorts of wishes and help (J. Q. Cao 2002, 378–400). In the site of one particular *xiang-zhen* of Feixiang County, near the eastern border of Henan and the neighboring province Shandong, a temple has been rebuilt on the site of an old ruined temple built in the revolutionary war. The newly completed temple was constructed with donations raised from many villages. Among the most generous contributors are *xiang-zhen* party officials. A stone stele recorded the history of this temple for Guanyin and Shakayamuni (Gautama Buddha). It is said that in this particular temple, sometimes in the early years of the Republican era, village leaders gathered to plan a massive armed uprising to fight the invading troops of a warlord (J. Q. Cao 2000, 309–400). Memory of this event is especially interesting, as Cao Jinqing notes, because recently there was a massive protest against a heavy tax being levied in the same *xiang-zhen* area. Worth noting is that temples seem to be a gathering place for local leaders, a phenomenon reminiscent of Yang's report and of Taiwanese temples where ritual circles were organized. The efforts to build such a worship center may imply the partial return of the traditional community network.

In his studies on Chinese religion, Yang viewed Western religion as a specific institution where the sacred and the profane are completely separated, whereas in Chinese religious society, religion is diffused into daily life. There is no sharp rupture between the sacred and the profane. In the same manner, Chinese cannot understand why there should be a claim of monotheism, which excludes all the other faiths (Yang 1967). Anyone who is familiar with the Chinese way of life would testify that in the Chinese mind religiosity demonstrated in devotion and reverence toward some transcendental force is more important than a total dependency on a set of values published by a particular deity. Such transcendental forces can be embodied in awesome feelings toward natural phenomena, heroic personalities, or ancestors. And often these figures can be blended and interchangeable, or, in Yang's term, diffused. Reflected in Chinese folk religion, deities are worshipped because they are admired or feared due to their deeds, characters, or powers. Therefore, deities of Buddhism, and Taoism, who are respectable and admirable personalities in the human world, are assigned to be in charge of certain natural forces (wind, rain, thunder, and so on). Thus, the Buddhist goddess Guanyin is virtually transformed into a merciful mother figure. Mazu, originally a deity who protected the fishermen and sailors, also acquired the title and the characteristics of an omnipotent, all-caring matron figure (D. Z. Chou 1983).

These deities are not loftily above daily life in the human world. They care for the well-being of the people and answer their prayers. A community needs spiritual protectors whose power is diffused everywhere and thus most helpful for answering prayers for peace and prosperity in their lives. People in the same community who share a similar environment would need the same protection. A ritual circle may be simply symbolizing the common need in a neighborhood, in addition to sharing an identity of the community of solidarity. In a community, through interaction, people share resources within boundaries; they also jointly protect the homestead from external threat. Activities such as collectively maintaining irrigation systems, organizing militias, raising funds for charitable purposes, and building joint ventures of *xiang-zhen* protections are all conducted within the framework of having the same spiritual values, embodied in the temple by a spiritual figure, that are linked by the network.

Local autonomy, in traditional China, is the delimiting boundary beyond which state power cannot unilaterally reach. Beyond this point, the state needs to negotiate with the society in order to exercise a certain extent of effective governance. The secular authority of the state, from the point of view of country folk, may reflect the same merits of such deified figures who shield the community from external encroachment. Cao finds that four villages achieved spectacular success in the development of joint ventures of *xiang-zhen* enterprises (in the cases of Nanjie of Linyi, Zhulin of Gongyi, and Liu Zhuang and Xiaoji of Zhangyang). He cities local people who say that such success should be attributed to the merits of certain local leaders, whose capabilities and moral character made people follow ardently toward the accomplishment of such success. In the session, Cao discussed the merits of the deified Guangong, a Shu-Han general who is admired by people for his gallantry, valor, loyalty to his master, and faithfulness to friends. Cao compared these trustworthy characteristics of defied figures to the personal merits of local leaders of the four successful communities. Likewise, Baogong, an incorruptible judge of the Song period, who is respected as a symbol of justice, is also regarded as a model for today's officials to follow (J. Q. Cao 2000, 146–65).

Neither Cao nor his informants have adopted the Weberian term "charisma" to describe such characteristics attributed to both the deified cultural heroes and the leaders of the successful villages. I venture to suggest that the character of diffused deities in Chinese folk religion is probably a reflection of the idealized charismatic leadership in daily life in which, due to the nondifferentiation of functions in a small community and intimate contacts therein, a leader leads in all aspects of life, regardless whatsoever of titles or positions assigned to such persons.

Amitai Etzioni, one of the advocates of modern communitarianism, points out that community solidarity is built on a network of social relationships among people who share certain sets of social meanings, including commonly shared values (Amitai Etzioni 1998, introduction). In the case of Henan communities, the commonly cherished values are manifested both in the characters of deities and the recognized merits of charismatic leaders. The network of social relationships is reflected in the lineage organizations where members trace their common ancestry by compiling lineage records. Collectivization in the Maoist days of the commune movement constituted the solidarity of sharing communal incomes. Although the communes are now dissolved and property is privatized, such memory would make village members willingly entrust resources to their leaders for the sake of building village enterprises collectively.

Communal solidarity makes Chinese local communities into collective entities, which are located between the individual members and the state. If somehow the state oversteps the thin line, or the state fails to rule effectively, Chinese peasants would rise en mass to resist the state authority. The Feixiang case illustrates such a memory. Again, the deities in folk faith may become the symbols of uprisings, while community solidarity may lend strength to the people to form massive protests and even to organize armed bands. In Chinese history, large-scale peasant uprisings are nothing but the combined force of community armed bands that emerged from basic cells of Chinese society. The list of such uprisings can be found in any Chinese dynastic history: Yellow Turban, Heavenly Master Cult, White Lotus, and so on. The latest of such movements, yet probably not the last one, was incorporated in the guerilla activities in the Communist revolution of our time; and, today, mass protests are reported to often happen in the countryside.

In summary, Yang and Skinner, in their studies of marketing systems in Shandong and Szechuan, respectively, provide a foundation for sociologists and anthropologists to discuss the local communities that have been the basic identities claimed by individuals in the vast land of China. The state in Chinese history is different from the nation-states in Europe in that the state authority could hardly reach hundreds of millions of individual subjects directly. The local communities have a bond of solidarity. Thus, the huge state of China is built on blocs of local communities, which also served as a buffer between the authoritarian state and the individual farmer in hundreds of thousands of villages.

The economic ties in the marketing network of local communities is only one of the several functions that have facilitated communal solidarity. Yang insightfully noticed the religious function of forming a local community. This observation probably led him to study Chinese folk religion. Indeed, in the cases of ritual circles in Taiwan, religious faith is the force that united local communities into extensive structures in which economic as well as political activities take place. I suggest that Taiwan had been a frontier province of the Chinese empire for centuries and that the state authority never was effectively exercised in the island. Large communal alliances in the form of ritual circles are not only local cells that served as a buffer between state and villages but also, by means of worshipping certain deities of diffused character, open channels through which a set of social values leads to communal solidarity. The state authority once overwhelmingly dominated village life. It is in the post-Mao period that villages have resumed their value in Chinese culture. The Henan cases of village organization and its function should be discerned as a revival of traditional values and communal commercial solidarity. Ironically, the success of the Communist revolution is often attributed to their strategy of taking root in rural China where the villages turned into guerilla bases against the Japanese occupation and the nationalist governance. The collectivization movement in Mao's day took place partly on the foundation of long-lasting communal solidarity. It is in the post-Mao period that villages have resumed the mechanism of the lineages and folk-faith. Such revival of communal solidarity, and thus collective action, has helped in the emerging rural economy.

The perennial prevalence of local communities in rural China appears truly impressive. Someday, communal solidarity may be a force for the Chinese to develop a grassroots democracy that could modify state authoritarianism. Who knows!

NOTES

Chapter 2: *Sociology in China and the Encounter of Civilizations*

1. Biographical update memorandum from C. K. Yang to the Department of Sociology, University of Pittsburgh, 1972.

2. Biographical update, 1972.

3. I appreciate assistance from Professor Chong Chor Lau of the Chinese University of Hong Kong on the history of the abolition of sociology in the People's Republic of China.

4. Nathan Sivin wrote about this in many of his publications. His remark comes from a colloquium at the University of Pittsburgh that was part of a series in the 1980s on science in different civilizations.

5. Biographical update, 1972.

Chapter 3: *Institutional Restructuring, Organizational Integration, and the Chinese Revolution*

1. See Parsons's summary on this part of Weber's career in Weber 1964, 78–86.

2. See the descriptive propositions in Perrow 1986, 260–62.

Chapter 5: *New Institutions in Practice*

1. We do not attempt to extract from the material gathered empirical data enabling a description of the situation of workers and employees in Shenzhen. The facts the claimants describe in the letters depict situations felt as so unfair and unacceptable that launching an appeal to local authorities seems justified. If such revelations, often depicting dramatic working conditions and extreme experiences, do exist and are even mentioned in national and local media, it is beyond the capacity of this analysis to estimate their frequency or discuss their causes.

2. *Conggxin zuzhi zhongcai jigou shouce*, 1995, 13.

3. *Renmin ribao*, June 5, 2002.

4. *Shenzhen tequ laodong zhidu shi nian gaige licheng*, 1991, 121.

5. Interview with head of "labor inspection brigade," Shenzhen, May 21, 1999.

6. The first figure is from "To Develop and Promote Healthy and Harmonious

Labor Relations," internal report of Shenzhen labor bureau, 1996; the second was provided during an interview with a head of the labor bureau, September 13, 2001.

7. *Zhongguo Laodong Nianjian*, 1997, 325.

8. Interview with member of Shenzhen municipality labor bureau, March 4, 1998.

9. The *sanlai yi bu*, or "three imports and one compensation" system, means that raw materials, patterns, and equipment are imported in exchange for compensatory trade.

10. The corpus collected comes from the labor bureau of the municipal government and therefore includes complaints regarding enterprises located inside *and* outside the special economic zone. Data are from the *Shenzhen tongji xinxi nianjian*, 90.

11. "Shenzhen shi laowugong diaocha" (Survey on migrant workers), Shenzhen municipality, 1997.

12. A 1997 survey by the All China Federal of Trade Unions (ACFTU) focusing only on rural migrants revealed a high degree of mobility: 44.6 percent had changed factories once, 32.7 percent had done so twice, and the remaining 22.7 percent had shifted from one enterprise to another three to nine times. This survey overemphasizes the part played by rural migrants working for state-owned enterprises since they represent 69.5 percent of all respondents. *1997 Zhongguo nongmingong wenti diaocha*, ed. ACFTU Policy Research Group, internal publication (Beijing, 1998).

13. Interview with claimants Mei Shengli, June 11, 1998; Ma Lisheng, March 10, 1999; Wang Leping, April 2, 1998.

14. Interview with Gao Geiwen, June 10, 1998.

15. Interview with Ma Lisheng, March 3, 1999.

16. *Gongren ribao*, September 20, 2002.

17. *Gongren ribao*, August 13, 2002.

18. *Gongren ribao*, September 25, 2002.

19. *Gongren ribao*, August 30, 2002.

20. *Gongren ribao*, August 6, 2002.

21. *Gongren ribao*, September 25, 2002.

22. *Gongren ribao*, September 3, 2001.

23. *Gongren ribao*, September 3, 2001.

Chapter 6: *Social Capabilities and Chinese Economic Growth*

The author gratefully acknowledges comments from conference participants, as well as financial and institutional support from the American Council of Learned Societies, Harvard University's John K. Fairbank Center for East Asian Studies, the National Endowment for Humanities, and the University of Pittsburgh's University Center for International Studies. This chapter draws on informative discussions with Cho-yun Hsu, Evelyn Rawski, James and Rubie Watson, and participants at a 1994 symposium sponsored by the University of Toronto and York University Joint Center on Modern East Asia.

1. Chinese sources give a rural population total of 868.7 million for 1998 (Yearbook 1998, 111).

2. Jean C. Oi identifies "the local corporate state" as being "directly responsible for the dramatic growth of rural enterprises" (1999, 99).

3. This perspective does not deny that education can be undertaken purely for its own satisfaction, in which case a student's expenditure of time, effort, and money becomes an element of consumption rather than investment. Empirical studies support the assumption made by human capital studies that investment motives predominate.

4. Evidence that female children have higher survival rates in districts of India with relatively high wage rates for adult females offers a particularly striking validation of the human capital perspective (Rosenzweig and Schultz 1982).

5. Chen and Myers (1976, 1978) offer many examples, including guild regulations specifying that "we will prohibit further commercial dealings" with violators (1978, 23).

6. Chen and Myers (1976, 11) translate a land contract dating from 1770 that requires tenants to "submit a report to the government requesting a survey for the farmland they have irrigated."

7. Material in the remainder of this paragraph comes from Hou (1975) as reviewed by Seidel (1978).

8. On Han agriculture, see Hsü (1980); on rice yields, see Perkins (1969) and Geertz (1966).

9. Potter (1968, 129) reports that kinsmen may be "so jealous of another villager's rise in wealth and prestige that they purposely do not patronize his store" and direct their business to outsiders instead.

Chapter 7: *Institutional Change and Income Inequality*

1. For market transition debate, see Symposium on Market Transition, *American Journal of Sociology* 101(4).

2. In sociology and economics, there are two main meanings of *institution.* Some scholars regard institutions as social relationships with high probability and long duration (Wallace 1994, 54–55). In this sense, Polanyi (1957) considers market, trade, and money to be three institutions. The other meaning of *institution* is developed in a new institutional approach in economics and sociology, defining the term as "the rules of the game in a society" that shape human interaction or govern social relationships.

3. "Institutional approach" as a paradigm rising recently embodies many versions of institutional theories. See Scott 1995, ch. 3.

4. For regulative aspects of institution, also see Scott 1995, ch. 3.

5. Szelenyi discovered differences in the rights over labor in the two types of society. See Szelenyi 1978, 74–75.

6. Some clarification with respect to labor and human capital is needed. When the term *labor* is used as a noun, it refers to labor capacity that is regarded as a kind of asset

or property (labor asset). Although *labor* and *human capital* are sometimes used synonymously in the literature of economics and sociology, it seems that they are different. In my view, *human capital* refers to labor capacity acquired through education and experience, exclusive of crude labor capacity.

7. Ownership of TVEs sponsored by rural governments is a field full of conflicts (Walder 1995). This issue will not be discussed fully here. However, what I want to emphasize here is the features of TVEs' capital and employees that essentially differ from those of state-owned enterprises. It is the contractual nature of TVEs that makes it possible for their entrepreneurs to "clearly calculate the costs of products in advance," like capitalist enterprises (Collins 1980, 928). At least in this sense, it seems reasonable to view TVEs as semiprivate firms. In addition, some comparative studies show that the behavior of TVEs in wage determination and employment is similar to that of private firms but different from that of SOEs (Gregory and Meng 1995; Peng 1992; Weitzman and Xu 1994).

8. See Dongjing Wang, "'Guojia shenfen' de jiongjing" [The Dilemma of "State Status"], *Beijing Ribao* [Beijing Daily], November 16, 2000.

9. The expansion of alienable private property rights in labor refers to the process that more and more economic activities concerning employment and distribution have been governed by the rules based on private labor rights. The state's specifying and enforcing such rights definitely cause this expansion. When the structure of rules remains constant, this expansion may also occur because of institutional competition that "would weed out inferior institutions and reward by survival those that better solve human problems" (North 1990, 7).

10. Urban collective enterprises in China were integrated into the state planning system and treated as state enterprises in the 1960s (Ji 1991, 290–92), and they were positioned in the bottom of the bureaucratic organizational hierarchy (Walder 1986, 43–46). Some urban enterprises emerged in the 1980s, and later "collective ownership" may have some essential differences from the traditional form.

11. Under state socialism, the state monopolized the entire economy. In the market-oriented transition, some industries have been opened for nonstate actors and thus become competitive. Corresponding to this change, the state sector has been divided into competitive units, one composed of competitive state enterprises and another composed of monopolistic state enterprises and other state organizations. Operational approaches specifying competitive and monopolistic state organizations will be discussed later in the chapter.

12. Zhou states: "On average," the advantages of "redistributors" may not decline relative to that of "producers" (Zhou 2000, 1143). Using the words *on average*, to me, seems to make the reasoning less reliable.

13. Revisions to the Constitution of the People's Republic of China concerning the position of the private economy illustrate this tendency. In the 1988 constitution, it was stipulated that the "private economy is supplementary to socialist ownership

economies." In the 1998 constitution, this stipulation was omitted. See *Renmin ribao* [People's Daily], April 13, 1988.

14. This is done through case selection according to the answer of the respondent regarding whether he or she was currently employed.

Chapter 8: *Categorical Sources of Income Inequality in Urban China*

1. China's Gini index of income inequality was less than 0.3 in the mid-1980s, lower than in developing countries in other parts of the world, and lower than in all developed capitalist countries combined (World Bank 1997b).

2. The World Bank (1997b), for instance, reported a Gini index of 0.347 for China in the mid-1990s, ranking it third in the world among major regions, only after Latin America and the Caribbean and sub-Saharan Africa regions, in income inequality. Other sources have reported a much higher figure for China's income inequality, often around 0.45. A national survey conducted in 1995 by a team of American and Chinese economists, for example, reported a Gini index of per capita income for China of 0.452, which is "higher than those for India, Pakistan, and Indonesia and perhaps about the same as that for the Philippines" (Khan and Riskin 1998, 247). The Gini index for the United States was reported at 0.447 in 1996 (Ryscavage 1999, 71).

3. China's measured income inequality in the mid-1990s was higher than that reported for the former Eastern European socialist countries, particularly those in the former Soviet Republics. But, unlike in the former Soviet Republics, China has not experienced an absolute decline in living standard or in life expectancy, and its increase in poverty was also much below the tenfold increase in Russia between 1987 and 1996 (Gerber and Hout 1998).

4. One estimate put local revenue from such sources at 500 billion yuan for 1996, amounting to about 7 percent of China's GNP in that year. Most of such income went for income and welfare of local residents (Yang 1997, 9).

5. Naughton put it this way: "Even though the danwei was required to turn over virtually all its surplus to the government, the reality was that the danwei had at least initial control of a large revenue stream, and the diversion of even a small proportion of that revenue could have a significant impact on the workers' standard of living. . . . 'Collective' benefits were seen as being ideologically preferable to individual wage increases" (1997, 175).

6. It was developed by Henri Theil in 1967 (Allison 1978) and calculates inequality by the following formula:

$$T = \frac{1}{n}\sum_{i=1}^{n}\left(\frac{x_i}{\mu}\right)\ln\left(\frac{x_i}{\mu}\right)$$

Where x_i represents an individual's income and μ is the mean income of all individuals.

Moreover, this index can also be decomposed into two parts:

$$T = \sum_{j=1}^{J} \left(\frac{p_j \bar{X}_j}{\bar{X}}\right) \ln\left(\frac{\bar{X}_j}{\bar{X}}\right) + \sum_{j=1}^{J} \left(\frac{p_j \bar{X}_j}{\bar{X}}\right) T_j$$

where $\bar{X}$ is the grand mean of income, $\bar{X}_j$ is the mean income for individuals in group *j*, and p_j is the proportion of individuals belonging to group *j*. The first item on the right side of the equation measures the between-group component of the inequality. Groups rather than individuals are used as the units. This item is therefore the value of inequality if everyone within each group, *j*, received the same income for that group. The second item on the right side of the equation is the weighted average of the within-group inequality measure for each group, T_j (Allison 1978).

7. In the survey, conducted by the Urban Social and Economic Survey Organization of China's National Bureau of Statistics, the questions asked changed over the decade, but they all included detailed information on income, personal background, and consumption expenditure. From the individual background data, group membership information (employment sector, geographic location, and industry) can be extracted. These data were collected by household bookkeeping, supervised by professional interviewers from the government statistical agencies and checked and aggregated monthly.

8. Conducted in 1993 by the National Research Center for Science and Technology Development of the Ministry of Science and Technology, the survey initially planned for a selection of ten work organizations in each of the 10 cities selected, with 40 employees in each of the chosen work organizations. The sampling procedure included three stages. First, 10 cities were randomly selected from 516 cities nationwide: Beijing, Shenyang, Wuhan, Guangzhou, Lanzhou, Chengdu, Shijiazhuang (above all national capital and provincial capital cities), and Baoding, Suzhou, and Luoyang (medium-sized cities). Then, within each of these cities, simple random sampling was used to choose ten work units. Finally, 40 employees were selected through a simple random sampling method in each work unit.

9. At the end of the interview process, 3,293 valid questionnaires were obtained, among which only 3,130 were identifiable, through a later process of data cleaning, as belonging to ninety-four unit organizations. Starting from these 3,130 cases, we further omitted those with missing income or other covariate variables at level-1 ($n = 569$; 409 with missing values in income, the dependent variable). At the same time, we limited our analyses to individuals with a formal job and between ages nineteen and sixty since in this analysis we were interested only in work organization stratification (excluded cases, $n = 14$). Cases with suspicious income (e.g., yearly income below six hundred yuan) were also excluded from our analyses ($n = 7$). Finally, we only kept work organizations that had at least 15 valid cases, since we needed a reasonable sample size at the first level (individual level) for our multilevel analysis (excluded cases, $n = 136$). In the end, 2,404 individual cases were used in the analysis. These individuals were distributed among eighty-one work organizations, and the number of individuals in each work organization varied from 15 to 38.

10. The Urban Household Income and Expenditure Survey drew its sample from

the list of urban households with permanent registration, and the Survey of Chinese Work Organizations only sampled those with a formal job in large organizations.

11. Over the decade after the mid-1980s, the average urban employee income of Guangdong Province has stood out as well above most other provinces in China. The interprovincial disparity based on these three provinces, nevertheless, may not be an exaggeration for all China, because while Guangdong is included, many poor provinces such as those in northwest China are also excluded.

12. Note that the inequality increase measured by the Theil index is more than that measured by the Gini index. The Theil index is more subject to income transfers between the extremes in the income distribution (Allison 1978).

13. Such a method allows the breakdown of all the variance in the dependent variable, in our case, income, to different sources. For example, such an analysis can tell us what proportion of the income difference among individuals is due to their gender or their educational attainment, as well as what proportion, if any, is due to the individual's employment sector or geographic location of employment and residence.

14. Base salary or wages are more subject to state wage policies than other labor incomes. Other labor incomes include bonuses, job subsidies and allowances, overtime pay, and incomes from secondary employment. These other labor incomes made up between 40 and 60 percent of total labor income among these employees during the decade.

15. Though based on a different sample, these results are fairly similar to Xie and Hannum's results for the same year (1996).

16. They are gender (male = 1), age, square term of age, Communist Party membership, and education (junior high school or below, senior high school, college). We intentionally have only three dummy variables for education because all individuals in this survey have a formal job in a relatively large work organization and thus our sample has higher educational level than the general population.

17. The first variable is organizational size. Size is divided into three groups, three hundred employees or fewer, between three hundred and five hundred, and five hundred employees and more. The second is ownership type of the work organization, which has three categories: state, collective, and private. State-owned/public work units include government agencies and state-owned firms; collective units include both large and small collective firms; private units include private firms and joint ventures. The third variable is rank within the bureaucratic hierarchy, which has the following five categories: ministry *(bu),* department *(ju),* division *(chu),* section *(ke),* and below section level or no rank. We dichotomize work units into high rank and low rank, with high rank including those at division level *(chu)* or above. Finally, based on the yearly amount of tax and profit per capita handed up to the state, we divide organizations into three groups according to profitability: low performance enterprises (less than five thousand yuan per capita), high performance enterprises, and nonprofit agencies (government and party agencies, research institutes, schools and universities, medical service centers, and other cultural services).

18. The reliability of our estimate for β_{0j} is defined as the average of the reliabilities of organizations:

$$\Sigma\left[\tau_{00}/(\tau_{00} + \sigma^2 / N_j)\right]/J,$$

where N_j is the number of individuals in jth organization, and J is the total number of organizations in our analysis. For more details on reliability, see Bryk and Raudenbush (1992, 63).

19. The labor bureau of one of Beijing's districts, for example, stipulated that at least thirty-five types of jobs should not be open to migrants. The Beijing Municipal Labor Bureau also made recommendations to local employers suggesting that the wages for laid-off urban employees not be below those of the labor cost of migrant laborers. *People's Daily,* overseas edition, May 25, 1998, 2.

20. The analysis for the United States is based on the 5 percent public use microsample data of the 1990 U.S. census, which includes employment and income information for 1989. We drew a random sample of 32 from a total of 262 Metropolitan Statistical Areas (MSAs). Only current employees are included in the sample. The number of individuals in the chosen sample is 53,634. We are deeply indebted to Professor Philip Cohen for his kind help in providing the U.S. census data and in selecting the sample for our analysis.

21. "The widespread practice of sharing a significant part of the proceeds from backyard profit centers among members of the same state agency suggests that, under certain circumstances, provision of public goods to group members may be necessary to sustain collusive collection action" (Lin and Zhang 1999, 224).

22. Xie and Hannum conclude, "we find the correlation between economic growth and overall earnings inequality to be moderate, in part due to the equalizing influence of the negative relationship between the returns to human capital factors and economic growth" (1996, 977). In other words, "bonuses and subsidies are distributed to workers mainly for their affiliations with profitable 8.work units" (1996, 983).

Chapter 9: *Local Response to a Global Agenda*

1. This chapter draws on fieldwork and interviews conducted in various parts of the mainland, including Guangzhou, Shanghai, Wenzhou, and Beijing from 1997 to 2000. With the assistance of research collaborators in China and by using the purposive sampling method, I have been able to identify interviewees who are informed and knowledgeable about educational development in mainland China.

2. Before the early 1990s reforms in higher education, Chinese citizens performing well on university entrance exams were entitled to free higher education; this changed in the mid-1990s when the CCP adopted a "user-charge" principle to recover costs.

3. In protests leading up to the 1989 June Fourth Incident, in Beijing's Tiananmen Square, citizens and university students complained, among other things, that the state's

financial support for higher education was inadequate and the reduction of state subsidies had increased the financial burden on university students. In response, the CCP intentionally controlled the number of self-support students.

4. The inequality of access to higher education that resulted from increasing tuition fees has led to social concern, and governments at both the central and local levels have adopted different strategies to help students from poor socioeconomic backgrounds continue their learning in higher education (see, for example, Agelasto and Adamson 1998).

5. By other approaches and models, I refer to different types of nonstate-run schools in the mainland that adopt different ways to finance and manage their schools (for details, see Mok 1998a).

6. In the Mao era, the CCP tightly controlled university course design and curricula. Hence, that a special "Teaching Material Working Committee" was established in recent years indicates that universities nowadays enjoy far more autonomy and flexibility than they did at one time.

Chapter 11: *When a House Becomes His Home*

This chapter was first published in *Popular China,* ed. Perry Link, Richard Madsen, and Paul Pickowicz (Rowman & Littlefield, 2002).

1. "A New Look at Housing," *China News Analysis,* October 1, 1998.

2. *China Daily,* January 7, 1991; *Beijing Review,* January 17, 1991; *Renmin ribao,* May 26, 1991; *Renmin ribao,* January 1, 1992.

3. The literature on women's subordination within their families is vast. One of the most comprehensive recent discussions was presented by Martha Nussbaum, in the Seeley Lectures in Political Theory, University of Chicago, February 1999.

4. Eighty-four of the one hundred families had at least one married child, and of these fifty-five shared a home with the married child. In 80 percent of the three-generation homes, the coresident married child was a son.

5. This is the observation of Columbia University political scientist Xiaobo Lu at the Columbia University Modern China Seminar, January 2000.

6. *Xinmin wanbao,* June 4, 1999.

7. This section draws on thirty-five brochures collected from 185 developers exhibiting in June 1999.

8. Advertisement for Yongde homes published in *Xinmin wanbao,* May 11, 1994.

9. A colleague in Shanghai said that this term could only be used for the taste of food and suggested that *pinwei* would be the better translation. In fact, I am simply quoting from the advertisement, and the idea that it is the foodlike taste of the female that attracts the male customer confirms my argument about a "male tilt."

10. In 1998 we designed and implemented a longitudinal study of consumer behavior among four hundred couples in four cities to examine how the consumer revolution

of the 1990s affected lifestyles among five occupational groups. In each city twenty-five families were randomly selected from residence committees in two to five different city districts from households headed by managers, professionals, blue-collar employees, and the self-employed. Over the year, each husband and wife was interviewed four times, and twice they filled out logs on one week's socializing activities. Here, I will use only the interview results from Shanghai. For financial support for the project, I thank the Henry Luce Foundation.

11. Interviewers asked each husband and wife during a separate interview: "Do you think every family must own the property rights of their own home? *(nin renwei meijia dou yinggai yongyou ziji zhufang de chanquan ma?)* The options were yes *(shi)*, no *(bu)*, and hard to say *(buhaoshuo)*.

12. Seven percent listed husband's father, 2 percent wife's father, 5 percent husband's mother, 2 percent wife's mother, 2.5 percent husband's brother, 3 percent wife's brother, 2 percent husband's sister, 3 percent wife's sister, 2 percent sons, and 1 percent a daughter.

13. Sixty-three percent of husbands but only 23 percent of women said the title or rental agreement listed their name.

14. A similar pattern of consumer purchases is found in all large cities from 1986 to 1990. State Statistical Bureau and East West Population Center, *Survey of Income and Expenditure of Urban Households in China in 1986* (Honolulu: University of Hawaii Press, 1989), 242–45; 1990 *Zhongguo Chengzhen Shumin Jiating shouzhu Diaocha Ziliao* (Beijing: Zhongguo tongji chubanshe, 1991), 225–28, 293–95.

15. I heard this remark on Shanghai Education TV at 11 PM, June 14, 1999. The program featured a male decorator answering questions from a studio audience about how best to furnish a home. Also of note was that at the conclusion of this program, the shopping channel took over this frequency and the first product to be promoted was a heavy-duty cleaning liquid for kitchens.

16. One especially rich source is from the Web site of Rongxin Decorators, which advertised in the newspapers as well as on the Web (www.rxjtzh.online.sh.cn).

17. *Shanghai Baijia Zhuanghuang*, ed. Li Yang (Shanghai: Shanghai renmin meishu chubanshe, 1996); *Shanghai Xinchao Jiating Zhuangshi* (Shanghai: Shanghai huabao chubanshe, 1996); *Xinbian Shanghai Jiating Buzhi Yi baili* (Shanghai: renmin meishu chubanshe, 1995); *Shanghai Jiating Shinei Zhuanghuang Jingxuan*, ed. Zhang Tianzhi (Shanghai: Zhongguo fangzhi daxue chubanshe, 1999); *Shanghai Jiating shinei Zhuanghuang Jingxuan*, ed. Zhang Tianzhi (Shanghai: Sanlian, 1998); *Shanghai Jiating Zhuanghuang Yishu*, eds. Chen Xuwei and Chen Guohong (Shanghai: Zhongguo fangzhi daxue chubanshe, 1999). I also purchased eight other magazines in the same stores between July 1997 and June 1999, but these were not published in Shanghai, so they are not reviewed here.

18. For example, among the seventy-two men who answered these questions, six said their parents had discussed the renovation plans, three said their parents had made some of the final decisions or purchased furnishings, and only one said his parents had managed the finances. Friends were exactly as likely as parents to play these

roles, except no friends managed the money. For women, parents played even less of a role: only one parent discussed the plan, one made the final decisions, one bought furnishings, and one managed the money.

19. Two friends who read a draft of this chapter and whose families live in China remarked that before the reforms high-level cadre homes also tilted toward displaying men's status and achievement. And one who had returned to attend the funeral of his grandmother noted that what struck him in his uncle's use of their homes was how the reforms have allowed them to "recapture their mother's house and turn it into a space for men's business."

20. *China Daily,* January 7, 1991; *Beijing Review,* January 17, 1991; *Renmin ribao,* May 26, 1991, and January 1, 1992.

21. GWYGB 1995, 70–73.

22. GWYGB 1997, 810.

23. *Renmin ribao,* September 14, 1951; *China News Analysis,* October 1, 1998, no. 1619.

24. One 1997 Xinhua article reported that 37.5 percent of city residents expected to buy an apartment through their unit, and another 26 percent expected to buy on the market. See *China News Analysis,* October 1, 1998, no. 1619. A 1998 Gallup poll in Chengdu, Beijing, Guangzhou, and Shanghai found that 15–18 percent planned to buy a home within the next twelve months. See Matthew Miller, "City Dwellers Hungry for Durables," *South China Morning Post,* January 14, 1999, online ed., document ID 19990113180151012; a follow-up survey in Guangzhou, Xian, and Wuhan indicated that 25 percent expected to purchase an apartment in 1999. CCTV, June 21, 1999.

25. Only 9 percent of husbands and 4 percent of wives answered no to the question "Do you think every family must have ownership of their own dwelling? *(nin renwei meijia dou yinggai yongyou ziji zhufang de chanquan ma).* When we compared the size, amenities, and number of rooms among families headed by each occupational category, owners did better. For example, among blue-collar men, owners averaged 2 rooms, renters 1.6; among professionals, owners average 3.0 rooms, renters. 2.1; and among managers owners averaged 2.5 rooms, renters 2.1. Similarly, among 26 owners, all but 1 had a private toilet, whereas among the 59 renters, 34 percent shared a toilet with at least 1 other household.

26. Among men, only 7 percent of renters but 24 percent of owners said they were very satisfied. Among women, the gap was 9 percent versus 25 percent. Using a five-point scale, male differences were significant at the .07 level.

27. Among men, 13 percent of renters but 42 percent of owners said they had private space; among women, 11 percent of renters and 31 percent of owners said they had it. Thus ownership significantly raised the likelihood of private space, but the gain for men was greater.

28. Among owners, the percentage of men who said they were a legal leaseholder was 69 percent as opposed to 60 percent among renters. For women, ownership also raised the number claiming to be leaseholders from 21 percent among renters to 27 percent among owners, but women remained in a clear minority.

29. In 1979 it was 3.6 square meters; in 1995, 8.1 square meters. *Zhongguo tongji nianjian* 1999, 317.

30. *Shanghai tongji nianjian* 1998 (Shenzhen: Zhongguo tongji chubanshe, 1998), 102

31. *Beijing Review,* January 14, 1991.

32. *Xinmin wanbao,* August 24, 1997.

33. Between 1978 and 1998, the average square meters per resident rose from 4.5 to almost 10. *Shanghai tongji nianjian* 1999, 85. By 1997 most urban households (70 percent) had self-contained apartments with their own kitchens, bathrooms, and private entrances (*Xinmin wanbao,* January 29, 1999).

34. By 1997 there were 861 buildings with twenty to twenty-nine floors, and 105 buildings with more than thirty. *Shanghai tongji nianjian* 1998, 102.

35. *China News Analysis,* October 1, 1998, no. 1619.

36. Miller, "City Dwellers"; CCTV, June 21, 1999.

Chapter 12: *Family Social Capital in Urban China*

Funding for this research comes from a Henry Luce Foundation grant (1997–2000). Two grants from the Research Grants Council to Yanjie Bian provided partial financial support for research assistants during various stages of data analyses. The authors thank their colleagues in the Chinese cities under study (Shanghai, Shenzhen, Tianjin, and Wuhan) for their collaboration in data collection, Hui Niu for her assistance in preparing the data file, and Yu Li for his able data management and statistical analyses.

1. In job-search studies, many researchers used name generators to identify and measure tie strengths and social resources of the helpers of job seekers (see Granovetter 1995; Lin 1999).

2. The resulting sample in each city is as follows: (1) party and government officials, eight households; (2) cadres in state nonprofit organizations, seven households; (3) managers in state firms, ten households; (4) managers in nonstate firms, ten households; (5) private business owners, five households; (6) professionals and technicians, twenty households; (7) blue-collar workers in industry, thirteen households; (8) staff and workers in commercial or service sector; and (9) families with a status of "migrant economic population," fifteen households.

3. Fifteen households were unavailable because they were out of town, on vacation, or visiting relatives in other locations.

Chapter 13: *When to Give and Why*

1. Indeed, the point can also apply to corporate family strategy in general. For instance, it has been argued that diversification, whereby children are urged by parents to choose different occupations, is one of the strategies that Chinese parents use to ensure maximum security (see Cohen 1996; Lee, Parish, and Willis 1994). The economic logic

that some parents invest more in one child than the other because of differing prospects of bringing benefits to the whole family rests entirely on the assumption that the child will identify with the family when he or she indeed becomes successful. Otherwise, the whole argument simply does not hold.

2. The young children who are under joint custody of their divorced parents present an interesting exception. As a result, their identification with both of their parents' newly formed families, speculated by Michael Hechter (1987), may be low.

3. In other places, Becker contends that caring and sharing makes combined resources of family members render more total utility than otherwise used (Becker 1973, 1974).

4. Hidden in the argument is an assumption that emotional attachment can well translate into economic cooperation. Just as parents provide economic resources to their children because of the tendency of parents' being altruistic toward their own offspring, part of which is obviously induced by their emotional bond, grown children, having been urged or "cajoled" by their parents over the long years of socialization to maintain a strong emotional bond with each other, are willing to contribute part of their resources to their parents, even when they have gained their economic independence. Thus, emotional attachment in a sense bears economic consequences: through assistance to each other, a parental family and a grown child's own family to a certain degree also become economically interconnected.

5. Also, following the reasoning of marginal utility, the utility of a certain service-type support provided to parents of frail health is much greater than that of the same amount of service given to healthy parents with little functional limitations. Hence, from the point of view that both parents and children wish to use their resources in such a way that the total utility is maximized, parents of good health see little utility in receiving service support.

6. For instance, according to Lee and Miller (1994), in the United States, inter-household transfer of resources, presumably mostly between older parents and grown children, has been overwhelmingly downward, from older ages to younger ones. The average annual per household transfer, in the form of gifts and bequest, is about $2,100. In other words, parents in the United States continue to bestow large amounts of resources to their already noncoresident children. Clearly, this suggests continued strong links between older parents and their grown children.

7. It should be noted here that, by sampling design, all child respondents interviewed lived in the Baoding city. The frequency of contact with parents would be lower if all children, including those outside of the city, were interviewed.

8. See Logan and Bian (1999) for a somewhat different interpretation.

9. In other words, meeting the material needs of parents in need may not be the only purpose, on the part of both parents and children, of money giving. A grown child may send money to his or her aging parents as a token of respect, or a gesture that his or her duty was fulfilled. Hence, old age itself may induce money giving (see Sahlins 1972).

REFERENCES

Agelasto, M., and B. Adamson, eds. 1998. *Higher Education in Post-Mao China.* Hong Kong: Hong Kong University Press.

Agricultural Yearbook 1980 [*Zhongguo nongye nianjian 1980*]. 1981. Beijing: Nongye chubanshe.

Albrow, M. 1996. *The Global Age.* Cambridge: Polity Press.

Allison, Paul D. 1978. "Measures of Inequality." *American Sociological Review* 43:865–880.

Anderson, E. N., and M. I. Anderson. 1975. "Folk Dietetics in Two Chinese Communities, and Implications for the Study of Chinese Medicine." In *Medicine in Chinese Culture,* ed. A. Kleinman, P. Kunstadter, E. R. Alexander, and J. L. Gale. Washington, D.C.: U.S. Department of Health, Education, and Welfare.

Arkush, R. David. 1984. "If Man Works Hard, the Land Will Not Be Lazy: Entrepreneurial Values in North China Peasant Proverbs." *Modern China* 10(4): 461–79.

Auslander, Leora. 1996. *Taste and Power: Furnishing Modern France.* Berkeley: University of California Press.

Balandier, Georges. 1999. "Introduction." In *Comment pensent les institutions* [How Institutions Think], by Mary Douglas. Paris: La Découverte.

Ball, S. J. 1998. "Big Policies/Small World: An Introduction to International Perspectives in Education Policy." *Comparative Education* 34(1): 119–30.

Baltodano, A. 1997. "The Study of Public Administration in Times of Global Interpretation: A Historical Rationale for a Theoretical Model." *Journal of Public Administration Research and Theory* 7(4): 623–26.

Baron, James. 1984. "Organizational Perspectives on Stratification." *Annual Review of Sociology* 10:37–69.

Baron, James N., and William T. Bielby. 1980. "Bringing the Firms Back in: Stratification, Segmentation, and the Organization of Work." *American Sociological Review* 45:737–65.

———. 1984. "The Organization of Work in a Segmented Economy." *American Sociological Review* 49:454–73.

Bearon, Lucille B., and Harold G. Koenig. 1990. "Religious Cognitions and Use of Prayer in Health and Illness." *Gerontologist* 30:249–53.

Becker, Gary S. 1973. "A Theory of Marriage: Part I." *Journal of Political Economy* 81(4): F813–846.

———. 1974. "A Theory of Marriage: Part II." *Journal of Political Economy* 82(2): S11–S26.

———. 1991. *A Treatise on the Family.* Cambridge, Mass.: Harvard University.

Bian, Fuqin, John R. Logan, and Yanjie Bian. 1998. "Intergenerational Relations in Urban China: Proximity, Contact, and Help to Parents." *Demography* 35:115–24.

Bian, Yanjie. 1994. *Work and Inequality in Urban China.* Albany, N.Y.: SUNY Press.

———. 1997. "Bringing Strong Ties Back In: Indirect Connection, Bridges, and Job Search in China." *American Sociological Review* 62:266–85.

Bian, Yanjie, and John Logan. 1996. "Market Transition and the Persistence of Power: The Changing Stratification System in Urban China." *American Sociological Review* 61:739–59.

Bian, Yanjie, John Logan, and Xiaoling Shu. 2000. "Wages and Job Inequalities in the Working Lives of Men and Women in Tianjin." In *Re-Drawing Boundaries: Work, Households, and Gender in China,* ed. Barbara Entwisle and Gail Henderson, 111–33. Berkeley: University of California Press.

Boltanski, Luc, 1990. L'amour et la justice comme compétences. Trois essais de sociologie de l'action. Paris: Metailié.

Bray, M. 1996. Counting the Full Cost: Parental and Community Financing of Education in East Asia. Washington, D.C.: World Bank and UNICEF.

Brinton, Mary C., and Victor Nee, eds. 1998. *The New Institutionalism in Sociology.* New York: Russell Sage Foundation.

Bryk, Anthony S., and Stephen W. Raudenbush. 1992. *Hierarchical Linear Models: Applications and Data Analysis Methods.* Newbury Park, Calif.: Sage.

Burt, Ronald S. 1984. "Network Items and the General Social Survey." *Social Networks* 6:293–339.

———. 1992. *Structural Holes: The Social Structure of Competition.* Cambridge, Mass.: Harvard University Press.

Cant, S., and U. Sharma, eds. 1999. A New Medical Pluralism? Alternative Medicine, Doctors, Patients, and the State. London: UCL Press.

Cao, Jinqing. 2002. *Huanghe Bian de Zhongguo* [China Along the Yellow River]. Shanghai: Wenyi Chubanshe.

Cao, Yang, and Victor G. Nee. 2000. "Comment: Controversies and Evidence in the Market Transition Debate." *American Journal of Sociology* 105:1175–89.

CCPCC. 1993. "The Program for Educational Reform and Development in China." *Zhonghun Renmin Gongheguo Guowuyuan Gongbao* 2:58–66.

Census and Statistics Department. 1983, 1992, 1996, 2000, 2002. *General Household Survey: Special Topics,* report nos. 2, 6, 7, 10, 15; and *Thematic Household Survey,* report nos. 3 and 8. Hong Kong: Government Printer.

Cerny, P. 1996. "Paradoxes of the Competition State: The Dynamic of Political Globalization," *Government and Opposition* 32(2): 251–74.

Chan, Anita. 1997. "Chinese Danwei Reforms: Convergence with the Japanese Model?" In *Danwei: The Changing Chinese Workplace in Historical and Comparative Perspective,* ed. Xiaobo Lü and Elizabeth J. Perry, 91–113. Armonk, N.Y.: M. E. Sharpe.

Che, Jishua, and Yingyi Qian. 1998. "Institutional Environment, Community Government, and Corporate Governance: Understanding China's Township Village Enterprises." *Journal of Law, Economics, and Organization* 14(1): 1–23

Chen, Fu-mei Chang, and Ramon H. Myers. 1976. "Customary Law and the Economic Growth of China During the Ch'ing Period." *Ch'ing-shih wen-ti* 3(5): 1–32.

———. 1978. "Customary Law and the Economic Growth of China During the Ch'ing Period" *Ch'ing-shih wen-ti* 3(10): 4–27.

Chen, Jieming. 1996. "Old Age Support and Intergenerational Relations in Urban China: Maintenance of Obligations Between Older Parents and Children." PhD diss., University of Michigan.

———. 1998. "Investment and Support: A Causal Analysis of Inter-generational Exchange Among Urban Residents" [Touzi yu shanyuang: Guanyu chengshi jumin daiji jiaohuan de yinguo fenxi]. *Social Sciences in China* [Zhongguo shehui kexue] 6:130–49.

Chen, Z. 1999. "Fifty-year of Education in the People's Republic of China." *Education Studies* [Jiaoyu yanjiu] 9.

Cheng, K. M. 1990. "Financing Education in Mainland China: What Are the Real Problems?" *Issues and Studies* 3(March): 54–75.

———. 1995a. "Zhongguo jiaoyu" [China's Education]. In *Zhongguo Shehui Fenxi* [China's Social Development], ed. X. M. Lee. Hong Kong: Hong Kong Educational Publishing Company.

———. 1996. "Markets in a Socialist System: Reform of Higher Education." In *Educational Dilemmas: Debate and Diversity*, vol. 2, *Higher Education*, ed. K. Watson, S. Modgil, and C. Modgil. London: Cassell.

———. 1997. "What Has Been Reformed? Review of Two Decades of Reform in China's Education." Paper presented at the Conference on Education and Development, Education and Geopolitical Change, New College, Oxford.

Cheng, Tiejun, and Mark Selden. 1994. "The Origins and Social Consequences of China's Hukou System." *China Quarterly* 139:644–68.

Cheng, Xiaonong. 1996. "Fanrong conghe erlai?—zhongguo jianji xianzhuang he qushi de fenxi" [Where Does Prosperity Come From?—Analysis of the Present Situation and Growing Trends in China's Economy]. *Dangdai Zhongguo Yanjiu* [Modern China Studies] 3(54): 18–61.

Cheung, Steven N. S. 1989. "Privatization vs. Special Interests: The Experience of China's Economic Reforms." In *Economic Reform in China: Problems and Prospects*, ed. James A. Dorn and Wang Xi, 21–32. Chicago, Ill.: University of Chicago Press.

China: A General Survey. 1979. Beijing: Foreign Languages Press, 82–86.

China National Institute of Educational Research. 1995. *A Study of NGO-Sponsored and Private Higher Education in China*. Beijing: UNESCO.

Chiu, Stephen W. K., K. C. Ho, and Tai-lok Lui. 1997. City States in the Global Economy: Industrial Restructuring in Hong Kong and Singapore. Boulder, Colo.: Westview Press.

Chou, De Zai. 1983. *Taiwan Zhi Shimiao yu Shenming* [Temples and Deities in Taiwan], vols. 1–4. Taipei: Taiwan Wenxien Weiyuanhui.

Chow, Gregory, 1987. "Development of a More Market-oriented Economy in China." *Science* 235.

Christiansen, F. 1996. "Devolution in Chinese Higher Education Policy in the 1990s: Common Establishment and the '211' Program." *Leeds East Asia papers* 36.

Clarke, Adele E., J. Shim, L. Mamo, J. R. Fosket, and J. R. Fishman. 2003. "Biomedicalization: Technoscientific Transformations of Health, Illness, and U.S. Biomedicine." *American Sociological Review* 68(2): 161–94.

Cohen, Myron L. 1976. *House United, House Divided: The Chinese Family in Taiwan.* New York: Columbia University Press.

———. 1996. "Changing Patterns of Family Division in Mainland China as Seen in a Hebei Village, 1950–1987." Paper presented at the Conference on Asian Population History, IUSSP Committee on Historical Demography and Academia Sinica, Institute of Economics, Taipei.

Coleman, James S. 1988. "Social Capital in the Creation of Human Capital." *American Journal of Sociology* 94(supplement): S95–S120.

Collins, R. 1980. "Weber's Last Theory of Capitalism: A Systematization." *American Sociology Review* 45:925–42.

———. 1991. "Women and Men in the Class Structure." In *Gender, Family, and the Economy*, ed. Rae Blumberg. Newbury Park, Calif.: Sage.

Congxin zuzhi zhongcai jigou shouce [Handbook on the Reorganization of Arbitration Bodies]. 1995. Edited by Research Group of the Legal Department of the State Affairs Councils. Beijing: Zhongguo fazhi chubanshe.

Cowgill, D. O. 1972. "A Theory of Aging in Cross-Cultural Perspective." In *Aging and Modernization*, ed. D. O. Cowgill and L. D. Holmes, 1–13. New York: Appleton-Century-Crofts.

Crissman, C. W. 1972. "Marketing in the Changhua Plain, Taiwan." In *Economic Organization in Chinese Society*, ed. W. E. Wilmott. Stanford, Calif.: Stanford University Press.

Croizier, Ralph C. 1968. *Traditional Medicine in Modern China.* Cambridge, Mass.: Harvard University Press.

———. 1970. "Medicine, Modernization, and Cultural Crisis in China and India." *Comparative Studies in Society and History* 12:275–96.

Csikszentmihalyi, Mihaly, and Eugene Rochberg-Halton. 1981. *The Meaning of Things.* Cambridge: Cambridge University Press.

Currie, J., and J. Newson. 1998. *Universities and Globalization: Critical Perspectives.* Newbury Park, Calif.: Sage.

Dale, R. 1997. "The State and the Governance of Education: An Analysis of the Restructuring of the State-Education Relationship." In *Education: Culture, Economy & Society*, ed. A. H. Halsey, P. Brown, H. Lauder, and A. J. Wells. Oxford: Oxford University Press.

———. 1999. "Specifying Globalization Effects on National Policy: A Focus on the Mechanisms." *Journal of Education Policy* 14(1): 1–17.

———. 2000. "Globalization: A New World for Comparative Education?" In *Discourse Formation in Comparative Education,* ed. J. Schriewer and Peter Lang. New York: Verlag der Wissenschaften.

Dale, R., and S. Robertson. 2000. "Regional Organizations as a Medium of Globalization of Education." Paper presented at the workshop Reflecting Globalization Effects on National Education Policy: The Perspective from East Asia, City University of Hong Kong, September.

Davis, Deborah. 1989. "My Mother's House." In *Unofficial China,* ed. P. Link, R. Madse, and P. Pickowicz. Boulder, Colo.: Westview Press.

———. 1993. "Urban Households: Supplicants to a Socialist State." In *Chinese Families in the Post Mao Era,* ed. D. Davis and S. Harrell. Berkeley: University of California Press.

Davis, Deborah, and Stevan Harrell. 1993. "Introduction." In *Chinese Families in the Post-Mao Era,* 1–22. Berkeley: University of California Press.

Davis-Friedmann, Deborah. 1985. "Intergenerational Inequalities and the Chinese Revolution." *Modern China* 11(2): 177–201.

———. 1991. *Long Lives.* Exp. ed. Stanford, Calif.: Stanford University Press.

Dean, Kenneth. 2003. "Local Communal Religion in Contemporary Southeast China." *China Quarterly* 173 (June 2003) 336–55.

DeFriese, Gordon H., A. Woomert, P. A. Guild, A. B. Steckler, and T. R. Konrad. 1989. "From Activated Patient to Pacified Activist: A Study of the Self-Care Movement in the United States." *Social Science and Medicine* 29(2): 195–204.

DiPrete, Thomas A. 1993. "Industrial Restructuring and the Mobility Response of American Workers in the 1980s." *American Sociological Review* 58:74–96.

DiPrete, Thomas A., Paul M. De Graf, Ruud Luijkx, Michael Tahlin, and Hans-Peter Blossfeld. 1997. "Collectivist Versus Individualist Mobility Regimes? Structural Change and Job Mobility in Four Countries." *American Journal of Sociology* 103:318–58.

DiPrete, Thomas A., and David B. Grusky. 1990. "The Multilevel Analysis of Trends with Repeated Cross-Sectional Data." *Sociological Methodology* 20:337–68.

Douglas, Mary, 1986. *How Institutions Think.* Syracuse, N.Y.: Syracuse University Press.

Duke, C. 1992. *The Learning University: Toward a New Paradigm.* Buckingham: Society for Research into Higher Education and Open University Press.

Eggersson, Thrainn. 1990. *Economic Behavior and Institutions.* Cambridge: Cambridge University Press.

Eisenberg, David M., Roger B. Davis, Susan L. Ettner, Scott Appel, Sonja Wilkey, Maria Van Rompay, and Ronald C. Kessler. 1998. "Trends in Alternative Medicine Use in the United States, 1990–1997: Results of a Follow-up National Survey." *Journal of American Medical Association* 280(18): 1569–75.

Ekong, D., and N. Cloete. 1997. "Curriculum Responses to a Changing National and Global Environment in an African Continent." In *Knowledge, Identity, and Curriculum Transformation in African.* ed. N. Cloete, J. Muller, M. W. Makgoba, and D. Ekong. Cape Town, South Africa: Maskew Miller Longman.

Elster, Jon. 1983. *Explaining Technical Change: A Case Study in the Philosophy of Science.* Paris: Cambridge University Press/MSH.

Epstein, E. J. 1991. "China's Legal Reform." In *China Review,* ed. Kuan Hsin-chi and Maurice Brosseau. Hong Kong: Chinese University Press.

Erwin, Kathleen. 2000. "Heart-to-Heart, Phone-to-Phone: Family Values, Sexuality, and the Politics of Shanghai's Advice Hotlines." In *The Consumer Revolution in Urban China,* ed. D. Davis. Berkeley: University of California Press.

Etzioni, Amitai, ed. 1998. *The Essential Communitarians Reader.* Lanham, Md.: Rowman & Littlefield.

Faulks, K. 1999. Political Sociology: A Critical Introduction. New York: NYU Press.

Favereau, Olivier. 1996. "Décisions, situations, institutions." In *L'interdépendance des niveaux de décision,* actes du colloque de Chantilly. *FORUM* (Université de Paris) 10(1).

Fei, Hsiao-tung (Xiaotong). 1939. *Peasant Life in China.* London: Routledge.

———. [1949] 1992. *From the Soil, the Foundations of Chinese Society.* Berkeley: University of California Press.

Ferlie, Ewan, Andrew Pettigrew, Lynn Ashburner, and Louise Fitzgerald. 1996. *The New Public Management in Action.* Oxford: Oxford University Press.

Fisher, Claude S. 1982. *To Dwell Among Friends: Personal Networks in Town and City.* Chicago, Ill.: University of Chicago Press.

Fisher, P., and A. Ward, 1994. "Complementary Medicine in Europe." *British Medical Journal* 309, 107–11.

Flynn, N. 1997. *Public Sector Management.* 3rd ed. Hempstead: Harvester Wheatsheaf.

Fraser, David. 2000. "Inventing Oasis: Luxury Housing Advertisements and Reconfiguring Domestic Space in Shanghai." In *The Consumer Revolution in Urban China,* ed. D. Davis. Berkeley: University of California Press.

Freedman, Maurice. 1974. "On the Sociological study of Chinese Religion." In *Religion and Ritual in Chinese Society,* ed. by Arthur P. Wolf. Stanford, Calif.: Stanford University Press.

Freeman, Linton C., and Danching Ruan. 1997. "An International Comparative Study of Interpersonal Behavior and Role Relationships." *L'Année Sociologique* 47:89–115.

Freidson, Elliot. 1970. *The Profession of Medicine.* New York: Harper and Row.

Fried, Morton H. [1953] 1969. Fabric of Chinese Society: A Study of the Social Life in a Chinese County Seat. New York: Octagon Books.

Fu, Min 1996. *Zhongguo zhengfu xiaochu pinkun xingwei* [Poverty Alleviation Actions by China's Government]. Wuhan: Hubei kexue jishu chubanshe.

Fukuyama, F. 1989. "The End of History?" *The National Interest* 16:3–18.

———. 1992. *The End of History and the Last Man.* New York: Free Press.

———. 1995. Trust: Social Virtues and the Creation of Prosperity. New York: Free Press.

Fulder, S. 1996. *The Handbook of Alternative and Complementary Medicine.* 3rd ed. Oxford: Oxford University Press.

Gallagher, Eugene B. 1995. "Toward an Analysis of Medicalization in the Global Context." In *Global Perspectives on Health Care,* ed. Eugene B. Gallagher and Janardan Subedi. Upper Saddle River, N.J.: Prentice Hall.

Gauld, R. D. C. 1998. "A Survey of the Hong Kong Health Sector: Past, Present, and Future." *Social Science and Medicine* 47:927–39.

Geertz, Clifford. 1966. Agricultural Involution: The Process of Ecological Change in Indonesia. Berkeley: University of California Press

Gerber, Theodore P., and Michael Hout. 1998. "More Shock than Therapy: Market Transition, Employment, and Income in Russia, 1991–1995." *American Journal of Sociology* 108:1–50.

Giddens, A. 1990. *The Consequences of Modernity.* Cambridge: Polity Press.

———. 1999. *Runaway World.* London: Profile Books.

Goldstein, Michael S. 2000. "The Growing Acceptance of Complementary and Alternative Medicine." In *Handbook of Medical Sociology,* 5th ed., ed. C. E. Bird, P. Conrad, and A. M. Fremont. Upper Saddle River, N.J.: Prentice Hall.

Good, Charles M. 1987. *Ethnomedical Systems in Africa.* London: Guilford Press.

Goode, William J. 1963. *World Revolutions and Family Patterns.* New York: Free Press.

———. 1982. *The Family.* 2nd ed. Upper Saddle River, N.J.: Prentice Hall.

Goody, Jack. 1990. *The Oriental, the Ancient and the Primitive.* Cambridge: Cambridge University Press.

Granick, David. 1990. *Chinese State Enterprises: A Regional Property Rights Analysis.* Chicago, Ill.: University of Chicago Press.

Granovetter, Mark. 1973. "The Strength of Weak Ties." *American Journal of Sociology* 78:1360–80.

———. 1995. "Afterword." In *Getting A Job.* 2nd ed. Chicago, Ill.: University of Chicago Press.

Green, A. 1999a. "Education and Globalization in Europe and East Asia: Covergent and Divergent Trends." *Journal of Education Policy* 14(1): 55–71.

———. 1999b. "East Asian Skills Formation Systems and the Challenge of Globalization." *Journal of Education and Work* 21(3): 1–21.

Greenhalgh, Susan. 1982. "Income Units: The Ethnographic Alternative to Standardization." *Population and Development Review* 8(supplement): 70–91.

Gregory, R. G., and Xin Meng. 1995. "Wage Determination and Occupational Attainment in Rural Industrial Sector of China." *Journal of Comparative Economics* 21: 353–74.

Griffin, Keith, and Renwei Zhou. 1992. *Chinese Household Income Project, 1988* (MRDF). New York, N.Y.: Hunter College Academic Computing Services (Producer). Distributed by Inter-University Consortium for Political and Social Research, Ann Arbor, Mich.

Grusky, David B. 1994. "The Contours of Social Stratification." In *Social Stratification: Class, Race, and Gender in Sociological Perspective,* ed. David B. Grusky, 3–34. Boulder, Colo.: Westview Press.

Guojia Tongji Ju [State Statistical Bureau, People's Republic of China]. 1994. *Zhongguo tongji nianjian 1994* [China Statistical Yearbook 1994]. Beijing: Zhongguo tongji chubanshe [China Statistical Publishing House].

———. 1996. *Zhongguo tongji nianjian* [China Statistical Yearbook]. Beijing: Zhongguo tongji chubanshe [China Statistical Publishing House].

Hajnal, J. 1982. "Two Kinds of Preindustrial Household Formation System." *Population and Development Review* 8:449–94.

Hammer, Andrew. 1990. "Four Hypotheses Concerning Contemporary Chinese Urbanization." In *Chinese Urban Reform, What Model Now?,* ed. R. Yin-Wang Kwok, William L. Parish, Anthony Gar-On Yeh, and Xu Xueqiang, 233–42. Armonk, N.Y.: M.E. Sharpe.

Hareven, Tamara. 1994. "Aging and Generational Relations: A Historical and Life Course Perspective." *Annual Review of Sociology* 20:437–61.

Hartley, D. 1995. "The 'McDonaldization' of Higher Education: Food for Thought?" *Oxford Review of Education* 21(4): 409–23.

Hay, Joel W. 1992. *Health Care in Hong Kong: An Economic Policy Assessment.* Hong Kong: Hong Kong Center for Economic Research, Chinese University Press.

Hayhoe, R. 1996. *China's Universities 1985–1995: A Century of Cultural Conflict.* New York: Garland Publishing.

Hechter, Michael. 1987. *Principles of Group Solidarity.* Berkeley: University of California Press.

Hedstrom, Peter. 1991. "Organizational Differentiation and Earnings Dispersion." *American Journal of Sociology* 97:96–113.

Held, D., A. McGrew, D. Goldblatt, and J. Parraton. 1999. *Global Transformation: Politics, Economics, and Culture.* Stanford: Stanford University Press.

Henkel, M. 1998. "Evaluation in Higher Education: Conceptual and Epistemological Foundations." *European Journal of Education* 33(3): 283–97.

Hermalin, Albert I., Mary Beth Ofstedal, and Ming-cheng Chang. 1992. "A Comparison of Alternative Approaches to Measuring Needs and Levels of Support Received Among the Elderly in Taiwan." In *Readings in Population Research: Policy, Methodology, and Perspectives,* ed. P. Krishnan, Chi-Hsien Tuan, and Kuttan Mahadevan, 295–310. New Delhi: B.K. Publishing.

Hirst, P., and G. Thompson. 1999. *Globalization in Question.* Cambridge: Polity Press.

Ho, Suzanne S. Y. 1985. "Dietary Beliefs in Health and Illness Among a Hong Kong Community." *Social Science and Medicine* 20:223–30.

Hou, Ching-liang. 1975. *Monnaies d'offrande et la notion de trésorerie dans la religion chinoise.* Paris: Collège de France.

Hsu, C. M. 1978. "Jishiquan zhi yu jutai hanren shehui de dutexing" [The Characteristics of Ritual Circles in Chinese Communities in Taiwan]. *Zhonghua wenhua fuxing yuekan* [Chinese Cultural Revival] 11(6).

Hsü, Cho-yun. 1980. *Han Agriculture.* Seattle: University of Washington Press.

Hu, Shih. 1934. *The Chinese Renaissance.* Chicago, Ill.: University of Chicago Press.

Hua, Ercheng. 1997. *Zhongguo jingji de ruanzuolu* [The Soft Landing of China's Economy]. Beijing: Zhongguo caizheng jingji chubanshe.

Huang, Shu-min. 1989. *The Spiral Road: Change in a Chinese Village Through the Eyes of a Communist Party Leader.* Boulder, Colo.: Westview Press.

Huff, Toby, ed. 1981. *On the Roads to Modernity: Conscience, Science, and Civilizations, Selected Writings by Benjamin Nelson.* Totowa, N.J.: Rowman and Littlefield.

Information Services Department. 2000. *Hong Kong 2000.* Hong Kong: Special Administrative Region Government.

International Social Survey Program. 1986. *Machine Readable Codebook: Social Networks and Support Systems.* Koln: Zentralarchiv fur empirische Sozialforschung.

Jessop, B. 1993. "Towards a Schumpeterian Workfare State? Preliminary Remarks on Post-Fordist Political Economy." *Studies in Political Economy* 40:7–39.

Ji, Long., ed. 1991. *Dangdai zhongguo de jiti gongye* [Modern China's Collective Industry]. Beijing: Dangdai zhongguo chubanshe.

Jones, P. W. 1998. "Globalization and Internationalism: Democratic Prospects for World Education." *Comparative Education* 34(2): 143–55.

Julius, D. 1997. "Will Chinese Universities Survive in the Emerging Market Economy?" *Higher Education Management* 9(1): 141–56.

Kalleberg, Arne L. 1988. "Comparative Perspectives on Work Structures and Inequality." *Annual Review of Sociology* 14:203–25.

Kam, Wing Chan, and Zhang Li. 1999. "The *Hukou* System and Rural-Urban Migration in China: Processes and Change." *China Quarterly* 159:819–55.

Kang, Xiaoguang. 1995. *Zhongguo pinkun yu fanpinkun lilun* [Chinese Poverty and Anti-poverty Theory]. Nanning: Guangxi renmin chubanshe.

Khan, Azizur Rahman, and Carl Riskin. 1998. "Income and Inequality in China: Composition, Distribution, and Growth of Household Income, 1988–1995." *China Quarterly* 138:221–53.

Kleinman, Arthur, Peter Kunstadter, E. Russell Alexander, and James L. Gale, eds. 1975. *Medicine in Chinese Cultures: Comparative Studies of Health Care Systems in China and Other Societies.* Washington, D.C.: U.S. Department of Health, Education, and Welfare.

Kogan, M., and Hanney, S. 2000. *Reforming Higher Education.* London: Jessica Kingsley Publishers.

Koo, L. C. 1984. "The Use of Food to Treat and Prevent Disease in Chinese Culture." *Social Science and Medicine* 18:757–66.

Krasner, S. 1999. "Globalization and Sovereignty." In *States and Sovereignty in the Global Economy,* ed. D. A. Smith, D. J. Solinger, and S. C. Topik. London: Routledge.

Kung, James Kai-sing. 1999. "The Evolution of Property Rights in Village Enterprises: The Case of Wuxi County." In *Property Rights and Economic Reform in China*, ed. Jean Oi and Andrew Walder, 95–122. Stanford, Calif.: Stanford University Press.

Kwong, J. 1996. "The New Educational Mandate in China: Running Schools Running Businesses." *International Journal of Educational Development* 16(2): 185–94.

Lam, Cindy L. K., Martin G. Catarivas, Clarke Munro, and Ian J. Lauder. 1994. "Self-medication Among Hong Kong Chinese." *Social Science and Medicine* 19:1641–47.

Landy, D., ed. 1977. *Culture, Disease, and Healing: Studies in Medical Anthropology.* New York: Macmillan.

Lardy, Nicholas R. 1983. *Agriculture in China's Modern Economic Development.* Cambridge: Cambridge University Press.

———. 1998. *China's Unfinished Economic Revolution.* Washington, D.C.: Brookings Institution Press.

Last, Murray, and Godfrey L. Chavunduka, eds. 1986. *The Professionalization of African Medicine.* Manchester: Manchester University Press.

Lau, Chong Chor. 1993. "The Chinese Family and Gender Role in Transition." In *China Review 1993*, ed. Joseph Cheng and Maurice Brosseau. Hong Kong: Chinese University Press.

Lau, Kwok-yu. 1994. "Urban Housing Reform in China Amidst Property Boom." In *China Review 1993*, ed. Joseph Cheng and Lo Chi Kin. Hong Kong: Chinese University of Hong Kong Press.

Laumann, Edward O. 1973. *Bonds of Pluralism: The Form and Substance of Urban Social Networks.* New York: John Wiley.

Lavely, William, and Xinhua Ren. 1992. "Patrilocality and Early Marital Co-residence in Rural China, 1955–1985." *China Quarterly* 130:378–91.

Lee, Ching Kwan. 1998. *Gender and the South China Miracle: Two Worlds of Factory Women.* Berkeley: University of California Press.

Lee, James, and Wang Feng. 1999. *One Quarter of Humanity: Malthusian Mythology and Chinese Reality.* Cambridge, Mass.: Harvard University Press.

Lee, Rance P. L. 1980. "Perceptions and Uses of Chinese Medicine Among the Chinese in Hong Kong." *Culture, Medicine, and Psychiatry* 4:345–75.

———. 1982. "Comparative Studies of Health Care Systems." *Social Science and Medicine* 16:629–42.

———. 1985. "Social Stress and Coping Behavior in Hong Kong." In *Chinese Culture and Mental Health*, ed. Wen-shing Tsang and David Y. H. Wu. Orlando, Fla: Academic Press.

———. 2000. "Socio-Cultural Factors in Medical Pluralism: Hong Kong's Chinese and Western Medicine as an Example" [in Chinese]. *Hong Kong Journal of Sociology* 1:1–28.

Lee, Rance P. L., and Y. W. Cheung. 1995. "Health and Health Care." In *Indicators of Social Development: Hong Kong 1993*, ed. S. K. Lau, R. Lee, and A. King. Hong Kong: Chinese University Press.

Lee, Ronald D. 1994. "The Formal Demography of Population Aging, Transfers, and the Economic Life Cycle." In *Demography of Aging,* ed. Linda G. Martin, and Samuel H. Preston, 8–49. Washington D.C.: National Academy Press.

Lee, Ronald D., and Timothy Miller. 1994. "Population Age Structure, Intergenerational Transfer, and Wealth: A New Approach, with Applications to the United States." *Journal of Human Resources* 29(4): 1026–63.

Lee, Yean-Ju, William L. Parish, and Robert J. Willis. 1994. "Sons, Daughters, and Intergenerational Support in Taiwan." *American Journal of Sociology* 99(4): 1010–41.

Lee, Yean-Ju, and Zhenyu Xiao. 1994. "Public and Familial Support for the Elderly in China." Paper presented at the annual meeting of the Population Association of America, Miami, Fla.

Leslie, Charles. 1980. "Medical Pluralism in World Perspective." *Social Science and Medicine* 14: 191–95.

———, ed. 1976. *Asian Medical Systems: A Comparative Study.* Berkeley: University of California Press.

Li, Qiang, 1999. "Occupational Mobility of Peasant Workers in Chinese Mainland." *Shehuixue yanjiu* 3:93–101.

Li, Shuhe, 1998. "Institutional Foundations for High Growth in China." In *China Review 1998,* ed. Joseph Y. S. Cheng, 339–62. Hong Kong: Chinese University Press.

Li, Yih-yuan. 1992. "In Search of Equilibrium and Harmony: On the Basic Value Orientation of Traditional Chinese Peasants." In *Home Bound: Studies in East Asian Society,* ed. Chi Nakane and Chien Chiao. Tokyo: The Center for East Asian Studies.

Liang, Jersey, Shengzu Gu, and Neal Krause. 1992. "Social Support Among the Aged in Wuhan, China." *Asia-Pacific Population Journal* 7:33–62.

Liang, Shuming. 1949. *The Essential Meanings of Chinese Culture.* Hong Kong: Zheng Zhong Press.

Lin, Mei-rong. 1988. "You jishiquan dao xinyang quan—Taiwan minjian shehui de diyu goucheng yu fazhan" [From Ritual Circle to Belief Circle—Foundation and Development of Folk Society in Taiwan]. In *Di san jie Zhongguo haiyang fazhan shiyan taohui lunwen ji* [Proceedings of the Third Conference on the History of Chinese Maritime Development], ed. Chang Yenhsien, 95–125. Taipei: Sun Yat-Sen Institute of Social Science and Philosophy, Academia Sinica.

———. 1989. "You jishiquan lai kan Caodun zhen de difang zuzhi" [On the Local Organization of Caodun Township from a Perspective of Its Ritual Circles]. *Zhongyang yanjiuyuan minzuxue yanjiusuo jikan* [Bulletin of the Institute of Ethnology, Academia Sinica] 62:53–114.

———. 1990. "Zhanghua Mazu de xinyang quan" [Zhanghua Matsu's Belief Circle]. *Zhongyang yanjiu yuan minzu xue yanjiusuo jikan* [Bulletin of the Institute of Ethnology, Academia Sinica] 68:41–104.

———. 1996. "Jishiquan, xinyang yu minzu zongjiao wenhua huodong de kongjianxing gou" [Ritual Circle, Belief Circle, and the Spatial Structure of the Cultural Activities of Folk Religions]. Paper presented at the conference Difang wenhua yu quyu fazhan [Local Culture and Regional Development], Commission of Cultural Reconstruction, Zhongyang University, Taipei.

———. 1999. "Taiwan guquxing jidian zuzhi de shehui kongjian yu wenhua yihan" [Social Space and Cultural Content of Regional Ritual Organizations in Taiwan]. In *Renleixue zai Taiwan de fazhan* [Development of Anthropology in Taiwan], ed. Hsu Chengkuang, 69–88. Taipei: Institute of Ethnology, Academia Sinica.

Lin, Nan. 1982. "Social Resource and Instrumental Action." In *Social Structure and Network Analysis*, ed. Peter V. Marsden and Nan Lin, 131–45. Beverly Hills, Calif.: Sage.

———. 1999. "Building a Network Theory of Social Capital." *Connections* 22(1): 28–51.

———. 2001. *Social Capital: A Theory of Social Structure and Action*. New York: Cambridge University Press.

Lin, Nan, and Yanjie Bian. 1991. "Getting Ahead in Urban China." *American Journal of Sociology* 97:657–88.

Lin, Nan, and Mary Dumin. 1986. "Access to Occupations Through Social Ties." *Social Networks* 8:365–86

Lin, Yimin. 2001. *Between Politics and Markets: Firms, Competition, and Institutional Change in Post-Mao China*. Cambridge: Cambridge University Press.

Lin, Yimin, and Zhanxin Zhang. 1999. "Backyard Profit Centers: The Private Assets of Public Agencies. " In *Property Rights and Economic Reform in China*, ed. Jean Oi and Andrew Walder, 203–25. Stanford, Calif.: Stanford University Press.

Lo, A., 1997. "Toward a Market-Oriented School System in Hong Kong: Impacts and Anticipated Consequences." Paper presented at the 14th annual Conference of HKERA, September.

Logan, John R., and Fuqin Bian. 1999. "Family Values and Coresidence with Married Children in Urban China." *Social Forces* 77(4): 1253–82.

Lu, Xueyi, ed. 2002. *Dangdai zhongguo shehui jieceng yanjiu baogao* [Research Report on Social Stratification in Contemporary China]. Beijing: Shehui kexue chubanshe.

Lucas, C. 1996. *Crisis in the Academy*. London: Macmillan.

Macfarlane, Alan. 1986. *Marriage and Love in England 1300–1840*. Oxford: Basil Blackwell.

Mann, Susan. 1997. *Precious Records*. Stanford, Calif.: Stanford University Press.

Marsden, Peter V. 1987. "Core Discussion Networks of Americans." *American Sociological Review* 62:266–85.

Meng, Xin, and Michael P. Kidd. 1997. "Labor Market Reform and the Changing Structure of Wage Determination in China's State Sector During the 1980s." *Journal of Comparative Economics* 25:403–21.

Mok, K. H. 1996. Marketization and Decentralization: Development of Education and Paradigm Shift in Social Policy. *Hong Kong Public Administration* 5(1): 35–56.

———. 1997a. "Marketization and Quasi-Marketization: Educational Development in Post-Mao China." *International Review of Education* 43(5–6): 1–21.

———. 1997b. "Private Challenges to Public Dominance: The Resurgence of Private Education in the Pearl River Delta." *Comparative Education* 33(1): 43–60.

———. 1998. "The resurgence of private education in post-Mao China." In *Social and Political Transformation in Post-Mao China*, ed. K. H. Mok and K. M. Yu. Hong Kong: Hong Kong Humanities Press.

———. 1999. "Education and the Market Place in Mainland China and Hong Kong." *Higher Education* 37:133–58.

———. 2000a. "Similar Trends, Diverse Agendas: Higher Education Reforms in Hong Kong, Taiwan, and Singapore." Paper presented at the University of Manchester, February.

———. 2000b. "Professional Autonomy and Private Education." In *Social and Political Development in Post-Reform China*. Basingstoke: Macmillan.

Mok, K. H., and D. Chan. 1996. "The Emergence of Private Education in the Pearl River Delta: Implications for Social Development." In *Economic and Social Development in South China*, ed. S. MacPherson and J. Cheng. Cheltenham: Edward Elgar.

Mok, K. H., and K. Y. Wat. 1998. "Merging of the public and private boundary: Education and the market place in China." *International Journal of Educational Development* 18(3): 255–67.

Mok, K. H., and A. Welch. 2001. *Socio-Structural Transformation and Educational Development in Asia Pacific Region*. Macmillan, Basingstoke.

Murdock, George P. 1949. *Social Structure*. New York: Macmillan.

Myers, John T. 1981. "Traditional Chinese Practices in an Urban-Industrial Setting: The Example of Kwun Tong." In *Social Life and Development in Hong Kong*, ed. Ambrose King and Rance Lee. Hong Kong: Chinese University Press.

Nakao, Keiko, and Judith Treas. 1994. "Updating Occupational Prestige and Socioeconomic Scores: How the New Measures Measure Up." *Sociological Methodology* 24:1–72.

Nathan, Andrew. 1990. "A Factionalism Model for CCP Politics." In *China's Crisis*, ed. Andrew Nathan, 23–37. New York: Columbia University Press.

Naughton, Barry. 1994. "China's Reforms: Structural and Welfare Aspects: Chinese Institutional Innovation and Privatization From Below." *American Economic Review* 84(2): 266–70.

———. 1997. "Danwei: The Economic Foundations of a Unique Institution." In *Danwei: The Changing Chinese Workplace in Historical and Comparative Perspective*, ed. Xiaobo Lu and Elizabeth J. Perry, 169–194. Armonk, N.Y.: M.E. Sharpe.

NBS (National Bureau of Statistics). 1996. *A Statistics Survey of China 1996*. Beijing: China Statistical Press.

———. 1997. *China's Statistical Yearbook 1997*. Beijing: China Statistical Press.

———. 2000. *China's Statistical Yearbook 2000*. Beijing: China Statistical Press.

Nee, Victor. 1989. "A Theory of Market Transition: From Redistribution to Markets in State Socialism." *American Sociological Review* 54:663–81.

———. 1991. "Social Inequalities in Reforming State Socialism: Between Redistribution and Markets in China." *American Sociological Review* 56:267–82.

———. 1996. "The Emergence of a Market Society: Changing Mechanisms of Stratification in China." *American Journal of Sociology* 101:908–49.

———. 1998. "Sources of the New Institutionalism." In *The New Institutionalism in Sociology*, ed. Mary C. Brinton and Victor Nee, 1–16. New York: Russell Sage Foundation.

Nee, Victor, and Sijin Su. 1997. "Institutions, Social Ties, and Commitment in China's Corporatist Transformation." In *Reforming Asian Socialism*, ed. John McMillan and Barry Naughton, 111–34. Ann Arbor: University of Michigan Press.

Niu, X. 1997. "The Practical Experience of the Non-Governmental Nanhua Industrial and Business College." *Chinese Education and Society* 30(1): 84–89.

North, Douglass C. 1981. *Structure and Change in Economic History*. New York: W. W. Norton.

———. 1990. Institutions, Institutional Change, and Economic Performance. Cambridge: Cambridge University Press.

———. 1995. "Institutional Competition." In *Locational Competition in the World Economy: Symposium 1994*, ed. Horst Siebert, 27–44. Tubingen: J.C.B. Mohr.

North, Douglass C., and Robert Paul Thomas. 1973. *The Rise of the Western World*. Cambridge: Cambridge University Press.

O'Brien, R. 1992. *Global Financial Integration: The End of Geography*. New York: Council of Foreign Relations Press.

Ohmae, Kinichi. 1990. *The Borderless World: Power and Strategy in the Interlinked Economy*. New York: Harper Perennial.

———. 1995. *The End of the Nation-State*. New York: Free Press.

Oi, Jean. 1993. "Reform and Urban Bias in China." *Journal of Development Studies* 29:129–48.

———. 1995. "The Role of the Local State in China's Transitional Economy." *China Quarterly* 114:1132–49.

———. 1999. Rural China Takes Off: Institutional Foundations of Economic Reform. Berkeley: University of California Press.

Oi, Jean, and Andrew G. Walder. 1999. *Property Rights and Economic Reform in China*. Stanford, Calif.: Stanford University Press.

Osborne, D., and Gaebler, T. 1992. *Reinventing Government: How the Entrepreneurial Spirit is Transforming the Public Sector*. New York: Plume Books.

Parish, William L., and Sarah Busse. 2000. "Gender and Work." In *Chinese Urban Life Under Reform: The Changing Social Contract*, Wenfang Tang and William L. Parish, 209–31. New York: Cambridge University Press.

Parish, William, and James Farrer. 2000. "Gender and Family." In *Chinese Urban Life Under Reform*, Wenfang Tang and William L. Parish, 232–70. New York: Cambridge University Press.

Parish, William L., and Ethan Michelson. 1996. "Politics and Market: Dual Transformations." *American Journal of Sociology* 101:1042–59.

Parkin, Frank. 1979. *Marxism and Class Theory: A Bourgeois Critique.* New York: Columbia University Press.

Parsons, Talcott. 1949. *Essay in Sociological Theory.* Rev. ed. New York: Free Press.

Peng, Yusheng. 1992. "Wage Determination in Rural and Urban China: A Comparison of Public and Private Industrial Sectors." *American Sociological Review* 57:198–213.

Perkins, Dwight H. 1969. *Agricultural Development in China, 1369–1968.* Chicago, Ill.: Aldine.

Perrow, Charles. 1986. *Complex Organization: A Critical Essay.* 3rd ed. New York: McGraw-Hill.

Peters, B. Guy, 1998. *Comparative Politics: Theory and Methods.* New York: NYU Press.

Piazza, Alan 1986. *Food Consumption and Nutritional Status in the PRC.* Boulder, Colo.: Westview Press.

Polanyi, Karl. 1944. *The Great Transformation.* Boston: Beacon Press.

———. 1957. "The Economy as Instituted Process." In *Trade and Market in Early Empires,* ed. K. Polanyi, C. Arensbery, and H. Pearson, 243–69. Glencoe, Ill.: Free Press.

Potter, Jack. 1968. *Capitalism and the Chinese Peasant: Social and Economic Change in a Hong Kong Village.* Berkeley: University of California Press.

———. 1974. "Chinese Shamanism." In *Religion and Ritual in Chinese Society,* ed. Arthur P. Wolf. Stanford, Calif.: Stanford University.

Powell, Walter, and Paul J. DiMaggio, eds. 1991. *The Institutionalism in Organizational Analysis.* Chicago, Ill.: University of Chicago Press.

Putnam, Robert D. 2000. *Bowling Alone: The Collapse and Revival of American Community.* New York: Simon & Schuster.

Putterman, Louis. 1993. *Continuity and Change in China's Rural Development: Collective and Reform Eras in Perspective.* New York: Oxford University Press.

Ratinoff, L. 1995. "Global Insecurity and Education: The Culture of Globalization." *Prospects* 25(2): 147–74.

Raudenbush, Stephen, and Anthony Bryk. 2002. *Hierarchical Linear Models: Applications and Data Analysis Methods.* 2nd ed. Thousand Oaks, Calif.: Sage.

Rawls John. 1958. "Justice as Fairness." *Philosophical Review* 67:169–74.

———. 1987. *Théorie de la Justice.* Paris: Seuil.

Report of the Preparatory Committee on Chinese Medicine. 1997. Hong Kong: Hong Kong Special Administrative Region Government.

———. 1999. Hong Kong: Hong Kong Special Administrative Region Government.

Revel, 1995. "L'institution et le social." In *Les formes de l'expérience. Une autre histoire sociale,* ed. B. Lepetit, 63–84. Paris: Albin Michel.

Rhodes, R. A. W. 1997. *Understanding Governance: Policy Networks, Governance, Reflexivity, and Accountability.* Buckingham: Open University Press.

Riskin, Carl. 1987. *China's Political Economy*. Oxford: Oxford University Press.
Robertson, R. 1992. *Globalization: Social Theory and Global Culture*. London: Sage.
———. 1995. "Globalization: Time-Space and Homogeneity-Heterogeneity." In *Global Modernities*, ed. M. Featherstone, S. Lash, and R. Robertson. London: Sage.
Rocca, Jean-Louis. 1999. "The Rise of Unemployment in Urban China: The Contradictions of the Labor Policy." *China Perspectives* 59:155–81.
Rodrik, D. 1997. "Sense and Nonsense in the Globalization Debate." *Foreign Policy* 107:14–37.
———. 1998. "Path-dependence and Capital Theory: Sociology of the Post-Communist Economic Transformation." *East European Politics and Societies* 12:107–31.
Rona-Tas, Ákos. 1994. "The First Shall Be Last? Entrepreneurship and Communist Cadres in the Transition from Socialism." *American Journal of Sociology* 100:40–69.
Rosen, S. 1997. "The Impact of Economic Reform on Chinese Education: Markets and the Growth of Differentiation." Paper presented at the Conference on Social Consequences of Chinese Economic Reform, John K. Fairbank Center, Harvard University, May.
Rosenau, J. N. 1992. "Citizenship in a Changing Global Order." In *Governance Without Government: Order and Change in World Politics*. ed. J. N. Rosenau and E. Czempiel. Cambridge: Cambridge University Press.
Rosenzweig, Mark R., and T. Paul Schultz. 1982. "Market Opportunities, Genetic Endowments, and Interfamily Resource Distribution: Child Survival in Rural India." *American Economic Review* 72(4): 803–15.
Ruan, Danching. 1993. "Interpersonal Networks and Workplace Controls in Urban China." *Australian Journal of Chinese Affairs* 29:89–105.
———. 1998. "The Content of the GSS Discussion Networks: An Exploration of GSS Discussion Name Generator in a Chinese Context." *Social Networks* 20:247–64.
Ruan, Danching, Linton C. Freeman, Xinyuan Dai, Yunkang Pan, and Wenhong Zhang. 1997. "On the Changing Structure of Social Networks in Urban China." *Social Networks* 19:75–89.
Ryscavage, Paul. 1999. *Income Inequality in America: An Analysis of Trends*. Armonk, N.Y.: M.E. Sharpe.
Sahlins, Marshall. 1972. *Stone Age Economics*. Chicago, Ill.: Aldine-Atherton.
Salais, Robert. 1998. "A la recherche du fondement conventionnel des institutions." In *Institutions et conventions. La réflexivité de l'action économique*, vol. 9, 255–92. Paris: Raisons Pratiques.
Sassen, S. 1999. "Embedding the Global in the National: Implication for the Role of the State." In *States and Sovereignty in the Global Economy*, ed. D. A. Smith, D. J. Solinger, and S. C. Topik. London: Routledge.
Schluchter, Wolfgang, ed. 1983. *Max Webers Studie über Konfuzianismus und Taoismus: Interpretation und Kritik*. Broschiert: Suhrkamp Taschenbuch.
Schmidt, V. 1995. "The New World Order, Incorporated: The Rise of Business and the Decline of the Nation-State." *Daedalus* 124:80–95.

Schultz, Theodore. 1961. "Investment in Human Capital." *American Economic Review* 51:1–17.

Schurmann, Franz, 1968. *Ideology and Organization in Communist China.* Berkeley: University of California Press.

Scott, Richard W. 1995. *Institutions and Organizations.* London: Sage.

Sebagia, A. 2000. "Governance, the State, and the Market: What Is Going On?" *Governance* 13:243–50.

Seidel, Anna. 1978. "Review of Hou 1975." *History of Religions* 17(3–4): 419–31.

Shanghai tongji nianjian, 1998. 1998. Shenzhen: Zhongguo tongji chubanshe.

Shenzhen tequ laodong zhidu shi nian gaige licheng [Ten Years of Reform Process of the Labor System in the Shenzhen Special Economic Zone]. 1991. Ed. Shenzhen Labor Bureau. Shenzhen: Haitian chubansshe.

Shenzhen tongji xinxi nianjian [Shenzhen Statistical Information Yearbook]. 2000. Beijing: Zhongguo tongji chubanshe.

Sher, Ada Elizabeth. 1984. *Aging in Post-Mao China: The Politics of Veneration.* Boulder, Colo.: Westview Press.

Sicular, Terry. 1989. "China: Food Pricing Under Socialism." In *Food Price Policy in Asia: A Comparative Study*, ed. Terry Sicular, 243–88. Ithaca, N.Y.: Cornell University Press.

Simmel, Georg. 1955. Conflict and the Web of Group-Affiliations. Trans. Kurt H. Wolff and Reinhard Bendix. New York: Free Press. (Originally published in 1922)

Skinner, G. William. 1964. "Marketing and Social Structure in Rural China." *Journal of Asian Studies* 24(1): 3–43.

Sklair, L. 1995. *Sociology of the Global System.* Baltimore, Md.: Johns Hopkins University Press.

———. 1999. Globalization. In *Sociology: Issues and Debates*, ed. S. Taylor. London: Macmillan.

So, Alvin Y. 1999. *Hong Kong's Embattled Democracy: A Societal Analysis.* Baltimore, Md.: Johns Hopkins University Press.

Solinger, Dorothy J. 1995. "The Chinese Work Unit and Transient Labor in the Transition from Socialism." *Modern China* 21(2): 155–83.

———. 1999. *Contesting Citizenship in Urban China: Peasant Migrants, the State, and the Logic of the Market.* Berkeley: University of California Press.

Sørensen, Aage B. 1996. "The Structural Basis of Social Inequality." *American Journal of Sociology* 101:1333–65.

Spilerman, Seymour, and Tormod Lunde. 1991. "Features of Educational Attainment and Job Promotion Prospects." *American Journal of Sociology* 97:689–720.

Spitze, Glenna, and John Logan. 1990. "Sons, Daughters, and Intergenerational Support." *Journal of Marriage and the Family* 52:420–30.

State Statistical Bureau. 1998. *A Statistical Survey of China.* Beijing: China Statistical Publishing House.

State Statistical Bureau and East-West Population Center, ed. 1989. *Survey of Income and Expenditure of Urban Households in China in 1986*. Honolulu: University of Hawaii Press.

State Education Commission (SEC). 1993. *Blueprint for Educational Restructuring in China.* Beijing: State Education Commission.

———. 1995. *Education Law.* Beijing: State Education Commission.

Stark, David. 1994. "Path Dependence and Privatization Strategies in East Central Europe." In *Changing Political Economies: Privatization in Post Communist and Reforming Communist States,* ed. Vedat Milor, 115–46. Boulder, Colo.: Lynne Rienner.

———. 1996. "Recombinant Property in East European Capitalism." *American Journal of Sociology* 101:993–1027.

Strassmann, Diana. 1993. "Not a Free Market: The Rhetoric of Disciplinary Authority in Economics." In *Beyond Economic Man,* ed. Marianne A. Ferber and Julie A. Nelson, 54–68. Chicago, Ill.: University of Chicago Press.

Swedberg, Richard. 2000. "Afterword: The Role of the Market in Max Weber's Work." *Theory and Society* 29(3): 373–84.

Szelenyi, Ivan. 1978. "Social Inequalities in State Socialist Redistributive Economies." *International Journal of Comparative Sociology* 19:63–87.

Tang, Wenfang, and William Parish. 2000. *Chinese Urban Life Under Reform: The Changing Social Contract.* New York: Cambridge University Press.

Tilly, Charles. 1998. *Durable Inequality.* Berkeley: University of California Press.

Topalov, Christian. 1994. *Naissance du chômeur. 1880–1910,* Paris: Albin Michel.

Topley, M. 1970. "Chinese Traditional Ideas and the Treatment of Disease: Two Examples from Hong Kong." *Man* 5, 421–37.

Trade Statistics. 1984. *Zhongguo maoyi wujia tongji ziliao, 1952–1983* [China Trade and Price Statistical Materials, 1952–1983]. Beijing: Zhongguo tongji chubanshe.

Treas, Judith, and Jieming Chen. 2000. "Intergenerational Support in Urban China: Living Arrangements, Financial Differentiation, and the Life Course." *Research on Aging* 22(3): 238–61.

Treiman, Donald J., and Harry B. G. Ganzeboom. 2000. "The Fourth Generation of Comparative Stratification Research." In *The International Handbook of Sociology,* ed. Stella R. Quah and Arnaud Sales, 123–50. London: Sage.

Tse, Daniel C. W. 2001. "Reviewing the Road-Map for Chinese Medicine." *Hong Kong Industrialist* 12:24–27.

Unger, Jonathan. 1993. "Urban Families in the Eighties: An Analysis of Chinese Surveys." In *Chinese Families in the Post-Mao Era,* ed. Deborah Davis and Stevan Harrell, 25–49. Berkeley: University of California Press.

van der Poel, Mart G. M. 1993. "Delineating Personal Support Networks." *Social Networks* 15:49–70.

Veseth, M. 1998. *Selling Globalization: The Myth of the Global Economy.* Boulder, Colo.: Lynne Rienner.

Wach, Joachim. 1944. *Sociology of Religion.* Chicago, Ill.: University of Chicago Press.

Walder, Andrew G. 1986. *Communist Neo-Traditionalism: Work and Authority in Chinese Industry.* Berkeley: University of California Press.

———. 1992. "Property Rights and Stratification in Socialist Redistributive Economies." *American Sociology Review* 57:524–39.

———. 1995. "Local Governments as Industrial Firms: An Organizational Analysis of China's Transitional Economy." *American Journal of Sociology* 101:1060–73.

———. 1996. "Markets and Inequality in Transitional Economies: Toward Testable Theories." *American Journal of Sociology* 101:1060–73.

Walder, Andrew G., and Jean C. Oi. 1999. "Property Rights in the Chinese Economy: Contours of the Process of Change." In *Property Rights and Economic Reform in China,* ed. Jean Oi and Andrew Walder, 1–26. Stanford, Calif.: Stanford University Press.

Wallace, Walter L. 1994. *A Weberian Theory of Human Society: Structure and Evolution.* New Brunswick, N.J.: Rutgers University Press.

Wallis, Claudia. 1996. "Faith and Healing." *Time Magazine,* June 24, 58–64.

Wan, Po-san 2003. "Subjective Well-being." In *Indicators of Social Development: Hong Kong 2001,* ed. S. K. Lau, P. S. Wan, M. K. Lee, and S. L. Wong. Hong Kong: Hong Kong Institute of Asia Pacific Studies, Chinese University of Hong Kong.

Wang, Feng. 2000. "Boundaries and Categories: Urban Income Inequality in China, 1986–1995." Paper presented at the Conference on the Legacy of Ch'ing-Kun Yang, Chinese University of Hong Kong, November–December.

———. 2003. Categories and Boundaries: Income Inequality in Urban China, 1986–1995. Unpublished monograph.

Wang, Feng, Xuejin Zuo, and Danching Ruan. 2002. "Rural Migrants in Shanghai: Living Under the Shadow of Socialism." *International Migration Review* 36(2): 520–45.

Wang, Shaoguang. 1995. "The Decline of Central State Fiscal Capacity in China." In *The Waning of the Communist State: Economic Origins of Political Decline in China and Hungary,* ed. Andrew Walder, 87–113. Berkeley: University of California Press.

Waters, M. 1995. *Globalization.* London: Routledge.

Watson, K. 1996. "Banking on Key Reforms for Educational Development: A Critique of the World Bank Review." *Mediterranean Journal of Educational Studies* 1(1): 43–61.

Watson, Rubie S. 1990. "Corporate Property and Local Leadership in the Pearl River Delta, 1898–1941. " In *Chinese Local Elites and Patterns of Dominance,* ed. Joseph W. Esherick and Mary Backus Rankin, 239–60. Berkeley: University of California Press.

Weber, Max, 1964a. *The Religion of China: Confucianism and Taoism.* Trans. and ed. Hans Gerth. With an introduction by C. K. Yang. New York: Macmillan.

———. 1964b. The Theory of Social and Economic Organization. New York: Free Press.

———. 1978. *Economy and Society,* vol. 1. Berkeley: University of California Press.

Wei, F. 1996. "The Great Tremors in China's Intellectuals Circles: An Overview of Intellectuals Floundering in the Sea of Commercialism." *Chinese Education and Society* 29(6): 7–104.

Weiss, Gregory L., and Lynne E. Lonnquist. 1997. *The Sociology of Health, Healing, and Illness.* Upper Saddle River, N.J.: Prentice Hall.

Weiss, L. 1998. *The Myth of the Powerless State: Governing the Economy in a Global Era.* Ithaca, N.Y.: Cornell University Press.

Weitzman, Martin L., and Chenggang Xu. 1994. "Chinese Township-Village Enterprises as Vaguely Defined Cooperatives." *Journal of Comparative Economics* 18:121–45.

Wellman, Barry. 1979. "The Community Question: The Intimate Networks of East Yorkers." *American Journal of Sociology* 84:1201–31.

Whitty, G. 1997. "Marketization, the State, and the Re-formation of the Teaching Profession." In *Education: Culture, Economy, and Society,* ed. A. H. Halsey, Hugh Lauder, Phillip Brown, and Amy Stuart Wells. Oxford: Oxford University Press.

Whyte, Martin King. 1975. "Inequality and Stratification in China." *The China Quarterly* 64:684–711.

———. 1990. "Chinese in Mate Choice in Chengdu." In *Chinese Society on the Eve of Tiananmen: The Impact of Reform,* ed. Deborah Davis and Ezra F. Vogel, 181–214. Cambridge, Mass.: Harvard University Press.

———. 1995a. "City Versus Countryside in China's Development." *Problems of Post-Communism* January–February 1996.

———. 1995b. "The Social Roots of China's Economic Development." *China Quarterly,* 144:999–1019.

———. 1996. "The Chinese Family and Economic Development: Obstacle or Engine." *Economic Development and Cultural Change* 45(1): 1–30.

Whyte, Martin King, and William Parish, 1984. *Urban Life in Contemporary China.* Chicago, Ill.: University of Chicago Press.

Williamson, Oliver E. 1981. "The Economics of Organization: The Transaction Cost Approach." *American Journal of Sociology* 87:548–77.

———. 1991. "Comparative Economic Organization: The Analysis of Discrete Structural Alternatives." *Administrative Science Quarterly* 36:269–96.

Wong, Christine P. W., Christopher Heady, and Wing T. Woo. 1995. *Fiscal Management and Economic Reform in the People's Republic of China.* Hong Kong: Oxford University Press.

Wong, Christine. 1992. "Fiscal Reform and Local Industrialization: The Problematic Sequencing of Reform in Post-Mao China." *Modern China* 18:197–227.

Wong, T. W., S. L. Wong, and S. Donnan. 1993. "Traditional Chinese Medicine and Western Medicine in Hong Kong: A Comparison of the Consultation Processes and Side Effects." *Journal of Hong Kong Medical Association* 4:278–84.

World Bank. 1990. *World Development Report 1990: Poverty.* New York: Oxford University Press.

———. 1992. *China: Strategies for Reducing Poverty in the 1990s.* Washington D.C.: World Bank.
———. 1994. *Priorities and Strategies for Education.* Washington D.C.: World Bank.
———. 1995. *Higher Education: The Lessons of Experience.* Washington D.C.: World Bank.
———. 1996. *Vietnam: Education Financing Sector Study.* Washington D.C.: World Bank.
———. 1997a. *Annual Report 1997.* Washington D.C.: World Bank.
———. 1997b. *Sharing Rising Incomes: Disparities in China.* Washington D.C.: World Bank.
———. 1998. *Annual Report 1998.* Washington D.C.: World Bank.
Wright, Erik Olin. 1997. *Class Counts: Comparative Studies in Class Analysis.* Cambridge: Cambridge University Press.
Wu, Guoguang, and Zheng Yongnian. 1995. *Lun zhongyang-difang guanxi* [On the Relationships Between Central and Local Powers]. Hong Kong: Oxford University Press.
Wu, N. 1996. Guangdong sili daixue fazhan chuyi [A Proposal for Private University Development in Guangdong]. *Gaojiao Tansuo* February, 40–44.
Wu, Xiaogang. 2002. "Work Units and Income Inequality: The Effect of Market Transition in Urban China." *Social Forces* 80:1069–99.
Wu, Z. 1997. *Guangzhou si jiaoyu fazhan zhanlue yinjiu di huigu jiqi rensi* [Review and Study of the Strategies of the Education Development in Guangzhou]. In *Zhanshe Xindaihua Jiaoyu Jiangsi—Guangzhousi Jiaoyu Fazhan Zhanlue Yinjiu* [Building a Strong Educational Province—Strategies of the Education Development in Guangdong], ed. Wu Ziyin. Guangdong: Guangdong Higher Education Press.
Xiang, Huaicheng, ed. 1999. *Zhongguo caizheng wushi nian* [Fifty Years of China's Public Finance]. Beijing: China Financial and Economic Press.
Xie, Yu, and Emily Hannum. 1996. "Regional Variation in Earnings Inequality in Reform-era Urban China." *American Journal of Sociology* 101:950–92.
Yan, Yunxiang. 1996. *The Flow of Gifts Reciprocity and Social Networks in a Chinese Village.* Stanford, Calif.: Stanford University Press.
Yang C. K. 1944. *A North China Local Market Economy: A Summary of a Study of Periodic Markets in Chowping Hsien, Shantung.* New York: International Secretariat, Institute of Pacific Relations.
———. 1959. *The Chinese Family in the Communist Revolution.* Cambridge, Mass.: MIT Press.
———. [1959] 1965. *Chinese Communist Society: The Family and the Village.* Cambridge, Mass.: MIT Press.
———. 1961. *Religion in Chinese Society: A Study of Contemporary Social Functions of Religion and Some of Their Historical Factors.* Berkeley: University of California Press.
———. 1975. "Some Preliminary Statistical Patterns of Mass Actions in Nineteenth-

Century China." In *Conflict and Control in Late Imperial China*, ed. Frederic Wakeman Jr. and Carolyn Grant. Berkeley: University of California Press.

Yang, Hongqiu. 1996. "The Distributive Norm of Monetary Support to Older Parents: A Look at a Township in China." *Journal of Marriage and the Family* 58:404–15.

Yang, Lien-sheng 1961. *Studies in Chinese Institutional History*. Cambridge, Mass.: Harvard University Press

Yang, Martin C. 1945. *A Chinese Village*. New York: Columbia University Press.

Yang, Mayfair Mei-hui. 1994. *Gifts, Favors, and Banquets: The Art of Social Relationships in China*. Ithaca, N.Y.: Cornell University Press.

Yang, Yiyong. 1997. *Gongping yu xiaolu, dangdai zhongguo de shouru fenpei wenti* [Equality and Efficiency, Income Distribution in Contemporary China]. Beijing: Today's China Press.

Yap, P. M. 1967. "Ideas of Mental Health and Disorder in Hong Kong and Their Practical Influence." In *Some Traditional Chinese Ideas and Conceptions in Hong Kong Social Life Today*, ed. M. Topley. Hong Kong: Hong Kong Branch of the Royal Asiatic Society.

Yearbook. Various years. *Zhongguo tongji nianjian* [China Statistical Yearbook]. Beijing: Zhongguo tongji chubanshe, annual.

Yee, A. H., and Lim, T. G. 1995. "Education Supply and Demand in East Asia: Private Higher Education." In *East Asian Higher Education: Traditions and Transformation*, ed. A. H. Yee. Oxford: Pergamon Press.

Yin, Q., and White, G. 1994. "The Marketization of Chinese Higher Education: A Critical Assessment." *Comparative Education* 30(3): 217–37.

Yuan, Z., and Wakabayashi, M. 1996. "Chinese Higher Education Reform from the 'State Model' to the 'Social Model': Based on a Sino-Japan Comparative Perspective." *Forum of International Development Studies* 6:173–200.

Zelin, Madeleine. 1990. "The Rise and Fall of the Fu-Rong Salt-Yard Elite: Merchant Dominance in Late Qing China." In *Chinese Local Elites and Patterns of Dominance*, ed. Joseph W. Esherick and Mary Backus Rankin, 82–109. Berkeley: University of California Press.

Zeng, Yi. 1991. *Family Dynamics in China: A Life Table Analysis*. Madison: University of Wisconsin Press.

Zhang, Buhong, and Zhang Gonghao. 1997. *Laodongfa xin leixing anli jingxi* [A Detailed Analysis of the New Types of Cases Related to the Labor Law]. Beijing: Renmin fayuan chubanshe.

Zhang, Tianzhi, ed. 1998. *Shanghai Jiating Shineizhuanghuang Jingxuan*. Shanghai: Shanghai Sanlian Shudian.

———. 1999. *Shanghai Jiating Shinei Zhuanghuang Jingxuan*. Shanghai: Zhongguo fangzhi daxue chubanshe.

Zhang, Z. 1996. "Summary of a Symposium on Nongovernmental Basic Education." *Chinese Education and Society* 29(5): 73–81.

Zhang, Zhanxin. 1997. "Reform of Public Agency Finance and Behavior of Revenue-Generating." Master's thesis, Hong Kong University of Science and Technology.

Zhongguo Chengzhen Shumin Jiating shouzhu Diaocha Ziliao, 1990. 1991. Beijing: Zhongguo tongji chubanshe.

Zhongguo Laodong Nianjian 1997 [China Labor Yearbook 1997]. 1998. Beijing: Zhongguo laodong chubanshe.

Zhongguo nongmingong wenti diaocha, 1997 [Survey on the Problems of Chinese Peasant Workers, 1977]. 1998. Beijing: Policy Research Office of the All-China Federation of Trade-Unions.

Zhou, N. 1995. "Strengthening the Connection Between Education and Economic Development: Major Issues in China's Educational Reform and Suggested Solutions." In *Social Change and Educational Development, Mainland China, Taiwan, and Hong Kong*, ed. G. Postilglione and W. O. Lee. Hong Kong: Centre of Asian Studies, University of Hong Kong.

Zhou, Xueguang. 2000. "Economic Transformation and Income Inequality in Urban China: Evidence from Panel Data." *American Journal of Sociology* 105:1135–74.

CONTRIBUTORS

Yanjie Bian is professor and head of Social Science and director of the Survey Research Center at the Hong Kong University of Science and Technology. Since 2003, he has led a team conducting a general social survey of China. His current research addresses the roles of social networks and social capital in China's economic transition.

Jieming Chen is associate professor of sociology at Texas A&M University, Kingsville. His research interests include family change, aging and health, and research methods. He recently expanded his research by participating in a major project on popular attitudes toward social inequality and distributive justice in China. He is writing an article on cohort differences in perceptions of social justice in China.

Deborah S. Davis is professor of sociology at Yale University, where she specializes in the study of contemporary Chinese society. Her publications include *The Consumer Revolution in Urban China* (2000), *Urban Spaces in Contemporary China* (1995), *Chinese Families in the Post-Mao Era* (1993), *Long Lives* (1991), and *Chinese Society on the Eve of Tiananmen* (1990).

Lizhu Fan is associate professor of sociology and executive secretary of the Center for Social Development at Fundan University, Shanghai. She specializes in the sociology of religion. She has published widely in both Chinese and international journals, and has edited several volumes of cross-cultural and cross-disciplinary research studies.

Burkart Holzner is Distinguished Service Professor Emeritus of International Studies at the University of Pittsburgh. His work in sociology focuses on the social construction of reality and international transformations. He was for twenty years the director of the University of Pittsburgh's Center for International Studies. He is the coauthor, with Leslie Holzner, of *Transparency in Global Change: The Vanguard of the Open Society* (2006).

Cho-yun Hsu is Professor Emeritus of History and Sociology at the University of Pittsburgh and a member of Academia Sinica. His research interests range from neolithic China to the cultural and socioeconomic changes in our world today, particularly the emerging technoscientific culture. His recent lectures on applied history and sociology are collected in several books that are on bestseller lists in Chinese communities around the world.

Hua Linshan is historian and associate researcher at the Center for Studies on Modern and Contemporary China, Paris. Among his publications is *A Sociological Investi-*

gation of China, 1911–1949, which he coauthored with Isabelle Thireau. His work focuses primarily on the Cultural Revolution and on recent institutional and normative changes in rural and urban China.

Ambrose Y. C. King is professor emeritus of sociology and former vice chancellor at the Chinese University of Hong Kong.

Chong Chor Lau is professor of sociology at the Chinese University of Hong Kong. His research interests include China's market transition and organizational changes.

Rance P. L. Lee has been teaching at the Chinese University of Hong Kong since 1965 and serving as advisory professor at Fudan University since 1995. At the Chinese University, he served as dean of social science for nine years and head of Chung Chi College for ten years. He is professor and chair of the Department of Sociology. His research interests include medical pluralism in Chinese culture and the impact of social structure on mental health.

Ka-ho Mok is chair and professor of East Asian Studies and director of the Center for East Asian Studies at the University of Bristol. He has published numerous works on comparative education policy and comparative policy and governance in East Asia. He is the author of *Education Reform and Education Policy in East Asia* (2006) and of articles published in internationally refereed journals, such as *Governance, Comparative Education Review, Comparative Education, Policy & Politics,* and *International Review of Education.*

Thomas G. Rawski is professor of economics and history and research professor at the University Center for International Studies at the University of Pittsburgh. He specializes in the development and modern history of China's economy, including China's reform mechanism and achievements, as well as specific analyses focused on productivity, investment, industry, trade, labor markets, and economic measurement. He is coeditor of *China's Great Transformation* (with Loren Brandt) and *China and the Balance of Influence in Asia* (with William W. Keller).

Wenfang Tang is associate professor of political science and chair of the China Council at the University of Pittsburgh. He is the author, with William L. Parish, of *Chinese Urban Life Under Reform: The Changing Social Contract* (2000) and *Public Opinion and Political Change in China* (2005). His articles have appeared in *American Journal of Political Science, Journal of Public Policy, China Quarterly, Problems of Post-Communism,* and *Journal of Contemporary China.*

Isabelle Thireau is professor of sociology and research director of the Center for Studies on Modern and Contemporary China at the National Center for Scientific Research, School for Advanced Studies in Social Sciences, Paris. She recently coedited, with Wang Hansheng, *Disputes in Chinese Villages: Forms of Fairness and Local Reconfiguration of Normative Spaces* (2001). Her current research explores labor and migration issues.

Zhanxin Zhang is associate professor at the Institute of Population and Labor Economics, Chinese Academy of Social Sciences. He is especially interested in social stratification and labor market segmentation in transitional China. His research currently focuses on Chinese rural migrants in cities.

Wang Feng is professor of sociology at the University of California, Irvine. His main research interests are social inequality in contemporary Chinese society and comparative and historical demography. His recent publications include studies on the economic and social consequences of China's demographic change, reexamination of China's one-child policy, and the impact of the Great Leap Forward famine and the Cultural Revolution on fetal losses in China.

Shaoguang Wang is professor of political science at the Chinese University of Hong Kong.

Tianfu Wang is associate professor of sociology at Tsinghua University.

INDEX